The Conduct of Social Research

The Conduct of Social Research

William B. Sanders
San Diego State University

Thomas K. Pinhey
California Polytechnic State University, San Luis Obispo

Holt, Rinehart and Winston
New York   Chicago   San Francisco   Philadelphia
Montreal   Toronto   London   Sydney   Tokyo
Mexico City   Rio de Janeiro   Madrid

ACKNOWLEDGMENT is gratefully made to reprint material from the following sources: *The Sociologists as Detective*, 2d ed., by William B. Sanders, Editor. Copyright © 1976 by Praeger Publishers, a Division of Holt, Rinehart and Winston. Reprinted by permission of Holt, Rinehart and Winston, CBS College Publishing. *Methods of Social Research* by Kenneth D. Bailey. Copyright © 1978 by The Free Press, a Division of Macmillan Publishing Co., Inc. *Analyzing Social Settings: A Guide to Qualitative Observation and Analysis* by John Lofland. Copyright © 1971 by Wadsworth Publishing Company, Inc. Reprinted by permission of Wadsworth Publishing Company, Belmont, CA 94002. From *Field Research: Strategies for a Natural Sociology*, pp. 99, 100, by Leonard Schatzman and Anselm L. Strauss. Copyright © 1973 and reprinted by permission of Prentice-Hall, Inc, Englewood Cliffs, N.J. The reference format (p. 415) from the inside cover of the *American Sociological Review*, reprinted by permission of the American Sociological Association. *Investigative Social Research: Individual and Team Research* by Jack Douglas. Copyright © 1976 by Sage Publications, Beverly Hills/London, with permission of the publisher. *The Structure of Sociological Theory*, rev. ed., by Jonathan H. Turner. © 1978, The Dorsey Press and reprinted by permission.

The Conduct of Social Research

Library of Congress Cataloging in Publication Data

Sanders, William B., fl. 1974–
    The conduct of social research.

    Bibliographies
    Includes index.
    1. Social sciences—Research. I. Pinhey, Thomas K.
II. Title.
H62.S335 1983   300′.72   82-11864
ISBN 0-03-058953-3

CBS COLLEGE PUBLISHING
Holt, Rinehart and Winston
The Dryden Press
Saunders College Publishing

For our families

Eli, Billy, and David
Donna, Stephenie, Holly, and Laura

Preface

What makes an event in our lives stand out against the background of the repetitive, routine days that make up most of our time? For the most part, such events are new experiences—special birthdays, first dates, honors, catastrophies, and the like. When we look back on our educational experiences, one class seems pretty much like another—a series of lectures, examinations, and perhaps some memorable insights. However, we might be hard-pressed to describe in detail a single day of any given class or even the class as a whole.

We have probably had more special experiences than most people, and the majority of those experiences have been connected with research. One of our first research projects occurred almost twenty years ago in a class that was conducting research in a mental hospital. A group of students were huddled together outside one of the older institutions, and we can vividly remember the screams of one of the patients. We were going in there!? That was exactly what we did, and in a series of experiences that are as clear today as they were back then, our first research opened the doors to a lifetime of discoveries, memories, and experiences equaled by few. Since that time, we have tramped through rural Louisiana interviewing farmers, observed courtrooms, conducted experiments on racism, ridden with police and outlaw bikers in high-speed chases, and watched victims of gang violence die. Obviously, not all of a researcher's experiences are happy ones and there have been times of danger, but there has always been insight and exposure to a broad spectrum of social life. And while we may not be able to recall the hours we spent coding data, we can vividly recall collecting it.

Our own experiences are in vivid contrast to so many of the stereotypes of research and research methods students hold. Too many view research methods as a course they have to take to fulfill a requirement rather than as an opportunity to explore the social world around them. Since research is the process of discovery, those who have been involved in research sometimes forget that the inherent interest in the process is not obvious to students. The emphasis has been on the precise techniques used by researchers without the connection to what these techniques ultimately accomplish. That is, rather than emphasizing the goals of research, the means—or methods—have almost become ends in themselves. Since the essential purpose of research is to acquire accurate information about some aspect of social life—to discover why people act as they do—it is important to keep a proper balance between the research methods and the goal of those methods. In this way, research can be understood in its proper perspective as a practical means to an end rather than as an exercise without a goal.

We wrote *The Conduct of Social Research* with a focus on the purpose of research methods. Basically, we believe that the student must understand that any methodology is a tool to test theory. Moreover, we think that theory is best understood as a means of explaining social behavior. Thus, the logical relationship between theory and research is between that of explanations of social behavior and devices to empirically test those ideas. Therefore, we begin with an explanation of what theory is and then show how it relates to research. Throughout the rest of the book, when we explain the various methods, we do so with respect to the goals of research in relation to understanding (explanations by theory) social behavior. In this way, the student will not come to see research methods as a tedious exercise, but rather as a very good way to test ideas.

Another balance we have attempted to achieve is that between quantitative and qualitative procedures. Far too often there will be lip service to such a balance after which the author will merrily fill the text with his or her favorite research technique. We have avoided doing so since one of us has focused on quantitative research and the other on qualitative, and we were not about to favor one side over the other. Furthermore, both of us have been involved in qualitative and quantitative research projects, and so even though we may have more experience in one type of research than another, we appreciate both kinds. (Besides, the qualitative half of our team is a computer nut!) Essentially, this approach is consistent with our view that the best method to use lies in the goals to be accomplished. In examining frequency and distribution, quantitative methods are generally more appropriate, but in describing processes, qualitative methods tend to be the best means. To have a single research method is analogous to the man who, because he liked the hammer, used it as the only tool to build a house. Without the use of a drill, saws, trowels, and other tools, the house he built was not a very good one. Similarly, the researcher with a single research tool is not going to do very good research. We have also included a chapter with several unique methods for unique research problems—specialized tools for specialized research.

Writing Style

The purpose of writing is to communicate, and in order to achieve communication, it is imperative that the writer consider the audience. In the preparation of journal articles and monographs there is a precise language and style with which most academics are comfortable. In those instances where the audience is other academics, we favor the objective albeit frequently turgid style one can find in almost any journal. However, the audience for this book consists of students and we have geared our presentation to them. This does not mean talking down or talking like students; it does mean writing in a clear expository way using appropriate and interesting examples. Although not an especially original approach to textbook writing, this approach is too frequently bypassed in research methods texts, where there is a tendency to be overly concerned with an imaginary journal reviewer who wants or expects a certain style. This is probably so because most publications that deal with research are written for professional journals, not for students. However, since both of us teach research methods, our "reviewer" was the typical student who is being introduced to the subject for the first time. Also, we attempted to provide examples of real research that students would find interesting. Since there is good research in both dull and exciting areas of social life, we saw no reason to avoid good research that was exciting.

Learning Aids

In addition to writing in a way students will understand, we sought to provide illustrations they could understand. A number of conventions in illustrating research procedures have been developed for communication to other researchers, not to students. Therefore, we created a number of different formats specifically for students. For example, in the chapter on experiments we have used nonconventional diagrams to explain the different kinds of experimental designs. Then, in a separate part of the chapter we have shown the conventional format used by researchers. In this way, we have been able to first show in a simplified way the different designs and then show the conventional format students will find in research articles. Throughout the book, we have adhered to the old adage that a picture (or diagram) is worth a thousand words.

Another technique we have employed is step-by-step design outlines. After reading a lengthy explanation of a method, students often fail to see how all the elements tie together or how to proceed from beginning to end. By providing a summary outline of a method, not only can the student better understand the research procedure, but he or she can see how all of the elements are linked. In addition, each chapter is summarized so that all of the important considerations are condensed.

Another teaching aid we have used is the placement of glossaries at the end of each chapter rather than at the end of the book. This has been done to reflect both the way in which research methods are taught and how students study. Typically, a class is broken up into several coherent parts with a number of chapters assigned each week or month. Since students prepare for examinations in terms of these segments, we chose to put the glossaries at the end of each applicable chapter. In this way, we hope students will better employ the glossaries and better learn the large number of new terms. However, the pages on which glossary definitions appear in the book are indicated in boldface type in the index. So, if the student wants to look up a term but is not certain which chapter it is in, he or she needs simply refer to the boldface index entry to locate the term in text.

Instructor Resource Guide

For instructors we have provided a resource guide, in which we have included a number of test items that measure students' progress; the guide includes everything from multiple-choice questions to glossary quizzes. Also, we felt it would be a good idea to provide an appendix of computer programs written in BASIC for those instructors who have access to microcomputers. The programs were written in APPLESOFT BASIC for the Apple II computer, but they can be easily adapted for other versions of BASIC if your university has different computers. Of course, we have provided some elementary instruction in the text itself for using the SPSS package.

Our purpose in *The Conduct of Social Research* has been to make the journey into research methods one which students will enjoy. For us, research has been an endless adventure, and it should be the same for all students. We believe that we have communicated this sense of discovery in this book; and so instead of being a course that students dread, we hope it will be the beginning of an exploration where those seeking knowledge are willing to go.

We are grateful to our reviewers for their detailed comments and for the many useful suggestions they made for improving the book: Mark Abrahamson, University of Connecticut; Frank Dane, State University of New York at Oswego; Bohdan Kolody, San Diego State University; Lawrence Rosen, Temple University; Richard Shankar, Stone Hill College; Darrell J. Steffensmeier, Pennsylvania State University; Ted Tannenbaum, Glassboro State College; William M. K. Trochim, Cornell University; and Brian Walsh, J. Sargeant Reynolds Community College.

W.B.S.
T.K.P.

Contents

The Conduct of Social Research

1

Knowledge and Social Science

Never has the need for the findings of **social science** been greater than in the past two decades. The population of the world is growing by geometric progression. Third World nations are moving from agrarian to industrial economies and everywhere social roles and social relationships are being redefined and transformed. To cope with these massive changes, we need to understand the social behavior that led to the new conditions and the implications of these changes for the future. The greater our knowledge of these new circumstances, the better we will be able to adapt to and control them. If our understanding is faulty, so too will be the methods we use for dealing with them.

The twentieth century abounds with examples of the application of scientific and technological knowledge to the needs of human social life. In 1969 the first human being set foot on the moon, and in the last few decades many diseases, such as polio, have been effectively eradicated. Microtechnology has made it possible for people to have on their desks the same kinds of computers that twenty years ago would have occupied several rooms. But when we look to social science knowledge, progress, while often dramatic, has been equivocal. For example, educational opportunities for minority groups have been increased as a result of social science findings. Such research demonstrated that low academic achievement of minority students is more a function of a poor educational environment than any inherent inability to learn. Yet the application of this knowledge in the form of busing to equalize educational opportunity has left many groups, both minority and nonminority, unhappy. Clear evidence has yet to be offered indicating that since busing was started minority students are getting more out of their education. In another area of inquiry, researchers have found a disproportionate amount of wealth and power concentrated in the hands of an elite group. Such findings, while underscoring inequities in a democratic society, do not provide practical answers to the problem identified. Likewise, in other areas of social life, social science research has provided us with knowledge about problems but has not supplied the solutions.

The challenge of employing the knowledge of social science is still present, however. For example, as energy supplies have become scarcer, it has become increasingly important to change patterns of energy consumption. This is especially true in the United States, where approximately 30 percent of the world's energy is consumed by 5 percent of the world's population. If our consumption of oil were reduced, say, by a gallon a person a month, the savings would be the equivalent of technological advances that would mean the production of almost 3 billion gallons of oil a year. The achievement of such goals in the future may well depend on what social science research is able to tell us about patterns of human social life. Thus, we can see that the practical application of social science can be as beneficial and as dramatic as the use of knowledge from other scientific sources.

Social Problems and Social Science Problems

Social researchers seek their knowledge through studying two different types of problems. On the one hand, there are **social problems**, or problems that people have to face in day-to-day living. Crime, pollution, poverty, and mental illness are social problems because they constitute obstacles to harmonious social life. On a more personal level, we can talk about social problems involving everything from how to fill our spare time to how to get a date for Saturday night. In contrast to social problems are **social science problems.** These problems have to do with theory, and they will be discussed in detail in Chapter 2. For now it is important to understand how the two types of problems differ and how they relate to social science research.

As an example, we will consider the different issues involved in examining crime as both a social problem and a social science problem. As a social problem, a crime is viewed as something that hurts victims, and we want to know how to stop it. We seek a variety of solutions from providing more and brighter streetlights to urging tougher court sentences for the perpetrators. From the social problems perspective we might ask such questions as "How much crime is there?," "Who are the victims?," and "What does crime cost the public?" Viewing crime as a social science problem changes our questions somewhat. Basically, the researcher wants to develop explanations of what causes crime—that is, theories that explain why crime occurs. One explanation might point to the social structure as the basic cause of crime while another might explain crime in terms of subcultural beliefs. If we are testing a theory of crime based on a structural explanation, we are likely to focus on the social class of the violator. On the other hand, if we are seeking to explain crime from a subcultural point of view, we will ask questions about the beliefs and values of persons who typically commit crimes.

In summary, social problems are defined by problems in society, while social science problems are defined by theoretical issues. For both kinds of problems we seek solutions through social science methodology and the knowledge it generates.

Social Science Knowledge

While much research ignores social science theory, here we will concentrate on research that attempts to build theory. The knowledge that is generated as part of social science theory is more general and more interconnected than other kinds of findings in social research, and as we will see in Chapter 2, it is guided by theory. While sometimes research begins with an unspecified problem and ends up adding to social science theory, the most valuable findings usually derive from research that begins and ends with the addressing of a theoretical problem.

A general aim of the social sciences is to establish relationships between social phenomena. Ultimately, findings from social science should be able to *predict* social patterns. To do this, researchers must uncover causal relationships between variables. By **causal relationship** it is meant that a particular characteristic or set of conditions determines another characteristic or set of conditions. As in math, a **variable** in social science is a quantity that has the capability of assuming more than one value. At this point most knowledge about causal relationships is based on statements of **probability**—the chance that an event will or will not occur. The whole issue of causality is complex; for now we will discuss it in terms of the kind of information research must uncover in order to establish causality, and we will define the key terms needed to understand the concept in social science.

Basically, three conditions must be met in order to establish cause and effect:

1. *Time order:* It must be shown that the cause (causal variable) precedes the effect (affected variable).
2. *Mutual patterned change or association:* It must be established that when one variable changes in a specified direction, the affected variable also changes in a specified direction.
3. *There is no other plausible explanation:* We can only say that one variable causes a change in another variable when we have eliminated other plausible explanations for the change.

We have seen that a variable is any concept, quantity, or item that has changing values. For example, *social class* is a variable with values of "upper," "middle," "working," and "lower." Another variable might be *career plans*, with values that include "professional," "business," "clerical," "skilled laborer," and so forth. A simple causal relationship between the variables *social class* and *career plans* might be stated as: "Social class determines career plans." In other words, we might say that depending on one's social class, different career plans are made. Schematically, the relationship is as follows:

Social Class ➡ Career Plans

In research, we refer to the variable that causes the change as the **independent variable** and the variable that is changed as the **dependent variable.** In this example, *social class* is the independent variable and *career plans* is the dependent variable, since we are saying that social class determines career plans.

Patterns of Social Action

If we gathered data to see whether career plans changed as social class changed, we might find the pattern of change we expected, but we would very likely find that the pattern is not perfect. We might, for example, discover that the career plans of the upper class are more likely to center in the professions or business and those of the working class are more likely to lie in skilled labor and clerical jobs, but that a portion of the upper class has plans to be skilled laborers and some working class members plan to enter the professions. That is why we must state any kind of relationship in terms of probabilities, or the statistical likelihood that a relationship will hold. We might, for instance, find that 80 percent of the upper class have career plans in the professions or business and 70 percent of the working class have career plans in skilled labor or clerical jobs. Such findings clearly show some kind of relationship between social class and career plans, but we must state the connection in terms of the probability that one class or another will choose a certain career.

In Chapter 2 we will see how theory points to the connections between variables and guides the researcher. Here it is enough to understand that researchers gather information with the purpose of discovering such relationships. On the theoretical level we simply make the connections, but in dealing with social problems we can apply the knowledge. Earlier we pointed out that by studying crime as a social problem we can try out various solutions for preventing it. However, if we have a theory to explain crime, then we know the roots of the problem; instead of a hit-or-miss approach using various hunches and guesses, we can go right to what our theory tells us are the basic causes of crime. In order for theories to be valid, of course, we must have valid information and knowledge. The rest of this chapter will examine the various types of knowledge available, showing how scientific knowledge is our best source of valid information.

Sources of Knowledge

Knowledge is only as reliable as the sources from which it derives. Whether the sources are firsthand or not, it is as important to know how the data were obtained as it is to have the information. This book will explain how the scientific method is employed, but like all other methods of obtaining knowledge, science should not be accepted with blind trust. Such unquestioning acceptance would not be in the spirit of scientific inquiry. Before examining the scientific method, however, we will consider various other sources of information.

Authority

When we obtain information from an **authority** we are relying on that person's or institution's social status as a guarantee that the data we receive are correct.[1] The authority itself can take a variety of forms—an oracle, a professor, a celebrity, a mystic, the Bible, government reports, the evening news on television. We believe the information because we believe in the source—because, for example, we *know* the authority has a special communication link with God or follows the scientific method rigorously or is simply honest and would not say something if it were not true.

An interesting example of authority as a source of knowledge concerns the Nobel Prize winner, physicist William Shockley, whose claims concerning the relationship between race and IQ have been widely reported in the press. Shockley argues—and some people believe him—that certain nonwhite minority groups are inferior in intelligence as a group to whites. His argument is based on comparative IQ tests administered to different ethnic and racial groups. As a Nobel Prize winner, Shockley is invested with a great deal of authority. Yet it is absurd to confer authority on the question of a link between intelligence and race on Shockley, who is a physicist. If a sociologist were to presume to lecture about physics, with no special training in that field and using questionable data as Shockley does, people would think the person mad, a crackpot not to be taken seriously. Even had the sociologist won the equivalent of a Nobel Prize in sociology it is doubtful that many people—least of all physicists—would give the person much credence. Many people might listen to the lectures, however, on the strength of the social status attached to a distinguished scholar.

In a memorable and succinct statement regarding authority as a source of knowledge, Groucho Marx in the film *Duck Soup* remarked, "Who are you going to believe—me or your eyes?"[2] The irony of Groucho's comment would appear sufficient to discredit authority once and for all, but we cannot dismiss authority so quickly. Consider the mistake it would have been if Europeans, after the voyages of Christopher Columbus, had relied on their eyes (and faulty observation) to conclude that the world was flat. Instead, they trusted the authority of Columbus, a well-known explorer, and obtained correct information. If we had to rely on our own senses for all of our knowledge and understanding we would obtain very little information. We count on others' authority and knowledge all the time.

Are we talking about two different things here, authority and expertise? Authority is a source deemed to be reliable because of social status, while expertise is a special ability or talent that a person has in a particular area. Yet the two are not entirely distinct, since to be accorded the status of authority a person typically must be able to demonstrate that he or she is knowledgeable in a certain area. Once authority is established, we assume expertise. In writing this book we assumed that those we cited have expertise in the methods they use and the findings they produce. We do not have the time to check every aspect of the findings to make sure their authority is based on expertise. Rather, we have trusted the social scientists whose findings we reported on the basis of the status they enjoy in their fields.

THE NEWS One of the most widely used sources of authority is the news, especially television news, because, for many people, it has replaced the newspaper as a major source of information concerning what is happening throughout the world. Most people believe what they see and hear on television news. After all, they are believing their eyes and ears and conclude that what is shown on the screen really happened. And most people tend to believe that if a story is not going to be accurately reported, it will not be allowed to be presented on television.

We are aware that the news could be censored and we could be flooded with propaganda in the guise of news. In Nazi Germany, Joseph Goebbels, Hitler's Minister of Popular Enlightenment and Propaganda, was able to control the information the German people received, mainly on radio but also through every other medium.[3] The people were convinced that Hitler and the Nazis could do no wrong and that the Jews, who made up only one percent of the population, were responsible for the problems that plagued Germany. These lies led to the Holocaust, and, subsequently, to the fall of Nazi Germany.

Americans, on the other hand, generally believe that since the United States has a free press, what is reported by the media is representative of what actually happens in the world. But is this really the case? In a study of television news production one researcher found that news presentations often distorted events by screening only certain shots and omitting others.[4] Thus, a news staff can misrepresent an entire event to such an extent that what the viewer sees amounts to a lie. For example, if the owner of a local television station supports one politician over another, the favored one can be shown positively and the unfavored one negatively. The news editor can focus on the favored politician giving clear, crisp answers to reporters' questions and omit shots of the same person stumbing over or evading questions, while doing the opposite to the opponent. In this way, the news can be manipulated for television audiences.

OTHER AUTHORITIES   In ancient societies authorities were more likely to be religious leaders, shamans, and persons who had some kind of spiritual connection with the supernatural. Spiritual authority is still to be found today in such personalities as evangelist Billy Graham and Iran's Muslim leaders, but modern sources of authority tend to take the form of the quantified document. "Official reports" have superseded spiritual leaders as accepted authority. Some reports are based on good scientific research, but others are manipulated to make a political point. For example, official police reports often reflect departmental policies rather than actual reported crimes. If the police want a certain type of crime to appear to increase or decrease, all they need do is change the criterion for a reported crime. For example, by recording all cases of purse-snatching as "petty theft" instead of "robberies," they can "decrease" the number of robberies. Thus, even though many official reports and documents are excellent sources of knowledge, to the extent to which we believe them because of their official status, our knowledge is based on a form of authority.

Common Sense

Another source of knowledge is **common sense.** Exactly what common sense is depends on whom one asks at a particular time. It may be common sense for some people that if one does not spank one's children they will grow up to be delinquents. "Spare the rod and spoil the child" is an example of the kind of folk knowledge that supports rearing children on the basis of corporal punishment. But common sense also tells us that "violence begets violence," and so folk wisdom also gives us the opposite advice on the same matter.

Perhaps the best way to characterize common sense is to say that it is the accumulated experiences, prejudices, and beliefs of a people. Its propositions are made up of proverbs, moral maxims, and wise sayings that "everybody knows" are true.[5] The problem with this source of knowledge is that it tends to be narrow and unsusceptible to any information or knowledge that would contradict it, even though common sense often contradicts itself, as in the example of the child-rearing advice. As evidence to support commonsense knowledge, examples are drawn in which common sense seems to have prevailed and everything else is ignored. For example, the old "commonsense" belief that women are bad drivers is supported whenever a woman backs through a garage door or has a similar accident. At the same time, the numerous instances of men doing the same thing are ignored, as is the fact that insurance rates are lower for women under 25 years of age than for men in that age group because women have fewer accidents. Because common sense does not concern itself with such considerations, it is not a reliable source of knowledge.

Other Nonscientific Sources of Information

The following nonscientific sources may be considered to be authority or common sense in certain contexts.

ADVERTISEMENTS Advertisements here include various types of commercial appeals, propaganda, and influence peddling. In their most familiar guise, advertisements are displays of wares or services purporting to provide information that will lead to consumer use. Television commercials use everything from claims of scientific proof to sex appeal to sell products or services, and while these claims no doubt contain some validity, they are only one-sided. That is, they cannot be considered to be useful knowledge because we are presented only with the positive aspects of the product or service. Likewise, propaganda and influence peddling are forms of advertisement, presenting one-sided and highly colored versions of positions.

While we may at first dismiss advertisements as a source of knowledge, many government decisions are made on the basis of lobbyists' one-sided presentations of their positions to legislators. Advertisements represent the kind of knowledge that is commonly useful in debate, where the emphasis is on winning a point, not on searching for truth. In science, whenever debates reach a point where one side is attempting to prove one hypothesis over another, then authority becomes simply a form of advertisement, aimed at gathering support and not knowledge.

MYSTICISM   The kind of knowledge generated by revelation, divine communication, or other contact with the supernatural is referred to as **mysticism** because there are no ways of verifying the validity of the information. Communications with the supernatural usually deal with some general moral edict and rarely produce practical information that can be tested empirically, such as the name of the team that is going to win the World Series.

INTUITION   When we have a hunch about something or know the right thing to do because it feels right, the knowledge is called **intuition.** For example, on meeting a new person a friend remarked that he felt there was something wrong with the individual. He could not pinpoint it, but his intuition told him the person could not be trusted. Later the individual proved to be highly trustworthy and the two later became good friends. The point of the example is that we rarely hear about intuition when it does not work, but rather only when it does. The false impression is thus created that intuition is more valid than in fact it is. A good test of intuition is at the horse races, where the results of choices made on intuitive knowledge can be seen quickly—though sometimes expensively.

The Scientific Method

At its core the **scientific method** is both simple and sensible, involving observation, induction, and deduction. There is nothing mysterious about it, and even though many people think of science as a world of computers, white coats, and laboratories, good science requires only the ability to make observations and systematic, logical decisions. Computers can help analyze huge amounts of data quickly, and they are used extensively in social science research, white coats serve only to protect clothes from spillage, and an elaborate laboratory only helps to control research conditions. As we will see, there is a good deal of difference between *being* scientific and trying to appear scientific.

EMPIRICAL OBSERVATIONS   The core of scientific knowledge is **empirical observations**—seeing, hearing, feeling, smelling, tasting—that is, obtaining information through the senses. We can *see* things to the extent that we can describe their features and/or measure them. Much of the empirical data gathered by social scientists reflect bits and pieces of a larger social phenomenon, the whole being empirically available only when all the parts are put together. We may not, for example, be able to observe social structure directly, but by making observations of individuals' social positions—their jobs, incomes, and backgrounds—we can empirically "see" the structure nevertheless. For example, we can "see" social stratification in looking at the different dwellings of the wealthy, middle class, and poor. It is possible to directly observe mansions of the wealthy on several acres of land, middle-class housing tracts on suburban lots, and cramped apartments of the poor in government projects and in tenements. Empirical data is different from knowledge based on unsubstantiated beliefs, mystical experiences, and other kinds of knowledge that cannot in some way be seen by others.

INDUCTION Empirical observations are employed to make inductions. **Induction** refers to building theory through the accumulation of observations. One takes several observations and makes a generalization, or summary statement, about what was observed. For example, criminologists have observed that men are more likely than women to commit armed robbery. By observing that the gender of the vast majority of armed robbers is male, criminologists were able to make an inductive statement to the effect that "most armed robbers are male." This simple generalization based on empirical observation tells us that there is some kind of *relationship* between being an armed robber and being male.

DEDUCTION The process of **deduction** involves going from the general to the specific and forming propositions about what we have seen as against what we have not seen but could expect on the basis of what we know. Deduction involves moving from premises, based on observations, to conclusions. Consider the following:

1. All rapists are men. (observation/premise)
2. Pat is a rapist. (observation)
3. Pat is a man. (conclusion, but not observed)

Assuming the validity of the first two statements, the third must be true. Of course, the premises may be incorrect in one way or another, and if that is the case, then the conclusion may be incorrect. For example, there may be women rapists, or Pat may not be a rapist. If either is true, then our conclusion may be incorrect.

A problem in deduction is the improper use of logic in deriving conclusions. One of the most common mistakes involves transposing key terms. For example, the following is a slight variation of our first deduction:

1. All rapists are men.
2. Pat is a man.
3. Therefore, Pat is a rapist.

The initial premise is *all rapists are men* and not *all men are rapists*, but the conclusion, together with the second premise, is based on the latter version of the initial premise. By transposing the key terms "men" and "rapists," the logic is lost. In developing scientific knowledge one needs to use care and not trip up on the logic after having made the necessary empirical observations.

While there is more to science than just observation, induction, and deduction, these procedures are the foundation of scientific inquiry. As we develop an understanding of social science research methods, it is important to remember these core principles and to ask, even as we have gone far beyond these basics, whether our methodology meets the fundamental requirements of science.

Social and Physical Data

Consider a rock rolling down a hill and a woman walking down the same hill. Observing the rock, we might assume that it was kicked loose somehow and began to roll, impelled by gravity. The woman is moving down the hill in a very different manner. She is not moving down the hill because of the pull of gravity, because we know that she could—unlike the rock—turn around and go back up the hill. We assume she is on her way somewhere—to work or to visit a friend or just enjoying walking outside. In other words, we assume that the woman has some kind of *meaning* to her actions and the rock does not.

Since there is a fundamental difference between social and nonsocial phenomena, it is necessary to use somewhat different procedures in social sciences than in the nonsocial sciences. In the latter we do not have to concern ourselves with the meaning of the things we observe, and our empirical observations can proceed independent of any questions about the subjective meaning inherent in the things we investigate. In observing the rock rolling down the hill, we wouldn't ask, "Is the rock on the way home or leaving home?"

If, however, we are studying basic forms of collective behavior, we will need to differentiate our observations not only on the basis of what is physically taking place but as to the meaning attached to the actions. Consider a group of people walking down the street. Depending on the meaning in the situation, the gathering could represent anything from protest marchers to a group of sightseeing tourists. The physical actions of the two kinds of groups may appear to be very similar, but once we understand the meaning of the actions in the context of the situation, we come to see the behavior of the two groups very differently.

VERSTEHEN   The process of coming to terms with the meaning of social action is what Max Weber called *Verstehen.* **Social action** is behavior by people that has some meaning or intention for the people engaged in that behavior. To observe social action it is necessary to determine what activities occur and the meaning of those activities. For example, in studying organizations sociologists look not only at the structure of an organization but also at its purpose and at the meaning of the various structures. In comparing organizations it would be absurd, for example, for a sociologist merely to point out behaviors in terms of arriving at and leaving work and not to mention that the comparison was between a meatpacking plant and a hospital.

Some people mistakenly assume that *Verstehen* is a form of subjective sociology. Sociologists study the *subjectivity* of the social actor in order to distinguish among different types of social action. The investigator, however, does not use the subjective point of view as a resource for gathering information; rather, the focus of the study is the subjective viewpoint of those being observed. In studying the American Civil Liberties Union and the Ku Klux Klan, sociologists come to understand the meanings and beliefs of *both* groups, but they do not take the beliefs of one group or the other as a tool for gaining knowledge. The beliefs *are* the topic.

SYSTEMATIC COLLECTION OF DATA So far it might seem as though it is possible to conduct social science research simply by living. After all, through our experiences we come to know and recognize different social patterns and their accompanying meanings. However, as we saw in discussing commonsense knowledge, the information we have based on our experiences often is not valid. Knowledge in social science means systematic collection and analysis of data. That is, the information must be gathered in accordance with some organized system. Suppose we want to find out about student attitudes toward the draft. If we asked our friends or just the people in our classes, we might have a very skewed view of what all students think. If a lot of our friends were in ROTC, we might come away thinking that most students favor the draft, while if most of our friends were in the humanities, we would probably find most of them to be antidraft. The answers we received would also depend on when we asked our question. If we asked shortly after an attack on the United States, such as the day after Pearl Harbor was bombed, most people would probably favor the draft, but if asked during a time of peace, most would probably be against it. In addition, our information would depend on how we asked the question. If we said, "I don't like the idea of a draft," and then asked, "What do you think?" we could expect a different pattern of response than if we asked simply, "What do you think of the draft?"

Systematic data collection requires that a standard of observation be used to collect all data. Only data that meet the requirements of the standard are considered valid for the purposes of analysis. In the example of student attitudes toward the draft, the researcher would take a sample of the population that represented all students; the researcher would make observations at different times; and if questions are to be employed, they would be worded in a specified manner in the same way. The exact plan and procedure for carrying out the research is called the **methodology.**

The Challenge of Social Science Research

The spirit of research in social science is one of discovery and understanding. Science is not a dogma, and like any other means of developing knowledge, it makes mistakes. Yet, science is designed to recognize its own mistakes, and all scientific findings should be critically analyzed. A single study, rather than being the final word on a topic, should be only the first, to be followed by further scientific inquiry. This approach is especially needed in the social sciences, where social change is a constant feature of the world. The challenge of social science research lies in uncovering the secrets of social order and change. Like our early explorations in space, social science is still on the frontiers of knowledge.

The opportunities for discovery in social science are broad and vast. Like all early explorers, the challenge is in the unknown, not the known, and there is more we do not know than do know of social life. Perhaps the most tantalizing aspect of such research is that rather than being across the galaxy, everything we must learn is right under our noses. We know about many aspects of social life, but we are constantly amazed at the complexity and diversity of that life. To some, like the early skeptics who could not accept the notion of a round earth, complexity is a reason for despair. Those people would prefer simple explanations for the complex problems of human social life. For others, though, the very complexity is the challenge. These researchers wish to unravel the mysteries of human life rather than shrink from them in dismay.

Summary

In this introductory chapter, we have tried to show that social science research methods are a sensible way to gather data about social behavior. At the base of the knowledge are theories based on observations and systematic logic. Through a systematic, organized process, new information is found, and the theories are refined and retested. Links and connections are discovered, and we begin to make statements about causal relationships. Such relationships are placed in a conceptual framework and still further explanations are developed.

Social science knowledge is differentiated from other sources of knowledge, such as common sense, authority, and mysticism. While social science may study these kinds of knowledge, it does not take them to be inherently valid, but rather sees them as tools used by laypersons to understand the world around them. They are not used for gathering social science data simply because they tend to be less valid sources of knowledge, but the fact that social actors employ such resources make them a topic of inquiry.

At the heart of it, social science methodology is simply a plan of study that will yield the best information possible. Its basic tenets are quite simple, and as long as we remember these points, no matter how complex a method used by sociologists, anthropologists, political scientists, or criminologists may appear, it is still based on methodologies we have discussed in this first chapter. In the following chapters we will see how the logical development of these principles are expanded into different kinds of research methods for a variety of research problems. However, it is important to remember the clear, simple logic behind them and their purpose of unravelling the enigma of social life.

Glossary

authority A source of knowledge that is considered reliable and valid because of its social status.

causal relationship The idea that a particular characteristic or set of conditions determines another characteristic or set of conditions.

common sense Knowledge based on the accumulated experiences, prejudices, and beliefs of a people. It is often contradictory and inconsistent.

deduction A form of logic that begins with a general statement of observed characteristics and arrives at a specific statement derived from the general one.

dependent variable A quantity that is caused to change by the state of another quantity. (See *independent variable*.)

empirical observation Information based on what our senses can actually record, either directly or indirectly. Excludes mystic and supernatural experiences, such as dreams and visions.

independent variable A quantity that implies or causes change in another quantity. (See *dependent variable*.)

induction Beginning with several observations and logically arriving at a general statement explaining the observations.

intuition An unobserved, unexplained hunch, idea, or feeling used as knowledge. Intuition can be the basis for concept or even theory, but it is unreliable for knowledge in and of itself.

methodology The scientific study of research techniques, instruments, and strategies for obtaining valid information.

mysticism Knowledge purported to come from communications with supernatural sources.

probability The likelihood or chance that an event will or will not occur. Statistics are used to specify quantitative probability.

scientific method Procedure for obtaining knowledge based on empirical observations and logical reasoning.

social action Human behavior that has meaning or intention for the person or persons engaged in the behavior.

social problems Conditions faced by members of a society that adversely affect their social welfare.

social science The study of social, cultural, and political behavior using scientific methods.

social science problems Questions or issues that are posed by social science theory and which are addressed through social science research.

variable A quantity that has the capability of assuming more than one value.

Verstehen Research that gathers information about the meanings of social behavior in addition to the patterns of behavior themselves.

1. Walter Wallace, *The Logic of Science in Sociology* (Chicago: Aldine and Atherton, 1971), pp. 11–12.
2. Reported in ibid., p. 13.
3. Ernest K. Bramsted, *Goebbels and National Socialist Propaganda: 1925–1945* (Ann Arbor, Mich.: Michigan University Press, 1965).
4. David L. Altheide, *Creating Reality: How TV News Distorts Events* (Beverly Hills, Ca.: Sage, 1976).
5. Peter Berger and Thomas Luckman, *The Social Construction of Reality* (New York: Doubleday, 1966).
6. Gustav Bergmann, *Philosophy of Science* (Madison, Wis.: University of Wisconsin Press, 1957), p. 31.
7. Kenneth R. Hoover, *The Elements of Social Scientific Thinking* (New York: St. Martin's Press, 1976), p. 67.
8. Max Weber, *The Methdology of the Social Sciences* (New York: Free Press, 1949), p. 74, and Stephen Mennell, *Sociological Theory: Uses and Unities* (New York: Holt, Rinehart and Winston, 1974), p. 23.

2

Social Theory and Research

The topics of social research are almost endless, and students can take a look at just about any aspect of social life they wish. Some interesting topics that students have studied include delinquent gangs, political lobbies, adjustments to retirement, college dating behavior, and criminal trials. One student studied traffic court, and when he received a speeding ticket, he used his knowledge of the informal court decision-making process to have his citation dismissed!

Choosing a topic of interest is only difficult insofar as there are so many things to study. The real difficulty is deciding what to do once a topic is chosen. Suppose a student wants to study college dating behavior. Most college students know something about dating from their own experiences, and if we stop to think about it, there are so many aspects to dating, it is difficult to know where to begin. Do we consider the fine interactions when male and female students meet or attempt to meet one another, or do we look at more general patterns, such as the number of times a month students date? Do we consider the elements of social class, ethnic background, age or are these really important? And what about sexual activities and dating? Is that a topic we should find out about, and if so, what aspects are significant? *The questions to ask become the first question to address.*

In this chapter, we will explain the relationship between theory and research. Theory tells us which questions to ask and what we will need to know to answer these questions. More than anything else, theory makes research *simpler*, not more difficult. Theory provides focus, direction, and organization to research, and without it, research would flounder for lack of purpose.

Theory-Research Relationship

When using the term *theory*, many people contrast theory with reality. That is, they might say, "Well that's just a theory, and we need to know about reality." Such statements tend to demonstrate ignorance about theory, for theories are statements about reality. Scientific and empirical theories are statements about reality based on observations and logic. In fact, we might even say that the most accurate statements about reality are theories.

Basically, we can define a **theory** as *a set of interrelated propositions (or generalizations) and definitions that serves to conceptually organize selected aspects of the empirical world in a systematic way.* Medical theories are generalizations about what medicines work best for certain diseases. Theories in physics are generalizations about relationships between physical matter. In the same way, theories in social science are generalizations about the way social behavior occurs. George Homans characterized propositions in sociological theory as "generalizations about how typical people act in typical situations."[1] In a theory of college dating patterns, a proposition might include the generalization that typical males ask typical females on dates in typical dating situations. If research were conducted on the basis of that proposition, the findings would probably confirm it. Indeed, we would be very surprised to find that the women *usually* asked the men for dates.

In a more detailed description of theory, Jonathan H. Turner explained it in terms of the following:

> Theorizing can be viewed as the means by which the intellectual activity known as "science" realized its three principal goals: (1) to classify and organize events in the world so that they can be placed into perspective; (2) to explain the causes of past events and predict when, where, and how future events will occur; and (3) to offer an intuitively pleasing sense of "understanding" why and how events should occur.[2]

To better understand this description of what theory does, we will break it down into its separate goals and examine each one separately.

Classification

The first part of theory is to classify and organize events and things in the world. In biology, animals are classified into fish, mammals, reptiles, and birds so that each category can be studied separately or compared with the other categories. In sociology, phenomena are **classified** into institutions, organizations, roles, and situations for the same purposes. Other social science **classifications** include values, beliefs, norms, ideologies, social class, ethnic group, and many more conceptual groupings useful for categorizing the many features of social actions and facts. In organizational theory, two sociologists, Peter Blau and Richard Scott, classified formal organizations according to which group is designated as the prime beneficiary of the organization: the owners, the members, the clients, or the public at large.[3] Such a classification helps in understanding the different structures of organizations based on comparisons between organizations in both similar and different categories.

Explanation and Prediction

Most social science theory can only predict events in general and is better at showing correlation than causation. However, the ideal of social science theory—to explain and predict phenomena—is the same as that of other scientific theories. For example, in medical science theory, a simple causal relationship can be shown to exist between light and dilation of the eye's pupil. The pupil contracts when light is shone directly on it, and it expands in the absence of light. This relationship exists in any healthy human's eye. Showing causal relationships and making **predictions** is somewhat more risky in social science since there is far greater social variation among people than significant physical differences. For example, in some groups there are strong norms prohibiting the use of alcohol, while in other groups it is expected, even demanded. Thus, depending on the group's norms, we can make predictions about drinking behavior, but we cannot make predictions for all people since their norms differ. Also, there is a far greater likelihood of social change than there is of a general physical change among people, and so it is necessary to have more general theory and also changing predictions. For instance, before 1965, criminologists could pretty well predict that white middle-class youths in high school and college would not use marijuana.[4] However, with the advent of the hippies and accompanying drug culture, the use of marijuana became very popular among middle-class youth. Therefore, the predictions had to change as the social norms and values changed.

Understanding

The third goal of scientific theory is to make things sensible or understandable. Once a theory has classified and explained causes in a given pattern of social behavior, it must provide some kinds of insight into it. In his theory of alienation, Marx provided an understanding of why workers in factories were unhappy with their lives.[5] He explained that because men and women no longer owned what they produced, and because, on the assembly line, they only participated in a tiny part of the overall process of production, workers came to feel apart or alienated from their work, other workers, and even themselves. This aspect of Marx's theory was not involved in classification or prediction, but rather it served to provide insight into how men and women felt—an understanding of a situation in life.

Theory as a Guide to Research Inquiry

Now that we can see what a theory is, we will be able to see how it helps in conducting social research. In order to understand this relationship, we will compare a better-known investigator of social life, the detective, with the social science researcher.[6]

To begin with, detectives do not ask for "just the facts," as the fictional Joe Friday did. Rather, in an investigation, detectives begin with some theory that gives them some idea of what facts to look for. Take for instance the investigation of a criminal homicide, and the eternal question of detective fiction, "Who done it?" Without some kind of theory, everybody in the entire world could be a suspect, but since detectives operate with theory, not only do they focus their investigation on certain people, they are able to center it around key questions. In the case of the typical homicide, detectives theorize that the killer is someone related to the victim. Such a theory is based on their past observations and experiences. As a result of this theory, they closely question husbands, wives, business partners, friends, and others who are related to victims. Now it may turn out that the murderer was a total stranger, but because of the assumptions of the detectives' theory, they begin their inquiry with friends and relatives of victims. As can be imagined, without *some kind of theory* to guide an investigation, literally billions of people could be suspected of a single murder.

Theory helps detectives "see" things that would otherwise be missed. Theory brings out the invisible. In a number of Sherlock Holmes adventures, the great detective was able to see much further because of his use of theory than Dr. Watson, Inspector Lestrade, or even the reader. In one story about a stolen race horse, Holmes noted that when the horse was taken, a dog at the farm did not bark. Dr. Watson pointed out that the fact of the dog's not barking had already been noted and so it had been impossible to pinpoint the exact time the horse was stolen. Watson's theory was that the dog would bark when somebody stole the horse, and by noting the time the dog barked it would be possible to tell when the horse was taken. When Watson found no one who had heard the dog bark, he dismissed the entire matter from his mind. It was Sherlock Holmes' theory that enabled him to *see* the significance of the silent dog. What was Holmes' theory? It was quite simple. Dogs are less likely to bark at people they know. The dog did not bark. Therefore, the dog probably knew the person who took the horse. Thus, instead of searching for a thief all over hither and yon, Holmes focused his efforts on the household of the farm from which the horse was taken and finally identified the culprit.[7] The point is that it was only due to Holmes' theory that the *fact* that the dog did not bark became relevant. *Theory tells you what is important to note.*

Consider a more complicated bit of theorizing by Sherlock Holmes to see how it tells what to look for, even when the clues are very well hidden. A woman had been found shot and killed on a stone bridge that spanned a large creek. A note found on her body indicated that she feared for her life from a certain man. Other than a fresh chip on the stone railing of the bridge, there were no other clues. No weapons, no footprints, and no witnesses. The obvious theory, based on the available data, was that the woman had been murdered by the person named in the note. However, in the course of his investigation it became clear to Holmes that the man suspected of the murder did not do it. In fact, he believed it was a case of suicide and the note was intentionally left to be found so that even in death the woman could have her vengeance. The problem was, how? What theory could lead to finding the solution to this case, and explain what could be seen and help find the unseen? Beginning with the theory that the woman committed suicide, Holmes began looking for evidence that would prove or disprove his theory. The woman had been shot, but no weapon was found where she had been killed. Problem: How do you shoot yourself and get rid of the weapon? If the woman had shot herself, the gun would have dropped by her side on the bridge and been prevented from falling over the side by the stone railing. She couldn't very well have shot herself and then thrown the gun in the water. But there's the chip on the stone railing. Holmes theorized that the poor woman had tied a weight to a string on one end and to the gun on the other. She then draped the weight over the railing and when the gun fell out of the woman's hand it was pulled over the side of the bridge and disappeared into the creek. This theory led Holmes to search the creek where he found the gun, string, and weight.[8] Again, the theory showed Holmes what to look for and where to look while at the same time providing a sense for the facts. The fact of the fresh chip in the stone now made sense in that when the weight pulled the gun over the railing, it chipped the stone. Without a theory all the facts in the world would not have helped Holmes, and in the same way social scientists who have no theory cannot tell what is and is not important.

Theory tells the social scientist what facts are relevant, what facts to look for, and what facts can be expected.[9] By looking at the same phenomenon with different theories, we can see that the relevant facts would be different. This does not mean that the findings are going to be contradictory; rather, because of the different *perspectives* generated by the different theories, different facts become relevant. There will be overlaps in most sociological theory, but the very same subject is simply researched differently.

An example of this can be seen in two studies of rape by sociologists. In the first study, two researchers took an "institutional" approach, their theoretical interests centering on the various agencies in society that responded when a rape occurred.[10] As a result of their perspective, their study led them to investigate the hospital's organization and procedures for examining rape victims, the police department's response to victims, the various rape crisis centers, and the operation of the criminal court in prosecution and defense of rape defendants. In the other study, the researcher took an "interactionist" perspective of rape.[11] Instead of focusing on institutions, this second perspective called for looking at interaction situations.[12] Thus, the researcher collected data on the different types of situations in which women were assaulted, the sequence of interaction contacts leading to sexual assault, and victim reaction to a rape assault. Each study generated a different kind of data because the theories focused on different dimensions and asked different questions. The theories told the researchers to look for different things.

Research as a Test of Theory

Theory tells research what facts to find, and the facts say whether or not the theory is correct. Columbus theorized that the world was round (a sphere), and he sailed west from Europe to test his theory. Had Columbus fallen off the end of the world, his theory would have been proven false.

The reciprocity between theory and research is cyclical in that theory points to relevant data, and the data either confirms or refutes the theory. If the theory is found to be inaccurate, the theory is reformulated, pointing to new areas of research where still further data are collected to test the theory.[13]

To see how this relationship works, we will look at Cressey's classical study of embezzlers.[14] Using intensive interviews as his primary method, Cressey talked with several convicted embezzlers. His questions were guided by his hypotheses, which were derived from Sutherland's theory of white-collar crime.[15] The first hypothesis stated that embezzlers would only violate trust once they had learned (rationalized) that the act really was not a crime but only a "technical violation."[16] Upon interviewing the embezzlers, Cressey quickly found that they were aware they had violated the law, and so he reformulated his hypothesis based on these initial findings. After revising the hypothesis, he found evidence that it too was inaccurate, and so he revised it again. After a number of revisions based on his continuing research, Cressey finally arrived at an **hypothesis** that could explain the experiences of the embezzlers he interviewed. His last hypothesis stated: "Trusted persons become trust violators when they conceive of themselves as having a financial problem which is non-sharable, are aware that this problem can be secretly resolved by violation of the position of financial trust, and are able to apply to their own conduct in the situation verbalizations which enable them to adjust their conceptions of themselves as trusted persons with their conceptions of themselves as users of the entrusted funds or property."[17] As can be seen, this last hypothesis was much more complex and significantly different from the first one Cressey used. However, by beginning with a theoretically derived hypothesis, the researcher had specific questions that could be asked and answered. Since the initial answers to the questions raised by the hypothesis showed that the hypothesis was incorrect, the researcher was able to reformulate his hypothesis until it reflected the experiences of the research subjects—the embezzlers. Schematically, we can see this relationship as follows:

Theory 1   Initial explanation of embezzlement
Research 1   Rejects initial hypothesis
Theory 2   Second explanation of embezzlement
Research 2   Rejects second hypothesis
Theory 3   Third explanation of embezzlement

Research 3   Rejects third hypothesis

-
-

Theory N   Nth explanation of embezzlement
Research N   Hypothesis confirmed

In each step, the theory guided the research, and the research guided the theory. In most research, the researcher does not go through the revision of hypotheses, but based on one person's findings, another researcher reformulates hypotheses or tests new theories to determine whether or not they are valid.

It is important to understand, however, that there is no complete certainty in developing and testing hypotheses; instead, there are trends in one direction or another that tell the researcher whether the theory is supported or not. The following illustration shows a pattern supporting an hypothesis, but it should be noted that not all of the cases go along with the pattern.

Hypothesis: **The elderly vote from a conservative perspective and the young vote from a liberal perspective**

Age Group	Young	Old
Vote		
Liberal	⊬⊦ ⊬⊦ |||	⊬⊦ ||
Conservative	||||	⊬⊦ ⊬⊦ ⊬⊦

As can be seen there are young people who vote as conservatives and old ones who vote as liberals. The pattern, however, is in the direction of the hypothesis. In the case of this hypothesis, the researcher would probably want to reformulate it to say, "The elderly are more likely to vote from a conservative perspective and less likely to vote from a liberal perspective than the young." Stated in this manner, the theoretical statement (hypothesis) better reflects the research findings.

Theoretical Concepts

The basic tool in both theory and research is the **concept.** While theory points in the general direction to which the researcher should look, concepts provide a more specific focus. What is a concept? Essentially, *a concept is an idea of* *social phenomenon derived from theory* (See Chapter 4). For example, "social class" is a concept that characterizes people's position in society in terms of power, wealth, and honor, and so is a "nonsharable problem" as discussed in Cressey's research above. Other social science concepts include social institutions, political party, family, social situations, groups, organizations, solidarity, value systems, norms, alienation, anomie, and social relationships. Different theories have different emphases on the same concept, and so the concepts themselves can have different meanings. Karl Marx's concept of social class emphasizes the economic dimensions of class, while Max Weber's class concept emphasizes the beliefs and values of class.[18] Both Marx and Weber recognize other elements of class than those on which they focus, for Marx talks about class consciousness and the different beliefs and values of classes while Weber recognizes the importance of the economic positions of different social classes. However, because of their different theoretical positions, their ideas about social class are different as well. Therefore, in discussing concepts, it is important to remember each is tied to a theory, and depending on the theoretical framework, the exact meaning of a concept will be different.

Herbert Blumer called concepts "fashioners of perception."[19] Concepts direct the researcher to see the social world in certain terms and configurations. In the rape studies we discussed above, one study examined rape in terms of the concept of "social institutions," the other in terms of "social situations." The research was directed in very different areas even though the studies were looking at the same topic. Each of the different researchers had their perceptions fashioned by the concepts they employed. It's something like putting on different-colored glasses. You look at the same thing, but because of the different tints in the glasses, things look slightly different.

Types of Theory and Data

Because different theories have different concepts and different meanings for similar concepts, the kinds of data collected differ as well. The data and what counts as data depend on the concepts and their meanings. Consider the different meaning of the concept of "motive" in psychological and sociological theories. In psychological theory, a motive is an inherent drive or need of the individual.[20] To a clinical psychologist it might make sense to attribute an extremely strong drive to work hard to the motive of trying to impress one's parents. The basic motive would be the "need to be loved by parents" and the expression of this motive is in the person's compulsive work habits. The *data* for the conclusion may be nothing more than the observation that the person worked abnormally hard. Or the psychologist might examine the person's past, and question the person about his or her feelings toward his parents and how they treated him or her as a child. Whatever psychologists take to be their data, though, it is grounded in the assumptions of their understanding of motive. In contrast to psychologists' use of motive, sociologists take a very different view of the same concept and count different things as "data." A sociological understanding looks at motives as being *accounts*[21] *or words in people's vocabulary that provide what are seen as good reasons for doing something.*[22] In other words, sociologists would be very interested in the actor's own reasons and the extent to which those reasons were accepted by others. For example, if a sociologist saw the same behavior of hard work that the psychologist saw, the former would be interested in what the person had to say about his or her work habits and would not attempt to probe for subconscious drives. If, to a researcher's question, "Why do you work so hard?" the person answered, "It'll help me get promoted faster," the sociologist would record the reply as an account. If to others the account was taken to be *reasonable*, then the sociologist would take that account as a socially acceptable motive.

THEORETICAL ASSUMPTIONS ABOUT THE NATURE OF SOCIAL DATA Using the example of the different assumptions psychologists and sociologists may have about human motives, we can see different underlying assumptions each has about the nature of human beings. The psychologist assumes an inner motivation system developed as part of the personality within the individual, and the sociologist sees a motivation system geared to a reasonable account for others. Each has a distinct notion of individual motives.

Researching a problem with different theoretical assumptions provides different pictures of the behaviors observed. Take dating behavior, for instance. The sociologist notes a girl "showing off" her boyfriend as a status symbol, and the psychologist notes the same behavior as fulfilling a need to be loved. The sociologist notes that it is interesting that wealthier men appear to be more "lovable" to women, while the psychologist notes that men of power and position can better meet an inner need for security in some women. Thus, looking at the same phenomenon, even when the description of the behavior is identical, different assumptions inherent in the theories give rise to very different observations.

THE PROBLEM OF REIFICATION When looking at the same behavior, including identically described activities, different theoretical positions lead to different observational conclusions. This is the problem of **reification.** In the context of research, reification refers to describing data in such a way that it confirms one's theory. For example, during the Vietnam War, the many instances of American troops killing Vietnamese civilians or Viet Cong prisoners of war was attributed by some to racism.[23] The concept of racism was applied to the unnecessary killing on the basis of the observation that the Vietnamese were of a different racial/ethnic group and racial epithets such as "gook" and "slope" were applied to them. To be sure, there was a good deal of racism on both sides during the war, but the use of racism theory as an explanation for the kinds of killing that occurred where there was no military or legal justification for them is only one possible theory, and there is evidence from other wars that such a theory may not be the most appropriate.

In World War II, for example, when the Americans were fighting the Germans, a "white" group, there were a number of instances in which American troops murdered German soldiers who had surrendered.[24] In virtually every war such killings occur, a product more of the situation created by the war, including the negative stereotypes of the enemy, than racism. When we look at civil wars in which people of the same race, language, and culture fight, we find no fewer outright murders than when different races fight. The Spanish Civil War is a good example of people of the same nation murdering one another in violation of the so-called "rules of war."

The point is not that racism cannot be a deadly excuse for murder during war, but rather when racism as a concept (or any other concept for that matter) is applied as an explanation, unless the application can be shown to be testably appropriate, it is nothing more than reification. For example, if the killings of innocent civilians or surrendered soldiers only occurred in wars where there were different races involved, then the concept of racism would be a viable explanatory concept. However, since this is not the case, racism is a poor concept for explaining the general unprovoked killing during war.

On the other hand, the concept of racism as well as other concepts are not reifications when it can be shown that the concept is testably the most appropriate explanation for understanding behavior. For example, in explaining the incarceration of Japanese-Americans in relocation camps during World War II, Harry Kitano explained the act in terms of racism.[25] Kitano pointed out the following:

1. The bulk of the Japanese-Americans who were sent to relocation camps were loyal Americans willing to fight the Japanese. Therefore, there was no military necessity for their internment.
2. Japanese-Americans in Hawaii, where they constituted a far larger proportion of the society and where they were employed in key positions necessary both for the war effort and civil functions, were not interned. Only where the Japanese-Americans were seen as a small minority compared to the whites, especially on the West Coast, were they interned. This further shows that there was no military necessity for the relocation of Japanese-Americans on the West Coast, for the Hawaiian Islands were far more vulnerable to attack by the Japanese.
3. No other groups, such as the German-Americans or Italian-Americans, were sent to relocation camps in large numbers even though the United States was at war with Italy and Germany. Moreover, since there were large numbers of German-Americans active in Nazi organizations, such as the American Bund, there would seem to have been better military reasons for sending them than the Japanese-Americans.

4. Because only nonwhite ethnics, the Japanese-Americans, were sent to relocation camps without valid military reasons, white racism on the West Coast explains the internment of the Japanese-Americans.

As can be seen by Kitano's argument and observations, he did not apply the concept of racism arbitrarily; rather, he showed, in a testable manner, how the concept explained what happened to the Japanese-Americans who lived on the West Coast during World War II. In this case, the application of the concept was *not* a reification.

Transforming Theoretical Problems into Research Problems

The most important step in social research is the first one: linking the research to a theoretical problem. Many students see social research as "doing a survey" or "making observations," but unless the research is directly tied to a problem in theory, it is of little merit or use. For example, one student wanted to "find out about student attitudes." First of all, there are millions of different attitudes one could possibly research. Second, even given a specific kind of attitude, there are several different dimensions of a single attitude, and it would be necessary to know the dimensions. Third, it would be necessary to know how attitudes are related to other variables, such as sex, age, major, social class, and any number of other conditions. Knowing the relevant variables would depend on the theory. Finally, it would be pointless to do research unless the results of the research could describe a theoretically relevant phenomenon or test relationships between theoretical concepts.

To get started in research, begin with the general theoretical problem and work it into a manageable **research problem.** In the case of the student who wanted to "find out about students' attitudes," she went back and worked up an interesting theoretical problem in the area of socialization. We will use her study to illustrate the steps in transforming a theoretical problem into a research problem.

The student's study concerned itself with primary and secondary socialization, and changing and traditional sex roles. Her theoretical problem involved the question of what happens during periods of social change in secondary socialization after a primary socialization in traditional molds. She transformed the theoretical problem into a workable research problem by asking whether women in traditional majors for women had different career plans than women in nontraditional majors. Primary socialization was assumed to be in the mold of the traditional woman's role (becoming a wife and mother), and the secondary socialization was indicated by the college major. By comparing women in majors that have been traditionally reserved for women planning domestic roles, such as home economics, with those that imply a career, such as business administration, it would be possible to see the effect of secondary socialization. One might readily expect that "of course" women majoring in business are going to have different career plans than women majoring in home economics, but when we stop to consider the wide variety of majors women have had in the past that never resulted in a career because of marriage and motherhood, it may not be as obvious as we may at first believe. Also, certain women might major in business as a way to find a husband who has high financial potential, while some women majoring in home economics might be interested in a career in consumer affairs. There are various measures that are taken in any research project to control for possible intervening variables we will discuss later in the book. Here, though, we will concentrate on how the student went from a theoretical problem to a research problem and then to a specific research design.

Step 1: *Statement of Theoretical Problem*   Stating the theoretical problem involves posing a question relating to some issues in theory. The student's question asked, "What effect does secondary socialization have on social roles after a primary socialization with different role expectations?"

Step 2: *Hypothesis*   From the problem, a statement is made about the relationship between conceptual variables. In our example, the student stated, "Secondary socialization will lead to changes in role expectations if the secondary socialization is in contrast to the primary socialization, but role expectations will not change if the secondary socialization is consistent with the primary socialization."

Step 3: *Operationalizing Concepts*   This step is the first one that links theory with research and is the first step in research design. It involves taking a concept and stating what will "count" in observation as that concept. By "count" we mean the observation will be recorded. The concepts requiring operationalization include (1) primary socialization, (2) secondary socialization, and (3) role expectations. The student chose to study female sex role expectations, dichotomizing the roles into "traditional" and "changing." The traditional role was characterized as that of a housewife and mother, the changing role that of a career outside the home. *The primary socialization was assumed to be in the traditional mode*, that of expecting women to be housewives and mothers. The secondary socialization was defined (operationalized) in terms of college education in majors that were considered to be either changing or traditional. The changing secondary socialization was seen to be in a business major (nonsecretarial) and the traditional in a home economics major.

Step 4: *Establishing Indicators*   Having operationalized the concepts, it is necessary to establish **indicators** that can be recorded as showing the concepts. At this point, the indicators make it possible to know what kinds of questions to ask on a survey, what activities to observe in the field, and what kinds of operations to employ in experiments. In our example, the student chose to indicate career choices by including questions about specific career plans and choices regarding conflict between the two. For example, one question asked, "If you were pursuing a career successfully in a city, and marriage would require you to move to another city where your future husband worked but which had few opportunities in your career, what would you do?" Other questions were more general, such as "What career plans do you have?", "For your development as a person, what is more important, a career or being a wife and mother?", and "Do you think the ERA Amendment is a good idea?" Simple questions, such as "What is your major?" established indicators of secondary socialization.

Completing the Design

The indicators having been established, the research instrument will now reflect the issues in the original theoretical problem. In later chapters we will go into greater detail as to how different designs are constructed, but for now, we can see how the researcher depends on theory to get the research project started. There are other details and considerations in setting up and executing any research project; however, once there is a clear statement of the theoretical problem and the concepts have been *operationalized*—defined as observable data—the researcher can see what is necessary to be observed. Compared to "finding out about students attitudes," which has absolutely no direction—no starting or ending point—the project examining women students' career plans is well focused. Were it not for a clear theoretical problem and concepts with which to work, the research would have floundered. As it was, and as is true with all research, the casting of research into a theoretical context makes the work all the simpler. Thus, rather than looking at applying theory as a chore to be done in the research process, it should be understood as a process that will make research a lot easier.

A Model of Logic in Social Science Theory and Research

Now that we have a general understanding of how theory and methods are interrelated, we will next present an integrated model based on the work of Walter Wallace.[26] As can be seen in Figure 2.1, theory and method complement one another, and in order to understand one component, it is necessary to understand the others.

There are a number of operations in the model that will be explained later in the book, varying according to the kind of method and theoretical problem, but for now, examine the model in terms of what we have discussed so far to get an idea of the general interconnections between theory and methodology. The informational components are shown in rectangles, and the methodological controls are shown in ovals. The arrows represent information transformations. Our main interest will lie on the right side of the diagram, beginning at the top with *theories*, and following the arrow to the right to *logical deductions*, on to *hypotheses* and further to *interpretations, instrumentation, scaling and sampling*, and finally to *observations*. Also, we will be interested in the path from *hypotheses* to *tests of hypotheses* and decisions to *accept or reject hypotheses*. The remaining portions of the diagram can be understood in terms of further developing theory from research findings, and while this is a crucial aspect of the theory-research interrelationship, our concern will focus on the other portions.

Looking at the diagram, we can trace our student's research project. Beginning with the theoretical problem of roles and primary and secondary socialization, she logically deduced her hypothesis. Next she operationalized

FIGURE 2.1
An Integrated Model of Theory and Research in Social Science

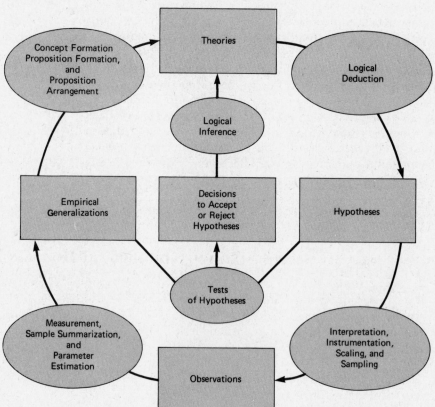

Source: Walter Wallace, *The Logic of Science in Sociology* (Chicago: Aldine-Atherton, 1971), p. 18.

her concepts to make her research instrument (interpretation and instrumentation). We will take up scaling and sampling later, along with the procedures for testing hypothesis, but for now, it is important to see how the student's project fit into the overall scheme of the model. Developing and refining theory is beyond the scope of this book, but it should be pointed out that any findings that are inconsistent with a theory call for theory or hypothesis reformulation, as we saw in the embezzlement study. In our example, the student found that *both* women from traditional and nontraditional majors for women were planning careers rather than confining themselves to becoming housewives. Her findings called for a reformulation of her hypotheses or perhaps taking an entirely different theoretical approach. The significance of her research lay in the fact that her findings were unexpected and therefore provided new knowledge and understanding of the changes in women's roles.

Summary

This chapter has attempted to show the relationship between social theory and methodology. The best way to understand this connection is in terms of theory providing a guide for research instead of being a troublesome ritual to be performed. Unfortunately, students sometimes miss the crucial role played by theory, and so in this chapter we have stressed the *practical* importance of beginning a research project with a clear theoretical goal. As we have seen, such a goal lays out what is needed in the research design.

At the same time that theory guides the research method, it is important that the research is not merely a reification of the theoretical concepts. True, theory provides a perspective on the social world, and different theories will give us different views, but the research should be designed to tell us whether or not that perspective is a true one. There is a difference between theory providing guidance and theory distorting or coloring our research.

Therefore, while theory guides research design, research, in turn, provides a test for theory. It tells us whether the predicted relationships and processes are accurate or not, instead of just constructing a view of the social world so as to confirm the theory. Research is always a *test* of theory, and we never should set out to *prove* a theory.

Because research tests theory, it in turn becomes a guide for theory. On the basis of research we can formulate and correct theory to guide future research. Surprises in theory occur whenever research finds something not expected by the theory, and rather than being cause for despair, findings that invalidate theoretical assumptions are as fulfilling as those that prove theory, for it is evidence of new discovery.

And so we have come full circle, from theory guiding research to research guiding theory, all of which occurs in the context of logical reasoning and empirical observations. A world of reason and evidence generate knowledge.

classification Placing conceptually similar phenomenon in common categories. General classifications use broad categories and specific classifications use narrow categories.

hypothesis Statement of relationship between two or more concepts and/or social patterns.

indicators Empirically observable and/or measurable events, actions, people, places, or things that can be recorded in relationship to research concepts and/or patterns.

prediction The ability to state what conditions will lead to a certain action. In social science, prediction is based on probability that an event will occur under certain circumstances. (*See causality* and *probability* in Chapter 1.)

reification Treating a concept, theory, or hypothesis in such a way that it is not tested by research but instead defined as true through operationalization. This is a common research problem and can be avoided by making sure that it is possible to disprove an hypothesis in the research design.

research problem A problem stated in such a way that it can be tested by research. Research problems are guided by implicit or explicit theoretical problems.

theory A set of interrelated propositions (or generalizations) and definitions that serves to conceptually organize selected aspects of the empirical world in a systematic way.

Notes

1. George Homans, "Bringing Men Back In," *American Sociological Review* 29, No. 6 (1964): 809—18.
2. Jonathan H. Turner, *The Structure of Sociological Theory* (Homewood, Ill.: Dorsey, 1974).
3. Peter M. Blau and W. Richard Scott, *Formal Organizations* (San Francisco: Chandler, 1962).
4. William B. Sanders, *Juvenile Delinquency: Causes, Patterns and Reactions* (New York: Holt, Rinehart and Winston, 1981).
5. Karl Marx, *Economic and Philosophical Manuscripts*, trans. T. B. Bottomore, in Erich Fromm, *Marx's Concept of Man* (New York: Ungar, 1963), pp. 85—196.
6. William B. Sanders, *The Sociologist as Detective: An Introduction to Research Methods*, 2nd ed. (New York: Praeger, 1976), pp. 3—4.
7. Sir Arthur Conan Doyle, Silver Blaze," in *The Annotated Sherlock Holmes*, Vol. II, ed. William S. Baring-Gould (New York: Clarkson N. Potter, 1976), pp. 261—81.
8. Sir Arthur Conan Doyle, "The Problem of Thor Bridge," in ibid., pp. 588—606.
9. Talcott Parsons, *The Structure of Social Action*, Vol. I (New York: Free Press, 1937) pp. 8—10.
10. Lynda Lytle Holmstrom and Ann W. Burgess, *The Victim of Rape: Institutional Reactions* (New York: Wiley, 1978).
11. William B. Sanders, *Rape and Women's Identity* (Beverly Hills, Ca.: Sage Publications, 1980).

12. Jack D. Douglas, Patricia A. Adler, Peter Adler, Andrea Fontana, C. Robert Freeman, and Joseph A. Kotarba, *Introduction to the Sociologies of Everyday Life* (Boston: Allyn and Bacon, 1980).
13. Parsons, op. cit. pp. 8−10.
14. Donald R. Cressey, *Other People's Money: A Study in the Social Psychology of Embezzlement* (Belmont, Ca.: Wadsworth, 1957, 1971).
15. Edwin H. Sutherland, *White Collar Crime* (New York: Dryden, 1949).
16. Cressey, op. cit. p. 27.
17. *Ibid.*, p. 30.
18. Karl Marx, *Das Capital* (New York: Random House [Modern Library], 1906, originally published in 1867): Max Weber, *The Theory of Social and Economic Organizations* (New York: Oxford University Press, 1947).
19. Herbert Blumer, *Symbolic Interactionism: Perspective and Method* (Englewood Cliffs, N.J.: Prentice-Hall, 1969), p. 155.
20. "Motive" in psychology is often used to denote a drive or inherent need common to all humans.
21. Marvin B. Scott and Stanford Lyman, "Accounts," *American Sociological Review* 33 (1968):46−62.
22. C. Wright Mills, "Situated Actions and the Vocabulary of Motives," *American Sociological Review* 6 (December 1940):904−13.
23. Michael Heer, *Dispatches* (New York: Avon, 1977).
24. Charles B. MacDonald, *Company Commander* (New York: Bantam, 1947, 1978).
25. Harry Kitano, *Race Relations*, 2nd ed. (Englewood Cliffs, N.J.: Prentice-Hall, 1980), pp. 258−63.
26. Walter Wallace, *The Logic of Science in Sociology* (Chicago: Aldine−Atherton, 1971), p. 18.

3

The Strategy of Research Design

There are over one and a half million people living in the city of Dallas, Texas, and there is ample evidence to suggest that the city's population will continue to increase over the coming years.[1] Because sociologists have traditionally associated the complexity of an organization with its size, we can hypothesize that Dallas is an extremely complex social system. Given such a large and complex city, it appears that it is also safe to imagine that if we randomly questioned a cross section of Dallas residents about what they believed to be important topics for social research that their answers would be as varied and as complex as the city they live in. We would expect that each person would suggest a somewhat different research topic. For example, one person from our sample might suggest that we study the opinions and attitudes of the American public toward the use of our country's natural resources. Another respondent might point out that drug abuse has become a major problem associated with the growth of the Dallas community, and that this topic would be more important than studying problems with the natural environment. As a researcher it is important to understand that each of the topics suggested by the members of our fictitious sample would require a different research strategy, what social scientists call a **research design.** In this chapter we explore the various kinds of research designs that are available, and we will see how the selection of a design is influenced by the goals of a research project, the time frame within which we plan to explore a topic, and the units of analysis we eventually select for study.

Research Design

The research design phase of a study includes the total *planning* for an investigation, to include sampling plans and data collection techniques. For instance, once a research problem has been stated, the researcher must begin to *plan* the methodological approach or tactic that will best address the problem he or she has selected for study. Of course, there are several approaches one can take for the study of a topic and it is the selection of the best possible approach for a study that constitutes the basis of a research design.

As an example, suppose we have decided to study *attitudes* toward some form of deviant behavior. For such a study it would probably be best to conduct a **survey** that would reach a large segment of the population. By selecting the survey as our research method, and assuming we used the proper procedures for drawing a sample, we could be reasonably positive that persons from all areas and social levels of the population would have the same chance of having their attitudes and opinions included in the study. This is important, because if our sample was not a representative one it would not accurately reflect the attitudes we were attempting to describe.

But suppose for a moment we had decided to study the deviant *behavior* itself and not simply public attitudes toward that activity. This change in our research problem would significantly alter the research design. For instance, suppose we decided to study drug abuse behavior and not simply attitudes toward it. First of all, it is obvious that the survey approach would be inappropriate because it would be far too difficult to obtain responses to a questionnaire dealing with such a sensitive issue. Indeed, people are generally unwilling to discuss personal problems with strangers, and in most cases "interviewers" are strangers to the persons they interview. A more productive approach would be one that guaranteed the placement of the researcher in the actual world of the drug abuser as either an observer or participant. Such a methodology, called *participant observation*, would allow us to observe firsthand the deviant behavior we were interested in (for example, drug abuse). Sociologist Laud Humphreys employed participant observation in his controversial study of "tearooms."[2] *Tearoom* is the name given to public restrooms used by some male homosexuals for sexual encounters. Humphreys observed (but did not directly participate) and made notes on fifty such encounters and reported that, although the men came to tearooms for a variety of reasons, they most often did so because they wanted their activities to remain *secret*. In this case direct observation by the researcher proved the most productive research design given the extreme sensitivity of the topic Humphreys studied.

Survey research and participant observation are only two of the many research methodologies you will learn about in this book and much more will be said about these methods in later chapters. What is important here is the understanding that there is no single research approach or methodology that is appropriate for every research question. One key rule we should remember is that *the research question dictates the research method and not vice versa.*

Several other aspects of a research question can influence the formulation of a research design, and it is the discussion of these aspects to which the remainder of this chapter is devoted. For example, what influence will the *goals* of a study have on its design? What designs can best be used to examine social change? And who or what can be studied?

Research Goals

The goal of a study can have a significant impact on the research design we construct, and there are several possible goals a researcher can have when studying a specific topic. For example, a sociologist might wish to *explore* a topic that had previously been unstudied. The simple *description* of a social activity could also be a research goal as could the *explanation* of certain social behaviors. Finally, a researcher might wish to conduct a **pilot study** in order to test a previously unused research technique.

The Exploratory Study

There are often occasions when a social scientist will conduct a study simply to explore a topic or question he or she is unfamiliar with. The goal of this type of research project is to examine an area new to the researcher or to "break new ground" when the topic has been unstudied by others.

As an example, sociologists had paid little attention to the relationship between society and energy consumption prior to the oil embargo of 1973.[3] At that time the price of gasoline in the United States increased dramatically and long lines at the gas pumps became the norm in many communities. However, because very little research had been conducted in that area, social scientists were unsure as to how the public would react to the long lines and possible energy conservation measures. It was believed that with the decrease in available energy sources several normal activities would have to be modified. For example, people would probably tend to car pool rather than drive their own cars to work or school. Findings reported from these early explorations provided new and valuable insights into the area and helped pave the way for more sophisticated and theoretically relevant studies. As pointed out in Chapter 2, *something* is needed to guide research—usually theory—but when there are no guides to follow, the researcher must explore.

However, there are other reasons for conducting an **exploratory study.** We may simply become curious about a phenomenon and study it to gain a better understanding of its occurrence. During the early 1970s, for example, some of our students became curious about "streaking": They conducted an exploratory study to discover just what type of student would run naked across a college campus and what other nonstreaking students thought about such people.[4] Although streaking may not appear to be as important an issue as the energy crisis, it is certainly one that can arouse a person's curiosity, and because it was a relatively new campus activity, no previous findings were available to help our students formulate a research design. In this instance an exploratory study was the most appropriate research avenue for them to follow. The students accomplished two things with their study. First, it satisfied their curiosity, and second, it provided a set of fingings for future students to use as the basis for a new and more thorough research project.

Exploratory studies are also useful in generating new hypotheses for future research. As in the example of the studies conducted during the energy crisis of 1973, more sophisticated and carefully conceived investigations are possible after the topic has first been explored. If nothing is known about a topic, it is difficult to hypothesize what is going on in that area. But after an exploratory study is completed, hypotheses can be stated prior to gathering new data, and this provides researchers with a better idea of the research questions that are important.

The Descriptive Study

As noted in Chapter 2, one goal of science is the classification of events or things in the world. For the social scientist this means the description of social events, institutions, groups, and behavioral patterns. Simply put, before we can classify events we must know what they look like.

At the beginning of this chapter we noted that the city of Dallas, Texas, had a population of over one and a half million persons, and that the city is still growing. This description helps us to understand what kind of community Dallas is, and its classification as a "big city" is made such easier because of it. The data used to describe Dallas came from the United States Census Bureau, whose research goal is the accurate description of the United States' population. Census data provide social scientists with a vast pool of information that can be used to describe almost every portion of our population. Because these data have been gathered since 1790, they are particularly useful in describing changes in the characteristics of our population.[5] By being able to describe and predict the growth of a geographic area, for example, sociologists can provide community planners with information useful in preparing solutions to the problems of future housing and employment needs.

However, there are many different kinds of **descriptive studies,** in addition to those using census data. For example, a survey could be used for the purpose of describing how people feel about a specific issue, or participant observation could be used as a method for describing a group's behavior. Almost all political candidates rely on the survey method of public opinion polls to describe the voting intentions of the electorate, while journalist Hunter S. Thompson used participant observation to describe the activities of the Hell's Angels.[6]

The Explanatory Study

Another goal of social science is the explanation of what is occurring in society. In some cases it is desirable to go beyond the simple description of an activity or social group and attempt to explain why people act or feel the way they do. Why is it, for example, that some students do well in school and others do not? To describe students as either "slow" or "sharp" does not answer the question of how we might help the slower or less interested students get better grades. But an **explanatory study** might research *why* some students do better than others and would help *explain* grade differences.

In one study that tried to explain differences in classroom performance, researchers asked, "Does it really matter what a teacher thinks about a student? If a teacher expects students to perform well, will they?" Apparently so, according to the evidence of a study designed to test the hypothesis that within a classroom those students from whom the teacher expects a great deal eventually perform as the teacher expects them to.[7] Researchers began the study by "giving a test" to most of the students in the school. The test was supposed to predict which students would "spurt" ahead in their learning activities in the near future. However, *there really was no such test!* The teachers in the school were given the names of students who were *supposed* to be the "spurters," and they were told not to reveal to other students or parents who these students were. But the names of these students were actually selected at random. At the end of the year the students were retested and those who had been "predicted" to spurt ahead made considerably higher scores than the rest of the school. It was concluded that the teachers had actually improved students' abilities simply by expecting improvement. Thus, differences in students' grades can at least be partially explained by the expectations of their teachers.

A single study is not necessarily restricted to any one of the three goals discussed thus far, and in fact, most studies are not. For example, a study could be designed to first distinguish between several categories of students, and once these student categories had been *described,* the study might then seek to *explain* why students wind up in one of these categories rather than another.

The Pilot Study

A **pilot study** is one that is conducted *prior to* an actual research project. Its goal is to avoid unforeseen difficulties that might arise from a research design. Stated differently, a pilot study is a *small* research effort designed to discover possible problems while there is still time to remedy them. For example, suppose we have selected a problem for investigation that requires the use of previously untested research instruments or equipment. Suppose further that we and our research associates were unsure of how our subjects or respondents would react to these untested methods. In this instance it is advisable to conduct a "dress rehearsal" of the study to ensure that we will be prepared to handle any problems that might occur during the actual study.

For instance, in preparation for a survey it is often a good idea to conduct a pilot study to *pretest* the clarity of the questions used in a questionnaire. Are our questions clear? Can they be understood? If the respondents taking part in the pilot study cannot easily understand the questions we have asked, there is still time to revise the questionnaire before going to the field for the actual study.

The pilot study can also be used to train interviewers and acquaint them with the instruments and procedures we have designed. And finally, a pilot study can be useful in determining if the questions we have asked or the procedures we have used will actually "get at" the information needed.

Sometimes the pilot study is confused with the exploratory study.

Remember that a pilot study is conducted when researchers are testing new methods and procedures, and when they are attempting to head off possible research problems that may be unforeseen. It is a *dress rehearsal.* An exploratory study is conducted when researchers are unfamiliar with the topic they wish to examine, and when they are breaking new ground in a previously unstudied area. It is more like an *adventure.*

In summary, research designs are simply the plans drawn up prior to actually conducting a study. These plans include every phase of the research project. As we have pointed out, the *goal* of a study can significantly influence a researcher's plan of action, and we have described several research goals: exploration, description, explanation, and pilot studies. However, these goals are not mutually exclusive and a research design can include one or all of them. Most importantly, research questions dictate research designs, and not vice versa.

Time Frames

Time is another important aspect of research design, and it too plays a part in dictating the plans needed for the successful completion of a research project. As with research goals, time is also a factor to be taken into account once a study problem has been identified. For example, if we wish to examine some aspect of social change, how will the time element fit into our research design? In order to detect change it is obvious that our design will have to include plans to observe the behavior in which we are interested *on more than one occasion.* On the other hand, if we are interested only in how people currently feel about an issue, it will be necessary to measure their attitudes *only once.* There are two ways, then, of looking at time within a research design: *cross-sectionally* and *longitudinally.* We will discuss each of these topics separately.

The Cross-Sectional Study

A **cross-sectional study** is one designed to examine a topic at *one point in time.* For instance, if we were concerned with attitudes toward environmental protection policies, we could sample a cross section of the population and then describe their attitudes and feelings toward various environmental issues, using our data for *only that given time.* Because time is a continuous phenomenon, a cross-sectional study can perhaps best be described as one that attempts to freeze the topic so that only that one slice of time is carefully examined. From this perspective a cross-sectional study can be seen as a "snapshot" rather than as a "motion picture," a term that would better describe longitudinal studies.

The Longitudinal Study

As suggested above, a study can also be designed to examine a phenomenon over an extended period of time, and this requires that the researcher make several observations rather than just a single "snapshot." This is the **longitudinal study,** which consists of several types: **panel studies, cohort studies,** and **trend studies.**

PANEL STUDIES   In a panel study the researcher will examine or question the *same group* of respondents at two or more different times. For instance, Dunlap and Dillman wanted to know if public attitudes toward environmental protection had changed since the early days of the environmental movement. In their research, respondents were interviewed first in 1970 and then again in 1974. Dunlap and Dillman were then able to compare responses from the same individuals at two different times to see if public attitudes had really changed as others had suggested. Their data indicated that there had been a change in public attitudes between the two time periods, and that the change was such that people appeared less concerned in 1974 than in 1970.

There are, however, some problems with the panel design that must be pointed out. For instance, although this basic design is still widely used in the social sciences to detect change, it contains certain inherent problems that can jeopardize a study's validity. The first of these problems is called the **history effect,**[9] the fact that between the first observation and subsequent observations several other change-producing events can occur. Stated differently, if our first observation and our second observation are made on different days, or during different years as in the Dunlap and Dillman study, then events between them may have caused the change we detect in our study. For example, if we measured attitudes toward the environment in 1970 and then again in 1974, we might *expect* a change in attitude because of the energy crisis of 1973. A problem would arise, however, if we had been trying to increase the public's concern with environmental issues through an educational program that also came about between the two observations. If this were the case, we might mistakenly attribute the negative change in public attitude to our program when it had actually been the result of other historical events (that is, the energy "crunch" in early October 1973, when the oil-producing states announced a cutoff of exports to nations supporting Israel and oil prices quadrupled).

Another problem with this design has been called the **maturation problem,**[10] a term coined to describe the biological or psychological processes that come about simply because of the passage of time between observations. The sample used in the Dunlap and Dillman study became four years older between 1970 and 1974, and if the age of a person is related to attitudes toward environmental policy, it might have been the maturation of the sample that caused the change and not actually changes in attitudes *per se.*[11]

Another problem—the **mortality problem**[12]—centers on the possibility that some members of our original sample might have moved and thus cannot be relocated for the second observation. Others may have died, which means that our second sample is somewhat different from the first and that the differences we detect may be the result of this change rather than a change in attitude. The maturation and mortality problems are generally associated with *experimental designs*, and they are more fully described in Chapter 8.

COHORT STUDIES   A cohort study is similar to a panel study except that the same respondents are not used when moving from the first observation to the next. Rather, cohorts, or identifiable subpopulations of the larger population, are examined over time. For instance, a sample of persons aged 20−25 could be surveyed in 1970, another sample of different persons 30−35 years of age in 1980, and finally another sample of individuals 40−45 years of age in 1990. Although each sample would not contain the same people (as was the case in the panel study design), each sample would contain persons *from the cohort who had been born between 1950 and 1955.* Of course, the assumption made for this type of study design is that cohorts share the same experiences through time, and thus changes in attitude can be monitored over several years.

TREND STUDIES   Finally, there is the trend study, in which we would examine trends (rather than respondents as in the cohort design) in attitudes or characteristics by simply comparing data from the general population over time. For example, Lowe and his associates wanted to examine possible changes in public attitude toward formal education for the years 1972 through 1978.[13] For their study they compared responses on educational-funding questions from a series of national public polls for each of the years they were interested in. By comparing the percentages of rural respondents who indicated that more educational funding was needed, the researchers were able to show that rural people had become more concerned about education over the years studied.

As with panel and cohort studies, there are some problems that should also be noted about trend studies. Specifically, it is often difficult to find a large number of surveys that cover several years and that also ask the exact same questions of their respondents. If the questions asked are not the same, they cannot be compared. Also noteworthy is the problem of finding surveys that asked questions several years ago that are seen as important issues today. This is currently the case with research related to the energy crisis and the environmental movement. Who would have thought to ask questions about car pooling in 1965 when gasoline was priced at thirty-five cents a gallon and no shortages were foreseen? A survey of this vintage containing such questions would certainly be valuable today.

Another important step in the formulation of a research design is the specification of the group of persons or things to be investigated. For sociologists there exists a wide variety of individuals or respondents who are appropriate for study. This is not to be confused with the wide array of topics available for study; rather, we are referring to who or what our **units of analysis** will be. More formally, a unit of analysis means the basic unit whose properties we choose to explore, describe, or explain. For sociologists this is generally the individual person or some aggregate of persons such as a city, an organization, or even an entire society. The unit of analysis, then, *is the basic unit we describe in our study.*

For example, you may have had reason to describe your hometown to a college roommate. In this situation you may have said something like, "It's a fairly large town, almost one hundred and fifty thousand people, and most of the folks in my hometown are involved in one way or another with agriculture." In this example, what is the unit of analysis? Since we have used the *individuals* in our hometown to describe its size, and their aggregate employment characteristics to describe the town's average employment pattern, our unit of analysis is the individual.

The Individual

For the social scientist the individual human being is almost always the basic unit of analysis. When it is necessary to describe a group, for example, we typically aggregate individual characteristics and responses and use an average score to depict the entire group. We say that the average grade for the class was 78 or that the typical respondent to our questionnaire was a white male. Additional examples using the individual as the unit of analysis would include descriptions of the student body at a university, the residents of rural areas in our home state, all mothers of teenage girls, or all people who ride motorcycles. If we keep in mind that the individual human being is generally the basic unit of analysis for the sociologist, we should better be able to remember that it would be difficult for a social researcher to go further *down* the scale of analysis when conducting a study. It would be difficult for a sociologist, for example, to do a study of the parts of the individual human body, although such a study would be appropriate for a medical researcher. For the social researcher, moving up the scale of analysis is another matter.

The Group

It is possible to move up the scale of analysis from the individual to the social group. This is, of course, different from using the aggregate responses or characteristics of individuals to describe group properties. For instance, we could use as our basic unit of analysis data from census tracts. In doing so we would not be able to reduce our data to the individual level because these additional data would not be available to us. What we could do is describe each census tract in terms of its average income or the percentage of its residents that were unemployed. Some additional examples of group-level units of analysis would include families, gangs, and cliques. If we wanted to describe a group's characteristics, however, it would be very similar to describing the characteristics of an individual. We could note the size of the group, its age, and any additional *group* characteristics that were of interest to us. It is important to note that when we use groups as our unit of analysis we cannot drop below the group level in our analysis. *The groups we are studying are the smallest units in our data set.*

The Formal Organization

Formal organizations can also be used as a unit of analysis. For example, we may wish to study all sociology departments in the United States that offer the doctoral degree. Individual departments could be characterized in terms of the number of professors they employ, the number of professional publications or papers produced by the organization each year, the number of doctoral and other advanced degrees conferred by the department, and the number and value of grants received by the faculty. There are many other examples of formal organizations that might be used as a unit of analysis. For instance, we could study drug stores, churches, or social fraternities on campus.

It is not only possible to describe these various units of analysis; it is also possible to manipulate their characteristics to help explain them. In the example of the study of sociology departments, we might discover that larger departments published more papers than smaller ones, and that they were able to attract more grant money. Smaller departments might be able to get their students through their programs much faster than the larger ones but they might not be able to bring in as much money to offer their students financial assistance.

When we have selected a topic for study, and when we have placed that topic within the framework of a theoretical statement, it is generally not too difficult to identify the unit of analysis. As *the* researcher, we will usually understand if we are studying departments of sociology or sociologists, individuals or communities, workers or corporations. What is often difficult to keep in mind is that we cannot assume that what is true at one level of analysis is true at another. This "jumping" from one unit of analysis—group data—to another—individual data—is called the **ecological fallacy,** that is, drawing conclusions about individuals based on the study of groups. For example, suppose we were interested in studying crime and had analyzed data for the census tracts in our hometown. We might find that more crimes are commit-ted in areas that were characterized by a high degree of unemployment. From these data we might be tempted to conclude that unemployed *persons* are more likely to commit crimes than those who are employed. In reaching such a conclusion we will run the risk of committing the ecological fallacy because in fact it may be that the employed portion of the population we have studied had been committing the crimes. The point is, we can never know which individuals are actually committing the crimes in our hometown based on group-level data only because we have drawn a conclusion from *group data and applied it at the individual level.* As an additional example, suppose we had data at the county level indicating a strong correlation between voting trends and income, and we discovered that counties with generally higher incomes tend to elect more Republicans while counties with lower income levels tend to elect more Democrats. To assume on the basis of these *group-level* data that the *individuals* within the counties necessarily behave in a manner analogous to the way their counties behave is another example of an ecological fallacy. We never know what individuals are doing based on the analysis of group-level data.

When we move in the opposite direction in drawing conclusions from an analysis, we run the risk of committing the **individualistic fallacy.**[14] Assume here that we have data at the individual level, and they indicate that younger persons are more favorably disposed to policy designed to protect wilderness areas. If we conclude from these data that legislators from states with generally young populations will vote favorably on wilderness protection legislation, we will again be "jumping" from one unit of analysis to another and run the risk of the individualistic fallacy. What is needed in both examples for the conclu-sions made is data from the level of analysis that is appropriate for such conclusions. Specifically, to understand how legislators will vote, we will need data gathered at the legislative level, and not simply for the group they represent. We cannot say that because a state has a generally young popula-tion, and because younger people tend to favor this type of legislation, that the legislators themselves will vote in this particular way. Although they may indeed do so, it cannot be concluded from the data at hand.

Scope

Finally, it should be noted that social scientific investigations vary in terms of the scope of their analyses, a factor related to the unit of analysis. For example, a psychologist will almost always use the individual as the unit of analysis in a study, but a sociologist is more likely to use the group as his or her unit of analysis. As we shall see later, when we study only a very few persons, our scope is somewhat limited and it is often difficult to generalize beyond the few people who took part in our investigation. This type of study is often said to have been conducted at the **micro** level. However, if we were going to study the characteristics of all communities in the United States over the size of twenty-five hundred persons, our study would be much broader in scope and we would have a much easier time generalizing to the rest of the population of the country. An investigation of this type is often referred to as a **macro** analysis.

To summarize our discussion of units of analysis, time has been shown to be an important aspect of the research design process. We have seen that there are several ways in which we can handle time within the framework of a research design. Some studies can be characterized as cross-sectional and others as longitudinal. In a cross-sectional study only one "slice" of the population at one point in time is examined. Of those studies characterized as longitudinal there are three varieties: panel studies, which examine the same group on two or more occasions; cohort studies, which examine persons from the same subpopulation over time; and trend studies, which generally compare similar data sets and responses to questions over time. We have also discussed some of the problems associated with longitudinal studies, and more specifically the problems associated with panel designs. We noted that a researcher might find change that had been brought about because of the history effect, the maturation of a sample, and mortality. For trend studies we noted that it was often difficult to find data and questions that are comparable from one survey to another. Further, we pointed out that there are three general units of analysis used in social research: the individual, the group, and the formal organizational level. A problem associated with units of analysis is that of moving from one level of analysis to another when drawing conclusions. This problem is called the ecological fallacy when we move from the group or organizational level to the individual unit and the individualistic fallacy when we conclude that what is true at the individual level is also true at the group or organizational level.

Research Motives

What is behind a social scientific study? What motivates the researcher and his or her associates to go to the field or to conduct a survey? Of course, as in an exploratory study, researchers are often curious about a topic and this motivates them to examine it more carefully. On the other hand, a researcher might become concerned about an issue and believe that it can be resolved by study. Basically, then, research can be classified into two general categories: **pure research** and **applied research.** Pure research involves developing and testing hypotheses that are intellectually interesting to the investigator and thus *might* have some application in the future, but have no direct application to a problem at the time the research is conducted. Applied research, on the other hand, is research with findings that can be applied to a problem of immediate concern.

Pure Research

Pure research is most often conducted to gain knowledge simply for the sake of gaining knowledge. In our earlier example of the streaking study, what aspects of the findings from that investigation could be used to solve a problem of immediate concern? Could the findings be used to stop streaking? Perhaps so, but the major objective of the study was not to *apply* the findings to that particular phenomenon; rather, it was to gain an intellectual understanding of the activity and to understand more about what people thought of streaking as a popular activity. The students who conducted the study were concerned with *understanding* streaking behavior and what others thought about it. Their *motive* for conducting the project can thus be classified as "pure" because no thought was given to the application of their findings to a problem of immediate concern.

Applied Research

Applied research is another matter. This type of research is directed toward finding solutions to immediate problems, and the findings from applied studies are generally used to aid policymakers and other government officials in making decisions about how to better run our towns, cities, and country. For these reasons applied research is almost always *funded* research. That is, because people in government are the persons who are generally most interested in the results of applied studies, they often make grants or contracts available to social scientists to study the problems they need solved. This means that social scientists are given money to research a specific topic, and that the government expects the study they have sponsored will be completed in a specified time. It also means that the findings will be made available to them immediately. Sociologists, for example, are often called upon to use their methodological skills to evaluate the effectiveness of the various social agencies our government supports. This type of applied research is called *evaluation* research (see Chapter 18).

It is important to note that pure and applied research styles are not mutually exclusive. There is no reason to believe, for example, that an applied research project cannot be as intellectually interesting to a researcher as a pure one. It is also very possible that the results of what is intended to be a pure research project can turn out to be extremely useful and applicable to problems of immediate concern. The major difference between the two is that with pure research projects the investigator is able to study what he or she believes is interesting. For the applied researcher, the selection of the topic for study is determined to a large degree by the person or group paying the bills. If our interests happen to coincide with the interests of a granting agency, we have found the best of all possible research worlds.

Selecting Research Methods for a Research Design

Up to this point we have discussed several factors that might influence the formulation of a research design. We have stressed the fact that the research question we ask will determine to a large degree the kind of design we will eventually formulate. We have noted, for example, that if a question deals with some aspect of social change, that some form of longitudinal study will be the best design to use, and we have suggested that if our question deals with a very sensitive topic that perhaps some form of participant observation would be our best bet. In this section we introduce you to some of the research methods that are presented later in the book and indicate, in a very general way, the strengths and weaknesses of each of them. Using this section as a guide, we should be better able to begin the formulation of a research design.

The Survey

Of all the methods available to the sociologist the survey is perhaps the most often employed. This method of gathering social data can be used for any of the goals we discussed earlier in this chapter: exploration, description, or explanation. The unit of analysis in the survey, however, is almost always the individual respondent. How does the survey handle the time element? This would depend on the way the method is used. As in the example of the panel design, if researchers can afford to conduct a follow-up survey or make additional observations, this technique can be a useful tool for the examination of certain aspects of social change. If we could locate existing data from surveys which asked respondents the same questions over a period of time, this method can also be at the heart of trend or cohort studies. As we shall see in later chapters, the survey is rather flexible in terms of the many ways in which it can be utilized. Specifically, survey research can be conducted in face-to-face interviews, over the phone, or through the mail. Because the survey can be used to reach a large number of persons, it is an excellent technique for studying attitudes and public opinion. The survey is discussed in Chapter 7.

The Experiment

This method is best suited for explanatory and descriptive studies but is used less often by sociologists than other methods. As we shall see in later chapters, social experiments are generally conducted in controlled settings. This means that experiments can become rather costly to the researcher. Because of the very nature of "experimental" designs, we shall see that this method is very useful in examining certain aspects of change, and the basic design of the experiment is at the heart of all studies dealing with this topic. Although there are variations in how this design can be employed, the basic unit of analysis is the individual. Experimental designs are presented in Chapter 8.

Content Analysis

This technique, which we have not mentioned up to this point, makes use of existing documents (novels, the text of a speech, diaries, comic books, letters) that were originally intended for uses other than research. This technique is not as costly as others because many documents appropriate for content analysis can be found in almost any library. Units of analysis for this method can vary from an individual level to a group level depending on the question we are asking. For example, if we wanted to explore changes in the methods used by sociologists in the studies they reported in professional journals, our unit of analysis would be the individual scientific article, and because sociology journals have been around for many years, it would not be difficult to use this method for detecting changes in the methods sociologists used over time. Content analysis is presented in Chapter 9.

Participant Observation

As mentioned earlier in this chapter, this is a social scientific method of systematic observation in which an investigator participates as a member of the group he or she is studying. Because it would be difficult to observe several persons at one time (as a city of some size), this technique is not well suited for studies directed toward measuring attitudes or public opinion. What this method will allow sociologists to do is to study groups that would otherwise be unwilling or unable to respond to a questionnaire. For example, if we wished to study the activities of very young children, some form of participant observation would be preferable to the survey as the basis of your design, essentially because very young children could neither read nor respond to the questions that are generally used in questionnaires. Also, and as we noted earlier, this approach is well suited for the study of sensitive issues that respondents might not wish to discuss with a survey researcher over the phone or on his or her doorstep in a face-to-face interview. If a researcher can gain entrance into the group he or she wishes to study, participant observation can be a useful research tool for studying deviant behavior and other sensitive topics. How does this method deal with the time dimension? Most anthropologists like to remain in the field for at least a year to observe behaviors throughout all the seasons. This can give the researcher some indication of what happens over time but it may not allow the observation of social change as such. It can also be a rather costly method if we consider that housing, food, and transportation must be provided when several researchers are in the field for extended periods. This method is presented in Chapter 10.

Mixing Methods for a Research Design

The terms *research method* and *research design* are used throughout the remainder of this book: they should not be confused. Keep in mind that a research design is a more general plan and that a single design may contain and require the use of several different methods. Research methods are more specific techniques, plans that are available for use within a single research design. For example, we could design a study that mixed both participant observation *and* survey research (two methods) in order to better answer a research question. Keep in mind that when we can strengthen a research design by including various methods that complement each other, we can have more confidence in the findings of the study when it is completed. Unfortunately, we do not always have the funds or the time to use all of the research tools that are available to us, and both time and money are key factors in the total research process.

Time, Money, and Research Designs

As suggested above, some research designs cost more than others, and some require a good deal more time to complete. Thus, two additional factors should be taken into account when considering a research project: *time* and *money.*

Time

Let us suppose, for example, that we have been hired to conduct research to help explain changes in public attitudes toward local plans for busing or some other issue of immediate importance, and let's suppose further that our findings are needed within the year so officials can begin planning for the future impacts of changing student populations and problems associated with transportation. Given that our findings are needed almost immediately ("We needed them yesterday"), this simple fact eliminates several possible study designs we might have otherwise selected. Specifically, it would be difficult to conduct a study over an extended period of time. This means that the traditional longitudinal study will have to be shelved, and that participant observation over an extended period will probably be out of the question as well. We'll have to select methods that are appropriate for generating reliable data in a short period of time, such as a telephone survey or the use of existing data of some kind.

The following are some questions you might wish to ask yourself before beginning a research project. They are intended to give you an idea of the methodological procedures that will work best for you and the research project you are thinking about doing.

What is the purpose of the study? Is your study exploratory, descriptive, or explanatory? Almost every one of the methods we have described would be appropriate for any one of the purposes listed above. However, the experiment is generally conducted when definite hypotheses have been generated from previous research, and therefore you would probably not select the traditional experiment as a means for exploring an area.

What is the scope of the study? By scope we mean the time period to be covered; that is, will your study be longitudinal or cross-sectional? If you plan to study change over a period of time, your design will have to be very different from one directed toward cross-sectional purposes. Depending upon the exact research question you're asking, the survey (at two or more different times), content analysis, and possibly participant observation will be your most useful selections.

How much time do you have? As we have suggested previously, if your project must be completed within a certain specified time period, your methods will be limited to those that can get the job done in as rapid a manner as possible. Most researchers who conduct polls for political candidates or for others who need information quickly select the telephone survey as their method for generating data to test questions of immediate concern.

What are the costs? It almost goes without saying that your efforts will be limited by the amount of money you have available to conduct your research. Simply put, you would not plan a national sample for a project if your funds were limited to only a few hundred dollars.

Money

Clearly, the funds available to conduct such a study will also dramatically influence what can and cannot be accomplished with a research project. If we are asked to conduct a statewide study of one kind or another, and our budget is limited to only a thousand dollars, then our selection of a research design will be limited to those that can be accomplished in an inexpensive way. We would again probably turn to a telephone survey, which is fast and relatively inexpensive, rather than a more complex multimethodological study.

Being realistic about the financial and time constraints that are placed upon us as we consider various research possibilities is also an important aspect of research design. Although it is beyond the scope of this book to make you an accountant or a time-study expert, it is wise to carefully consider both of these aspects when preparing a study proposal. If you are a student, for example, and your term paper is required by the end of the semester, you pretty well know what your time frame will look like and you should construct your design accordingly. Furthermore, if you're a student and are not working with an enormous bank account, you will heed your financial constraints and select problems that do not require you to fly to various parts of the country to conduct interviews or gather data of other kinds. Simply put, time and money constraints must each be carefully considered before a research design can be considered complete.

Summary

In this chapter we have introduced the design phase of social scientific research. We have tried to show that research questions determine the kind of plans that are needed to best answer the research questions asked. The goals of a study, the time frame we hope to address, the identification of units of analysis, the motives behind an investigation, and some of the various methods available to the social scientist have each been discussed. The main point we have stressed is that there is no single research methodology appropriate for all questions, and that one of the most important parts of a study comes at the very beginning when our plans are initially made. This phase occurs long before the researcher goes to the field.

We have briefly introduced some of the methods that will be discussed at length later in the book, and we have suggested when these methods should be used and how they are attached to research questions. The survey, for example, was presented as being most appropriate for examining public attitudes and opinions because it reaches a larger portion of the population than some of the other methods one might select. The experiment, on the other hand, is typically conducted in controlled settings rather than in the field, and is effectively used to detect change. Content analysis uses data that are not necessarily intended to be used in sociological studies (books, journals, letters, the content of a speech) and is not as costly as some of the other methods we described. It, too, can be used to examine change. Participant observation places the researcher into the actual group or setting he or she is trying to study. The scope of this variety of investigation is at the micro level, whereas the scope of most surveys is said to be at the macro level of investigation. When persons cannot read or understand the questions that we would otherwise include in a questionnaire or when our topic is a very sensitive one, it is probably best to turn to some form of participant observation when designing a study.

Each study asks a somewhat different question, and each study generates its own particular research problems that we must plan for. By carefully planning a study before going to the field, several problems are solved, and a more accurate answer can be provided to the question under investigation. Without road maps, travelers would become lost and it would take them a much longer time to reach their desired destination. Without a research design, researchers can also become lost, and research questions can remain unanswered for an unnecessarily long period of time. By carefully planning the route we will take we can reach our destination and answer our research questions. This is accomplished through a research design.

Glossary

applied research Research designed to find answers and solutions to problems of immediate concern. This kind of research can be *applied* to the various problems of society (compare with *pure research*).

cohort study Similar to a panel study except that the same respondents (or panel) are not used when moving from one point in time to the next. Rather, cohorts or identifiable subpopulations of the larger population are examined over time. For example, persons aged 20–25 could be surveyed in 1970, and another sample of persons 30–35 years of age could be sampled in 1980, and an additional sample taken of persons 40–45 years of age in 1990. These samples or cohorts could then be analyzed to see what changes in attitudes or beliefs came about over time.

cross-sectional study A study that is designed to examine a topic at only one point in time (contrast with *longitudinal study*).

descriptive study A research project that has as its purpose the accurate description of various social events, institutions, groups, and behavior patterns. Descriptive studies simply tell us what a particular social "thing" looks like.

ecological fallacy Making conclusions about one unit of analysis based upon the study of another unit of analysis. Generally this term refers to "jumping" from the group-level of analysis to draw conclusions about individual behavior (compare with *individualistic fallacy*).

explanatory study A research project that has as its purpose the explanation of certain social events and occurrences. This type of study will generally conclude with an explanation of why certain people behave as they do under certain social conditions.

exploratory study A research project that has as its purpose the discovery of insights and knowledge in an area that has previously gone unstudied. When a researcher is "breaking new ground" it can often be said that he or she is conducting exploratory research.

history effect Refers to the fact that between first and later observations several change-producing events can take place causing a researcher to reach faulty conclusions. The example we gave suggested that possible declines in public support for environmental protection could be caused by various historical events taking place between measurements of public concern taken at points in time separated by several years (see Chapter 8).

individualistic fallacy This refers to "jumping" from the individual level of analysis to make conclusions about group-level data (compare with *ecological fallacy*).

longitudinal study A study designed to examine data gathered at several different points in time to detect possible change (contrast with *cross-sectional study*).

macro Refers generally to the study of large-scale social systems and patterns of interrelationships within and between systems, including, for example, national and international forms of social organization (contrast with *micro*).

maturation problem A term coined to describe the biological or psychological processes that come about simply because of the passage of time between observations. For example, respondents grow older or get hungry as time goes by.

micro Refers primarily to the study of small-scale social systems or to the study of small groups (contrast with *macro*).

mortality problem Refers to the problem of losing members of a sample from time one to later observations because they cannot be located. Respondents may have moved or even died and their exclusion from later samples may cause a significant change in findings (see Chapter 8).

panel study A form of longitudinal study that examines the same panel (or sample) of individuals at two or more points in time.

pilot study A "mini" study conducted prior to an actual larger study. It is designed to avoid unforeseen difficulties that might arise from an untested research design. This type of study is often used also to test new methods and research procedures that have not been previously tried. A pilot study is a "dress rehearsal" for a larger study, and is often used to "pretest" major research projects.

pure research Research designed to gain knowledge simply for the sake of gaining knowledge (contrast with *applied research*).

research design The initial planning of a research project based upon the various goals of a particular study and the research problem being asked. This process can also be thought of as the *tactics* you will employ to gather and analyze a specific data set.

survey One type of research design. The term *survey* generally refers to the methods of asking questions to a sample of respondents, either in face-to-face interview situations, by mail, or even over the phone. This is a good technique for determining public opinion and attitudes because it generally takes into account a larger portion of the population (see Chapter 7).

trend study Similar to cohort studies, but in this case you would examine trends in attitudes or characteristics by simply comparing data from the general population over time (compare with *panel* and *cohort* studies).

unit of analysis Refers to the group of persons or things to be analyzed. For sociologists this generally refers to the individual human being. However, it is possible to study units other than individuals, and researchers often focus on groups or formal organizations when attempting to answer research questions.

1. T. Lynn Smith and Paul E. Zopf, Jr., *Demography: Principles and Methods* (Port Washington, N.Y.: Alfred, 1976), p. 98.
2. Laud Humphreys, *Tearoom Trade: Impersonal Sex in Public Places* (Chicago: Aldine and Atherton, 1969).
3. See, for example, Otis Dudley Duncan, "Sociologists Should Reconsider Nuclear Energy," *Social Forces* 57 (1978): 1—22.

Notes

4. Michael D. Grimes, Thomas K. Pinhey, and Louis A. Zurcher, "Note on Students' Reactions to 'Streakers' and 'Streaking,' " *Perceptual Motor Skills* 45 (1977): 1226.

5. Smith and Zopf, op. cit., p. 11.

6. Hunter S. Thompson, "Hell's Angels: Hoodlum Circus and Statutory Rape of Bass Lake," in *Observations of Deviance*, Jack D. Douglas, ed., pp. 131−145 (New York: Random House, 1970).

7. Robert Rosenthal and Lenore Jacobson, *Pygmalion in the Classroom* (New York: Holt, Rinehart and Winston, 1968).

8. Riley E. Dunlap and Don A. Dillman, "Decline in Public Support for Environmental Protection: Evidence from a 1970−1974 Panel Study," *Rural Sociology* 41 (1976): 382−390.

9. Donald T. Campbell and Julian C. Stanley, *Experimental and Quasi-Experimental Designs for Research* (Chicago: Rand McNally, 1963), p. 5.

10. Ibid., p. 5.

11. Thomas K. Pinhey and Michael D. Grimes, "Comment on the Decline in Public Support For Environmental Protection," *Rural Sociology* 44, No. 1 (1979): pp. 201−203.

12. Campbell and Stanley, op. cit., p. 5.

13. George D. Lowe and Thomas K. Pinhey, "Do Rural People Place a Lower Value on Formal Education?: New Evidence from National Surveys," *Rural Sociology* 45, No. 2 (1980): 325−331.

14. See Claire Selltiz, Lawrence S. Wrightsman, and Stuart W. Cook, *Research Methods in Social Relations*, 3rd ed. (New York: Holt, Rinehart, and Winston, 1976), pp. 439−440, for a discussion of the individualistic fallacy. See W.S. Robinson, "Ecological Correlations and the Behavior of Individuals," *American Sociological Review* 15 (June 1950): 351−57, for a presentation and description of the ecological fallacy.

4

Conceptualization and Operationalization

Moving from abstract theory to the actual conduct of social research is perhaps the most difficult task for the beginning sociologist to grasp. How, for example, does a researcher move beyond the theoretical realm of social scientific study to the process of making observations in the concrete world? How does one actually go about *seeing* what theory directs us to see? As has been pointed out in earlier chapters, the sociological attachment to theory is a strong one, and it is this strong attachment that distinguishes what we do as sociologists from what those in the "public opinion industry" seek to accomplish. For those who are simply interested in what people think about an issue there is little need for theory to guide their work, but as sociologists our work must be grounded within some theoretical frame of reference in order that it "make sense." Simply put, *theory guides research* for the social scientist but this is not always the case for the person who simply wants to measure public opinion.

But the question remains, "How does one start with only a fuzzy idea about what they want to study and end up with a successfully completed research project?" In this chapter we introduce the process of moving from theory to practice. We show how one starts with theory and moves to a clearly defined set of variables that can both be seen and measured in the social world. Two important notions are introduced in this chapter. First, the idea of **concepts,** and second, the term **operationalization.**

The Concept

What is a concept? How do concepts work? First of all, concepts are the basic building blocks of theory, and it is the logical linking together of concepts that makes theory.[1] A concept can be a word or a set of words that expresses a general idea concerning the nature of something or the relations between things (see Chapter 2). For example, a concept can provide a category for the classification of phenomena or it can simply point researchers in the general direction they should follow. In this sense, a concept is a tool that can sensitize the researcher to the aspects of the world he or she has selected for study.[2] For instance, *polyandry* is a concept describing a form of polygamous marriage in which one woman may be married to several men at the same time. This concept sensitizes researchers to a specific category of women—those who have more than one husband—and points researchers in a general direction concerning the nature of what is to be looked for when trying to identify a person who would fit into this or another category. Simply put, if we have one category for women with more than one husband, we should also be sensitized to those who have only one husband or perhaps none at all. According to theorist Jonathan Turner, however, there are two kinds of concepts. First, there are **abstract concepts**, which refer to the very *general* properties of phenomena. By *abstract* it is meant that the concept does not refer to a particular place, time, or event. Second, there are **concrete concepts**, which refer to *particular* individuals and interactions. Turner points out that the importance of abstractness can be illustrated by the fact that people had observed that apples fall from trees for centuries but did not really understand why the phenomenon occurred until the abstract concept of gravity was introduced. This conceptualization allowed for many similar occurrences to be visualized within the context of the gravity concept, which, as we know, explains much more than simply why apples fall from trees. We can see from Turner's example that abstract concepts are not restricted to only one situation or event, but are applicable to a much wider range of occurrences as well. Concrete concepts, on the other hand, are "fixed" in time by their reference to particular phenomena and, as a result, are sometimes not as theoretically useful as their more abstract counterparts.

An Example

Let's look at concepts in a less formal way. For instance, are you sitting in a chair? Even if you are not, think for a moment about the word *chair* and imagine that it represents a key concept for a theory we are working with. What kind of chair have you conjured up in your mind? How have you mentally *constructed* the concept "chair"? Do you see a rocking chair? An easy chair? A high chair? An electric chair? We are reasonably sure that everyone can mentally picture *a* chair but we cannot be sure that all of us have conjured up a picture of the exact same one. In this example we can see that the word *chair* expresses only a general idea about the nature of the item we are interested in. We have been sensitized by the concept and we can see that it points only to the *general properties* of chairs, by which we mean the attributes of characteristics that *all* chairs have in common—legs, a seat to sit on, and possibly arms. However, if our theory were to more clearly specify what the concept "chair" should look like, we would be moving down the ladder of abstractness to a more concrete concept which might enable all of us to visualize almost the exact same chair every time. For example, if the concept described our chair as having four rather tall legs with a tray attached to the front on which utensils for the feeding of infants were placed, our mental construct of the concept would be much clearer and definite, and we would agree more often when we saw this type of chair in a social setting. Now the concept "chair" has been made less abstract and more concrete, and in fact now refers to a particular category of chairs: the high chair.

A Sociological Example

Because sociologists seldom study chairs, let us look at an example of a concept in sociology. A classic example can be found in the work of Emile Durkheim, who examined suicide to see if he could detect a relationship between a person's propensity for suicide and his or her social surroundings.[3] For his study, Durkheim developed a single concept that linked together several hypotheses regarding suicide. It was hypothesized that persons were more likely to commit suicide during periods of rapid social or economic change, that soldiers were more prone to suicide than civilians, and that among soldiers officers were more likely to commit suicide than enlisted men. Males were also hypothesized to commit suicide more often than females, Protestants more likely than Catholics, single persons more often than married persons, and divorced or widowed persons more likely than those who were either married or single.

Durkheim linked together all of the above hypotheses using the concept of "social integration," which points to the general depth of a person's involvement with a social group. Persons can be extremely well integrated into a group, for example, or they can experience a very low level of integration into a group. They can also experience some confusion concerning their status within a group, which can be the result of a sudden crisis that disrupts traditional interaction routines.

Thus "social integration" can be seen as pointing to how tightly people are bound into groups. It sensitizes researchers and points them in the general direction they should follow. Because "social integration" is not tied to any one specific time, group, or place, it can be said to be an *abstract concept* and should therefore be applicable to a much wider range of occurrences than simply suicide. More specifically, this concept influenced Durkheim's decision to look at *variations* in social integration and to see how these different levels of social integration were correlated with the incidence of suicide.

From his initial studies Durkheim developed three additional concepts. He found that when persons were very tightly bound to a social group, and when, for example, their commitment to a group superseded personal satisfaction, they were prone to *altruistic suicide.* Because the rank of military persons usually increases with their commitment and integration into the military organization, this new concept helped explain why officers were more prone to suicide than enlisted men. An often-used example of this category of suicide is the Japanese kamikaze pilot.

The second concept developed from Durkheim's work was labeled *egoistic suicide*, which is motivated by a very low level of social integration into a group. When people are not committed to a group, they often feel isolated and alone and believe they have little to live for. This concept was used by Durkheim to explain why Protestants were more likely to commit suicide than Catholics. More specifically, Protestantism emphasizes self-reliance and the independent judgment of the individual more than Catholicism does. Another difference is that Catholicism more clearly spells out the rules of its church, thus giving its members a sense of understanding and of belonging to the group. Among these rules is a strict ban on suicide.

Anomic suicide, the last concept Durkheim developed in his classic study, refers to the disruption that can occur in a person's social circumstances. When there are sudden changes brought on, for example, by physical catastrophies, war, the loss of a member of the family, or a very close friend, then, according to Durkheim, persons are more likely to commit anomic suicide.

The importance of our discussion of Durkheim's work can be seen in two ways. First, it illustrates how the relations among concepts can be described; second, it shows how Durkheim used concrete concepts to describe the different categories of suicide. By making his concepts more concrete we can more clearly see what kinds of social integration are related to various forms of self-destruction. In a very similar way we tried earlier to show that there can be a general and more abstract conceptualization of a chair as well as a more specific and particular conceptualization of the same object.

Conceptualization

From the above example we can see that Durkheim not only used concepts to help in his study of suicide but that he also left these concepts for all sociologists to use in future studies. Durkheim **conceptualized** suicide so that we can classify each case we observe into one of his three conceptual categories. Each of these categories (anomic suicide, egoistic suicide, and altruistic suicide) has been clearly spelled out by Durkheim so that we can identify these forms of self-destruction when we examine the social world. *When we conceptualize we clearly spell out and define what it is we mean when we use a certain concept or term.* For example, if we intended to use *social integration* in a study of behavior, we would have to clearly indicate what we meant by the term. We might say, then, that when persons were integrated into a group, they performed specialized activities as members which were interrelated and complementary to other members' specialized ways of behaving.

Thus far we have tried to show that concepts are the theoretical tools that sensitize researchers to the general areas they should be looking at when conducting a study. A concept is simply a word or a set of words that express a general notion about the nature of "things." Concepts can be abstract and are thus not tied to a specific place or event. They can also be concrete and refer directly to particular individuals, interactions, and settings. Durkheim used a single concept to tie together several different hypotheses concerning suicide, and from his subsequent investigations he was able to conceptualize some of the various forms of self-destruction that we currently examine in sociological studies. By conceptualization is meant the process whereby we clearly indicate what we mean when we use certain terms or concepts in a study.

Theorist Jonathan H. Turner uses the following example to clarify the uses of concepts in sociology. Perhaps his example will help you to more clearly understand how they are utilized in the conduct of social research:

> The concept "conflict" asserts that varying forms of hostile interactions exist in the social world. The concept "social unit" reveals that individuals are organized into different types of collective patterns. The concept "solidarity" denotes the fact that social units evidence different degrees of internal cohesion and unity. The following theoretical statement allows scientists to see the *relation* among these concepts: "The greater the degree of conflict among social units, the greater the degree of solidarity in each unit." Several features of this statement should be emphasized. It is abstract, because it does not talk about a specific conflict among particular units in a given time and place. It transcends time and space. And it is a theoretical statement, because it asserts a relationship among three social phenomena: "conflict," "social units," and "solidarity."

Adapted from Jonathan H. Turner, *The Structure of Sociological Theory*, rev. ed. (Homewood, Ill.: Dorsey, 1978), pp. 20.

But how do we move from abstract concepts to the practice of social research? To understand this aspect of the process we will have to explore some additional terms.

The Variable

The concept "social integration" points researchers in the direction they should be looking and gives a general idea of what it is they should be looking for. For this concept, we are looking for variations in the strength and intensity with which one is integrated into a group. We can say, then, that we would expect persons to be bound or integrated into a group to some variable degree. If persons are attached to groups in a variable way, then these attachments are assumed to differ—or vary—from one observation to the next. It can be thought of as the opposite of a **constant**.[4] A variable is a type of concrete concept that varies and takes on different values. A constant never changes and thus has only one value. As individuals our attachments to groups vary, and if we could measure such "differing" group attachments for all of us we would find that we each had a different "social integration" score. This score is called a variable. For example, if an English class takes a test, and each student receives a score on the test, we can say that the score is a variable because it has taken on a somewhat different value for each student in the class. Again, suppose we had an interest in the age of each of the persons in our class. If we went to each person and asked them their age we would get as many different answers as there were persons in the room. Even if our fictitious class contained a set of twins we would still expect that no two persons would have been born at the exact same time. As can be seen, a social variable can take on several values. Additional examples of variables that can be measured in the classroom are years of education, sex, ethnicity, major, and political party preference. Even when some of the class members share a common trait, such as political preference, we can still see that there is variation between these categories of people because the political variable itself can take on several different values. There are several kinds of variables that should be noted. The "kind" of variable we use will be influenced by how we wish to use it. The most common distinction between variables is made between the *independent* and *dependent* variable.

The Dependent Variable

The **dependent variable** is the one the researcher is usually most interested in. It is the variable we are trying to explain, describe, or simply understand. It is generally the *focus of our study*. For example, when Durkheim conducted his study of suicide, his dependent variable was the incidence of suicide itself. If we wish to understand more about attitudes toward the natural environment, our dependent variable would be "attitudes toward the natural environment."

Another way of thinking of dependent variables is to consider that our main variable, the one our study is focusing upon, *is dependent upon other variables for its explanation.* For instance, if we wanted to understand more about status attainment, that is, about how people go about gaining their social position in society, we might select as our dependent variable a respondent's annual income. This would be an *indicator* of one's social position, but what other variables would we use to explain why income varied from one person to the next? What is income a consequence of? What other variables would income depend upon?

One key variable found to predict a person's income is educational level. If an individual has a high level of formal education, he or she generally has a somewhat higher level of income than persons of lower educational attainment. General intelligence, race and ethnicity, occupational status, and several other variables can also be used to help explain a person's income.
Importantly, we can see that a person's income *depends* upon how much education he or she has as well as upon the combination of several additional variables.

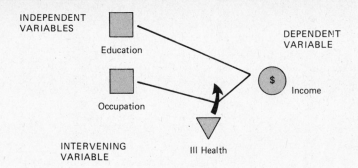

INDEPENDENT VARIABLES

Education

Occupation

DEPENDENT VARIABLE

$ Income

INTERVENING VARIABLE

Ill Health

FIGURE 4.1
Variables

The Independent Variable

Variables in a study that are used to explain other variables are called **independent variables,** the variables used to explain or account for variations in the dependent variable. What was Durkheim's independent variable in our example of his study of suicide? Most would agree it was "social integration." He used social integration to explain difference in suicide rates, his dependent variable. Again, when we tried to account for a person's social position we used educational level as an independent variable for explaining why some people have more income than others.

Intervening Variables

We can also think of dependent variables as occurring after some preceding variable, which we have called an independent variable. In a "causal" hypothesis, for instance, independent variables occur before the dependent, and some would argue that they were the variables that "caused" the dependent variable. **Intervening variables** are those that come between the independent and the dependent variables. For example, suppose we had hypothesized a relationship between one's educational attainment and one's eventual income level. We might hypothesize that, as the educational level increased so would the income level of our respondent. It is possible, however, that some variable might intervene between the independent variable (education) and the dependent variable (income) which would change our stated relationship. What variable or variables might intervene between a person's education and eventual income that could cause some change in the relationship we had hypothesized? If a person had a high level of formal education but had taken a job that was relatively low on the occupational status scale, his or her income would be somewhat lower than we would expect. Thus one's occupation can be seen as an intervening variable between education and income. Some additional factors that might intervene between one's education and income could be health problems, economic depression, or simply a change in occupation.

In later chapters we will see how variables are used to detect differences in attitudes and various forms of behavior among respondents in a sample (see Chapter 13). We will see that as one variable increases in its magnitude, so will the magnitude of other variables. For example, as a person's educational attainment increases, so usually does his or her average income level. However, as one's educational level increases, the desire to have more than two children has been found to decrease. These are examples of *positive* and *inverse* relationships, and they are described in greater detail in Chapter 13.

The Derivation of Variables

How does a researcher go about locating the variables that are appropriate for a study? As pointed out in Chapter 2, researchers generally start with a theoretical statement about some problem of interest and work from there. The problem selected for research, however, may have come from our everyday observations, which may have caused us to become curious about the topic in the first place. At that point we could have turned to some body of theory to help us understand what we had observed. Theory, as we have pointed out, is really nothing more than a very accurate description of reality, and it is comprised of concepts. Concepts are simply words or sets of words that express general ideas about things in the world. The task is to "see" what the concepts are pointing to and concepts typically lead researchers to the variables they will use in their study. Let's look at another example.

Suppose we are interested in the relationship between one's socioeconomic status (SES) and one's political party preferences. Suppose further that we have noticed in our everyday activities that persons from higher SES backgrounds tend to be more politically conservative than those from lower SES backgrounds. With this observation in mind we could have gone to the work of some theorist to see if they could provide some theoretical insight into our question of SES and politics. For instance, drawing from Weber's work, sociologist Gerhard Lenski defined "social class" as "an aggregation of persons in a society who stand in a similar position with respect to some form of power, privilege, or prestige."[5] In other words, some people, because of a similarity in occupation, income, or education, set themselves apart from the rest of society. Over time, these people become differentiated from the others, and become tightly integrated into a separate social stratum or class. As sociologists we would understand that people who are ranked in specific social classes display very similar social styles in their handling of day-to-day experiences. Such "classes" of people tend to hold similar values, live in similar areas, have similar occupations, and, in short, tend to display a common set of class interests. Because persons at higher levels in the social stratification system often have a greater interest in maintaining the status quo, perhaps this is why we have noticed their reluctance to support more liberal, change-oriented political candidates. Although in this example we have an interest in the political attitudes of respondents, for the sake of brevity we shall deal only with the SES concept. The task now is to logically derive from the concept the variables we will want to measure when we conduct our study.

Seeing SES

What does the concept "SES" generally point to? According to Lenski's conceptualization it has something to do with one's "power, priviledge, or prestige." But these aspects of the concept are themselves still rather abstract and it is our task to move down to a level that is more concrete and observable. What are some concrete examples of one's "power, privilege, or prestige"? The most powerful persons in our society are generally those with the most money. These are also the same persons who enjoy a great deal of prestige and privilege. They are also those who can afford higher levels of formal education. For example, David Rockefeller appears to have a great deal of money and is also the powerful and prestigious chairman and director of the Chase Manhattan Bank of New York. In addition, he is a member of the board of directors of the International Banking Corporation, of the National City Foundation, of the First New York Corporation, of the First National Corporation, of the Kimberly-Clark Corporation, of the Northern Pacific Railway Company, of the National Cash Register Company, of Pan-American World Airways, and of the Monsanto Company.[6] Given our knowledge of Mr. Rockefeller's family's political activities, we can conclude that he is very likely to be a Republican, a political preference that would coincide with our original observation. We should now be able to see that SES generally points to an individual's income level, formal educational attainment level, and occupational status.

We have moved, then, from the abstract concept of social class or SES to the concrete concepts or variables of education, income, and occupation. As we shall see in the next chapter, these variables can rather easily be measured and observed in the social world.

Note that a single concept does not necessarily "point" to only one variable or indicator, and that in our example of SES we were able to easily locate three variables that were indicative of the SES concept. This is not an unusual discovery given that concepts are general terms and thus can point to several variables that could adequately reflect the nature of the term employed. As in our example of the chair, each of us was able to mentally construct a *chair*, but we were never sure if we all pictured the exact same one. With SES we all form a mental picture of what one's social position should look like and what should go along with that position. Some of us, however, might place more importance on one aspect of SES than another. In every case, we must clearly spell out or conceptualize what it is we will be looking at when we tell others that we are using a certain concept.

Operationalization

We have noted that when we conceptualize, we clearly spell out and define what it is we mean when we use a concept. **Operationalization** refers to the same process when applied to the description of variables. However, operationalization also includes the "how-to" aspects of variable definitions and can be seen as a recipe that others could follow to obtain the same research dish. For instance, if we are interested in studying SES, as in the example above, we will have to tell others just what we used as a measure of SES. This is not unlike baking a pie and writing down the recipe so that others can make the same kind of pie. In our recipe we might tell our readers to cut up ten apples, to add exactly a cup and a half of sugar, and so on. In our operationalization of the concept "SES," we will also have to tell our readers what went into the process. We might tell them that we used annual income in dollars, educational level in actual years of school attended, and some measure of the prestige of respondents' occupation as our recipe for SES. In both cases we would want to tell our readers *exactly* what ingredients we used so that they could follow and replicate what we had done.

To operationalize a variable, then, means that the researcher provides an *operational definition* of the *empirical observations* that will be necessary to "see" that variable in the social world. Generally, we understand that a researcher can "see" what has been defined when respondents answer questions—usually from a questionnaire—that will place them within some specified category. For example, we might operationally define "political party preference" as the respondent's reply to the question, "Which political party do you prefer?" We could operationally define "formal education" as the response to the question, "How many years of school have you completed?" And we could operationally define age as the response to the questions, "How old were you on your last birthday?" or "In what year were you born?"

The major problem we can have with operational definitions is being sure that what has been defined will actually capture what the original concept intended for measurement. Specifically, we should always work to make as good a fit as possible between the abstract concepts we deal with and the concrete concepts or variables that will actually be observed. The correspondence between these two levels, what we call an **epistemic relationship,** is vital. Such a relationship can never be measured or truly known, but it is up to the researcher to make this "fit" as logically close as possible (see Figure 4.2).

For example, in a study of the relationship between social class and political party preference, what if we operationally defined political party

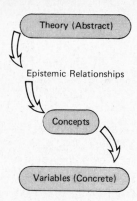

FIGURE 4.2
Relationship of
Theory,
Concepts, and
Variables

preference as a respondent's answer to the question, "How old were you when you first voted in a national election?" Although this question certainly has something to do with a person's political activities, it is hardly representative of a strong epistemic relationship between the concept "social class" and political ideology. A better question might be, "Which party did you support in the last election? Did you support the Democratic party, the Republican party, or some other party?"

A Note on Observation

From a researcher's point of view, the term *observation* is not restricted to only the direct observation of a social activity or event. By observation, we can mean one of several things and the direct method of observation is only one way of "observing" the social world. Other methods of observation were pointed out in the preceding chapter, including the use of previously gathered information such as content analysis or in the reanalysis of existing survey data as discussed in our examples of longitudinal studies. Simply asking questions and receiving responses to them is another way of observing, and this can include telephone and mail surveys as well as face-to-face interviews. By observation, then, we can mean any one of these three basic techniques: the direct observation of the activity or phenomena we wish to study, the reanalysis of existing documents, and the question-answer methodology of the survey. As we have noted, each of these modes of observation has its advantages and disadvantages, and one technique will usually be selected over another based upon the research question we have asked. Direct observation, for example, would *not* be a good methodology if our unit of analysis was at the macro level. A desire to study a problem at the micro level, however, could easily lead a researcher to some form of direct observation.

Levels of Measurement

Operational definitions depend primarily upon the answers respondents give to a set of predetermined questions that have been selected because of their epistemic relationship to abstract concepts. Questions can be asked in any number of ways, and the answers to these questions can result in various *levels of measurement.* For example, one question that is almost always used at the beginning of a questionnaire asks respondents to indicate their sex. The sex of a person can be very important from a theoretical point of view, as in Durkheim's study of suicide, wherein women were hypothesized to commit suicide less frequently than men. As stated earlier, a concept can provide a means for categorizing events or "things" in the world, and the sex variable allows for the classification of each respondent into one of two categories: male or female. This is an example of the lowest level of measurement, the nominal level. There are four levels of measurement discussed here: *nominal, ordinal, interval,* and *ratio.*[7]

The Nominal Scale

The **nominal scale** of statistical measurement is considered the crudest level as it allows only for the placement of objects or "things" into categories, but these categories must be *mutually exclusive* and *exhaustive.*[8] By mutually exclusive we mean that if we can place an item into one of the variable's categories, we have automatically excluded it from any of the others. For example, if we had surveyed a sample of students using a series of questions that contained one asking them to indicate their sex, we would expect that our respondents could be placed in only one category or the other and not in both. A person would be either a male or a female. Another example would be political party preference. In this case our respondents could be placed into one of several categories—Democrats, Republicans, Independents, the Peace and Freedom party, and so on—but none of our respondents could be classified into more than one of these categories. Additional examples of variables at the nominal level would be religious affiliation, marital status, or the response to questions that would lead to the placement of respondents into a "yes" or "no" category.

The term *exhaustive* refers to another property of nominally scaled variables and indicates that all possible categories have been included within which to classify respondents. For instance, in our example of political party preference we indicated that persons could be placed into one of four political categories. However, we could have listed several additional categories and, in fact, if we had thoroughly researched political parties in the United States we probably could have filled several pages with the possible political affiliations respondents could indicate. In doing so we would have *exhausted* all the possible categories of political parties available in this country, and this is exactly what is meant when a nominally scaled variable is said to be exhaustive. It simply means that we can classify all of our observations into one of the values that the variable can take on.

The Ordinal Scale

The **nominal scale** allows for the classification of objects into categories based on some property of the "thing" we are studying. It allows us to distinguish only between one value on the scale and another. However, we are never sure how much these categories differ. For example, if we had an interest in studying religion and we used a "religion" variable in our study, and we classified respondents into groups of Catholics, Baptists, Druids, and Methodists, we would be unable to tell which persons in our sample were *more* religious than others. Stated differently, we would not know who had more religion or who had less religion. This is the value of the **ordinally scaled** variable—it adds the property of "more or less than" to our ability to simply classify respondents.[9] If we can logically *rank-order* the values of a variable, then we are working with ordinally scaled data. Examples of this variety of variable would be social class, prejudice, political ideology, and even age. We could say, for instance, that some people were older than others or that some were more liberal than the rest. Specifically, we could classify our respondents into categories that could be logically rank-ordered. Respondents could be placed into the "older" group, the "middle-aged" group, and the "younger" group. Using the political ideology example, we could rank-order respondents as "liberal," "middle-of-the-road," or "conservative." Persons could be "upper-class," "middle-class," or "lower-class." Water can be "hot," "warm," "cool," or "cold." We can see that ordinal variables maintain the same mutually exclusive and exhaustive properties of the nominal scale but they also have the property of allowing us to rank the groups or categories such that we can say one group possesses *more of some quality* than members of another category. What you cannot say is exactly how much more or less of some quality a group has. For example, we could say that the "older" group had more age than the "younger" group but we would not know exactly how much more age it had.

The Interval Scale

Some of the variables we use allow us to indicate "how much more" one group will have of an attribute than another.[10] This level of measurement, called the **interval scale,** can tell us the interval or distance between one score and another. Suppose we had not simply placed respondents into age categories as in the previous example, but that we had gathered data based on their "age in years at their last birthday." If our sample were large enough and if we had taken a representative cross section of the population, we would expect to have persons of almost every age included in the study. If we placed all the persons that shared the same age into a group or category, we would exhaust all the possible age categories in our sample and they would be mutually exclusive as well. After we had arranged our data in this fashion we could continue by placing our age categories into a rank-order. Now if we took a single person from any one group and compared his or her age to another person's age taken from any other group, we would be able to tell exactly how much older (or younger) one respondent was than another. Given that each group was made up of persons of the same age, we could also tell how much older or younger one group was than another.

As can be seen from our example, the interval scale of measurement takes on the properties of both the nominal and the ordinal scales. Specifically, it allows for the mutually exclusive and exhaustive classification of variables as well as their rank-ordering. Added to these properties is the ability to see exactly how much more of an attribute one value of a variable will have than another. Using intervally scaled data we can say, for instance, that because Tom is thirty-five years old and Dan is twenty-five, there is a ten-year age difference between them. If we had used an ordinal scale all we could have said was that Tom was "older" than Dan.

The Ratio Scale

We have seen that as we move up from one level of measurement to the next we take with us the properties of the lower levels. When we discussed the nominal level, we talked simply about classifying or naming events or things in the world such that no two "things" went into the same group if they did not share similar attributes, and that all possible categories were available for classifying people into these groups. When we moved to the ordinal level, we added the ability to rank-order the values of a variable, and we maintained the properties from the nominal level. When we moved to the interval level we found that we were able to say "how much" different one value was from another. At the **ratio scale** or level of measurement we add the additional property of a *true zero point*.[11] Examples of variables with a true zero point are the number of times we attend fraternity meetings during the semester, the number of campus groups we belong to, and the number of times a person has been married. As is obvious from these examples, most variables that meet the requirements for interval level data are also appropriate for use at the ratio level, but each of our examples has the additional quality that a response could be "zero." For example, if we took all the persons in the class and began to arrange them into categories based upon the number of times each of them had been married, we could begin at the nominal level and simply divide the class into those who were currently married and those who were not. Such a classification would meet the nominal requirements of mutual exclusivity and exhaustiveness. However, we could also arrange the class into groups based on the rank-order of the number of times they had been married by classifying our classmates into groups of "high" numbers of marriages and "low" numbers of marriages. We are now operating at the ordinal level of measurement. We could then move to the interval level by simply classifying each person according to the actual number of times they had gone to the altar. Some may have been married three times, others twice, some only once, and others never. Since one of the values of our marital variable is a true zero point, and some of our class had zero marriages, this measure can be said to be at the ratio level of measurement.

At this point it is important to note that there are several reasons for paying such close attention to levels of measurement. As we shall see in later chapters, one reason is that there are certain important statistical techniques that require data to be at a specific level before they can be properly analyzed. One rule that is best to follow when going through the operationalization process is to measure all variables at the highest possible level. If all the data gathered in a study were at the interval level, there would be no problem in reclassifying it into nominal or ordinal scales. However, it is impossible to move back up the measurement scale when original data are gathered at the lowest level. In the following chapter we will discuss how to ensure that needed data are at the highest levels of measurement.

TABLE 4.1   Levels of Measurement

Level of Measurement	Nominal	Ordinal	Interval	Ratio
Can objects be determined to be equal or unequal?	Yes	Yes	Yes	Yes
Can objects be rank-ordered?	No	Yes	Yes	Yes
Can distances between objects be determined?	No	No	Yes	Yes
Does the scale have an absolute zero point?	No	No	No	Yes

Although it is almost impossible to simply follow a diagram or a set of rules or instructions for "seeing what a theory intends for you to see," we can outline general steps that can be taken to accomplish this process. Not all studies are alike nor are they as simple as they may appear when reading about them, and problems of conceptualization and operationalization can be difficult and tedious to solve. However, after selecting a question for study, and after going to the theory books for insight, you might begin with the following:

Step 1   Identify the concepts you wish to work with; *write them down.*
Step 2   Conceptualize these concepts by writing down what is meant when they are used in your study.
Step 3   Make a list of the various aspects of the social world to which these concepts point or sensitize you to.

Step 4 Operationally define the variables that have an epistemic correspondence to the concepts selected; *write down each variable, the concept it is associated with, and possible questions or observations that could be used to "get at" that concept.*

Step 5 Indicate the level of measurement the variables will assume.

Summary

In this chapter we have described the process of moving from highly abstract theory to the concrete world of social research. We have shown that there are two kinds of concepts a researcher can derive from theory: the abstract and the concrete. Abstract concepts do not refer to specific times and places but are more general and merely sensitize researchers to the general properties concerning the nature of a social thing. Concrete concepts are less general and can refer to specific times and places. They are more specific and they make clear what it is the researchers should look for in the social world they are studying. If a concept or term used in a study is conceptualized properly, there is little doubt as to the meaning a researcher intends for it to have.

Concepts indicate which variables should be used in a study. Variables are things that vary, that can take on several values, and they are themselves very concrete concepts. Three kinds of variables were discussed: the dependent variable, which is usually the focus of a study; independent variables, which are used to explain the different values taken by the dependent variable; and intervening variables, which can intervene or come between the independent and the dependent variables.

We also discussed techniques for discovering variables through the careful examination of the concepts selected for study. A researcher should first identify the concepts that are appropriate for the study and then clearly indicate what they will mean when they use that concept or term. Then a list should be made of what the concept sensitizes you to when looking around the concrete world. One should then operationally define the variables that have a logical epistemic correspondence to the concepts being used. Finally, we should note the level of measurement these variables will assume.

Levels of measurement include the nominal level, which allows us to classify or categorize the values of a variable into mutually exclusive and exhaustive groups. The ordinal level of measurement allows us to rank-order the values of a variable as well as to maintain the properties of the nominal scale. The ordinal scale can be interpreted in terms of a "more or less than" relationship among the values of a variable but does not indicate how much of a difference there is. The intervally scaled variable, however, allows us to indicate in some known unit of measurement (inches, years in school, age in years) how much different one value is from another. Finally, the ratio level of measurement adds a true zero point to the properties of the other three scales.

concept A word or set of words that expresses a general idea concerning the nature of something or the relations between things; concepts are the building blocks of theory. There are two kinds of concepts: abstract concepts, which refer to the very general properties of phenomena, and concrete concepts, which refer to particular individuals and interactions (see also Chapter 2.)

conceptualize To clearly spell out and define what is meant when we use a certain concept or term.

constant A constant has only one value and does not change from one observation to the next. If we studied a group of women about their occupational aspirations, the sex of the respondents would be constant from one observation to the next because all of the members of the sample would be females. (See *variable*.)

dependent variable The variable the researcher is usually most interested in; the variable we are trying to explain; usually the focus of the study.

epistemic relationship The logical linking between the abstract concepts you are studying and the concrete variables you are using to measure the concepts.

independent variable Variable(s) used in a study to explain other variables.

interval scale When it is possible to detect the distance between the magnitude of one score and another. Using intervally scaled data we can say, for example, that one person is five years older than another and not simply that one is older (ordinal scale). (See *nominal*, *ordinal*, and *ratio* scales.)

intervening variable Those variables that can come between the dependent and independent variables. For example, a person's occupation could intervene between his or her educational level and income. (Compare to *dependent* and *independent variables*).

nominal scale The lowest level of measurement; provides only a set of exhaustive and mutually exclusive categories, as when you examine the variable marital status. You can place persons in one and only one of the marital status groups: you are married, single, divorced, widowed, or living together, but you can't be placed into two of these categories at one time. Additional examples of nominal variables would include political party preference (Democrat, Republican, and so forth), religion (Baptist, Catholic, and so on), and sex (you can be only in the category male or female). (Compare to *ordinal*, *interval*, and *ratio scales*.)

operationalization The "how-to" aspects of defining variables. That is, operationalizing is telling others exactly what you did to measure or observe a variable.

ordinal scale When we can begin to rank-order the categories of a variable from high to low but not actually know the distance between them. Respondents could be ordered according to age as "older," "middle-aged," and "younger." (See *nominal*, *interval*, and *ratio scales*.)

ratio scale Has the properties of all the other levels of measurement (mutually exclusive and exhaustive categories, rank-ordering, and knowing the interval between observations) plus a true zero point. (Compare to the *nominal*, *ordinal*, and *interval scales*.)

1. Jonathan H. Turner, *The Structure of Sociological Theory*, rev. ed. (Homewood, Ill.: Dorsey, 1978), pp. 2−5.
2. Herbert Blumer, *Symbolic Interactionism: Perspective and Method* (Englewood Cliffs, N.J.: Prentice-Hall, 1969).
3. Émile Durkheim, *Suicide: A Study in Sociology*, trans. John Spaulding and George Simpson. (New York: Free Press, 1951).
4. J. Turner, op. cit., p. 5.
5. Gerhard Lenski, *Power and Privilege: A Theory of Social Stratification* (New York: McGraw-Hill, 1966), pp. 74−75.
6. Thomas R. Dye, *Power and Society* (North Scituate, Mass.: Duxbury Press, 1975).
7. Hubert M. Blalock, Jr., *Social Statistics*, rev. ed. (New York: McGraw-Hill, 1979), pp. 15−19.
8. Ibid., pp. 15−16.
9. Ibid., pp. 16−17.
10. Ibid., pp. 17−19.
11. Ibid., pp. 18.

5

The Measurement Process

Yardsticks, rulers, and tape measures are all familiar "measurement" instruments that we apply to various physical objects as we go about our daily routines. Sociologists also use various instruments to measure the concepts and variables they routinely study, but their instruments are somewhat different and less familiar than the rulers and yardsticks we learned about in grade school. As noted in the previous chapter, sociologists often use questions from survey questionnaires to operationalize the variables they have derived from theory. The direct observation of behavior can also be used. In any case, the sociologist's measurement instrument is often the questionnaire rather than the more familiar measurement tools noted above. The purpose of this chapter is to introduce some of the techniques and problems that are associated with the measurement of social behavior. For example, how does a sociologist measure religiosity or racial prejudice when these "things" are not physically present in the world? We know that geologists and chemists can take physical substances to their labs to weigh and measure them, but how does a sociologist take religiosity to his or her office to gauge its size or configuration? What are the rules of measurement for the social sciences, and how do we measure what we cannot physically grasp and place against a yardstick or upon a scale?

Measurement Terminology

As in any other area of science, the practice of social measurement has generated its own set of specific concepts and terms. Some of these terms are already familiar to us, but their meanings within the context of research are sometimes confusing for a beginning methodologist. The following discussion is presented to familiarize you with some of the key measurement terms that will be used throughout the remainder of the book.

The Questionnaire

When researchers use the term **questionnaire,** they are referring to a form or document that contains a set of questions, the answers to which are to be provided personally by respondents.[1] If the interviewer writes or records a respondent's answers on the document, it is called an **interview schedule.**[2] Questionnaires are also referred to as *research* or *measurement instruments.* For the most part, questionnaires are used in survey research, but they are also used in field research settings, and some social experiments as well.

The Item

An **item** is a question or a set of questions that appear on a questionnaire. Sometimes called a *questionnaire item*, this term refers simply to the statements we ask respondents to answer so that we can measure their attitudes, characteristics, beliefs, and so forth.

The Scale

According to George and Achilles Theodorson, an attitude **scale** is a device designed to quantitatively measure the intensity with which an attitude is held by respondents.[3] There are various types of attitude scales, each differing somewhat in form and method of construction. However, all attitude scales are designed to generate a numerical score for each respondent that indicates their position on some attitude continuum. Specifically, a scale can be said to weigh the degree to which a respondent is either favorably or unfavorably disposed toward a group of persons, an idea, or some form of social behavior.

The Index

When social scientists refer to an **index** they are generally talking about measuring a phenomenon that cannot be observed directly and that is comprised of several different dimensions.[4] For example, it is assumed that one can measure the social status of respondents by determining their occupations, income, or educational levels. Any one of these factors can be used as an index of social status, a "thing" we cannot directly observe. However, it is clear that there are several indicators of this phenomenon and thus it is possible to create several indices of the same thing. For example, frequency of church attendance could be used as one index of religiosity. But if religiosity is believed to include more than simply attending church, another index could be created to add a further dimension to the concept being measured. When we use only one index to measure a phenomenon, we refer to that as a *simple index*. When indices are combined to include several indicators of a phenomenon, they are called *composite or multiple-factor indices*. A complete discussion of the methods and techniques for developing and creating attitude scales and indices is presented in Chapter 14.

Validity

We can best think of **validity** as the correspondence between what a measuring device is supposed to measure and what it really measures. This concept is discussed in greater detail later in the chapter.

Reliability

Reliability refers to the consistency of a measure, that is, whether it measures things in a reliable way time and time again. Reliability may be measured by giving a test to the same respondents more than once to see if the same results emerge each time or by comparing different parts of a test or scale that are supposed to measure the same thing. It is important to note that a measure may be reliable but not valid. This concept is also discussed in more detail later in the chapter.

A Definition of Measurement

The conduct of sociological research rests on the assumption that we can measure whatever it is we are attempting to study. However, how do we measure alienation, religiosity, or attitudes toward abortion? If we wished to measure desk tops or the height of a door we know there are agreed-upon tools for doing so, and we reach for tape measures and yardsticks and we talk about known units of measurement like inches, meters, feet, and yards. But when we wish to measure alienation there is no agreed-upon tool we can use, and our problem becomes the creation of our own measuring devices such that other researchers will agree we have reasonably, accurately, reliably, and validly measured the variables we are using.

S. S. Stevens has defined **measurement** as "the assignment of numerals to objects or events according to rules."[5] In the previous chapter we found these rules were associated with levels of measurement, and that four such levels (nominal, ordinal, interval, and ratio) exist. Our task is to follow and understand these rules when we go about assigning numerals to the social events we are studying. For instance, if we wanted to measure a person's socioeconomic status (SES) we could begin by assigning to that individual a measure of his or her annual income. Because a person's annual income is at the interval level of measurement, we know the rules associated with that measure. Specifically, we know that the distances between one person's income and another's can be determined, and that incomes can be rank-ordered, as well as used to distinguish the "poor" from the "rich" respondents in a sample. If we had wanted to measure sex, on the other hand, we would have only been able to distinguish between respondents who were women and those who were men because such an indicator follows the rules of nominally scaled variables.

Observations and Measurement Levels

After variables have been identified and clearly defined, it is necessary to begin thinking about which questions or observations must be used to operationalize them. Questions can be asked in any number of ways, and the way in which they are asked determines how responses will be scaled. As we have pointed out earlier, whenever possible it is best to obtain data at the highest level of measurement because it is easier to collapse interval data into nominal or ordinal data, and impossible to transform nominal or ordinal data into interval data. The task is one of making observations that will be at the highest levels.

An Example

Suppose we intended to study some aspect of religion, and we wished to measure *religiosity*. This term or concept might first direct us to look at a person's religious affiliation to see what category of religion they could be classified under. By simply asking, "What is your religious preference?" however, we will gain information at only the nominal level when we would prefer to gather data at the higher interval or ratio levels of measurement. What questions can we ask to better measure respondents' religiosity? How can we ask a question that will give us *more* information than simply what religion a person is?

There is considerable doubt that knowing only what religion a person prefers actually measures how religious that individual is. Nearly all of us would respond to a question asking that we indicate our religious preference, but this type of question can only reveal that we *have a religion*, and not how strongly we feel about it. Asking respondents to indicate *how often* they attend worship services, however, might help us reach a better epistemic correspondence between our eventual observation and the concept "religiosity" that we are attempting to measure. This will also allow us to do a great deal more than simply classify respondents into categories of religion because such a measure would now be at the interval or ratio level. (See Figure 5.1).

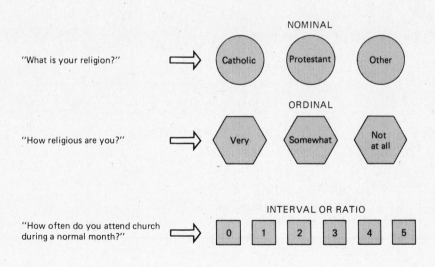

FIGURE 5.1
Three Ways to
"Get At"
Religion

Measuring Political Ideology

Another example of asking questions that will generate higher levels of measurement can be seen in observations dealing with the political ideology of respondents. The concept "liberalism," for instance, certainly brings to mind a person's political party preference, and we generally assume that Democrats are more liberal than Republicans. However, it is possible that our assumption about "liberal Democrats" is a faulty one, and that in some parts of the country Republicans and Democrats are not as different from one another when compared to their counterparts in other regions of the United States. How can we better ask a question that will more directly "get at" how liberal respondents really are? One method would be to ask respondents to place themselves on some form of political liberalism scale:

In general, how would you characterize your political orientation? Are you:

Radical right	( )1
Very conservative	( )2
Moderately conservative	( )3
Moderately liberal	( )4
Very liberal	( )5
Radical left	( )6
Other (please state): _____	( )7
Don't know	( )8

This question generates data at the ordinal level of measurement and gives the researcher more information than a question asking for only a person's political preference. A response to this question makes it possible for the researcher to classify each respondent into a category of "political orientation" as well as to rank-order individuals in terms of self-assigned political attitudes. By cross-tabulating respondents' political party with this measure it is now an easy task to find out which party contained persons who believed they were "very conservative" or "very liberal." In later chapters we show that by moving to the higher level of measurement we have also made it possible to utilize more powerful analysis techniques.

A Note On Direct Observation

The above examples focus on the use of questionnaires and "items" for operationalizing and measuring variables. However, this is not the only method available for gathering data that can be quantified. By assigning numerals to events, rather than asking questions, for example, a researcher can simply observe the behavior or actions that he or she wants to study. Rather than use a questionnaire as the research instrument, researchers can use an *observation schedule.*[6] An observation schedule is an instrument prepared and used by an observer to help make direct observations systematic and quantifiable. For example, it is sometimes difficult to question children about their beliefs; thus, it is often better to directly observe their activities in order to understand their behavior. In a study of sex and aggressive behavior among children, a student developed an observation schedule to be used while observing children at play in a school sandbox.[7] Through careful observation of the children, the researcher was able to record on an observation schedule the number of times a child of a particular sex made an aggressive act toward another child. (See Figure 5.2.) The researcher was then able to see if boys were more aggressive than girls, and if one sex picked on another more often than expected by chance alone. The observation schedule also makes it easier to observe behavior when more than one observer is working on the same project. By indicating on the observation schedule what it is that is to be observed, researchers can "switch" observers to see how reliable their observations really are. Chapter 10 contains a more elaborate discussion of the use of observation schedules. An example of an observation schedule is presented in Table 5.1:

TABLE 5.1   Observation Schedule

	Aggressive Boys	Aggressive Girls
Boys	|||	||
Girls	|||||	|||

Asking Questions

Asking questions is one of the most often-used means for measuring social variables. However, there are several ways to ask questions and several problems to be avoided when beginning to think about the construction of a measurement instrument.

The Open-Ended Question

Some questions can be asked that are *open-ended*, meaning no response category is made available for respondents. This technique allows respondents to give their own answer to the question asked and ensures that we have not put words into the mouths of the people being questioned. This method of asking questions will generally result in a more detailed response than we would receive if we asked questions using a closed-ended technique, but both methods have their advantages and disadvantages. An example of an **open-ended question** is, "What do you believe is the most important issue facing the United States government today?"

The Closed-Ended Question

Closed-ended questions or fixed-choice questions include *response categories* for respondents. Respondents are directed to select one of the response categories as their answer. With the increased use of computer analysis in sociology, this method has become very popular because it makes responses uniform from one individual to the next, and this means that questions can be analyzed faster and easier. When preparing fixed-choice questions to measure a variable, the researcher must keep in mind the rules of measurement discussed in Chapter 4. For instance, response categories must adhere to the rule of being mutually exclusive and exhaustive. For example:

"What do you believe is the most important issue facing the government of the United States today?"

Improving and protecting the environment	( )	1
Improving and protecting the nation's health	( )	2
Solving the problems of the big cities	( )	3
Halting the rising crime rate	( )	4
Dealing with drug addiction	( )	5
Improving the nation's education system	( )	6
Other (please state): _____	( )	7
Don't know	( )	8

When it is logical to do so, response categories can adhere to both the rules of the nominal scale and the ordinal scale and categories can be mutually exclusive, exhaustive, *and* rank-ordered.

Differences Between Open-Ended and Closed-Ended Questions

The major difference between the open-ended and closed-ended questions become clear when it is time to analyze the data. Because response categories are uniform when using the closed-ended methodology, this technique usually results in fewer analysis difficulties. On the other hand, the open-ended question tends to generate more detailed and individualistic responses from the persons we are interviewing, but they tend not to put words into the mouths of respondents the way a fixed-choice question can. Open-ended questions, however, are certainly more difficult to analyze because respondents are not restricted to a list of categories as in closed-ended questions. When we are unsure as to what categories would be appropriate for a question or we are studying an area that has gone unstudied prior to our analysis, the open-ended question can help generate categories for future fixed-choice alternatives. Because questionnaires generally contain several questions, we usually find both types appearing on a research instrument. A more detailed explanation of the best way to use and construct items for questionnaires is presented in Chapter 7.

In summary, most of us are familiar with the idea of measurement but have probably given little thought to the measurement of social variables. We have introduced some of the terminology of measurement as well as some of the problems researchers can encounter when trying to measure social behavior and attitudes. Questionnaires contain items that can be used to construct various scales and indices. An attitude scale weighs a respondent's favorable or unfavorable feeling about something, while an index is used to measure properties that cannot otherwise be directly observed and are multidimensional. Measurement for the social sciences is not unlike any other form of measurement in that it involves the assignment of numerals to objects or events according to certain specified rules. When we begin to assign numerals to the social world, it is best to do so at the highest levels of measurement because this guarantees that the greatest amount of information will be gathered. We have also noted that the questionnaire is not the only instrument that can be used for the measurement of social behavior, and we showed how an observation schedule can be used to help in the systematic collection of "observed" data. We have also introduced two general ways of asking questions: the closed-ended question and the open-ended question. We pointed out that when using the closed-ended questioning technique, response categories must follow the rules of measurement and be exhaustive and mutually exclusive. We now turn to some of the more specific problems associated with asking questions to measure social "things."

Questions to Avoid

Perhaps the most important aspect of constructing items for questionnaires is making sure they are clearly written and unambiguous. This is where the pretest of research instruments can be most useful. However, there are several pitfalls that can be avoided prior to testing our items for clarity.

The Double-Barreled Question

Double-barreled questions are single items that contain two questions when they should contain only one. This type of question should be avoided at all costs and can be "weeded out" of a questionnaire long before going to the field with the study and generally long before the research instrument is pretested. Double-barreled questions give themselves away because they almost always contain the words "and" and "or." For example, "Does your school's athletic program have a recruitment policy for men *and* women?" This question is difficult for respondents to answer if their school has only one of the two kinds of recruitment policies described in the question. How does a respondent answer when her school maintains a recruitment policy for males only, but is working on a new policy to include female athletes as well?

Suppose we have asked a question that requires respondents to agree or disagree with the statement "This university should abandon its football program *and* spend that money on the sociology program." Again, it is difficult to respond to this question if we really want the school to abandon its football program but at the same time believe the money should be equally distributed among the various departments on campus. When double-barreled questions are spotted, it is best to rewrite them, making two items instead of one.

The Leading Question

Items should be constructed in order to minimize the probability of biasing a respondent's answer by leading him or her to a particular answer. We should not ask, "You smoke marijuana, don't you?" A better question would read, "Do you smoke marijuana?" We should also be careful when we refer to authority figures in the context of questions. For example, "The majority of medical doctors in the United States believe skipping breakfast is harmful: do you agree?" The wording of this **leading question** makes it difficult for a respondent to do little more than agree with the statement. After all, how can we disagree with the majority of medical doctors in the United States?

The Relationship Between Items and Respondents

When we ask respondents to provide information relevant to our research topic, we are assuming they are competent to do so. We assume the people we are questioning have given some thought to the issues we are dealing with, and that they can indeed respond in a reliable way. For instance, if we planned to measure student attitudes toward the draft as part of a research project, we would not select a group of persons who are above the legal age for the draft for our sample. Respondents could hardly be expected to provide reliable data on an issue that does not affect them. If respondents are not students, this is another good reason for not including them in a study of student attitudes as they cannot be competent to provide student opinions. Keep in mind also that some questions are difficult for anyone to answer and that such questions should always be avoided. For example, questions that require respondents to rely solely upon memory for their answers should be carefully considered before use as items in a survey. "How old were you when you first realized that people died?" "How many calories did you usually consume per day when you were ten years old?" and "What was the size of a hospital in which you were born?" are examples of this variety of question. Almost no one is competent to answer them.

Another important aspect of preparing items for measurement instruments and general questions for questionnaires is keeping in mind that the questions themselves must be relevant for at least most of the respondents.

When we are attempting to measure an attitude that is not relevant to our respondents, we can expect our final "measurement" to *not* reflect the true attitude we are trying to probe. For example, if we wanted to know more about "the law" in our hometown, who would we speak with to get the most reliable picture of law enforcement activities? If we began by interviewing people who lived in neighboring communities we would no doubt be misled. Of course, we could measure *their* attitudes, but they would probably know very little about what went on in our local police station because they would not have given much thought to how a police department operated in another town.

Items Should Be Short and Positive

One key rule to keep in mind when preparing items for a measurement instrument is to *keep them as brief as possible.* Complicated and very long items should be avoided because respondents will generally not take the time to go over a question that appears confusing and overly long to them. Keep in mind that when we interview respondents or ask them to take their time to fill out our questionnaire, we are asking them to work for free! The faster a person can accurately respond to our questionnaire, the better off we will be. *Write items as briefly and as precisely as possible.*

Negative items in a questionnaire can often cause unnecessary confusion for respondents and result in misleading information. It is best to phrase questions in a positive manner. If asked to agree or disagree with an item such as "Professors should not be rated for their teaching ability," respondents will often "read over" the word *not* and will answer the question as if it had been a positive one. Although some respondents will certainly understand the question and will respond as we intended them to, others will answer that they "agree" with the statement when they actually "disagree" with it. This is like trying to measure the length of a tabletop with a tape measure that is difficult to read. The same table will be described differently each time it is measured because the instrument (the tape measure) will be read differently each time it is used. Short and positive questions will generally result in the most accurate and best-understood items on a questionnaire.

How Good Are Our Measures?

Once we have constructed the items we need for a questionnaire, and after we have pretested them for clarity, there remains the problem of whether or not they will actually measure what it is we are trying to measure. Our research instrument can be compared with other measurement devices in that it will be used to assign numerals to various things in the world, but a questionnaire is unlike other measurement instruments in that it is not always an agreed-upon yardstick for measuring things as straightforward as the top of a table. When we reach for a ruler or tape measure, we can be fairly certain that when we use it our results will come out in "inches" or "feet" and that other people will agree that we have accurately measured whatever it is we were working with. If people disagree with our measurement, they can check it themselves with their own tape or yardstick. If they believe our instrument was wrong, for example, they could use their own instrument to "check" our work. This is not as easily done in the social sciences as it is in table measuring.

Reliability

In the discussion above we noted that if a person didn't believe our measurements were correct, he or she could check them by using his or her own ruler or yardstick. The person who brings another yardstick to check our work believes that such a measurement instrument is a reliable one in that it has given accurate results time and time again. Specifically, if we had a yardstick that gave us three different lengths of a tabletop when three different measures were taken, we would believe that yardstick to be an unreliable one, and we would discard it and replace it with one that gave us the same results each time we (or anyone else) used it. Such a yardstick would be considered reliable.

The term **reliability** refers to the property of a measurement instrument such that, when applied over and over again, it will yield the same result each time it is used.[8] If the instrument does not yield the same results time and time again, it is an unreliable yardstick and should be discarded or rebuilt. For example, suppose we have constructed an item to measure how strongly people feel about abortion laws in the United States, and that after applying this item to an individual we discover that our respondent is "pro-abortion." Now suppose we return to this respondent later the same day and reapply the same item we used earlier. If we discover that our respondent is now "anti-abortion," we would suspect that our item was unreliable.

Direct Observation and Reliability

Let us imagine we had not selected the survey methodology as our research design, and that we had decided instead to observe directly the activity we were interested in studying. In this case it is possible we might not actually "see" what is taking place and report that one thing is happening when it is actually some other activity we are observing. For instance, if we wished to study aggression among children and we started by observing them at play in the schoolyard sandbox, we might at one point interpret an aggressive act as a playful one, and at another time of playful one as aggressive. In this case, as in the example dealing with the abortion item, our measure would be unreliable because the same behavior resulted in a different measure each time it was observed.

Several normal aspects of the measurement process can contribute to problems of reliability for the sociologist. For example, different interviewers can come up with different observations while using the same research instrument, and different observers can come up with different observations of behavior even when they have been watching the same activity. The social sciences, like no other science, depend primarily upon the human as the main measurement instrument, and since it is human behavior we are trying to study, it is often difficult to remove individual biases and predispositions from the measurement process. Interviewers and observers tend to see and hear things in their own way, and it is often difficult to obtain agreement among researchers as to what is really going on in the research setting. How, then, is it possible to build reliable research instruments?

There are a number of ways in which we can improve our confidence in the reliability of our measures. As noted earlier, we could begin by being fairly positive that our respondents were competent to answer the questions we were asking. If respondents are not competent to respond, our measures will certainly not be reliable ones, even though you have received several "answers." An additional method to improve chances of obtaining a reliable measure is that of asking more than one question designed to get at the same information. In other words, it is possible to "check" the reliability of an item by using composite or multiple-factor indicators. If one of the indicators does not correspond to the others, that is, if five items from a six-item composite measure each place our respondents into a number of distinct categories but one item does not classify them into the same groups, that single item is probably not a reliable measure. However, it is not always necessary to develop a composite index to check for reliability. We could simply ask the same question in a slightly different way at a different point in the research schedule to determine the reliability of items. If our "slightly" different question results in a significantly different response, we have a problem with reliability.

Using indicators or scales from previously successful studies of the same phenomenon is yet another method of improving the probability that our measures will be reliable ones. If we can locate an attitude scale that has been used several times and has also obtained the same results each time, then we could use that same scale and expect the same reliable results. However, it is always a good idea to pretest an instrument even if the instrument has been used before. As in our earlier discussion of pilot studies (Chapter 3), it is always best to acquaint interviewers with the instruments we are using by putting them through a dress rehearsal of the study. Because interviewers can sometimes be at the root of reliability problems by not understanding what the study is about or by being unfamiliar with the research schedule, their training can help reduce reliability problems.

Validity

When researchers talk about the *validity* of an item they are referring to its ability to actually measure what it is supposed to measure, and if we are trying to measure one thing with a question, but that question is really measuring something else, then that measure is not a valid one. For example, it is possible that by asking respondents to indicate if the government is spending "too much," "about right," or "not enough" money on a list of social problems, we are measuring respondents' attitudes toward government spending rather than concern with one of the problems on our list. Although it is difficult to check the validity of a measure, in most cases it can be done.

To begin with, if measures appear to be valid, that is, if they appear logically to be measuring what we are trying to measure, they are possibly valid. This is called **face validity.** When on the *face of it* a measure appears valid, it is said to have face validity.

Another method of checking the validity of an item is to check the measure against an independent and accepted criterion of the same characteristic. For example, income could be used to check the validity of a measure of economic success or grade point averages could be used to check the validity of a measure of educational success. As another example, if we had used a scale to measure racial biases and found those who had scored "high" on our scale (as very prejudiced) were members of the Ku Klux Klan, we might conclude that our scale had measured what it was supposed to measure.

There are several additional kinds of validity that researchers are concerned with besides face validity. We have listed some of these below with a brief explanation and examples of how they may be validated.

CONSTRUCT VALIDATION   When researchers talk about construct validation they are referring to the determination of the accuracy of a measure by showing that its scores will separate individuals into categories previously determined by some theory. For example, if a theory indicates that persons with higher incomes will be placed within a politically more conservative group, and they are indeed placed in that group when income and political attitudes are compared, this is an example of **construct validation**. This is similar to our earlier example of discovering that the persons who scored high on a scale designed to measure prejudice were actually members of the Ku Klux Klan, except that construct validity relies solely upon theory for validation.

CONCURRENT VALIDITY   This refers to the ability of a scale or index to produce results that are in keeping with those from some criterion that is observed at the same time the scale is administered. A scale of this sort would be used to determine the current status of an individual. For example, we may wish to distinguish between persons who, at the time we take our measurements, are well adjusted in their marriages and those who are in need of marriage counseling. If our test can distinguish those individuals who differ in their present state of mind, our measure is said to have **concurrent validity.** However, we are often concerned with predicting the future status of respondents, and this leads to a consideration of predictive validity.

PREDICTIVE VALIDITY   When we refer to **predictive validity** we are concerned with the ability of a measure to give us results that are in keeping with some criterion that may be observed at a future time. For example, we may be concerned with predicting which high school students will do well in college. This means that the scores derived from our measures will be used to predict a future status instead of a current one. The validation of this type of measurement would be similar to those used when concerned with concurrent validity: we would check our measures against additional empirical observations. Stated differently, we could begin by discovering which traits corresponded to college performance and measure these traits in a sample of high school seniors. Those who shared the same traits as individuals who had previously been measured and who had also done well in college would probably be admitted and those who did not might be advised to take remedial course work. Of course, the final validation of such a scale or index would come only with the eventual success of the students who had been tested.

CONVERGENT VALIDITY   This term refers to the quality of a measure when results based on it correspond to the results of a different measure designed to measure the same thing. For instance, if the results of one scale designed to measure alienation correspond to the results of a different scale designed to measure alienation, we can say there is a degree of **convergent validity.**

DISCRIMINANT VALIDITY   When we are concerned with **discriminant validity,** we are concerned with the ability of our measures to measure only one particular thing and not any others. To validate this type of measure, we could develop additional measurement devices designed to measure the opposite of what we were trying to actually get at. For example, if we were concerned with political attitudes, we might develop a scale designed to measure political liberalism. Our final scale, however, might actually be measuring something else very similar to political liberalism and in order to gain more confidence in our original measure we might develop a political conservatism scale. If these two scales correspond in their grouping of respondents, that is, if the political liberalism scale places one group from our sample into a liberal category and the conversatism scale places another group from our sample in the conservative category, we can say there is a degree of discriminant validity. Stated differently, our combined scales could be said to validly discriminate between political liberals and conservatives. Liberals should score low on the conservative scale and high on the liberal scale. Conservatives should score high on the conservative scale and low on the liberalism scale.

CONTENT VALIDITY   **Content validity** refers to the notion that the items on a scale or index actually represent the content of the attitude or behavior that is being measured. For example, the concept "alienation" contains several different dimensions: powerlessness, social isolation, and normlessness. Content validation requires that each of these dimensions be clearly specified and that each of them be represented by several items. In some cases, we might wish to treat each of them as a separate variable, independent from a single scale. This would be especially so if we had even more than the three constructs that are said to comprise a single variable. However, when we are concerned with content validity, we should attempt to clearly indicate (that is, operationalize) what the relationships between these concepts are. Thus we might return to the idea of convergent validity, and ask ourselves if the entire group of items correspond to one another, or to discriminant validity, where items represent very different measures. This, of course, takes us back to construct validation, where we are concerned with the determination of the accuracy of scores to separate individuals into meaningful groups based on theoretical predictions.

Summary

In this chapter we have introduced several aspects of the measurement process. We have discussed basic measurement terminology, and we have defined the measurement of social variables as the assignment of numerals to objects or events according to a set of rules. These rules comprise the rules of measurement discussed in Chapter 4, and we discovered that by carefully wording items for a questionnaire we can achieve the highest levels of measurement. We have also indicated which types of questions to avoid: the leading question and the double-barreled question. Closed-ended questions and open-ended questions were also compared. The observation schedule was also discussed, and we suggested that this kind of research instrument could be used to help make direct observations as systematic as possible. However, the most important topics covered in this chapter focused on the reliability and validity of the items used as measurement devices in both scales and indices.

Reliability was defined as the property of a measurement instrument such, that when applied over and over again, would yield the same result each time it was used. If different results emerge from the same instrument, it was said to be unreliable. Validity was defined as the property of an item or measurement instrument to actually measure what it is we are trying to measure. Several forms of validity were discussed, including face validity, construct validity, concurrent validity, predictive validity, convergent validity, discriminant validity, and content validity. Although these types of validity do not exhaust all the varieties of validation that concern social researchers, they should provide an indication of how we go about being as positive as possible so that we are actually getting at what it is we are trying to measure. If we carefully consider what it is we are trying to measure, and if we keep in mind the various points made in this chapter, we should have more success in our research efforts. We hope now that the yardsticks and rulers of sociology have taken on a more familiar appearance and that your understanding of the use and construction of these tools is a better one.

closed-ended question A question asked of respondents that includes response categories for them to check.

concurrent validity The ability of an item to produce results that are in keeping with those from some criterion that is observed at the same time the item is administered.

construct validation The determination of the accuracy of items by showing that the scores on them will separate individuals into categories determined by theory.

content validity When items in a scale or index actually reflect the content of the attitude or behavior that is being measured.

convergent validity When results of one measure designed to measure an attitude correspond with another item designed to measure the same attitude or behavior.

discriminant validity The ability of an item to measure one and only one particular thing and not any other things.

double-barreled question Single items containing two questions when they are supposed to contain only one. For example, "Does your school's athletic program have a recruitment policy for men and women?" This kind of question usually contains the words "and" and "or."

face validity When, on the face of it, a measure appears to be valid.

index An index is used to measure a phenomenon that cannot otherwise be observed directly. For example, we cannot actually see the SES of a respondent so we utilize measures of income, educational level, and occupational status as indexes of SES.

interview schedule If the interviewer writes or records the respondents' answers, that document is called an interview schedule.

item An item is a question or set of questions that appear on a questionnaire; items are used to measure attitudes, beliefs, and similar variables.

leading question A question worded in a way that biases a respondent's answer. For example, "You smoke marijuana, don't you?"

measurement The assignment of numerals to objects or events according to rules.

open-ended question A question asked on a questionnaire when no response category is provided for respondents.

predictive validity The ability of an item to give results that are in keeping with some criterion that may be observed at a future time.

questionnaire A form or document that contains a set of questions, the answers to which are to be provided personally by respondents.

reliability The consistency of a measure, whether it measures things reliably time and time again. If an instrument is reliable, we'll get the same results each time we use it to measure the same thing.

scale An attitude scale is a device designed to quantitatively measure the intensity with which an attitude is held by respondents. It provides scores that indicate the position of a respondent on an attitude continuum.

validity The correspondence between what a measuring device is supposed to measure and what it really measures.

1. Fred N. Kerlinger, *The Foundations of Behavior Research,* 2nd ed. (New York: Holt, Rinehart and Winston, 1973), pp. 412−414.
2. Ibid.
3. George A. Theodorson and Achilles G. Theodorson, *Modern Dictionary of Sociology* (New York: Thomas Y. Crowell, 1969), p. 367.
4. Ibid., p. 198.
5. S. S. Stevens, "On the Theory of Scales of Measurement," *Science* 103 (June 7, 1946: 677−680.
6. William B. Sanders, *The Sociologist as Detective: An Introduction to Research Methods* (New York: Praeger, 1976), p. 91.
7. This example was taken from a student project directed by one of the authors.
8. Claire Selltiz, Lawrence S. Wrightsman, and Stuart W. Cook, *Research Methods in Social Relations* 3rd ed. (New York: Holt, Rinehart and Winston, 1976), pp. 181−194.
9. Ibid., pp. 169−181.

6

Elementary Sampling Procedures

The basic procedures and terminology required for sampling from large populations are outlined in this chapter. We should begin by noting that although sampling is usually associated with large-scale survey research, the procedures presented here are appropriate for use in sampling *anything* and can be used within the context of any research design. The chapter begins with the presentation of a sampling problem, and we then introduce sampling terminology. Probability, randomness, the use of random numbers, standard error, sampling frame construction, and numerous probability and nonprobability sampling techniques are also discussed.

Whom Do We Interview?

When the construction of a questionnaire is complete, and after it has been checked for clarity and interviewers have been trained in its proper use, the logical question becomes, "Whom do we interview?" It turns out that there is much more to conducting a survey than simply going out onto the sidewalk, stopping the first person who walks by, and interviewing him or her. First of all, we would quickly discover that if we did simply go out onto the sidewalk and begin talking to the people who passed by, we wouldn't talk to just *anybody*. Rather, the persons we would select for interviews would probably fit into the same social categories we would fit into ourselves. We would select those persons who appeared the most comfortable to talk with, who appeared less threatening than others, and who were as much like us as possible. In short, we would probably not select members of the Hell's Angels, winos, or shady-looking characters as our interviewees.[1] Instead, those persons we perceived as being the easiest to talk with and the easiest to interview would be the individuals we would select for our respondents. The problem with this kind of "sample" is that it is a *biased* one because it would contain only the responses of people who appeared "comfortable" to us, who appeared easy to talk with, or who weren't threatening to us in some way. The **sample** would be an **unrepresentative** one because it would not reflect the characteristics of the larger population we were actually trying to study.

This is a common problem beginning researchers often encounter. We know we have to interview someone in order to gain the information we need for a study, but where do our respondents come from if they aren't the folks we encounter on the street? Interestingly, much of the knowledge we gain through our everyday interaction comes to us by way of biased and unrepresentative samples of the human universe. For example, in the classroom we sometimes hear people say things like, "But everyone *I* know wants to vote for Senator Powers, so surely he is the people's choice," or "No one *I* know would ever do a thing like that, so it must not be a very good thing to do." What these students are saying is that their opinions and ideas coincide with those of the people they are most often around. But who are we most likely to spend our time with? People we feel are comfortable to be around: our friends, neighbors, fellow students, and the like, are those persons with whom we spend our time. Sociologists, however, cannot base their findings on only the opinions and responses of friends, colleagues, and family or the people they are "most like." As we shall see, what is needed for a scientific study is a group of respondents who are representative in their characteristics of some larger population that is of interest to the researcher. Unless we intend to study "people walking by" who are "comfortable" to talk with, responses gained by such "sampling" practices will be of little use. The task of the sociologist is to gather data that are representative of some greater population so that conclusions can be drawn about that population and not simply for an unspecified group within it—such as the few people who just happened to walk by when we started doing interviews. **Sampling,** the systematic selection of individuals or things from the total population, allows sociologists to do just that.

A Sampling Problem

Imagine we have already graduated from college and have obtained a job with the Long Life Light Bulb Company. Our new job is to check the quality of the light bulbs that are manufactured so the company can continue its advertising campaign as the world's leading manufacturer of "long life" bulbs. It would be an excellent idea for the company to know the actual life expectancy of the light bulbs they manufacture, and it is our job to discover just what that real life expectancy is. How will we handle this job? What will we do to come up with a figure that will reflect the actual life expectancy of Long Life Light Bulbs?[2]

We could take each bulb as it came off the assembly line and plug it in until it burned out, recording the length of time that each bulb remained burning. However, this would leave *no* light bulbs for the company to sell as they would eventually all burn out! Another possible solution would be to take only one bulb from all that have been manufactured, plug it in until it burned out, and report that span of time as the average time a Long Life Light Bulb would last. However, how confident would we feel basing our conclusions on just one light bulb? Could that single bulb have had an unusually long life for a Long Life bulb or could it have had an extremely short one? By examining only the single bulb we would never know.

The point is we can't check *all* the bulbs, and we can't depend upon only *one* to gain the information needed. This is also true for sociology. Indeed, as we look around the social worlds we live in, we quickly realize it would be impossible to ask each and every person to respond to a research questionnaire. Intuitively, we also understand that by asking only one of those persons to respond, our data would not be valid. Proper sampling procedures can help us to solve these problems.

A Sampling Solution

One way to get around the problem with the light bulbs would be to systematically sample one of every one hundred bulbs that came off the assembly line, plug them in and let them burn until they went out, and then calculate the average life expectancy from that sample. We could then *infer* from the sample what the average life would be for the total number of bulbs produced. This is the basic reason we take samples: *to make inferences about some larger population of interest.* In our example above we are interested in drawing conclusions about the nature of a certain population of light bulbs (Long Life Light Bulbs). We realized we couldn't examine each and every bulb that was produced, and so took a systematic sample of the bulbs, found their average age, and then inferred that the total population of bulbs would have the same life span.

In sociology we do the same thing that was done in the light bulb example. We realize we can't talk to or observe everyone, so we sample a portion of the population we are interested in studying, carefully examine the sample, and then make inferences about the population from which the sample came. For example, if we had an interest in understanding the outcome of a local election, we could sample a portion of the local population, and from that sample predict who would win. By knowing beforehand what the political makeup of the local area was, we could make our sample representative by sampling in proportion to the numbers of Democrats, Republicans, and other political parties that were to take part in the election process. (See Figure 6.1.) As we noted earlier it is *not* a good idea to base predictions on the responses of only those we are comfortable being around, as those persons usually express the same values and beliefs we do, thus making that kind of sample a biased one. In the same vein, if we asked a group of respondents who they planned to vote for, *but we asked only respondents who were Democrats,* our conclusions would be biased. We would predict that

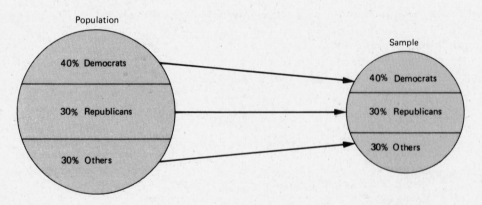

FIGURE 6.1
A
Representative
Sample

the Democratic candidate would win when we hadn't asked who the Republicans or the "others" taking part in the election planned to support.

The examples given thus far suggest that there are actually several ways in which a sample can be taken. We discussed how it would be possible, for example, to take one of every one hundred light bulbs produced and use these bulbs as a sample. We also indicated that if we had some prior knowledge of a population, we could arrange our sampling procedures such that the eventual outcome would be representative. Both of these examples reflect actual sampling procedures that are used by sociologists: the **systematic sample** and the **stratified sample.** However, before we begin our discussion of sampling procedures, let's examine some of the terms and concepts that are associated with them.

The Technical Terms of Sampling

In our examples we have used several terms that you may or may not be familiar with. For instance, we have referred to "populations" and "samples" without offering a formal definition for either concept. The purpose of this section is to introduce some of the technical terms that are associated with the selection of respondents for large-scale survey studies. However, as noted in the introduction, the terms and procedures that we will outline in this chapter are appropriate for sampling *anything,* including social groups, census blocks, or any other objects that are needed in a sample.

The Sampling Element

As noted in Chapter 3, one of the beginning steps in setting up a research design consists of specifying the persons or things we intend to study. According to Bailey, the objects of study are called *the units of analysis.*[3] These units are also called **sampling elements,** a term that refers to the elements or units about which information will be gathered. The sampling elements for sociologists are almost always the individual human being, but they can also be groups, clubs, formal organizations, or almost any "thing" that we are interested in studying.

Populations

The sum total of the sampling elements is called the **population** or **universe.**[4] When researchers talk about populations from a sampling perspective, then, they are talking about the total number of cases with a given characteristic or set of characteristics from which a sample is drawn. For example, if we wished to study student feelings about the draft, the population we would theoretically be dealing with would be *all* students no matter where they were. However, by clearly spelling out a specific class or subgroup of students we can define our sampling universe into a more workable form. For instance, we could specify our population as *all students registered for classes at this university as of June 1, 1984.* Now our population is clearly defined, and we know what our sampling elements consist of as well as where our respondents will come from. As we shall see, by clearly understanding what our population is at the beginning of a study, we will be in a much better position at the conclusion of a project to draw inferences that will make sense.

Sampling Units

A **sampling unit** is either a single sampling element or an aggregation of elements. In a simple random sample, the sampling units are generally the individual cases that comprise the sample. However, in a **multiple-stage sample,** the first stage, called the primary sampling units, are aggregates or clusters of cases such as geographic areas or specified groups from within which the final sampling units (individual cases) are selected. As an example, suppose we wanted to study *persons* within a certain state. We could start by first sampling counties within the state, and then from within each county we could select cities, and from the cities we could sample census blocks, and from the blocks we could sample households, and finally from each household we could select the actual individuals we would interview while conducting our study. The sampling units at each stage of this example would be (1) counties, (2) cities, (3) blocks, (4) households, and (5) individuals. When talking about the various stages within a complex sampling design such as the one described, it is wise to distinguish between the various stages by referring to them as **primary, secondary,** and **final sampling units.**

The Sampling Frame

A **sampling frame** is a complete list of all the units from which a sample is taken. For example, if we wanted to study the members of the Rural Sociological Society, we could use their membership roster as a sampling frame. If we wished to draw a sample of students from our university, we could use the student roster as a sampling frame. In the example above that deals with selecting a multiple-stage sample, the sampling frame for the primary stage was a list of all counties in the state from which the final sample was to be drawn. Obtaining a sampling frame for a study can be a difficult task. Some examples of possible sampling frames include telephone directories, city directories, membership rosters, or any kind of complete and up-to-date list of the units we intend to study. However, because "all members" are not always on a club's roster, and since not all people have telephones or telephone listings, it is difficult to come up with a sampling frame that actually includes the total defined population. In practice, researchers often attempt to obtain as many possible sampling frames as they can, and then from this collection select what is believed to be the best one for their study.

Observation Units

An **observation unit** is an element or a collection of elements from which data are collected.[5] The unit of analysis and observation units are usually the same in sociological studies. However, it is possible this correspondence would differ from one study to the next. For example, a researcher could interview heads of households to gather data for an entire family. In this case, the observation unit would be the "household head," but the unit of analysis is still the individual family member.

Variables

As previously noted, variables are things that vary, that take on different values—such as age, marital status, and religion. A variable is opposed to a constant, which does *not* take on different values and does not vary. What is important here is the understanding that *variables are used to describe sampling elements* taken from some specified population. Therefore, variables can refer to units other than simply individual human beings. Stated differently, variables can be used to describe variations among census block characteristics, group characteristics, or individual characteristics.

Parameters and Statistics

A **parameter** is the summary description of a variable *for a population.* Because we seldom know the parameters of populations, we estimate them using data from samples. More specifically, a parameter would be the average age of *all* students at a university at some specified time (June 1, 1984). Because students are frequently changing schools, and because they grow older each day, it is almost impossible to measure the average age of a university's population. However, we can take a sample of students, calculate the average age of the sample, and *infer* or *estimate* the average age of the students for the total university population using a statistic. Whereas a parameter represents a summary description of a population, a **statistic** represents a summary description of a sample. As in the example above, we might never know the age parameter of a population, but by using proper sampling techniques we can estimate parameters and report them using statistics such as the arithmetic average or mean age of the sample.

Sampling Error

Even the best sampling techniques seldom result in statistics exactly equal to the population parameters they are supposed to estimate. However, in most cases we are able to estimate the degree of error we can expect in our samples.

Although **sampling error** is more fully discussed later in the chapter, a brief and simple example may help you grasp what this concept implies.

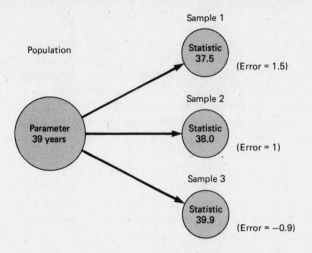

FIGURE 6.2

Imagine we actually knew the parameters of a population; for example, we know its average age is 39 years. Now, suppose we have drawn a sample from that population and have calculated an average age for that sample of 37.5 years. First of all, we can see the sample has yielded an average age very close to the parameter we were trying to estimate, and we are only 1.5 years away from the "average age" of the population. For this sample, then, there is an error of 1.5 years (39 − 37.5 = 1.5 years) and we can imagine that if several samples were taken from the same population, that the error would vary from one sample to the next. (See Figure 6.2.) The logical question becomes, "How well does our specific statistic represent the parameter we are estimating?" The calculation of the standard error answers this question for us, and we describe the calculation of the standard error later in this chapter.

Probabilistic Selection

The main goal of sampling is to arrive at the best possible estimates of the parameters of a population. It would be highly impractical to interview or make observations of an entire population, so our task is to come up with a representative sample that allows us to draw inferences about the population in which we are interested. We have also noted that bias can creep into a sample if it is not drawn properly. **Random sampling,** or the random selection of sampling units, allows us to overcome these problems.

Randomness

The term **randomness** or *random* refers to the occurrence of events in an unpredictable order. Also, it is assumed the occurrence of one event does not affect the occurrence of another, and that each event occurs independently.[6] For instance, in a series of coin tosses one cannot predict the order in which heads or tails will appear based on the outcome of one flip of a coin because one flip is independent of any other flip. We often hear people say that because a coin has repeatedly turned up heads, that it is time to bet on tails because of the "law of averages." This is a poor argument and we might call it the "gambler's fallacy."[7] Because a coin has no brain, it is impossible for it to know how many times it has come up heads during a series of flips. Consequently, if a coin continues to come up heads, it is certainly not time to bet on tails; rather, it is time to put your money on heads! We suggest this bet under the assumption that something is wrong with the coin; it is perhaps weighted so it comes up heads more often than we would expect by chance alone. In any event, the fact that the coin came up heads a large percentage of the time is absolutely lost on the coin because it simply does not know it is "time to come up tails."

When we use the notion of randomness in the selection of a sample, we also assume each time an individual is selected, his or her selection is independent of all other selections, and the selection of one person will in no way influence the selection of another.

In our definition of randomness we introduced the notion of the "unpredictable" occurrence of events. If we consider each selection of a respondent for a sample as a single and independent event, we can see that each time we select a person to be included, that too is an unpredictable occurrence. This property of random selection ensures that persons will not be included in a sample because of a bias on the part of the researcher.

A Note on Using Random Numbers

Sampling often entails the use of a **table of random numbers** (see Appendix A) for the selection of elements from sampling frames. A table of random numbers is just what the name implies: a table containing numbers that have been placed there in a completely random fashion. The purpose of this brief section is to describe such a table and how it is used in research projects. Suppose, for example, that we wanted to randomly select a sample of 100 respondents from a population of 500 individuals. The following steps indicate how this is done:

Step 1   Number the members of the population from 1 to 500; now the task is to select the 100 persons needed for the sample from the numbered sampling frame.

Step 2   Determine the number of digits needed for the random numbers to be selected; in the example there are 500 persons in the population, so we will need to use three-digit numbers to ensure that every person in the population will have a chance of being selected; if we had 1,000 persons in the population, we would have to use a four-digit number (000−999); if we had 10,000 possible respondents, we would need a five-digit number, and so on.

Step 3 Using the Table of Random Numbers (Appendix A) create three-digit numbers from the five-digit numbers listed by using only the first three numbers in any single digit; for example, if a digit reads 36697, read only the first three numbers, 366; if we wanted to, we could decide to use the last three digits of a number rather than the first three (that is, in our example, 697); either method would work just as well.

Step 4 Now close your eyes and, using a pencil or your finger, point to the table and start the selection process wherever the pencil or your finger falls; it is also possible at this step to simply select *any* column number and row number and use this as a starting point.

Step 5 Move through the table in any manner you feel comfortable with, either down the columns from the starting point, or up the column, or across from right to left, or from left to right; it is important, however, that once we have decided on a pattern of selection to stay with it and not change horses in the middle of the stream; also, when we get to the bottom of a column (or to the top, depending on how we have decided to do it), make sure the move to the next column is made the same way each time (that is, "when we get to the bottom of a column, we will move to the top of the next one and continue selecting cases").

Step 6 Now that we have decided where to start and how to progress through the table, begin to select the 100 cases needed for the sample; if numbers are encountered that do not "fit" into the sampling scheme, such as the number 678 (our population contains only 500 persons), ignore them and continue moving down (or up) the column until a number that does fit into the scheme is located (450, for example); continue selecting numbers until a total of 100 *randomly* selected cases is reached.

Probability

When we randomly select persons from a population to be included in a sample, we are ensuring that each person in the defined population has the same *chance* of being selected. The term *chance* can be equated with the idea of probability. Thus, we can rephrase the above sentence to read, "When we randomly select persons from a population to be included in a sample, we are ensuring that each person in that population has the same *probability* of being selected." **Probability** refers to the likelihood that out of a specified number of equally likely and mutually exclusive occurrences, some event will take place. Probability is therefore like a proportion; *the proportionate frequency with which a given outcome is expected out of the total frequency of outcomes.* Stated statistically, the probability of an event (E) can be expressed as a ratio of the frequency (n) of any particular event to the total number (N) of trials in which the event might occur (Probability of an *Event* $= \frac{n}{N}$).[8] For example, suppose we have an interest in studying the sociology majors attending the University of Guelph. If there is a roster of these individuals available to us (a sampling frame), then we will know exactly how many students there are, and what the expected outcome would be for the selection of each person for the sample. If there were 75 students majoring in sociology at the University of Guelph, we would know each individual would have a 1/75 chance of being included in our sample. *Probabilities are like proportions.* In this case we are talking about the proportion of times a selection for our sample would be expected, given the total number of persons from which these selections could be made. The total number of persons from which we are selecting is 75, and each selection is a single, independent event. If we plan to sample 25 of these students for the study, and we do not exclude a person's name from the sampling frame each time one of the 25 selections is made, each individual would have the same chance of being included in the sample. The important aspect of knowing what chance respondents have for being included in a sample lies in the fact that such knowledge provides researchers with the ability to estimate the *error* a sample might contain.

Standard Error

Measurement based on sample data always contains some error. The important question, then, is how much error? Stated differently, how well do our statistics estimate a population's parameters? We can understand this by exploring a few additional sampling concepts: sampling distributions and the normal curve.

Sampling Distributions

A listing of all possible outcomes of an event is called a **sampling distribution.** For example, suppose we had three coins and we wished to know what *all possible outcomes* of a single "flip" of all three coins would be. If we look at all the possible combinations of heads and tails that can come up in a flip, and if we record all these combinations, we will have created our own sampling distribution:

Flip	Coin One	Coin Two	Coin Three	Number of Heads
A	Tail	Tail	Tail	0
B	Head	Tail	Tail	1
C	Tail	Head	Tail	1
D	Tail	Tail	Head	1
E	Head	Head	Tail	2
F	Head	Tail	Head	2
G	Tail	Head	Head	2
H	Head	Head	Head	3

As can be seen, three coins can result in several combinations of heads and tails, ranging from a result of "zero" heads to "three heads" (or zero tails to three tails) in a single toss of the coins. Because we know that the probability of an event is nothing more than a ratio of the frequency of an occurrence to the total number of trials in which it can occur, we can calculate the probability of obtaining any one of the heads—tails combinations. Let's suppose we are concerned with the possible combinations of heads. We should first note two important things. First, there are *eight* combinations of heads and tails possible (from A through H); and second, the range of *heads* obtained in any single flip runs from zero to three. These figures allow us to calculate the probability of obtaining any combination:

Number of Heads Occurring For All Flips		Frequency	Probability
0 Heads (occurred 1 time)	=	1/8	P (0) = .125
1 Heads (occurred 3 times)	=	3/8	P (1) = .375
2 Heads (occurred 3 times)	=	3/8	P (2) = .375
3 Heads (occurred 1 time)	=	1/8	P (3) = .125
			1.000

If we examine all the outcomes of the coins after they have been theoretically tossed, we note in one case there are zero heads, in three cases there is one head, in three cases there are two heads, and in one case we obtain three heads in a single toss. By making each of these into a ratio to the total number of possible outcomes (that is, 8), we have calculated the probability of obtaining from zero to three heads for a single toss of the three coins. Specifically, the probability of obtaining zero heads in a single toss is .125 or about 12.5 percent. We would have the same chance of coming up with three heads in a single toss. The probability of coming up with one or two heads is the same: .375 or about 37.5 percent in both cases.

The Normal Curve

We have used only three coins in our example. What would have happened if we had used 20 coins? 30? Or 100? The proceess demonstrated would have been somewhat more difficult to complete but the result would have been the same: the outcomes would have distributed themselves in a normal form. By *normal* we mean the outcomes would have formed a *normal or bell-shaped curve*. Normal curves have certain known mathematic properties and almost anything you can imagine will distribute itself in a normal or bell shape. We also know that beneath a normal curve slightly more than 68 percent of the cases will always be distributed around the center of the distribution:

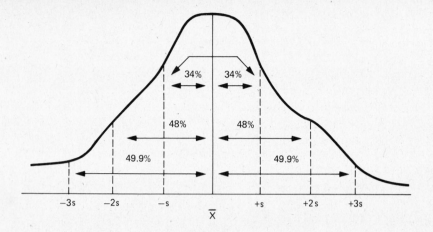

FIGURE 6.3
The Normal
Curve of
Distribution

We will discover later that this information will help us see just how accurately our statistics estimate the parameters of a population, and using our earlier example of the three coins, we can also demonstrate just how closely a distribution can approximate a normal curve.

To do this we first create an *X axis* consisting of the number of times a certain combination of heads were obtained in our theoretical toss of the coins:

| 0 | 1 | 2 | 3 | (X) |

Next we add a *Y axis* consisting of the actual probabilities we calculated earlier:

Now we add a "histogram" with the beginning shape of the normal curve superimposed over it:

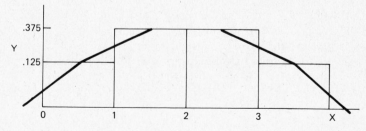

As can be seen, even when using only three coins, the outcomes of all the possible combinations of heads and tails begins to approach a normal distribution.

An Illustration

Suppose we are sampling respondents for a survey, and not simply trying to figure out the total possible combinations of heads and tails that would turn up when tossing three coins. Suppose, further, that we have a population consisting of 1,450 persons, and from this population we draw a random sample of size n = 12. If we compute the mean age for this sample (the arithmetic mean) we find it is 23.9 years:

35	40	
15	13	
16	26	
25	19	$\bar{X} = 23.9$
18	10	
20	50	

How certain can we be that this sample average is an accurate estimation of the population average? How much confidence can we have in our sample statistic? Is it possible the sample we have taken does not reflect the population we are interested in? To address this problem we must explore the variations that exist in the sample. We can do this by calculating the standard deviation for our age data. The **standard deviation** is a measure of spread or dispersion that tells us how the scores we have collected differ from one another. Whereas the arithmetic mean (an average) tells us what the *typical* case in a sample looks like, the standard deviation tells us how *different* the scores are.

The Standard Deviation

The following formula is used to calculate the standard deviation:

$$s = \sqrt{\frac{\sum_{i=1}^{n}(x_i - \bar{x})^2}{n-1}}$$

Where the symbol s is used to represent the standard deviation, and x is used to indicate any particular score, $\bar{x}$ represents the mean, and n the total number of persons in the sample. The standard deviation for our sample is calculated as follows:

Step 1 Calculate the mean by summing all the scores and dividing that number by the total number of cases in the sample; the sum of all the ages in the sample is 287 and the size of the sample is 12; the mean is therefore 287/12 = 23.9 years.

Step 2 Subtract the mean from each of the age scores in the sample as follows:

X (age scores)	$(X-\bar{X})$	$(X-\bar{X})^2$
35− 23.9 =	11.1	123.1
15	−8.9	79.21
16	−7.9	62.41
25	1.1	1.21
18	−5.9	34.81
20	−3.9	15.21
40	16.1	259.21
13	−10.9	118.81
26	2.1	4.41
19	−4.9	24.01
10	−13.9	193.21
50	26.1	681.21
287	00.0	1596.81

Step 3 Now square each of the differences obtained as indicated above, and sum them.

Step 4 Divide the total by $n - 1$, which is the total number of persons in the sample (n = 12) minus one (11). This calculation gives us 145.16.

Step 5 Take the square root of the sum of the squared deviations from the mean score (1596.81). This calculation yields a standard deviation of 12.

Characteristics of the Standard Deviation

The standard deviation has certain distinct properties that should be kept in mind. First, it will always result in a positive number. Second, it measures variability (or spread) in the same units as those of the original observations. But most important, no matter how the original observations are distributed, the mean plus or minus 2 standard deviations $(\bar{X} + 2s)$ will always include at least 95 percent of the observations, and the mean plus or minus 3 standard deviations will always include 99 percent or more of the observations. Also, we interpret the standard deviation as an index of variation. Thus, *the larger the standard deviation, the greater the variation (or spread) of the scores in the sample.*

If there is *no variation in the scores collected, the standard deviation is always zero:*

	X Scores	$X - \bar{X}$	$(X - \bar{X})^2$
Scores Do Not Differ; No "Spread" or Variation	5	0	0
	5	0	0
	5	0	0
	5	0	0
	5	0	0
	25	0	0

The mean of the five scores listed above is 5 (25/5 = 5), and if we subtract this score from each individual score, we obtain a zero in each case. Of course, the square of zero is zero, and when we divide zero by n − 1 we again obtain a zero. And the square root of zero is, of course, zero. Thus, *there is no variation in our sample of five scores.* (See the example of standard deviation in the box on pages 106−107.)

Suppose, again, that we are sampling respondents for a survey. And suppose our population consists of 1,450 persons, and that from this population we take a random sample size n = 30. If we compute the mean age for this sample, we find it is 29 years:

35	40	62	24	35
15	13	31	13	14
16	26	38	56	15
25	19	41	65	22
18	10	12	72	21
20	50	10	18	36

$\bar{X} = 29$

But how certain are we that this statistic is an accurate estimation of the true population average (the parameter)? How much confidence do we have in this sample statistic? To address these questions we use our knowledge of both the *sampling distribution* of our sample statistic, in this case the sampling distribution of "means," and the *standard error* of the sample statistic.

Reflect back to the example where we noted that if several samples were taken from a population, each would yield a somewhat different statistic. From this we can see we are actually talking about "all possible combinations" of heads and tails that can come up in a single toss of three coins. In other words, if we drew *all possible samples* of n = 30 from the population, if we calculated the average age for each one of these ($\bar{X}$), we would then have created a distribution of means:

Sample Number	X̄ (Average)	Difference
1	28.5	10.5
2	31	8
3	27	12
.	.	.
.	.	.
.	.	.
N	n	N

Now consider each of the average scores for each of the samples we had taken as a *variable,* and imagine that all of these averages constitute a sample itself. If this were the case we could compute the average age *for the sample of average ages.* Let us suppose we drew 100 samples of size n = 30 from a population of 1,450, and we now have 100 average age scores (one for each sample). If we compute the "mean" of all of these, we call the result the "grand mean" or the grand average of all the mean scores. This is now our best estimate of the true population average (parameter). Of course, we never really know the *population* average or mean (parameter) when we are using sample data. Only in *our example* do we know the *population* mean is 39 years. We can see that several of our sample scores differ from this parameter. These figures allow us to see how much our scores *deviate* from the grand mean, and this deviation is called the **standard error.** Assume this special statistic has a value of 5.5.

As seen in Figure 6.4, the larger curve represents the population, and the smaller curve the distribution of means from the sample of means (n = 100). Although we never really know the parameter for the population, in the example it is 39 years. The mean or average score for the smaller curve is 44.5 years. Now, because we know what proportion of a distribution lies beneath a normal curve, we can establish how "close" our sample mean is to the

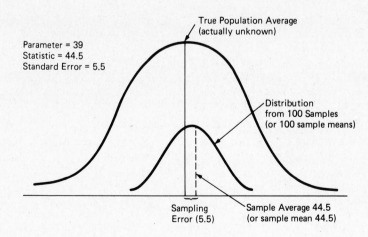

FIGURE 6.4 Relationship of Population Average to Sample Average

population mean. Specifically, we know the distance from the estimated mean to plus or minus one standard error will *always* include the true population mean 68 percent of the time. Stated somewhat differently, we know 68 percent of all sample means lie within one standard error of the true population mean, and conversely, since the grand mean of all sample means is our best estimate of the true population mean, we can also say the true population mean will fall within the range of $\overline{X}$ (the mean average), plus or minus the standard error, 68 percent of the time. We can also say we are 68 percent confident our sample mean estimates the true parameter within one standard error of the parameter we are attempting to estimate.

Calculating the Standard Error

The standard error is related to both the standard deviation in a sample and to the sample size. If there is very little variation among scores, and if the sample is a very large one, we will obtain very little error in our estimates. We can calculate the standard error as follows:

$$\text{Standard Error (SE)} = \frac{S}{\sqrt{n-1}}$$

where S is the standard deviation for a sample, and n is the sample size. For our sample of 12 individuals, the standard error would be:

$$SE = \frac{12}{3.32} = 3.61$$

Confidence Intervals

We can now use the standard error to place a confidence interval around the mean score we have calculated for the sample.

Think of a **confidence interval** as the "range" within which you would be confident that a score actually existed. For example, walking down the street we might see a person and estimate her age to be 21 years. Of course, we could not be positive the estimate was exact. We would have more confidence if we said, "I'm sure her age is *between* 19 and 25 years." This is the way a confidence interval works; it provides a range of scores within which we are confident the parameter we are trying to estimate actually lies. The wider the range, the more confidence we will have that that score is actually there.

This is accomplished as follows:

$$\text{Confidence Interval (CI)} = \overline{X} \pm SE\ (1.96)$$

Researchers generally distinguish between values representing a population and values obtained from a sample. In notational form, this distinction is generally symbolized by using Greek letters for population values and Roman letters for sample values. The mean is symbolized by the Greek letter μ (mu) and the standard deviation σ (sigma) when referring to populations. For samples, these values are distinguished by the notations $\bar{X}$ for the mean and s for the standard deviation. Note also that N is used to denote the size of a population and n the size of a sample. The table below will help you to understand the notations used when sampling.

Distributions	Mean	Standard Deviation
Sample	$\bar{X}$	s
Population	μ	σ
Sampling	μ	$\dfrac{\sigma}{\sqrt{n-1}}$

As can be seen above, the standard error is the same as a standard deviation, although it refers to the deviations of a sampling distribution and not of a sample.

Where CI is used to represent our confidence interval, $\bar{X}$ the mean for the sample, and 1.96 the number of standard deviations, we will add and subtract to the mean to provide an interval between which we will be certain to find the parameter we are attempting to estimate at least 95 times out of every 100 samples we draw. When applied to the example, the following results are obtained:

23.9 $\pm$ 3.61 (1.96) =

23.9 $\pm$ 7.08 = 16.82 to 30.98

We now conclude that the chances are 95 to 100 that the actual mean will be found *within* the interval 16.82 to 30.98. We are now reasonably sure that our interval will *catch* the true mean, since only 5 intervals in 100 constructed in this way will fail to do so; if it does not, something has happened which would occur only 5 times in 100 cases, and this seems like a reasonable risk to take. We can use the figures listed below to establish various confidence intervals. The derivation of these numbers, however, is beyond the scope of this book.

To establish a 68 percent confidence interval, use 1.0; to set up a 95 percent confidence interval, use 1.96; to establish a 99 percent confidence interval, use 2.58. And finally, the standard deviation and standard error are again briefly reviewed at the end of Chapter 15.

So far in this chapter we have focused on the *reasons* for sampling. We have argued that we couldn't ask or measure everything or everyone in a population, for example, and we also wouldn't have much confidence in asking or measuring only one element from that population. We have argued that samples must be drawn in a way to avoid bias, and that samples should be representative of the population being studied. In other words, the purpose of sampling is to come up with a manageably sized group of respondents that come from a known and clearly defined population such that estimates of the characteristics or parameters of the population can be made. The various terms and concepts used within a sampling context were also examined. We found the terms "population," "universe," and "sample" took on different meanings from normal use when used within a research framework, and that "statistics" and "parameters" referred to summary figures that described samples or populations, respectively. The concepts "randomness" and "probability theory" were also introduced, and we found by selecting elements randomly we could overcome problems of bias. Probability was compared with chance, and we noted that in a proper sample, every respondent has the same chance of being included. Finally, we demonstrated the use of the standard error in checking to see just how confident we could be in estimates of population parameters.

Constructing a Sampling Frame

It is obvious a sample cannot be any more accurate than the sampling frame it is drawn from. As pointed out earlier, a sampling frame is a complete list of all the units from which a sample is taken. However, it is very difficult to obtain accurate and complete lists of this kind. When researchers begin a study, the generation of a complete sampling frame is one of the most important tasks encountered. Where do such lists come from? What are some of the problems associated with finding and using a sampling frame? How are they constructed? In this section we discuss some ideas of how sampling frames are constructed.

Sources for Sampling Frames

One important rule to remember when beginning to construct a sampling frame is that every person or object of analysis in the population should be listed—*but only once!* If a person is listed more than once, his or her chances of being included in the final sample are increased, and this can result in an unrepresentative sample. For example, one of the most often-used sources for sampling frames is the telephone directory, but names in a phone book are often listed more than once. People have separate telephones in their homes, businesses, and for their children. Also, many poor people do not have phones, and upper-level SES persons often do not have their numbers listed. And people without telephones share similar characteristics, just as people who do not list their numbers make up a distinguishable social group. For example, single women often do not list their telephone numbers. In short, the telephone directory can exclude various people from a sampling frame because of the "telephone behavior" associated with these groups of people.

It is obvious that it is very difficult to obtain accurate sampling frames for large studies. However, an additional source is available to researchers: the information provided by the U.S. Census. Although the accuracy of census data will depend upon when the census was conducted, the major advantage of using this as a beginning point is that these data indicate the *location* of persons with special characteristics. For example, census data indicate the percentages of persons from various ethnic groups living within certain known boundaries, and this makes the sampling of specific groups somewhat easier and more accurate. Specifically, a benchmark is provided to see if the final sample is representative of the population when census data are available for comparison. It is also noteworthy to mention that households and residences are far more stable than are their mobile human owners, and when lists of residences can be coupled with knowledge from census data, more accurate and precise sampling frames can be generated.

When specialized investigations are conducted, sampling frames can be easier to prepare. For example, if we were interested in studying some form of formal organization, sampling frames could be generated from organizational membership rosters. Schools are also a good source of information when beginning a sampling frame, especially when studying forms of education or the behavior of children in general. Membership rosters from churches, employee lists from local factories or businesses, fraternity or sorority membership lists, club rosters of all kinds can be used for sampling frames if and when they are up-to-date and complete, and when members are not listed more than once.

Lists of registered voters, automobile and property owners, welfare recipients, permit and license holders of all kinds, street directories, and tax rosters are also good beginning points for creating sampling frames. Each of these lists are, of course, subject to the same problems associated with any other source: they must be complete, up-to-date, and must not exclude certain groups of people. For instance, if we used a list of property owners from our hometown to generate a sampling frame, we would have to keep in mind that "poor" people would be underrepresented in our sample and the more affluent members of the community would be overrepresented. Also, many people do not vote or own automobiles, and this too can confound a sampling frame. Members of lower SES families often do not vote or register to vote as often as higher SES persons, and poor people are less likely to own cars than are individuals with more money. However, if these facts are taken into consideration, and if we are careful to not generalize beyond our data, and if our sampling frame is clearly spelled out for others to understand, the above sources can be very helpful in building a sampling frame.

Designing Samples

After reading several pages about the importance of sampling frames, and about clearly defined "populations" and sampling error, you are probably beginning to wonder just how one goes about designing a sample. It turns out that there are several ways to do this. However, sampling methods are generally categorized into two broad categories: **probability sampling** and **nonprobability sampling** (see Table 6.1).

Probability Designs

THE SIMPLE RANDOM SAMPLE   The simple random sample (SRS) is the basic sampling design used in almost every social scientific study. Statistical analyses of data almost always depend upon samples drawn randomly. How does one go about drawing a random sample? As Bailey notes, all that is required to conduct a SRS, after an adequate sampling frame has been constructed, is to select respondents without showing bias for any of their personal characteristics. As suggested earlier in this chapter, randomness is not a "hit-or-miss" method of simply interviewing anybody who walks by. Such a technique could only result in a biased sample that was not representative of the total population. First, the researcher must be positive each individual in the population is listed once and only once on the sampling frame. We then assign a number to each individual on the list, and using a table of random numbers or some mechanical procedures such as computer-generated random numbers, we make the selections. For small samples this can be done by

TABLE 6.1   A Summary of Sampling Designs

Probability Designs	Nonprobability Designs
The Simple Random Sample	Accidental Sampling
The Systematic Sample	Purposive Sampling
The Stratified Sample	Snowball Sampling
Proportional Stratified	Quota Sampling
Disproportional Stratified	
Cluster Samples	

writing each person's name on a slip of paper, and then drawing the number of slips of paper randomly from a hat until we reach the number of individuals needed for the sample. However, what happens to an individual's probability of being selected in a sample after half of the slips of paper have been taken from the hat? Or after half of the respondents have been selected using a table of random numbers or a computer-generated list? Given our knowledge of probability, we understand the last person in such a sample would have a higher probability of being included than the first person selected. We have now encountered a new question: Should we replace a name after it has been drawn from the hat, or should we leave it out?

SAMPLING WITH AND WITHOUT REPLACEMENT   Sampling without replacement is called **simple random sampling** (SRS), and SRS is considered an adequate method if the probability of an individual's selection is equal at any particular stage of the sampling process. However, if we were to begin with a sampling frame consisting of 500 elements, we can see the first element to be selected would have a 1/500 chance of being selected. What happens after we have taken 200 names from the list? What is the probability of being selected for the sample then? It is 1/300, which means there is a somewhat greater chance of being included in the sample. This would be true only if the names of the respondents were *not* returned to the sampling frame. If the names were returned, the probability would remain the same for each person selected. Of course, if a name is selected that has already been included in the sample, that name is returned to the sampling frame, and another name is randomly selected. However, if the population size is relatively large, and the sample size is relatively small, the difference in the probabilities of selection from the beginning to the end of the sampling process is usually very slight, and sampling without replacement is an appropriate procedure to follow.[10]

THE SYSTEMATIC SAMPLE   In **systematic sampling,** another sampling technique often used by sociologists, the researcher simply goes down the list of sampling elements and selects every kth individual, starting with a randomly selected case. For instance, if we wanted to select a sample of 100 persons from a list of 1,000, we would take every tenth name on the list for our sample. The first selection, of course, would be made using a random sampling technique called a **random start.**

This form of sampling is much simpler than random sampling whenever a sampling frame is extremely long and a very large sample is required. As Blalock points out, it is extremely difficult to find the 512th name in a telephone book using the random sampling process.[11] However, if the ordering of the sampling frame obtained can be considered random with respect to the variables we intend to measure, a systematic sample is equivalent to a simple random sample.

There are some problems to be avoided when using the systematic sampling technique. First, the elements from the sampling frame may have been ordered in such a way that a pattern occurs. For example, persons could have been listed according to their status in some group (that is, privates, sergeants, captains, and so forth), and therefore a **skip interval** (the distance between the elements selected for the sample) might be selected such that only one type of person would be included in the sample. If individuals were listed in ten-person groups, and the first person listed for each group was the leader of that group (the sergeant), and our skip interval was 10, *every person in the sample would be a sergeant.* Of course, such a sample would not be representative. If patterns of this kind are noticed prior to beginning the sampling procedure, the list should be "shuffled" or a "middle start" should be used.

A second problem to avoid has to do with the actual names appearing on a list. For example, most lists are in alphabetical order (that is, telephone listings, city directories, and the like) and certain ethnic groups may have an undue proportion of names beginning with the same letter (O'Neill, O'Reilly, O'Toole, O'Malley). This can create bias in a sample if a researcher is not careful. However, in the case of alphabetical ordering, we often have something similar to a stratified sample, wherein ethnic groups are grouped together.[2] By taking every kth respondent we are likely to obtain a proper representation for each group for the final sample. In any event, when using this method it is wise to carefully examine the sampling frame before beginning to make selections. If you detect a pattern or trend in the way names or elements are listed, take the proper precautions.

THE STRATIFIED SAMPLE   In stratified sampling, researchers begin by dividing the elements of the population into categories or groups, and then independent samples are selected from within each of the "stratum" or groups created. When using this design, keep in mind the rules associated with the nominal scale of measurement: groups should be defined in such a manner that each respondent or element appears in only one of the groups, and all possible groups should be included. There are two kinds of stratified samples: the *proportional stratified sample,* in which the sampling fractions for each group are equal, and the *disproportional stratified sample,* in which they are not equal.

Proportional stratified sampling is used to assure that a representative sample is obtained. Suppose, for example, we know there are 500 Democrats, 300 Republicans, and 200 Independents in a population. If a simple random sample of 100 respondents were taken from this population, we would certainly not expect to obtain exactly 40 Democrats, 30 Republicans, and 20 Independents. We would be especially concerned with the proportion of the sample made up of the political Independents because they constitute such a small number. If we wanted to study political liberalism, and we realized political party played a major part in determining one's political attitudes, we can see that a proportional stratified sample with sampling strata for each of the three political groups of 1/10 would probably yield more reliable results than a simple random sample. Specifically, we would feel assured that each proportion of the population we had an interest in would be fairly represented. Because the Independents make up such a small part of the total population, we could now be sure they would be equally represented, that they would not be passed over in our analysis. Importantly, when conducting a proportional stratified sample, the researcher must know in advance what the sizes of the population strata are. This means researchers are often restricted to simple variables such as sex, age categories, or the area of residence of respondents when stratifying a sample. This information, of course, is obtained from census data.

In disproportional stratified sampling we make use of different sampling fractions to modify the number of cases selected in order to further improve the efficiency of the design. For example, suppose we wished to compare the Democrats, Republicans, and Independents in our final sample with respect to their specific voting activities on a local issue. If we selected the SRS or the proportional stratified sampling design we would expect *too few* Independents in the sample to make meaningful comparisons. Therefore, we would

PROPORTIONAL STRATIFIED SAMPLING

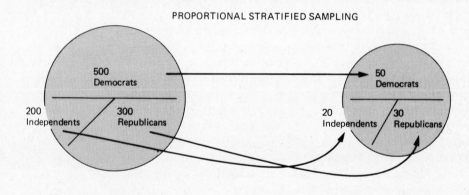

DISPROPORTIONAL STRATIFIED SAMPLING

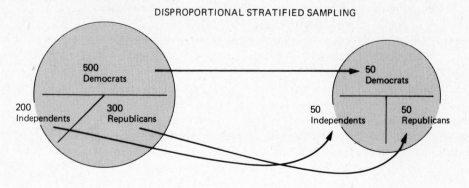

FIGURE 6.5
Examples of
Stratified
Samples

turn to the disproportional stratified design and select *equal* numbers from within each of the political groups. We might select, for example, 50 persons from each group such that enough respondents would be available to make comparisons of scores between each political strata. Whereas the proportional stratified sample assures representativeness with respect to the variable upon which the sample is stratified, the disproportional stratified sample makes possible a more efficient comparison of strata. One disadvantage of stratified samples is that researchers must have accurate knowledge of the population before the stratification process can take place.

CLUSTER SAMPLES In stratified sampling we separate the population into groups called strata and we sample from every group. However, sometimes it is advantageous to divide the population into a large number of groups, called *clusters,* and to sample among the clusters. For instance, we might divide the state into counties, and then select a number of counties for our sample.

This means we do not sample our elements directly, but we sample *clusters or groups of elements* instead. For instance, we would use a random selection process among clusters, and then select elements from the clusters that had been selected. The aim of **cluster sampling** is to select clusters as heterogeneous (unlike) as possible but small enough to cut down on such expenses as the costs of obtaining sampling frames and the expenses of travel for conducting interviews.

Cluster samples can become very complex in their design, but, in general, they are easier and less expensive than the other designs we have discussed so far. In a *multistage* cluster sample, several individual samples are drawn. For instance, we could begin by taking a random sample of high schools within a school district, and then, from within each school, take a simple random sample of classes. And finally, interviewers could be instructed to select and interview every tenth student in a class. In a sample to be used to study public opinion for an entire state, counties could first be randomly selected, then census tracts within counties, then census blocks within the tracts, and then every third house on every block, and then every adult member at each of the households could be interviewed. As can be seen, when large populations are involved, cluster sampling techniques can be used when sampling frames are unavailable. National samples, state samples, samples of large cities and counties, and communities of all kinds can be sampled using this method when no list of elements can be located.

SOME TECHNICAL COSTS OF THE CLUSTER SAMPLE Although cluster samples can be very efficient and less costly than other designs, there are some technical costs associated with its utilization. As you will recall, every sample contains a certain degree of sampling error. Therefore, if several independent samples are taken to obtain a final sample of respondents, then the *cumulative* sampling

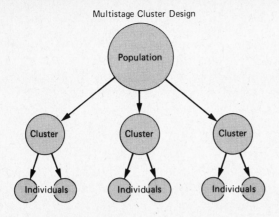

Multistage Cluster Design

FIGURE 6.6
Multistage
Cluster Design

error of all of the samples taken at the different stages of a multistage sample can contribute to a rather large sampling error among elements in the final sampling stage. While cluster samples are efficient, they are also less accurate.

A summary of the basic probability sampling procedures presented thus far and some of their advantages and disadvantages is provided in Table 6.2.[13] We turn now to some nonprobability sampling techniques.

Nonprobability Designs

The obvious disadvantage of using nonprobability sampling techniques lies in the fact that the probability of an individual being selected is not known, and researchers cannot claim a sample as representative of a larger population. It is therefore difficult to generalize when using these techniques since it is impossible to estimate the degree of departure between one's sample and a population. In other words, one cannot calculate sampling error using nonprobability sampling methods. However, the advantage of nonprobability sampling is it is not very complicated and therefore not very expensive. Also, these techniques can be adequate if a researcher has no desire to generalize or when conducting a pretest of instruments for a larger study to be conducted at a later time.

ACCIDENTAL SAMPLING   In this type of nonprobability sample the researcher simply selects the nearest persons as his or her respondents. **Accidental sampling** technique is also called *convenience sampling*, and one example of its use can be seen in captive audience samples that use introductory classes as the respondents for student studies. This technique is often used to gain a better understanding of the "populations" who attend specific meetings or who frequent shopping malls and so forth.

TABLE 6.2   Summary Sampling Chart for Probability Samples

Type of Sample	Sampling Procedures	Advantages and Disadvantages
1. Simple Random	To each population member, assign a unique number; select elements using random numbers.	Requires a minimum of knowledge of the population in advance; free of classification error, and easy to analyze and compute error.
2. Systematic	Use natural ordering of population; select random starting point between 1 and the nearest integer to the sampling ratio, and then select elements at interval of nearest integer to sampling ratio.	Simplicity of taking the sample is an advantage; must watch population ordering with respect to pertinent variables to ensure representativeness.
3. Stratified	Select from every sampling unit at other than last stage a random sample proportionate or disproportionate to size of sampling strata.	Proportional assures representativeness; disproportional is more efficient for comparison; requires accurate information on population.
4. Cluster	Select sampling units by random procedures; ultimate units are groups; select these at random and take a complete count of each.	Characteristics of clusters as well as of population can be estimated; low in terms of field cost if clusters are geographically defined; however, this design requires that each member of population be uniquely assigned to a cluster; inability to do this can cause the duplication or the omission of individuals.

Source: Modified from Russell L. Ackoff, *The Design of Social Research* (Chicago: University of Chicago Press, 1953), p. 124.

PURPOSIVE SAMPLING   When a researcher uses his or her own judgment about which respondents to select, and picks only those who meet the *purpose of the study*, he or she is conducting a **purposive sample.** If we intend to study a very specialized profession that few people know about, we would purposely select for our respondents only those who had firsthand experience with the area we had an interest in. If we wished to study only the rural people in a state, we might select only the rural counties when conducting the primary stage of a multistaged sample.

SNOWBALL SAMPLING   This sampling design is often used in "observational" and community studies, and is conducted in various stages. In the first stage, persons having some desired characteristic are identified and interviewed. These respondents are then used as "informants" to identify other individuals who qualify for inclusion in the sample. The second stage consists of interviewing these persons who in turn supply the researcher with additional names, and so forth. The term *snowball* comes from the analogy of a snowball, which begins very small but becomes larger as it rolls down a hill. Note that it is possible to select respondents randomly from within each stage of the **snowball sampling process,** making this a probability sample. This design could be used to generate a "sample" of persons who might not otherwise be easily found. For example, this technique could be used to locate the individuals who made decisions about communities but who were not "visible" community leaders.

QUOTA SAMPLING   This type of sample is often used in public opinion surveys, and at first glance it appears to be the same as a stratified sample. For quota samples, an interviewer is given a *quota* to fill when in the field. For instance, an interviewer is instructed to obtain interviews with "25 males who have an annual income of more than $9,000," or "who are under 21 years of age." *The selection of these persons is left entirely to the interviewer.* As has been pointed out earlier, because interviewers are human, they are likely to select those persons who are the most convenient and easy to talk with, and the resultant sample is usually a biased one. For this sampling method, then, researchers first decide which group or groups of people are important for the study, and then set quotas for each group that are proportionate to its representation in the population. After the quota has been established, interviewers simply go out and locate the appropriate number of individuals with the desired characteristics, and include them in the study. In a study of college students, for example, we could set quotas proportionate to the number of persons in a given class (freshmen, sophomores, juniors, and seniors), and then have interviewers find the persons from within each student class category to fill their quotas. Of course, we would expect our interviewers to avoid unfriendly students and restrict their samples to friends, fraternity brothers, persons who were not accompanied by large dogs, and so forth.

Summary

The focus of this chapter has been sampling. We have seen that there are two general headings under which various sampling designs can be classified. The first is probability sampling, where researchers know the probability of a respondent's becoming a part of a sample. The second is nonprobability sampling, where the probabilities of selection are not known by the investigator. Under the probability heading are placed simple random sampling (both with and without replacement), systematic sampling, stratified sampling, and cluster sampling. Accidental sampling (also called convenience sampling), purposive sampling, snowball sampling, and quota sampling were classified as nonprobability sampling designs. When a sample is drawn using a nonprobability technique, researchers will have a difficult time generalizing from their data, and sampling error cannot be estimated. Generalizations and estimates of error, however, can be handled rather easily with probability designs.

Sampling frames were also discussed, and we argued that no sample can be any better than the sampling frame from which it is drawn. Several possible "lists" were presented that could be used as a starting point for the creation of a sampling frame. City directories, telephone books, student rosters, employee lists, and lists of welfare recipients were all examples given of possible sampling frames. However, these lists often contain names that appear more than once, and in some cases sampling frames are biased against certain classes of people. For example, persons from lower SES homes often do not have telephones, and persons from higher SES groups often do not list their telephone numbers, and thus both situations can bias a sample.

Census data were suggested as a source for verifying the representativeness of a sample. Because census data can give a researcher a general picture of the characteristics of populations within certain known boundaries (that is, census tracts or blocks), it makes possible not only the verification of a sample but also provides data necessary for stratifying samples. These data can also be used when preparing a quota sample.

The terms *population* and *sample* were introduced, and we showed that it was necessary to clearly define the population we were interested in generalizing to before beginning the sampling process. The objectives of sampling are to overcome bias, to create representative samples, and to provide estimates of population parameters that are described using statistics. In short, because we can never really know the parameters of a population, we must estimate them using samples and statistics. We can't ask *everyone* in the population the questions we would like, and we can't depend upon only *one* or a *very few* respondents when drawing our conclusions. We must take samples that are representative of some clearly defined population of interest, drawn in a random fashion such that estimates can be made about the likelihood of our statistics adequately describing that population's parameters.

If we summarize the process of sampling into a series of steps a researcher could take, it would look like this:

Step 1 Identify and clearly define the population you wish to generalize to; if you are not concerned with generalizations, select a nonprobability sample (they are less complex).

Step 2 Determine exactly what it is you will want to do with the sample data and select a sampling design; if you wish to compare groups *within* the sample, you would select the disproportional stratified design, but if you want a representative sample and are not interested in such comparisons, select a proportional stratified sample, and so forth.

Step 3 Now that you have clearly defined the population and what you want from your data, begin to look for a list appropriate for a sampling frame: telephone directories, city directories, club and school rosters, lists of employees, auto registration records, census data, and any complete and up-to-date list showing all members of the population (but only once) are beginning sources for a sampling frame.

Step 4 Using random selection procedures (if conducting a probability design), select the elements from the completed sampling frame.

Step 5 Calculate the sampling error for the sample data to indicate the confidence you have in the estimates made about the population.

At the beginning of this chapter we noted there was much more to conducting a survey than simply stopping people in the street for interviews. As we have shown, one of the key elements in survey research (although not restricted to surveys alone) is the sampling process, which makes it possible to generalize to populations and gives researchers a degree of confidence in their findings. In the next chapter we discuss the various forms survey research can take. Each of the survey techniques we discuss will depend upon a properly selected sample of respondents.[14]

Glossary

accidental sampling When we select the nearest live persons as our respondents; this is not a probability sample. Also called *convenience sampling.*

cluster sampling When we sample among clusters rather than among individuals.

confidence interval Used to place a range around a statistic to tell researchers how much confidence they have in it; used with the standard error.

multiple stage sample When several individual samples are taken before coming to the final sampling stage. Also called *multistage sample.*

nonprobability sample A sample drawn in such a manner that we cannot indicate the probability of an individual being selected.

normal curve A bell-shaped curve with certain important properties; we know the proportion of cases under a normal curve and can find how likely an event is to take place using it.

observation units An element or a collection of elements from which data are collected; in sociology, usually the individual human being.

parameter A summary number used to describe a population.

population or universe The sum total of the sampling elements; if we wanted to study husbands in America, our population would theoretically include all husbands in the United States; a population or universe is what we want to generalize to upon the completion of a study.

primary, secondary, or final sampling units These terms indicate the various stages in a sampling design.

probability Refers to the likelihood that out of a specified number of events, some event will take place; a ratio of possible events to actual occurrence of events. The probability of an event can be determined as follows: $P = n/N$

probability sample A sample drawn such that we know the "chance" each individual in a population has of being selected.

purposive sampling When elements are selected using judgment about which respondents are needed in a sample; this is not a probability sample.

quota sample When an interviewer is given a quota of a certain type of individual to interview.

randomness The occurrence of events in an unpredictable order.

random sampling The random selection of sampling units.

random start When we begin a systematic sample, we start with a random position on the sampling frame.

sampling The systematic selection of individuals or things from the total population of things or persons to be studied.

sampling distribution When all possible outcomes of an event are listed.

sampling element The objects of study; the persons or things that we intend to study can be called units of analysis.

sampling error A method of estimating the degree of error in a sample to see how much confidence we have in the statistic we have calculated.

sampling frame The list of the population from which a sample is taken.

sampling units Either a single sampling element or an aggregation of elements.

simple random sample When sampling is conducted without replacement of those drawn back to the sampling frame.

skip interval The distance between the elements being selected in a systematic sample.

snowball sample A multistaged design in which we ask a group of individuals to provide the names of others to be sampled or interviewed.

standard deviation A measure of dispersion or variation in a sample; the larger the standard deviation, the greater the variation of a variable.

standard error A method used to detect the error in a sample (see *sampling error*).

statistic A summary number used to describe a sample.

stratified sample When elements of the population are divided into categories, and samples are taken from the various stratum.

systematic sample When we select every kth element from a sampling frame; as in every tenth individual from a list of fraternity members.

table of random numbers A table containing a series of numbers that have been placed there completely at random; used in sampling.

unrepresentative sample One that does not reflect the characteristics of the larger population being studied.

1. The assumption we are making, of course, is that you yourself would not fit into one of these social categories.
2. Michael A. Malec, *Essential Statistics for Social Research* (New York: Lippincott, 1977), p. 4, has used a similar example.
3. See also Kenneth D. Bailey, *Methods of Social Research* (New York: Free Press, 1978), p. 69.
4. Claire Selltiz, Lawrence S. Wrightsman, and Stuart W. Cook, *Research Methods in Social Relations* (New York: Holt, Rinehart and Winston), p. 512.

Notes

5. Bailey, op. cit., p. 69.

6. Hubert M. Blalock, Jr., *Social Statistics*, rev. 2nd ed. (New York: McGraw Hill, 1979), p. 124.

7. Ibid., p. 119.

8. Malec, op. cit., p. 62.

9. Bailey, op. cit., p. 76.

10. Blalock, op. cit., p. 557.

11. Ibid., p. 558.

12. Ibid., p. 559.

13. Russell L. Ackoff, *The Design of Social Research* (Chicago: University of Chicago Press, 1953), p. 124. See also Delbert C. Miller, *Handbook of Research Design and Social Measurement*, 3rd ed. (New York: David McKay, 1970), pp. 57–58.

14. Several sources other than the ones cited here are available for students interested in more reading on the sampling process. See, for example, Morrise H. Hansen, William N. Hurwitz and William G. Madow, *Sampling Methods and Theory* (New York: Wiley, 1953); Leslie Kish, *Survey Sampling* (New York: Wiley, 1965); Arthur F. Mace, *Sample Size Determination* (New York: Reinhold, 1964); William Mendenhall, Lyman Ott, and Richard L. Scheaffer, *Elementary Survey Sampling* (Belmont, Ca.: Wadsworth, 1971); Slonim J. Morns, *Sampling in a Nutshell* (New York: Simon and Schuster, 1966); and Seymour Sudman, *Applied Sampling* (New York: Academic Press, 1976).

7

Survey Research Methods

One of the most frequently employed methodologies in sociology is the social survey. Most of us have taken part in survey research as respondents to various types of questionnaires or interviews. A **survey** is a data-collection method that asks questions of a sample of respondents, generally at a single point in time, using either a questionnaire or an interview.[1] When **questionnaires** are used in survey research, they are **standardized** so that all respondents are asked the same questions in as close to the same way as possible. This chapter describes in detail the construction of standardized questionnaires and examines the two basic types of survey research that sociologists conduct— the self-administered questionnaire and the interview. The **self-administered questionnaire** asks respondents to give written answers to prearranged questions, while in the **interview** the researchers ask questions and record the answers themselves. The merits and problems of both techniques are spelled out so that the researcher will have some basis for selecting the method that will best suit his or her needs.

When Is the Survey an Appropriate Research Tool?

When the objective is to measure public opinion or to reach a large proportion of a population that could not otherwise be observed directly, the survey is a useful research tool. If the research topic focuses on the attitudes of the public toward some issue, then the survey is the best bet for a basic design. When proper sampling techniques are used, the survey method will enable a researcher to *estimate* statistically public opinion on important issues, so that generalizations can be made to the total population from which the sample was drawn. The survey thus has a distinct advantage over some other sociological techniques because it makes possible *inferences* to a known universe of possible respondents that can be determined before the study is conducted. Other methods (for example, some forms of direct observation) can be restrictive when it comes to generalizations because the samples are too small or not representative of larger populations, as when probability samples cannot be drawn. However, there are also problems associated with the survey, as we shall see later in the chapter.

Questionnaire Construction

Although questionnaires can be used in other forms of research, they are most often associated with the basic survey design. The material presented here, it should be noted, can be applied to several additional designs and methods and is not restricted to survey research projects alone. For example, the general appearance or format of a research tool is highly important whether the instrument is used in a survey setting or for recording direct observations. Stated differently, proper format is important no matter who is supposed to use the instrument, the respondent or the researcher. Remember, the questionnaire is a *measurement* device, so it should be clear enough in presentation and *format* for anyone to understand it. If it cannot be easily understood by either respondents or interviewers, it will be of little use in measuring anything. An improperly constructed questionnaire can confuse respondents and obscure the data that are being sought. It is possible for a research instrument to be so confusing that the respondent will throw it away or at best respond to only a few parts of it. If one keeps in mind that the basic task when preparing research instruments is to make them as easy to use as possible, one will go a long way in obtaining complete and usable data. When we ask respondents to reply to our questions, whether in a face-to-face interview or with a self-administered questionnaire, we are asking them to work for us for nothing. It behooves us, therefore, to make that work as easy for them as possible by preparing well-thought-out, clearly written questionnaires.

Response Formats

There are two methods, as we have seen, of setting up response "categories" for a research instrument (see Chapter 5). One technique is the **open-ended question,** which is constructed to elicit a free response from a respondent rather than one limited by suggested alternatives. The other is the **closed-ended** or **fixed-choice question** method,[2] in which the respondent's answers are limited to stated alternatives or choices. The alternatives may be simply "yes" or "no" or they may provide for several degrees of approval or agreement with an item or they may be presented as a series of alternatives from which respondents are instructed to "pick" the one that is closest to their position. The following are examples of various forms of fixed-choice response category formats.

BOXES: Check the appropriate *box:*

1. My class standing is: Freshman ☐ ; Sophomore ☐ ; Junior ☑; Senior ☐ ; Graduate ☐

BLANKS: Check the appropriate *blank:*

2. My class standing is: Freshman ___; Sophomore ___; Junior ✓ ; Senior ___; Graduate ___

CIRCLE: Circle the appropriate *number:*

3. My class standing is: Freshman 1; Sophomore 2; Junior ③; Senior 4; Graduate 5

BRACKETS: Check the appropriate *item:*

4. My class standing is: Freshman ( ); Sophomore ( ); Junior (✓); Senior ( ); Graduate ( )

When a respondent's check is contained within the boundaries of a box, or between brackets, there is little doubt as to where they have placed themselves in response to a question. If we are unclear as to where a respondent has "checked" an answer, it will be difficult to conclude that his or her response adequately measured what we hoped it would.

When respondents are asked to check blanks (as above), they can sometimes become confused about which blank belongs with which item when the response categories are listed side by side. Spacing can usually solve this problem. With sufficient space between one response category and another, respondents can more clearly see which item belongs to a particular response. A better technique, however, is to place the response categories below one another:[3]

Check the appropriate box:

1. My class standing is:
   Freshman   ☐
   Sophomore   ☐
   Junior   ☑
   Senior   ☐
   Graduate   ☐

The most obvious problem with this format is that it requires a great deal of space, and this means that more of one's research budget will be spent on paper. Also, a very long questionnaire may discourage respondents to the point where they will ignore it, thinking it will require too much trouble to fill out. If an instrument is to be used in a mail survey, increased length and paper can also mean more weight and therefore more postage both for sending the questionnaire to the respondent and for returning it to the researcher. A good approach is to construct a pretest questionnaire, deferring decisions concerning the final format until the instrument has been tested on a small sample of respondents who are similar to the population to be studied. If the questionnaire is clearly understood in a pretest, modifications will not be needed. However, if some of the items are "missed" by pretest respondents, or if there is some confusion about what goes where on an instrument, the questionnaire format can be modified before continuing with the study.

Note that question formats of this type are essentially the same whether they are used in face-to-face interviews or in self-administered questionnaires. We saw in Chapter 5 that the reason for using face-to-face interviews instead of self-administered documents with this variety of question is to reach respondents who are unable or unwilling to fill out questionnaires. Very young children, persons unable to read or write, and those for whom English is a second language are examples of respondents who would not be able to complete a self-administered questionnaire.

Open-ended questions are designed to permit a free response from a respondent. Because the question simply raises an issue but does not provide or suggest any alternatives for an individual's reply, respondents can answer in their own terms and within their own frames of reference. The following is an example of an open-ended question:

This next question is on the subject of work. People look for different things in a job. What would you *most* prefer in a job?

_____

_____

_____

_____

_____

Advantages and Disadvantages of Open- and Closed-Ended Questions

There are generally two arguments for using open-ended questions in attitude surveys. First, closed-ended questions constructed prior to going to the field may fail to provide an appropriate set of alternatives that are meaningful to respondents in substance or wording. As Schuman and Presser have pointed out, this possibility leads to the recommendation that survey questionnaires *begin* with open-ended questions in pilot or pretest studies, while the responses that result can then be used as a basis for developing a meaningful set of final closed-ended alternatives.[5] The second argument is that respondents are apt to be influenced by the alternatives that a researcher gives them, so that a more valid reflection of respondents' attitudes toward an issue may be obtained when people are allowed to answer for themselves. Schuman and Presser have also noted that there are some variations to these basic arguments, which include discussions of the desire to avoid "social desirability" effects, and a concern to prevent mechanical choices or simply guesses rather than individual feelings about a topic.[6]

Open-ended questions, however, are not as easy to administer as close-ended questions and take much longer to analyze and respond to. For example, to evaluate open-ended questions, categories for analysis must be derived from the handwritten responses from relatively large samples. This is a costly and time-consuming process because "coders" must be trained to place responses into "categories" before further analysis can begin. When compared to the simple process of tabulating precoded responses to closed-ended questions, analyzing open-ended questions is complex.

Closed-ended questions, on the other hand, have the advantage of ensuring that the answers given are within a frame of reference that is relevant to the purpose of the study and in a form that is legible and easy to analyze. Consider the question, "About how often do you go to church, on the average?" When no response categories are provided, such diverse answers might be obtained as "only when my wife makes me go," "not too often," "on special holidays," "when there is a wedding," "every Sunday," or "every day of my life." If the purpose of the question had been to measure *frequency* of church attendance, the above answers would be of little use. If, however, we had provided alternative response categories such as "once a week," "once a month," and so forth, the respondents would have been able to answer within the context we intended. Thus the provision of alternative responses can make clear to respondents the intent of the question, and therefore minimize confusion. This feature can reduce the numbers of "failed to respond" and help keep response rates up.

Fixed-choice questions can also be advantageous when dealing with sensitive issues. For example, questions to which numbers are appropriate responses—such as income, number of years of school completed, and age—may be viewed as sensitive topics by some respondents. We can, of course, easily deal with such questions using open-ended techniques ("How old were you on your last birthday?" "How much money did you make last year?"). And the resulting responses would be at the highest level of measurement. The advantage is that closed-ended alternative response categories would *reduce* the measurement level to the ordinal scale (see Chapter 4), and information would be inevitably lost. When income categories must be synthesized, for analysis or for graphic presentations, the task can be taken care of after the data have been collected, even when the original question was asked in an open-ended way. If we had started with *ordinal* response alternatives, however, we would never be able to return to the *interval* level of measurement (see Chapter 4). The advantage of the closed-ended question about income (or age, or education, for that matter) is that while a respondent might refuse to provide an exact income figure in an open-ended question, he or she would be somewhat more likely to respond within some range of income *if the alternative is available*, for example, "between $15,000 and $21,000."

Tables 7.1 and 7.2 summarize the advantages and disadvantages of closed-ended and open-ended questions, respectively.

TABLE 7.1   A Summary of the Advantages and Disadvantages of Closed-Ended Questions

Advantages	Disadvantages
1. Standardized—easy to code and analyze.	1. Respondents sometimes "guess" at answer rather than provide true feelings.
2. Usually "clearer" to the respondent; result in more complete set of responses and increased response rate.	2. Can be frustrating to respondent if appropriate category is not provided; response rates may thus be reduced.
3. Can be useful when used with sensitive questions because "ranges" can be provided within which respondents can reply.	3. Too many response categories can confuse respondents *and* interviewers.

Source: Adapted from Kenneth D. Bailey, *Methods of Social Research* (New York: Free Press, 1978), p. 105.

TABLE 7.2   A Summary of the Advantages and Disadvantages of Open-Ended Questions

Advantages	Disadvantages
1. Useful when categories are unknown or when *too many* categories are needed.	1. Responses are not standardized; results are difficult to code and analyze.
2. Allow respondents to qualify their own responses. Answers can be in respondent's own words and can be self-expressive.	2. Respondents must have fairly advanced writing skills to respond to questions.
3. Good for dealing with complex issues that need detailed response.	3. Time and effort are required on the part of respondent. More paper required and thus increased costs.

Source: Adapted from Kenneth D. Bailey, *Methods of Social Research* (New York: Free Press, 1978), p. 106−107.

Contingency Questions

Several other question-asking techniques are available to the researcher. For example, there are times when a question will be appropriate for only a limited number of persons in a sample but will be irrelevant to others. The determination of who is and who is not supposed to respond to certain questions is decoded by a filtering or screening method called a **contingency question.** If, for example, we were studying some aspect of criminal behavior, we might use a screening question such as, "Have you ever been arrested?" The next question could be, "How old were you when you were arrested?" or "For what were you arrested?" The second question is a contingency question because the answer to it is *contingent* upon the answer to the first question. The directions for respondents to this question might read as follows: "If you answered 'yes' to this question, go on to question 2; if you answered 'no' to this question, skip to question 3."

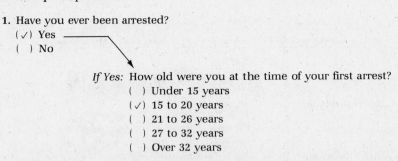

1. Have you ever been arrested?
   (✓) Yes
   ( ) No

        If Yes: How old were you at the time of your first arrest?
                ( ) Under 15 years
                (✓) 15 to 20 years
                ( ) 21 to 26 years
                ( ) 27 to 32 years
                ( ) Over 32 years

If we keep in mind that we are trying to make the job of responding as easy as possible for the respondent, we can see that by using contingency questions we can eliminate the confusion that might result because of questions that did not appear relevant to everyone in a sample. For example, the question, "Have you ever had an abortion?" would not be relevant to the male respondents in a sample. A carefully prepared contingency question, however, could be used to "weed out" the persons who had not actually experienced abortions. Contingency questions can also be used to further separate a sample into its various parts. For example, such a question could be included in the second part of a question that had already filtered out a special group within the sample. Thus, the second question itself becomes a screening question:[7]

1. Have you ever been arrested?
   (✓) Yes
   ( ) No

   a. If *Yes:* How old were you at the time of your first arrest?
      ( ) Under 15 years
      (✓) 15 to 20 years
      ( ) 21 to 26 years
      ( ) 27 to 32 years
      ( ) Over 32 years

   b. *If you were under 15 years:* Where were you at the time of the arrest?
      ( ) In a small city (under 50,000)
      ( ) In a medium-sized city (50,000−250,000)
      ( ) In a suburb near a large city
      ( ) In a large city (over 250,000)
      ( ) Don't know

Matrix Questions and Inventory Formats

We often ask questions that require a response about more than one person. This is often the case when our observation unit is different from our final unit of analysis. For example, we might want to ask one member of a group about the other members of the group. To avoid confusion we could use the **matrix question** (also called a **grid technique).** In setting up this type of question, a box is often used:

Name	Age	Sex	Rank in Organization
Jim	32	Male	President
Tom	29	Male	Member
Linda	28	Female	Member
Donna	30	Female	Member

Instructions for using grid format questions would read: "Please give me the name, age, sex, and rank of each member of your organization. Please list the person with the highest rank first." Since, with the grid format, information about than more one person can be collected using a single question, the result is a saving of space used on a questionnaire, as well as of money. If, however, instructions for the use of the question are not clear to both respondents and interviewers, confusion is likely. *Be sure that all questions are accompanied by a set of appropriate instructions for respondents and interviewers.*

Just as we often ask questions that require information about more than one person, we also ask questions requiring respondents to indicate more than one answer. This kind of question uses an **inventory format.** An inventory is simply a list of items to be checked or marked by respondents.[8] For example:

We are faced with many problems in this country, none of which can be solved easily or inexpensively. I'm going to name some of these problems, and for each one I'd like you to tell me whether you think we're spending too much on it, too little, or about the right amount. Are we spending too much, too little, or about the right amount on:

	Too Little	About Right	Too Much
A. Space exploration program		✓	
B. Improving the environment	✓		
C. Improving the nation's health		✓	
D. Solving the problems of the cities		✓	
E. Halting crime		✓	
F. Dealing with drug addiction		✓	
G. Improving the educational system		✓	
H. Improving conditions of blacks		✓	
I. Foreign aid			✓
J. Welfare[9]		✓	

When possible, it is generally a good idea to use an inventory question when, as in the example, the same answer format can be used for the entire series of questions to be asked. This type of question can actually save space on a questionnaire, since the instructions need be given only once, and the format itself saves space because several questions are actually being asked at one time.

Questions can be asked in any number of ways, but as we indicated in earlier chapters, it is best to ask questions such that responses can be scaled at the highest levels of measurement. Although we have already introduced some of these techniques, additional examples are given here.

Nominal Questions

Most of the questions we have dealt with in this chapter have been asked such that responses can be measured at the *nominal level* (see Chapter 4). The response format for this kind of question is usually easily understood by both respondents and interviewers. Responses are used to place an individual into a category such as "male" or "female." For example:

What race do you consider yourself?

White	☐
Black	☐
Mexican-American	☑
American Indian	☐
Puerto Rican	☐
Asian	☐
Other	☐ Please state _____

Instructions for this question should indicate that a respondent is supposed to "check" the appropriate box. Examples of variables that are measured at the nominal level on questionnaires would include marital status, race, sex, and any response that requires a simple yes-or-no answer or that places a respondent into a mutually exclusive category that appears on an exhaustive list of alternatives. Of course, with this kind of format a researcher must be concerned with the number of categories that are employed. For example, too many categories can both confuse the respondent and occupy more space than we might otherwise like to devote to the question. On the other hand, if too few categories are used, the one the respondent feels is the appropriate answer may not be among them. We can address this problem by conducting an adequate pretest of our research instrument, or in the case of face-to-face interviews, placing the categories on a card that is separate from the question-naire. After a question is asked that has several possible alternative responses, a card containing the response categories is handed to the respondent, who is instructed to select the one he or she believes is most appropriate for the question. When asking questions that are somewhat sensitive, such as those dealing with a respondent's income, several income categories can be placed on a card, and each possible income response could be accompanied by a letter or number. When the respondent finds his or her income "range" on the card, rather than responding with actual yearly income, he or she can be instructed to give only the number or letter that is appropriate for that income range. This method gives the respondent an easy way to respond to a sensitive question, and it saves the researcher money that would otherwise go into paper and printing.

As in the sample question concerning the race of the respondent, a category for "other" should always be included. Such a practice makes the list exhaustive, and when the "other" category is accompanied by the instruction "please state," we are in a position to analyze the responses to see if we have missed an appropriate and significant category.

Ordinal Questions

Several items on questionnaires are measured at the **ordinal level,** and the response categories for such questions do not differ significantly from those used in nominal questions. The ordinal response is at a higher level of measurement than the nominal response, however, because of the way in which the question is asked and the "ordering" of the response categories. Some examples of this type of question and possible response categories are listed below.[10]

Should divorce in this country be easier or more difficult to obtain than it is now?

Easier □
Stay as is □
More difficult □
Don't know □

What about sexual relations between two *adults* of the *same* sex—do you think it is always wrong, almost always wrong, wrong only sometimes, or not wrong at all?

Always wrong □
Almost always wrong □
Wrong only sometimes □
Not wrong at all □
Other (please state) □ _____
Don't know □

Do you agree or disagree with this statement: Women should take care of the country and leave running the home up to men?

Strongly agree □
Agree □
Neutral □
Disagree □
Strongly disagree □

The following are additional examples of ordinal categories that might be used when constructing an item for a questionnaire:

1. Very important/important/somewhat important/not important
2. Always true/often true/seldom true/never true
3. Often/sometimes/almost never/never
4. Excellent/good/all right/poor/bad

This type of item requires that a researcher make some decisions about how to "order" response categories, whereas with the nominal format such categories are determined objectively. That is, the categories for our earlier item on race were determined as a function of the actual existence of race in the social world; the response categories for the examples just given, however, are determined by the researcher with only a little help from the objective world. After all, there are no ordinal categories for measuring attitudes that can be observed as easily as can a person's sex or race. It is such considerations that make measuring attitudes (as opposed to, say, determining the sex of a respondent) the complex task that it is.

Before turning to questions that generate interval-level data, we will give one more example of ordinal response categories. An alternative format for ordinal questions is to list responses as a *continuum*, with labels only at the extremes. For example:

> We hear a lot of talk these days about liberals and conservatives. I'm going to show you a seven-point scale on which the *political* views that people might hold are arranged from extremely liberal—point 1—to extremely conservative—point 7. Where would you place yourself on this scale?

Extremely
Liberal

Extremely
Conservative

The instructions for such a question would ask respondents to circle "the appropriate number." A similar technique can be called a "thermometer" question. The difference between this kind of response category and what we have thus far presented is that the thermometer question places a zero category in the middle, with negative points on the left and positive points on the right:

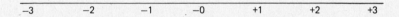

−3	−2	−1	−0	+1	+2	+3

The advantage of using this type of response category is that a respondent who has "no opinion" or feels "neutral" about an issue can circle the zero. If we did not have this category available, a respondent who had no real feelings about a topic would have no clear way of responding. If we had used one of the methods presented above, for example, and a respondent felt neutral about the question, where would he or she place a response? Another advantage is that more categories can usually be employed than could otherwise be used, and there is no need to think up titles or labels for them.

Another method of obtaining data at the ordinal level is to have respondents rank-order a list of items presented on the questionnaire. For example, respondents might be asked to rank what they believe to be the most important problems in their community from a list of alternatives:

> The following are some of the problems faced by citizens of our community. Please order them in terms of their importance to you, from 1 for the most important to 6 for the least important:
>
> _____ Air pollution
> _____ Violent crime
> _____ Drug addiction
> _____ Traffic
> _____ Noise
> _____ Property taxes

A disadvantage of this format is that the order of the alternatives can affect the respondent's ranking of them. One method to keep this from happening is to list alphabetically or at random and then rotate the items as they are listed from one group of instruments to another. Thus, the first item on one instrument would be the second, third, and so forth, on subsequent instruments. Of course, this way of handling the format is rather costly, and it is only a partial remedy at that.

Interval Questions

Intervally scaled questions can theoretically have as many responses as there are persons in a sample. For example, if we asked the age of each individual in a sample of 100 persons, we could conceivably obtain 100 different answers, assuming the sample was not restricted to adults or some other special group in the population. This means we cannot have a special category for all the possible responses that we might receive because we would have *too many*. Of course, we might use an open-ended question and avoid the use of a responses category format altogether. For example, we could simply ask respondents to indicate their age on their last birthday. Such a question would be ideal if we were concerned with all possible "ages" that appeared in the sample. Sometimes a researcher wishes to know only the approximate age or income group into which a respondent fits rather than actual age or income figures. In this case the task is to create categories that are neither too broad nor too numerous. By reducing categories to very narrow limits, we increase the number of categories needed for the questionnaire, requiring more space and costing more money. If the categories are very broad and thereby reduce the total number of categories to be used, we run the risk of losing a great deal of information. For example, suppose a researcher who is preparing a questionnaire wants to ask about the ages of the respondents but is more interested in *age groups* than in the actual ages of the persons in the sample. Perhaps his or her concern is with ages at first marriage rather than simply with people's age *per se.* The question might be as follows:

1. Are you currently married, widowed, divorced, separated, or have you never been married?

   Married ☑
   Widowed ☐
   Divorced ☐
   Separated ☐
   Never married ☐

   a. *If ever married:* How old were you when you first married?

   ten to nineteen years ☐
   twenty to twenty-nine years ☑
   thirty to thirty-nine years ☐
   forty to forty-nine years ☐
   fifty to fifty-nine years ☐
   sixty to sixty-nine years ☐
   seventy to seventy-nine years ☐
   eighty or above ☐

In the example the numbers are written out, but numerals are also used:

10−19/20−29/30−39/40−49/50−59/60−69/70−79/80+

In most cases each grouping will cover the same *width*, or age range. In the above example, each group spans 10 years except the last one, which picks up persons who were married when they were 80 years old or older. This category has an unknown width or range because persons who were married at 102 years, say (a somewhat unlikely event), would fit into it, which means the range is greater than 10 years. This kind of category is called an **open-ended category.**

Notice also that in the example no categories overlap, for example, 10 to 20 years, 20 to 30 years, 30 to 40 years. With this format people who were married when they were 20 years old, for example, would fit into two categories (the first and the second); the same is true for the age categories. For this reason the first number of a category ends in zero and the last number should end in four or nine. This practice ensures that each respondent will fit into only one category.

Just as sometimes it is best to measure age at a group level, the same is true when asking questions about income. As we have seen, income can be a sensitive area for some respondents, so that it is often wise to give income ranges from which respondents may select one rather than a direct question asking for actual income figures. Income categories, however, are not always presented with the same ranges or widths as age categories. Researchers often use income intervals that differ in width for some categories because income categories are often based on known "average" incomes for a population. For example, if the average income for a population was known to be around $20,000, we would not use this figure for the last category in a list (that is, $20,000 +) because we would lose too much information from respondents who earn above this average figure. Researchers should also carefully consider which income group they are most concerned with in a study. If the focus is to be persons under the poverty line, and that line is drawn at $6,000 a year, one would not present a category of 0 to $7,000 because it would obscure or "mix" the poverty portion of the sample with the portion above the poverty line. An example of income categories is presented below. A researcher who is unsure about average incomes and is not interested in any specific group within the population can make all income categories the same width or use an open-ended question. If knowledge of the population is available, however, and one is concerned about certain income groups, the following type of category should be considered:[12]

> In which of these groups did your total *family* income, from *all* sources, fall last year—in 1982—before taxes, that is? (Interviewer hands card to respondent.)
>
> **A.** under $2,000 ☐
> **B.** $2,000−3,999 ☐
> **C.** $4,000−5,999 ☐
> **D.** $6,000−7,999 ☐

E. $8,000−9,999	☐
F. $10,000−12,499	☐
G. $12,500−14,999	☐
H. $15,000−17,499	☐
I. $17,500−19,999	☐
J. $20,000−24,999	☐
K. $30,000 or over	☐

Survey Research Questions: A Summary

The focus of this chapter has thus far been on the construction of research instruments. We have suggested that when researchers are interested in reaching a large proportion of the population or when they are trying to measure public attitudes, that the survey is an appropriate research tool. Questions should be written clearly and a questionnaire should be formulated such that using it will be easy for both the respondent and researchers. Several response formats have been discussed. We reviewed the uses of open- and closed-ended questions, and illustrated several response formats that might be used. The advantages of using fixed-choice items include the fact that they are standardized questions and are easy to code and analyze after the question-naire has been administered. We also noted that fixed-choice questions are usually clearer for the respondent and much easier to understand because of the response categories that are included. This helps to increase response rates and makes data more complete. However, we also noted that closed-ended alternative formats can be associated with a respondent's guessing at answers rather than giving his or her own response. This is a major problem with closed-ended items. Another problem we noted was that sometimes a researcher has not included all the possible alternative responses to a fixed-choice question, and that this can frustrate respondents. Too many alternatives can also be a problem when using the closed-ended format.

Open-ended questions, however, were suggested for use when research-ers didn't know how many categories to use or when too many would otherwise be needed. Also, when a very detailed answer to a complex question is required, the open-ended question was suggested as the format to use. Open-ended questions allow respondents to qualify their answers and make them more personal. However, because such responses are not standard from one questionnaire to the next, open-ended questions can be difficult to code and analyze. When using open-ended questions, it is also assumed that respondents have the writing skills that are necessary to respond. When the assumption of fairly advanced writing skills is made, several possible re-sponses can be lost because of respondents not being able to understand English or because they are too young to have learned to read or write. The time and effort that is required to respond to such questions is also a disadvantage, and when a great deal of space is required for responses to open-ended items, it can require additional paper and increase costs.

Contingency questions, matrix or grid questions, and a review of nominal, ordinal, and interval response catergories were also presented. We noted that there are really several response formats available to the researcher for each of these kinds of questions, ranging from open-ended to fixed-choice with variations of both types between the ends of an open to closed continuum. "Thermometer" responses catergories and having respondents rank-order lists of items are examples we illustrated that would fall between the ends of this continuum.

The Ordering of Questions on Questionnaires

When interviewers record respondents' answers directly on the questionnaire, the document is called an *interview schedule*. The set of items that make up a questionnaire or interview schedule can consist of several different kinds of open-ended and fixed-alternative questions. These questions, however, are not simply placed on a research instrument in a random order, for the order in which they appear can have a dramatic effect on respondents' answers. Which questions should be asked first? Which would be better left for last? Should an open-ended question be asked before or after closed-ended questions? The following are guidelines for determining the order of questions:[13]

1. *Place sensitive and open-ended questions toward the end of a questionnaire.* If the research instrument begins with sensitive questions, respondents may react negatively and refuse to continue with the questionnaire. However, if sensitive questions fall late in the questionnaire, respondents will have already answered most of the other questions, so that if they refuse to go on, at least part of the information is given.

Open-ended questions should also be placed at the end of the instrument because they take time and effort to complete since respondents must write out their answers. A person who encounters such questions at the beginning might well be turned off and discard the questionnaire, thereby lowering response rates and creating an incomplete data set.

2. *Ask easy-to-answer questions first.* The opening questions should be nonthreatening to respondents, be clearly written, and have distinct response categories. Questions that deal with facts—sex of respondents, marital status, occupation, educational background, and so forth—are best asked first rather than those dealing with beliefs, attitudes, or opinions. In other words, the first questions should be *easy* questions that require very little thought. In general, opening questions should not touch on sensitive areas such as income, religion, or race. Bailey suggests making the first questions as interesting as possible in order to "stimulate" respondents to complete the questionnaire.[14]

3. *Ask information needed for subsequent interviewing first.* Questions that tax a respondents' memory or that deal with other members of his or her family or social group are best placed early in the questionnaire. The information derived can then be used to "personalize" later questions. For

example, if the observation unit is a household head and information is being sought on the total household, the questionnaire might begin by asking for the names of all the children in the family. Armed with this information the researcher can go on to ask, "How old is Billy now?" or "Where did Danny go to school when he was in kindergarten?" By obtaining the names of family members first and placing them in order of their birth, the researcher can usually "jog" a respondent into remembering more detail than by simply asking "Where did your children go to school?"

4. *Place questions in logical order.* If the concern is with obtaining information about job history, asking about a respondent's jobs in a logical sequence starting from the first job and progressing to the present job—or vice versa—will make it easier for the person to answer. Asking questions out of sequence, such as starting with the second or fifth job, can be confusing. When questions will cover several distinct areas—for example, job history, marital history, history of childhood illnesses—they should be grouped into logical categories and not scattered throughout the questionnaire. That is, ask questions that are alike or that go together at one time and then move on to the next topic.

5. *Avoid establishing a response set.* The fourth guideline suggests that a logical order of questions be established and that questions that are alike be asked in groups with similar questions. Bailey notes, however, that this rule may be broken whenever a researcher believes that by establishing a particular order of questions a response set will emerge.[15] A **response set** is a tendency on the part of a respondent to reply to items in a particular way, regardless of the content of the question or the "correct" answer. For example, a **social desirability** response set would be one where a respondent would agree with statements that are socially desirable and supported by social norms. However, the social desirability response set can be corrected (after a pretest) by changing the wording of questions rather than changing the order. Other examples of response sets include the tendency to answer "yes" rather than "no" or "agree" rather than "disagree" on *all the items.* This problem can also usually be corrected by changing the wording of the questions.

Still other response sets can be caused by the ordering of questions. For example, sequences of questions that are asked in a similar way and with a similar response format can produce responses such as a tendency to "check" only the lefthand column, or to alternate from "agree" to "disagree" with every other item. When asked about the income derived from first job to present occupation, Bailey notes, respondents have a tendency to increase the income they report with each subsequent job, whether or not the income actually increased. Bailey's remedy for response sets due to question sequence includes changing the order of questions:

> If response bias due to question sequence is suspected or demonstrated in a pretest, the researcher has little recourse but to change the order. He or she can randomize question order or vary the question and/or answer format from question to question. The disadvantages of this are that the respondent's train of

thought may be broken, he or she may be confused by having to switch from one format to another, and much more labeling of response categories may be required. However, it may be worthwhile to do so if the response set can be broken. Another possible advantage of mixing question types and orders is that the added variation may make the questionnaire less boring for the respondent and motivate him or her to finish it.[16]

There is a delicate balance between grouping questions and running the risk of establishing response sets and mixing questions to avoid response sets. Pretesting and careful thought can usually aid the researcher's judgment in this area.

6. *Use pairs of questions to check reliability.* Pairs of questions, usually one stated negatively and one positively, are generally used to check for reliability. We might ask, "Marijuana should be decriminalized (agree or disagree)" at one point in our questionnaire and "Marijuana should not be decriminalized (agree or disagree)" at a later point. If the question is unreliable, a respondent might disagree or agree with *both* questions. Paired questions can help the researcher detect unreliable questions, which can be removed from the questionnaire after a pretest or ignored during data analysis. Obviously, reliability-check questions cannot be placed together because respondents would quickly catch on to the tactic and make their responses consistent. Nor should such questions be placed in an ordered sequence, such as a positive question always first and a negative one always last. Rather, the order should be determined randomly. When respondents detect these questions, they will deliberately answer them in a consistent way, thus defeating the purpose of the questions; or they will spend time "flipping" back through the questionnaire to see how they answered earlier questions, or they will interpret such questions as "trick" items intended to catch cheaters. Of course, there are no "right" or "wrong" answers on a questionnaire, but the *idea* that they might be can cause respondents to become frustrated and refuse to respond to further questions.

7. *Place scale items according to response required.* Questionnaires often contain large numbers of items that are part of a scale, and the researcher will have to decide if these items are to be placed together or listed separately on the instrument. If the scale items can be presented in a single group, the same response format may be used for all the items, and a different response category will not be needed for each question. This format presents a "neat" package for respondents and appears to be a logical tactic to employ. There is, however, a strong argument for scattering the items throughout the question-naire. If all the items are presented together, respondents might look for a pattern of answers or try to guess what is being measured and answer according to what they think the researcher wants. Again, there is a delicate balance between placing items in groups and spreading them out over the instrument, and the researcher will have to decide which approach to use after pretesting has been completed.

8. *Vary questions by length and type.* It is often wise to vary questions to question format, response format, length, and whether they are open-ended or

closed. While this method can help maintain a respondent's interest, it can also make an instrument more difficult to respond to—and the researcher's task is to make the respondent's job as easy as possible.

9. *Determine whether the funnel technique is applicable.* The **funnel technique** of ordering questions is often employed in questionnaire construction. This method calls for the use of broad and general questions (open-ended questions) at the beginning of a questionnaire or item sequence, and then narrowing the document by asking specific questions (fixed-choice questions) about the same topic that include response categories. This kind of questioning is similar to the contingency questions discussed earlier in this chapter. By asking broad questions at first, a researcher can determine who should continue to the more specific items.

Level of Wording and Item Construction

Just as the order in which questions appear can affect answers, so can the wording of questions have an impact on the data we receive. The first rule to be kept in mind when writing questions is the rule of *parsimony:* the shortest question that conveys what is intended is the best bet. Just as exceedingly long questionnaires can confuse and frighten a respondent, so can very long and confusing questions. Such questions also take up a great deal of room and cost both money and data. We have already talked about *double-barreled questions* and *leading questions* in Chapter 5. The rules associated with avoiding these kinds of questions should also be kept in mind when preparing a questionnaire.

One aspect of questionnaire construction that we have not talked about is the actual wording of the questions. Are there certain words or kinds of words that should not appear on questionnaires? Is there a *level of wording* that should be kept in mind when preparing items? We will briefly discuss the aspects of item construction related to this problem.

Are Long Words Needed?

When preparing items for a research instrument, keep in mind that not all respondents will be familiar with the same words that we and our colleagues use. The level of wording in an item can confuse respondents if we are not careful to keep our words at the appropriate level. For example, we shouldn't use the word "vocation" when we can use the word "job" or "occupation." Or shouldn't ask, "What is your regular remunerative employment?" when we could ask, "What is your current occupation?" However, there are two sides to this coin. We should also keep in mind that just as there are high-level words—often called fifty-cent words—there are also low-level words, and they too can confuse and frustrate respondents.

Is Slang Appropriate?

Just as we shouldn't ask, "What is your regular remunerative employment?" we should also *not ask* "What'cha do for your bucks?" Just as the level of wording can confuse some respondents, slang can also be misunderstood. Usually, slang expressions and words are associated with different classes of people or different regions of the country. If we are working in an area where a word or expression is accepted by the larger population, we will have to come to a decision about using it in our questionnaire. However, it is best to avoid slang whenever possible. Remember, our role is that of the scientist, and it would appear to some respondents that we were being less than scientific by using slang terms and expressions in a research setting.

Write Questions at the Respondent's Level

When we know who will comprise our sample and have an understanding of their background and general educational level, we can write questions at a level tailored especially for them. If we are dealing with a special group, for example, it would not be difficult to accomplish this task. For instance, if we wanted to study college professors, we could probably get away with using long, more difficult words than if we were dealing with a less educated portion of the population. On the other hand, if we were preparing to study seventh-grade truants or juvenile delinquents from the inner city, our wording of questions would be at a much lower level. However, one should be careful not to offend these distinct populations by using their terms and expressions in an improper way. Remember, you're the researcher, and researchers don't use offensive language, slang expressions, or terms that are unfamiliar to respondents.

One final note: Remember that census data are available that can provide an indication of the educational level of the populations we will be dealing with, unless we plan to look at a very unusual group. Before preparing questionnaires or interview schedules, it is wise to check available data on the population to see what it looks like. Census data can provide descriptions of a community's educational level, its racial composition, and its average age. Since each of these variables can be associated with special words and expressions, they can provide clues about an appropriate level of wording long before we go to the field.

Instructions

Every questionnaire and interview schedule should contain instructions for either respondents or interviewers. Introductory comments and clearly written examples of how to respond are also important parts of a research instrument. Instructions about how to answer questions are especially important for self-administered questionnaires because there will be no interviewer present to help respondents when they are "filling-out" the instrument. Therefore, it is best to begin an instrument with instructions for its use. We should instruct respondents, for example, in exactly how we want questions answered; if questions are to be marked with a check or an X or if responses are to be circled. If we have open-ended questions on our questionnaire, it is a good idea to let respondents know about the length of answer we are looking for. Of course, one clue to the desired length of a response will be indicated by the space provided.

If an instrument is divided into subsections that deal with various topics (health history, job history, and so on), each section should be accompanied with its own set of instructions and an introductory statement. For example, "Now we would like to ask you about your occupation," or "We would like to know a little about you, your age, your occupation and if you're married or not. The next few questions should be checked in the appropriate places."

There will also be times when special questions will be asked, and they will need special instructions. For example, when we are using contingency questions, we will have to be very clear in giving instructions. This is also true when asking respondents to rank-order a list of items, or to select the most important items from among several possibilities.

Now that we have covered the basics for constructing research instruments, it is time to take a look at the various forms a survey can take. As has been noted earlier, there are some interviews that are conducted face-to-face, and others that are handled through the mail or over the phone. We can therefore divide surveys into two general categories: **the self-administered questionnaire** and **the interview.**

Self-Administered Questionnaires

There are two basic ways in which questionnaires can be used in self-administered situations: the **group survey** and the **mail survey.**

The Group Survey

In the group survey, questionnaires are handed out to a group of respondents who are in the same place at the same time. Many of us may have taken part in this type of survey when questionnaires have been given out in one of our classes or to a group of employees or some other group situation where it would be easy to simply hand everyone an instrument, briefly go over the instructions with them, give a few examples, and let the respondents do the rest. If there is some confusion over an item, a respondent can raise his or her hand, and the researcher is there to clarify the question. Of course, this could not happen using the mail survey because no interviewer or researcher is present. This demonstrates the need for clearly written and tested instructions, and points up a weakness of the self-administered survey. Specifically, when there is no interviewer present to guide a respondent through a questionnaire, there is an increase in the probability that some questions will not be understood, and that they may not be answered.

The Mail Survey

The basic methods associated with conducting a mail survey are probably known by most of us already. It is not very much different from paying the bills we receive every month! Basically, a questionnaire is prepared and sent through the mail to a sample of respondents, accompanied by a cover letter, instructions, and a stamped and return-addressed envelope. Respondents are instructed to complete the questionnaire and send it back to the researcher. Even with the increasing cost of using the mail services, this method is generally an inexpensive one when compared with other survey techniques, and we can cover a very wide geographical area by using the postal service. Imagine when it would cost to send a letter to another country, and then compare that cost with the cost of sending an interviewer to accomplish essentially the same task. Using the mail survey method, it is also possible to reach people who otherwise could not (or would not) be interviewed. For example, it would be possible to gather data from persons who were in prison, or from community leaders who claimed they didn't have the time to submit to a face-to-face interview. Note that we say it is *possible* in these situations to reach these kinds of people through the mail, although specific situations would definitely have to be taken into account before attempting to conduct studies such as those in our example. Keep in mind, however, that when we send a questionnaire to a person it does not necessarily mean that he or she will complete it and send it back. In fact, even when we receive a completed questionnaire, it does not always mean that the person we sent it to has *filled it out!* It could have been completed by a secretary, one of the respondent's children, his wife or her husband, or anybody who might have found it and decided to answer your questions. This constitutes another of the mail survey's major drawbacks. Others would include the fact that not everybody can read or write, and therefore would be unable to complete and return our questionnaire. Relatively low costs and the ability to reach a large number of people over a very large area, however, make the mailed questionnaire one of the most often-used survey techniques available. A summary of the advantages and disadvantages of mailed questionnaires is presented in Table 7.1.

MAKE THEM EASY TO RETURN   The basic task of the researcher using the mail survey methodology is to make certain that respondents return a completed questionnaire. There are several techniques that can be used to ensure that happens, and there are several factors we can "control" to increase the response rates. Some factors found to influence responses are:

1. The sponsorship of the questionnaire.
2. The attractiveness and clarity of the questionnaire format.

3. The length of the questionnaire.
4. The nature of the accompanying cover letter requesting cooperation.
5. The ease of filling out the questionnaire and mailing it back.
6. Inducements offered to reply.
7. The interest of the questions to the respondent.
8. The nature of the people to whom the questionnaire is sent.

As Selltiz and her coauthors summarize, "Attractively designed question-naires that are short, clear, and easy to fill out; interesting to the respondent; simple to return; sponsored by prestigious groups; personalized with regard to the cover letter, envelopes, and the questionnaire itself; and presented in a context that motivates the respondent to cooperate are most likely to be returned."[17]

SPONSORS If we can obtain a known and prestigious sponsor for our survey, such as a well-known college or university, this tends to legitimatize our study, and respondents are more willing to participate. Heberlein and Baumgartner have reported that sponsorships from government organizations, in general, favorably affect mail survey response rates.[18] Our task, then, is to locate and gain permission from a prestigious or government sponsor before putting our questionnaire in the mail.

CLARITY It stands to reason that a clearly written questionnaire in an attractive format will help increase our response. If questions cannot be understood or if the printing is smudged and difficult to read, people will have a hard time filling it out. Some researchers use colored paper for their questionnaires to make them appear more attractive, but evidence that this tactic increases response rates is inconclusive. However, if we are conducting a large-scale mail survey that covers a large number of regions or geographical areas (such as rural, urban, and metropolitan areas), we can color-code questionnaires for each area to improve our recordkeeping procedures when

TABLE 7.1   Advantages and Disadvantages of the Mailed Questionnaire

Advantages	Disadvantages
1. Usually saves time and money	1. Lacks flexibility
2. Can be completed at the respondent's convenience	2. Can result in low response rate
3. Ensures anonymity of respondent	3. Respondents can't check with interviewer; interviewer can't check with respondents
4. Is standardized	4. No control over interview environment
5. Eliminates interviewer bias	5. Difficult to use complex questionnaire format
6. Allows respondents to check on the information they are giving you	6. Possible bias sample
7. Has accessibility of respondents over wide geographical areas	

the instruments are returned. If the colored paper is attractive enough to increase response rates even by a small percentage, it may be worth the effort.

QUESTIONNAIRE LENGTH   The length of a questionnaire is another important consideration to take into account when preparing a mail survey. When questionnaires become very long, they become more costly to mail, and some respondents can be scared off by their length. However, Heberlein and Baumgartner have argued that the perceived importance of a questionnaire may be associated with its length. That is, respondents might not take a one-page survey very seriously, but would believe that a somewhat lengthy instrument was an important one. It would be best for us to balance as much as possible the cost of a lengthy questionnaire against the benefits of the additional data we are attempting to gather. It would also be wise to carefully consider the population we will be working with. If, for example, it is one that is relatively high in educational level, a fairly long questionnaire may not be as frightening as one that is sent to a lesser educated group. However, keep in mind that longer questionnaires with more items *clearly increase the cost factor* and this can exert a modest influence on our return. In fact, *there is about a five percent reduction in the final response rate for every additional ten pages added to a mail questionnaire.*

PERSONALIZED LETTERS   Just as there are several ways of putting together a research questionnaire, there are several ways of putting together the cover letters that accompany them. They too can be of different lengths and written at different levels. One of the most controversial aspects of preparing cover letters is whether they should be personalized or not. A personalized letter is one that is addressed to the respondent, using his or her actual name, and not "Dear Sir or Madam," for the salutation. Personalized letters are also signed by the researcher, and made to at least appear as if they had been written especially for each individual respondent. This kind of letter is obviously a costly one, and our question becomes one of whether or not personalization actually increases response rates, making the cost worth the effort. Researchers have found that personalization can increase response rates, but the increase is only a slight one. More important then personalization, it has been argued, is the actual content of the letter. Letters that are written in a "permissive" rather than a "firm" style seem to elicit better responses than letters that are "short" and to the point. It has also been reported by some that handwritten signatures make no difference in the return rates received from mail surveys. In short, it is the content of the letter that is more important, not the trappings of colored paper, signatures, and the like.

PAYING RESPONDENTS   What about the practice of paying respondents to fill out our questionnaire; that is, actually including money in our package of questionnaire and cover letter? Several researchers have examined this possibility and have found that inducements of this kind can help increase returns. However, if we included 25 cents in each of the questionnaires we sent out, our costs would soar dramatically, and some respondents would keep the quarter we had sent them and still not return our questionnaire. Additional prizes or rewards can be offered, however. For example, we could promise to send our respondents a copy of our findings, which may induce them to complete the questionnaire and return it to us promptly.

Our best bet is to make our letter as appealing as possible and hope that respondents are as interested in our study as we are. Most of us don't have the extra research funds required for any other form of inducement anyway, since we are usually working on a very tight budget. In fact, being a student with very little money and badly needing a grade on a class project may be a better inducement than anything else we can think of. If respondents are interested in the study, from the description and information we provide them in our cover letter, they will generally be more than happy to return a questionnaire. It has been found, for example, that the first persons to return completed questionnaires are generally those who demonstrate the greatest interest in the subject of the study. Persons who aren't very excited about a study's topic will usually put our questionnaire aside and can eventually forget about it all together.

We have discussed several of the problems associated with getting a good response to a mailed questionnaire. We have pointed out and discussed several of the factors that a researcher can "control" when conducting this kind of study. However, two additional aspects of the mailed questionnaire should be mentioned before we turn to another topic: the monitoring of our returns and follow-up mailings.

MONITORING RETURNS   After we have constructed our questionnaire, tested it, prepared a cover letter to be included in our package of instructions, and return-addressed and stamped envelopes, and after all our questionnaires have been sent out to the sample previously drawn, we should expect to begin receiving returns. At this point, we will have to monitor the questionnaires as they are sent back to us. By this we mean that we should begin to carefully record the varying rates of return among our respondents. We can easily do this by preparing a **return graph**,[19] which will allow us to monitor the rates of our response as well as provide us with a record that can be used to indicate the success of follow-up mailings, and when additional "reminder" mailings should be sent out. We can construct a return graph by simply indicating on a piece of paper with an X and Y axis the number of days the questionnaire has been out, and the number of questionnaires that have been returned on any particular day. By doing this, and keeping tabs on returns, we will find that most questionnaires are returned early in the research project, tapering off as time goes by, and increasing slightly after follow-up mailings have been sent out. Such records are good to have when we begin analyzing our data, since persons who return data early may be different from those who returned questionnaires late, and all of the respondents who returned questionnaires are probably much different from those who did not return them at all, late or otherwise. If we assume that people who return questionnaires very late are more like those who never return them at all, and that both of these groups are significantly different from the respondents who returned them within only a few days, we have the beginnings of a design to check for bias in our sample. When coupled with additional information on the population we are studying—taken from census data, for example—we have a very useful tool for helping to more adequately describe our sample and ensure against bias (see Figure 7.1)

FOLLOW-UP MAILING Sending out "reminders" to respondents who have yet to fill out and return our questionnaire is an excellent way to increase the overall response rate. Usually about two or three weeks after the initial mailing, and after we have consulted our return graph and detected a significant tailing off of returns, it is wise to conduct a **follow-up mailing.** We have found that after about two weeks (or about ten days), a postcard reminding respondents that we had sent them the questionnaire, and that we would like them to complete it and send it back, increases response rates almost immediately, albeit a rather slight increase. After an additional week or so (depending on what we

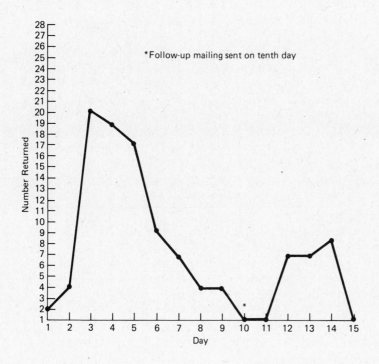

FIGURE 7.1
Return Graph
for Mail
Questionnaires

can read into our return graph), we can send a new questionnaire and cover letter to respondents who have yet to send back our original document. When we say that we will need a new cover letter, we mean that it will have to be rewritten to explain that this is a follow-up mailing. We would include in this mailing the same items as in the original mailing: addressed and stamped envelopes for returning questionnaires, any inducements we have decided to send, instructions, and the like. Although follow-up mailings can increase research costs considerably, they can return a good deal of data also.

ID NUMBERS   There are a few ways in which we can handle follow-up mailings. Basically, we can affix some form of identification number to each of the questionnaires sent out. This number should correspond to the address of the particular respondent we are dealing with. When his or her questionnaire is returned, we would simply check the number on our list. When we decide that it is time for a follow-up mailing, we would consult our list of numbers and addresses and send follow-up mailings to only those who had not returned questionnaires. Beware of the fact that some respondents will notice that there is an identification number attached to their questionnaire, and some will cross it out before sending it back because they are afraid that they will lose their anonymity, and you will know how they answered your questions. You can overcome this problem in part by explaining in your cover letter or in your questionnaire instructions that the ID number is only for recordkeeping purposes, and that anonymity is ensured. When we have promised to send an inducement to those who have returned the questionnaire, we can inform respondents that this number will be used only for ensuring they receive what we have promised them. In some cases it might be best to not mention the ID number at all, since pointing it out might cause respondents to notice what they would probably have overlooked anyway, and they might suspect that something devious is going on. This is a decision researchers have to deal with themselves; there are no hard-and-fast rules about such things. Of course, we could forget about such numbers completely, and when it is time to send out a follow-up mailing, send it to the entire sample, regardless of whether certain respondents had returned their questionnaires or not. A well-written cover letter can explain to those that had returned them why we had sent them an additional questionnaire. Of course, conducting follow-up mailings in this way can be costly when working with large-scale samples, and this fact will have to be kept in mind when we are designing a project.

WHAT KIND OF RESPONSE RATE CAN BE EXPECTED?   A question that many beginning researchers ask is, "What kind of response rate can I expect using this type of survey as my methodology?" Heberlein and Baumgartner recently reviewed 98 different studies that used the mailed questionnaire technique and reported the average response rate to be 60.6 percent.[20] Given that this is an average, we can expect to at least obtain a return of 50 percent, and some

TABLE 7.2   Advantages and Disadvantages of the Self-Administered Questionnaire

Advantages	Disadvantages
1. Usually less expensive	1. Not everyone can read or write: this eliminates certain groups from your study
2. Requires less skill to administer	
3. Can cover a wide area for a limited amount of cost	2. Response rates to mailed questionnaire can be low
4. Usually uniform and standardized from one respondent to the next; makes it easy to analyze	3. Because there is no interviewer present, confusion over questions cannot be remedied during its administration
5. Can reach "special" groups	

researchers have reported returns of 80 percent and more. Much of this depends upon the nature of our sample. If our sample is composed of persons who are very concerned with the topic of our study, and if the issue we are investigating is a popular one, response rates will probably be fairly high. If the issue we are studying is not of interest to the members of our sample, and if our questionnaire is not clearly written with good instructions, and if it is not properly packaged to make its completion and return as easy as possible for respondents, our return will more than likely be very low.

Before turning to a discussion of interview surveys, let us look at the steps one would take to complete a mail survey:

Step 1   Prepare questionnaires following the rules presented in this chapter.

Step 2   Draw a sample following the instructions presented in Chapter 6.

Step 3   Prepare a return graph and send out questionnaires.

Step 4   Keep track of returns and prepare for follow-up mailing(s).

Step 5   Send out follow-up mailing(s).

Step 6   After a predetermined time has been reached, cut off the survey and prepare to begin analysis; one of our first tasks, then, will be to check for bias in the sample.

If the basic rules and procedures presented here are followed, we can expect to obtain a return rate of at least 50 percent and probably better.

Interviewer-Administered Questionnaires

The Interview Survey

In an **interview survey,** trained interviewers ask questions of respondents rather than have the respondents read them and write the answers themselves. Interviews are generally handled in a face-to-face context, and usually in the home of the respondent, but interviews can also be conducted over the telephone. We will discuss both of these methods in this section.

THE INTERVIEWER   One very distinct advantage of the interview survey is its high response rate, which can be as much as 85 percent and sometimes higher. It is usually more difficult for a respondent to refuse an interview when the researcher is at the front door, and when respondents aren't able to be interviewed at the time the researcher is present, an appointment for an interview at a later date can be made. Data are generally more complete from interviews because well-trained interviewers will "probe" respondents for answers when they don't understand the questions. The presence of the interviewer also cuts down on the confusion that can come about when resondents are asked to read the questions themselves, and write the answers too. Interviewers can also add to the data by making observations on their own. For example, they could note the race or sex of a respondent and not actually ask such questions. Notes can be taken on how respondents are dressed or on what possessions are in their homes. More importantly, a well-trained interviewer can make notes on the attitude of the respondent toward the interview itself, if these kinds of data are important for a study. By being there, interviewers can note several important points that would otherwise be lost, and they can help respondents when help is needed, making a more complete data set with relatively few "don't knows" and "failed to responds."

INTERVIEWING   The objective of the interviewer, and the major assumption that all interviewers work under, is that each interview will be exactly the same from one respondent to the next. This is similar to the idea that mailed questionnaires are "standardized" for all respondents. To obtain anything like "the exact same interview" for each contact that is made in a large-scale survey requires that interviewers be trained prior to going to the field. Interviewers should practice interviewing. They should become more than simply familiar with the questionnaire; they should know it very well and should have practiced using the research instrument several times before going to the field. They should learn to ask each question in exactly the same way, in the same order, and in a neutral manner. They should not *lead* respondents by including their own phrases or opinions, and responses should be recorded in the exact same way from respondent to respondent. This means in the same order and using the same techniques for each person interviewed. If a probing question is required for an item, it should be used in the same way, using the same wording each time.

DRESSING FOR THE PART   Interviewers should try to dress in a way that is not offensive to respondents, and in every case should attempt to dress in the way the respondents themselves might dress. In general, they should be neat in their appearance, not too dressed-up, but not in shorts and sandals (unless that's the way we expect our respondents to be dressed). Above all, interviewers should be as pleasant as possible. Remember, an interview is like any other form of social interaction in that interviewers and respondents are exchanging ideas. However, the ideas that are being exchanged in a formal interview are almost always the ones that the interviewer "brings up" for conversation. When we conduct other forms of business, we generally try to be as pleasant as we can, even when receiving a speeding ticket. The same goes for face-to-face interviews.

ADVANTAGES AND DISADVANTAGES OF INTERVIEW SURVEYS   Several of the advantages and disadvantages of the interview survey are summarized in Table 7.3. Note that because there is an interviewer present who can help respondents and make interesting observations while in the field, that the face-to-face interview is considered somewhat more flexible than mailed questionnaires. As has been pointed out earlier, a higher response rate and more complete data are also associated with the interview survey. Because the interviewer has "control" over the interview (that is, more so than if the questionnaire had simply gone through the mail to respondents) he or she can be at least partially assured that there is some standardization associated with this methodology. That is, questions can be asked in the same order from one interview to the next, but if the questionnaire had been sent through the mail, question order could be reversed or respondents could "skip" from one question to another. As we have seen, the order in which questions appear can make a difference on the answers you receive.

Another advantage worthy of mention is the fact that the exact time taken to interview a respondent can be recorded on the interview schedule itself, as well as the exact time of day and the date upon which the interview occurred. If something important were to take place during the conduct of a survey (that is, if a war broke out, if there was an important election, or some other noteworthy event), then we could compare responses both before and after

---

TABLE 7.3   Some Notes on Approaching the Respondent for Face-to-Face Interviews[21]

1. Tell the respondent who you are and whom you represent, and show them some identification (university name, for example).
2. Tell respondents what it is you are doing, what the study is about, and try to stimulate their interest. Tell them that their responses will be confidential, and that their names and addresses will not be associated with their answers.
3. Tell respondents that they were selected using a scientific sampling procedure, and that their input is needed for the survey.
4. Interviewers are sometimes given letters to send in advance to notify respondents of the interview. When possible, carry newspaper clippings of past survey results to indicate the importance of your study.
5. Be positive. Assume that the respondent has the time to give you an interview, and ask, "I would like to come in and talk with you about this," rather than, "May I come in?" or "Should I come back later?"
6. Then ask the questions from your instrument *as they are worded, and in the order they are presented on the interview schedule. Don't lead respondents; be adaptable, responsive, and friendly.*

---

that event took place to see what effect it had on the attitudes or opinions of the members of our sample. Also, knowing how long an average interview will take can be helpful in training new interviewers by giving them some idea of what to expect while in the field.

When interviewers are present, a more complex and thorough question-naire can be used. This means our data can be "finer" than the broad kinds of things we would otherwise expect from simpler mailed instruments. However, there are several obvious disadvantages that go with the interview survey. For example, interviewers must be paid, and if we intend to conduct a large-scale study, we will need several of them. They will have to be transported to the field, housed, and fed, and this takes time and money. As well, if we are not careful in training our workers, interviewer bias can slip in. Interviewers can misunderstand a respondent's reply and possibly record it incorrectly if they're not fully trained and familiar with the instrument being used. As noted earlier, questionnaires should be designed so they are easy for anyone to understand and use, and this includes interviewers as well as respondents.

Several additional disadvantages include the fact that respondents will sometimes see the interviewer as intruding on their privacy, causing them a certain amount of inconvenience. There is also a certain loss of anonymity associated with the face-to-face interview. That is, it is often difficult for respondents to sit in their own living rooms and talk to a complete stranger about their personal sex life, but this is a somewhat less difficult task if we are given the time and privacy mailed questionnaires provide.

One final point about the disadvantages of the interview survey: it is often difficult to reach respondents we would like interviewed. Specifically, with the mailed questionnaire and several stamps, we can reach people across the United States and around the world, but with the interview survey we will need transportation and housing to conduct the same study. Certain groups can also be difficult to "find" and interview using the face-to-face approach. Executives with very little time and four secretaries trained specifically to keep people from bothering them represent another example of the kind of respondent that is often difficult to reach in person. Through the mail, however, it might be easier.

The Telephone Survey

One of the major advantages of the **telephone survey** is that it can be extremely fast to complete. If a bill to reinstate the draft were to be signed today, and we wanted some idea of what the public thought about the signing, we could quickly pull a random sample from the telephone directory and have an answer in a few hours. Essentially, the telephone survey is the fastest technique social scientists have for gathering data, and to do it we don't even have to leave our offices. This means we can save money too, since the cost of a long-distance phone call is certainly less expensive than traveling to the respondent. Although there are some problems associated with the sampling

TABLE 7.4   Advantages and Disadvantages of the Face-to-Face Interview

Advantages	Disadvantages
1. Does not require that respondent be able to write	1. Expensive; interviewers cost money and so does transportation
2. Can yield a better "sample" of the population	2. Requires interviewing skills; interviewers must be trained
3. People are generally more willing to respond if they don't have to write anwers, and are only asked to talk	3. Interview situations are not standardized
	4. Can be seen as pressuring respondent for answer

procedures that are often used in the telephone survey, it offers speed and an attractive price tag. The sampling problems were pointed out in the last chapter, and are associated with the sampling frame that is most often employed in studies of this kind: telephone directories. As we have noted, there are people who don't have telephones or telephone listings, and there are also people who have several phones. These factors, as we now know, can confound our sampling design and result in an unrepresentative sample. However, this does not always have to be the case. For example, some researchers have begun to use random dialing techniques to overcome the problem of unlisted numbers, and machines have been devised that randomly dial combinations of numbers that are appropriate for the geographical area they wish to study. This eliminates at least part of the sampling problem.

ANONYMITY   The telephone survey also offers a certain degree of anonymity for respondents, which can be lost in a face-to-face interview. It is often easier to talk about a sensitive subject when we don't have to look an interviewer in the eye! However, one additional problem should be noted: people tend to believe that we are *not* really conducting a survey when we call them, that we are some kind of "crank" caller or that we are soliciting for some business in the area. This is a problem with no immediate solution but we suggest that you be as polite and sincere as possible when making calls, and that you be very familiar with the interview schedule before picking up the phone. The telephone survey is a quick and inexpensive method for gathering information. If used wisely, it can be a profitable choice for a survey that must be done quickly.

Summary

Of necessity, this chapter has been a long one because survey methods are essential to the social sciences, and because there has developed around them a fairly complex and detailed methodology which we have actually only touched upon here. As often as possible we have summarized the main points associated with each of the topics discussed. We have tried to include as many examples of survey research techniques as we could possibly fit in. However, there is much more to survey research than reading about it and looking at examples. Now that we have gained an understanding of what the social sciences are about from a methodological point of view, now that we understand the link between theory and research, what a "sample" is (and what it is not), and how to construct a research instrument, the time is approaching for us to select a problem for study and to begin putting together our research design. It may be time, as we say, *to get your hands dirty.* If we follow the rules and ideas provided here, our research projects should reach successful conclusions, so have no fear. Simply review our examples, give them some thought, and begin a design. Because you probably won't have much money for your first research effort, you will more than likely wind up selecting a self-administered questionnaire for a design. If you are a student, you will probably have only a semester or even less time to conduct a project, and this too will influence the methodology selected. In any event, only after your hands have been soiled, and after you have gone through the process of preparing and conducting a survey, be it a self-administered or face-to-face interview, will you begin to truly understand the complexities and fine points of this research tool.[22]

Glossary

closed-ended question An item to which respondent's answers are limited to stated choices or alternatives (see *open-ended question*).

contingency question A question designed to screen or filter out only those respondents who are supposed to answer the question; a response to the question is contingent upon the response to a previous question.

follow-up mailings Sending reminders to respondents who have yet to return a mail questionnaire.

funnel technique The use of broad and general questions at the beginning of a questionnaire or item sequence and then narrowing the question by being more specific.

group survey When questionnaires are handed out to a group or subjects who are in the same place at the same time.

interview The researchers ask and record the answers themselves.

interview survey Trained interviewers ask questions of respondents rather than have respondents write answers.

inventory format A technique used when a question requires more than a single response from subjects; a list of items to be checked or marked by respondents.

mail survey When questionnaires are prepared and sent to respondents through the mail.

matrix question Used when responses are required from or about more than one person; also called *grid technique* because responses to the question are placed in a grided box.

open-ended category When a category is used ending with "and above" or "and older." At the end of an age range this could be "75 years and above."

open-ended question Constructed to elicit a free response from a respondent rather than one limited by suggested alternatives (see *closed-ended question*).

response set The tendency of respondents to reply to items in a particular way, regardless of the content of questions.

return graph A technique used to keep track of the returns to a mailed questionnaire.

self-administered questionnaire Asks respondents to give written answers to prearranged questions.

social desirability When a respondent would agree with statements that are socially desirable and supported by social norms rather than say what he or she actually believes.

standardized questionnaires All respondents are asked the same questions in as close to the same way as possible.

survey A data collection technique that asks questions of a sample of respondents, generally at a single point in time, using either a questionnaire or an interview.

telephone survey When surveys are conducted by telephone; a very fast way to conduct a survey.

Notes

1. George A. Theodorson and Achilles G. Theodorson, *Modern Dictionary of Sociology* (New York: Thomas Y. Crowell, 1969), p. 395.
2. See Howard Schuman and Stanley Presser, "The Open and Closed Question," *American Sociological Review* 44, No. 5 (1979): 692–12, and references quoted therein.
3. Kenneth D. Bailey, *Methods of Social Research* (New York: Free Press, 1978), p. 111.
4. This question was adapted from the National Opinion Research Center General Social Surveys, 1972–1978: Cumulative Codebook (Roper Public Opinion Research Center, Yale University: New Haven).
5. Schuman and Presser, op. cit., pp. 692–712.
6. Ibid., pp. 692–712.
7. Earl R. Babbie, *The Practice of Social Research*, 2nd ed. (Belmont, Ca.: Wadsworth, 1979), p. 319, suggests the use of arrows to direct respondents. This is not a hard-and-fast rule when preparing contingency questions, however.
8. Bailey, op. cit., p. 110.
9. This example was adopted from National Opinion Research Center.
10. This example was adopted from National Opinion Research Center.
11. See also Bailey, op. cit., p. 114.
12. This was adopted from NORC data.
13. These guidelines were adopted from Bailey, op. cit., pp. 118–121.
14. Ibid., p. 93.
15. Ibid.
16. Ibid.
17. Claire Selltiz, Lawrence S. Wrightsman, and Stuart W. Cook, *Research Methods in Social Relations*, 3rd ed. (New York: Holt, Rinehart and Winston, 1976), p. 297.
18. Thomas A. Heberlein and Robert Baumgartner, "Factors Affecting Response Rates to Mailed Questionnaires: A Quantitative Analysis of the Published Literature," *American Sociological Review* 43, No. 4 (1978): 447–462.
19. Bailey, op. cit., also provides a useful discussion of the return graph; see page 147.
20. Heberlein and Baumgartner, op. cit.

21. Bailey, op. cit., pp. 168–169.
22. There are several additional sources available for students who wish to read more about the survey process. See, for example, Charles Backstrom and Gerald Hursh, *Survey Research* (Evanston, Ill.: Northwestern University Press, 1963); Herbert Hyman, *Survey Design and Analysis* (New York: Free Press, 1955); N. A. Oppenheim, *Questionnaire Design and Attitude Measurement* (New York: Basic Books, 1966); and Herbert F. Weisberg and Bruce D. Bowen, *An Introduction to Survey Research and Data Analysis* (San Francisco: Freeman, 1977).

8

The Experiment

Of all of the methods identified with scientific thinking, the experiment is the most familiar. Your first introduction to science was probably an experiment conducted to show you the power of the scientific method. A common demonstration experiment in elementary schools involves giving children plants and having half the class put theirs in the sun while the other half place theirs in the dark. They are *shown* the relationship between the light and a plant's health by comparing the growth of plants in the sun with the demise of those kept without light. The simplicity of the experiment and the strength of its logic have made it a model of scientific research from elementary school to university research labs.

In social science research, there are difficulties in conducting experiments with human subjects, especially on a large scale. In psychology, there are numerous experiments, but most deal with animal subjects such as pigeons, monkeys, and mice. Social psychologists do small-group experiments in special laboratories with human subjects, and there are a number of interesting field experiments in sociology that take place in ongoing social situations. Understanding the experimental method and its application in the social sciences is very important, for this method, better than any other, can clearly demonstrate relationships between variables. Moreover, the scientific logic of experiments is a consideration in every method employed by social scientists.

The Logic of Experiments

The most compelling feature of experiments is their logic. Essentially, the logic of experiments holds that if the only difference between two identical groups is the experimental condition applied to one group and not the other, any differences in the two groups after the introduction of the experimental condition must be due to the experimental condition. The goal of experiments is to demonstrate the presence or absence of a causal relationship between two or more variables. Using the experimental method, it is possible to isolate a single variable (the experimental one) while keeping everything else the same. Thus, the *control* over variables possible in experiments allows the researcher to isolate one variable at a time to find the effect of one upon another.

In the logic of experiments we can best see the relationship between the independent variable and the dependent variable discussed in Chapter 4. The independent variable is manipulated by the experimenter, to see what effects it has on the dependent variable. For example, in an experiment by a social psychologist, the researcher wanted to see what effect a film would have on students' attitudes.[1] The film was about prejudice, showing it in a negative light, and the experimental hypothesis stated that after seeng the film, students would be less prejudiced. In this case, the independent variable was the film and the dependent variable was the attitude of the students. Schematically, we can see the relationship in the following diagram:

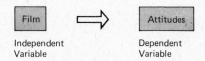

Since we have the independent variable labeled as "film" one may wonder how it can vary—after all, if we call something a "variable," it should be able to change. In this case, the independent variable can be either "film" or "no film." (Of course, films vary in their content, but for this experiment only exposure to a single film was manipulated.) The following illustrates this variation:

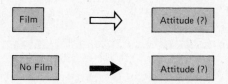

As we can see, this experiment is very much like the one with the plants in the light and dark, but instead of having "light" and "no light," this experiment has "film" and "no film." The dependent variable in the social science experiment—attitude—has two states, "more prejudiced" and "less prejudiced," while the plant experiment had conditions in dependent variables of "healthy" and "not healthy." Taken all together, the experimental logic would appear as follows, comparing the plant and prejudice experiments:

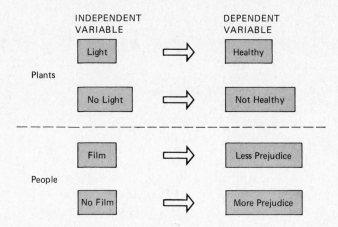

In the plant experiment, we saw that there was clear evidence of the effect of light because we assumed that all the seeds came out of the same batch. Had the seeds in the experiment been different, we would not have been certain whether the plants in the dark were unhealthy because of the lack of light or because of bad seeds. Likewise, how do we know in the study of prejudice that the researcher did not have groups that were more or less prejudiced to begin with? Using random selection, the researcher selects two groups from the same population, giving the researcher two roughly equal groups, both of which are given a test to measure attitudes after initial selection. By giving the same test *after* only one of the groups saw the film, the researcher is in a position to conclude that any differences in the two groups' test results was due to the film.

Experimental Design

To begin looking at experimental designs, we will start with the classic design,[2] which fits the requirements outlined in the logic of experiments. We will take each part of the classic design separately and build it up into the complete model.

Control and Experimental Groups

In order to assess the effect of an independent variable on a dependent variable in experiments, it is necessary to compare groups that were subjected to different states of the independent variable. In experiments, the independent variable is called the **experimental variable** or **experimental condition** or **treatment.** Discussing experiments, we refer to a group either being introduced to the experimental variable or not. The group introduced to the experimental variable is called the **experimental group,** and the group not introduced to the experimental variable is called the **control group.**

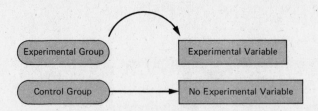

SELECTING GROUPS The most basic condition in selecting the control and experimental groups is that they are similar at the beginning of the experiment. If there are differences between the groups at the outset, then it is impossible to tell exactly what effect the experimental variable had, for the differences after the experiment may be due to the different groups selected. There are two procedures in which experimenters choose experimental and control groups in attempting to ensure that both groups are similar.

The first procedure, called **matching,** involves selecting subjects of similar characteristics and making sure there is an equal number in both the control and experimental groups. For example, in a study of school performance and teaching techniques, a researcher may want to match two groups on the basis of their grade averages. If there are 40 subjects available for the experiment and 10 are "A" students, 10 are "B" students, and 20 are "C" students, the experimenter will make sure that both the experimental and control group have 5 "A" students, 5 "B" students, and 10 "C" students. In this way, the researcher will know that both groups are equivalent in terms of their school performance.

MATCHED GROUPS

	Control Group	Experimental Group
"A" Students	5 ⟵⟶	5
"B" Students	5 ⟵⟶	5
"C" Students	10 ⟵⟶	10
Total	20	20

In matching the students, the researcher is using only a single dimension, *school performance*, since the experiment is measuring school performance as the dependent variable. It is possible that the entire control group is made up of girls and the experimental group boys. Of course the experimenter may wish to match the two groups on several dimensions so that the chance of having the experimental and control groups differing is reduced on other dimensions not being measured but which nevertheless have an effect on the outcome. But the problem is deciding which characteristics to match, for even though it is clear that the groups *must* be matched on the dependent variable—school performance—it is not clear what other factors might creep into the experiment if the two groups are not equal in other dimensions. For example, if the researcher has the control group from one school and the experimental group from another school, even though both groups have the same distribution of grade averages, one school may have different standards or grading criteria than the other. As a result, a student who has an "A" average in one school might have only a "B" average had he or she gone to the other school.

In trying to figure out all of the possible differences in matching a control and experimental group, a researcher could become totally confused, since the more differences are looked for, the more can be found. However, the researcher, while attempting to minimize original differences in the groups, realizes that every single aspect of the group cannot be the same. In order to minimize differences other than the key dependent variable, *random assignment* to create similar control and experimental groups is used. This procedure of choosing groups for experiments is based on the same logic we discussed in .Chapter 6 for making random samples. Using a table of random numbers (see Appendix A), or any other random selection device, such as flipping a coin with the "heads" going to the control group and "tails" going to the experimental group, the researcher selects each group. The probability that each group will be equal depends on the number of subjects available— the greater the number of subjects, the higher the probability that the experimental and control groups will be similar. At the same time that random assignment will match the key dependent variable, the researcher is also better assured that any other intervening variables will also be matched. If there are any other characteristics that may get in the way of seeing the effect of the experimental variable, each group will have roughly the same number of such characteristics and therefore they will cancel each other out.

The main problem with using random assignment without matching is that there is always the chance that there will be significant differences in the groups in terms of the key dependent variable. This is especially true with a small number of subjects. What most experimenters do is to use a combination of matching and random assignment. On the key dependent variable, the researcher matches the two groups, but then randomly assigns the matched subjects to the experimental or control groups. In this way, he or she is assured of having matched groups for examining the effects of the experimental variable while at the same time being better assured that any intervening variables are evenly distributed between the experimental and control groups. The diagram on page 167 shows how random assignment and matching are employed together. An equal number of "A" students is randomly selected for the experimental and control groups, and the same is done for the "B" and "C" students.

Pretest, Experimental Variable, and Posttest

As we saw in discussing the logic of experiments, experimental researchers have to compare the experimental and control groups before and after the introduction of the experimental variable. In order to do this with any faith in the effect of the experimental variable, the two groups must be tested before the introduction of the experimental variable. The initial comparison is called the **pretest.** After the selection of the two groups, experimenters administer a pretest so that they will have precise information with which to compare the groups later.

Once the groups are selected and pretested, the experimenter *introduces the experimental condition to the experimental group only.* As we saw, the experimental condition represents the independent variable of interest, and since the researcher wants to find out the effect of the experimental variable, it is controlled by introducing it to one group (experimental) and not the other (control).

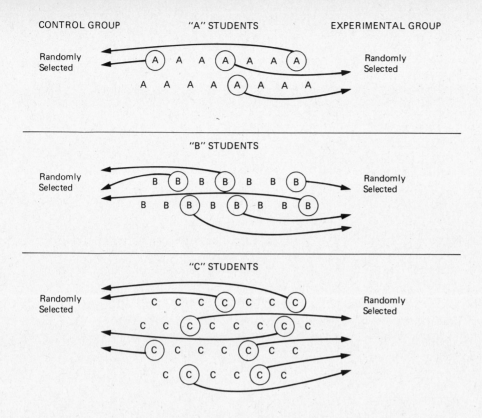

CONTROL GROUP   "A" STUDENTS   EXPERIMENTAL GROUP

Randomly Selected   A A A A A A A   Randomly Selected

A A A A A A A A

"B" STUDENTS

Randomly Selected   B B B B B B B   Randomly Selected

B B B B B B B B

"C" STUDENTS

Randomly Selected   C C C C C C C   Randomly Selected

C C C C C C C C

C C C C C C C

C C C C C C

After the experimental condition is introduced to all of the subjects in the experimental group, the experimenter then administers the **posttest** to all of the subjects in *both* groups to compare them a second time to see if there are any differences related after only one has been subjected to the experimental variable. The posttest is exactly the same as the pretest. For example, in the experiment measuring the film's effect on attitudes of prejudice, the researcher gave each group a test measuring prejudice before and after the experimental variable was introduced. It was the same test, since the researcher was using the test as a measurement of the dependent variable— prejudice. Had the experimenter given different tests, he or she would not have known whether any differences resulted from the different tests or from the experimental variable.

Once the experimenter has given both groups the posttest, he or she compares the results on the pretests and posttests. If the experimental group has changed from the pre- to posttests, and the control group has not, then the experimenter can attribute the differences to the experimental variable. On the other hand, if both groups have the same results on the posttest, then the experimental variable has not had any significant effect.

The following diagram and summary constitute all of the features and steps in the **classic experiment.**

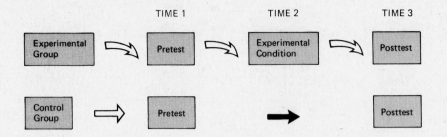

TIME 1   TIME 2   TIME 3

Experimental Group ⟹ Pretest ⟹ Experimental Condition ⟹ Posttest

Control Group ⟹ Pretest ⟶ Posttest

Step 1   Select a control and experimental group using matching and/or random assignment.

Step 2   Give the control and experimental groups a pretest.

Step 3   Introduce the experimental variable to the experimental group and do nothing to the control group.

Step 4   Administer the posttest (same instrument used in the pretest) to both the control and experimental groups.

Step 5   Compare the results of the posttests to determine the effect, if any, of the experimental variable. The differences are assumed to be caused by the experimental variable since that was the only difference between the two groups between the pretest and posttest.

Problems with Experiments

The advantage of experiments over other methods in social science research is that they can isolate and control variables in order to show causal relationships between them. To be sure, it is more accurate to say that causal relations are best *implied* by the method, but still, the best argument for using experiments rests on their ability to demonstrate causal relationships. However, when a researcher claims to have shown such a connection between an independent and dependent variable, he or she has to be in a position to reject competing explanations for an observed change in the dependent variable. In other words, what has to be shown is that the change that occurred was due to the experimental variable and not something else.

In assessing the worth of an experimental finding, we must look to the internal and external validity of the experiment. Experimental **internal validity** refers to whether the independent variable actually had the effect observed. Sometimes experimenters either lose control of the variables under examination or overlook an intervening variable that could have had more effect on the outcome than the experimental condition. The other problem with the validity of experiments concerns whether or not the findings can be generalized to all social behavior or whether they are only valid in the experimental setting. This problem of generalizability in experiments is referred to as **external validity.** Both of these problems of validity plague experimental research, and in order to deal with them, we must be aware of what they are. In this section, we will examine the various problems that affect experimental validity.

Artificiality

One of the most often-cited problems with experimental reserch is that it creates its own world that cannot be generalized to the world outside of the **laboratory.** In other words, since the environment created by the experiment is unlike the social world, experimental findings lack external validity. For example, in experiments examining violence on television and violence in real life, the experimental situation where violence is shown to children is different from the normal social world where television violence is viewed.[3] In the experimental situation, children watch violent and nonviolent television scenes without adults interpreting and supervising the activities. However, in the normal television viewing situation, children are not only supervised, but the violence on television is usually interpreted for them by adults. In experiments dealing with television violence and violence by children, children were found to be more likely to engage in aggressive play when shown violent programs than nonviolent programs.[4] However, when children start aggressive play at home while watching violence on television, parents will usually intervene and interpret the violence on television as "stupid," "something that dummies do," or some similar statement that interprets the violence in a way not done in experimental situations. Depending on the family's values, the violence is either seen as something to avoid or something to be used in problem-solving; therefore, the child "sees" the violent activity through the "lenses" of family values. When we examine violence in society, we find a disproportionate amount of direct interpersonal violence in the lower socioeconomic classes, and even though there is no significant difference between the exposure to television violence in the upper and lower social strata, there is a good deal of difference in the actual amount of violence.[5] Thus, when experimental findings do not conform to what can be observed in the larger social world, the problem can be in the **artificiality** of the experimental environment.

Demand Characteristics

Another interesting aspect of the experimental situation was discovered by Stanley Milgram in his famous experiment regarding authoritarian personalities.[6] In his experiment, Milgram told subjects that he was testing a new teaching device which produced increasing dosages of electrical shock to be administered to experimental subjects. The electric shocks were fake and the person receiving the shocks was a confederate of the researchers, but the subjects did not know this. Milgram found that most of the subjects were willing to give lethal doses of electrical shocks to an unknown person, either voluntarily or on the orders of the experimenter. Although the electrical shocks were not real, the subjects thought they were. The important finding was that the subjects were willing to administer such shocks in near-lethal and lethal doses. When questioned as to why they were willing to do so, the subjects said that since it was an experiment, they did not think they would be told to do anything wrong, especially expressly commanded by the experimenter. All of the subjects claimed they would not do such things under normal conditions. It was the scientific aura of the experimental situation that led them to trustingly do what they were told. Thus, whenever experimental subjects act as they believe the experimenter wants them to, we refer to these compelling circumstances as the **demand characterisics** of the experimental situation.

Uncontrolled Changes

A second type of problem encountered in experiments has to do with changes over which the experimenter may or may not have control. For example, in one experiment, the experimenter burned a hole in his suit about halfway into the experiment. He had met half the experimental subjects without the hole (a small cigarette burn in his lapel) in a certain suit he always wore during the conduct of the research, and he wanted to meet every other subject in the same outfit just to cancel out any changes that may have been a result of different clothes.[7] However, such minor changes can be considered normal trouble in experiments, but other changes, especially significant ones, are more serious for they affect the internal validity of the experiment. We will examine some of the common changes that occur.

MORTALITY   In experiments that take place over a long period of time, subjects will sometimes drop out. If the people who drop out are different from the people who continue the experiment, this will have an effect on the outcome. For example, if research is being conducted on authoritarian personality and the people who drop out of the experiment tend to be those with less authoritarian personalities, the posttest will show that the *overall* scores on authoritarian personality scales will be higher.

HISTORY Sometimes there will be changes in the world outside of the experiment that will affect the experiment more than the experimental variable, giving rise to changes in both the experimental and control groups. For instance, if a researcher is involved with an experiment measuring attitudes toward capital punishment, an especially heinous crime may occur that will shock people so much that they may change their attitude toward capital punishment. The mass murders involving the Manson Family, Son of Sam, and John Gacy were so shocking that people who were normally against capital punishment changed their minds. Such events can totally obscure any changes caused by the experimental variable.

MATURATION In dealing with groups going through natural changes, especially the rapid ones that take place in childhood, the differences between a pretest and posttest may be due to **maturation.** College students often change their attitudes as they mature from "kids" to "adults," and changes on posttests may reflect this maturation. Since so many experimental findings are are based on college student subjects, these naturally changing attitudes can pose a problem.

TESTING EFFECT Under certain circumstances, the pretest will affect the subjects so that they will alter their attitudes. In the experiment examining the effect of a film on racial prejudice discussed earlier, the researcher found hat *both* the control group and the experimental group had changed their attitudes so that the measured amount of prejudice was greatly reduced.[8] What appears to have happened is that when the subjects in both groups took the pretest, the test itself made them examine their prejudices. As a result, the test affected the control group enough so that there were no significant differences between them and the experimental group who had viewed the film.

The Solomon Four-Group Design

In order to overcome many of the problems facing the classical experiment in social sciences, a researcher developed the Solomon-Four design.[9] Instead of having a single control and experimental group, the Solomon-Four has two of each, for a total of four groups of subjects. One experimental and control group is treated exactly the same as in the classical experiment, and the other set is only given the experimental variable and posttest. The following diagram outlines the components and procedures in the Solomon-Four:

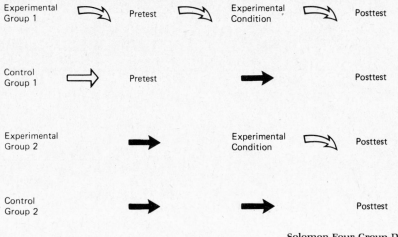

All of the groups are selected on the basis of random assignment to maximize similarity, since without a pretest for Experimental and Control Groups 2, it is difficult to have matching without risking some kind of testing effect. The purpose of this design is to test for any effect of the testing device itself. If the pretest does influence both Experimental and Control Groups 1, it can be seen in the comparison with Experimental and Control Groups 2. This is so because the second set of groups had no pretest to possibly influence them.

Standard Experimental Notations And Various Designs

In the text we have used nonstandard notations in the diagrams for purposes of explanation. The standard notations used in experiments are shorthand ways of communicating different types of designs. The following are the basic symbols used in talking about experiments and examples of different types of designs.

O = Observation

X = Experimental condition or treatment

$O_1 \ldots O_n$ = Subscripts refer to observational or experimental order
$X_1 \ldots X_n$

For example: O_1 means the first observation and O_2 means the second observation. In the classic design O_1 is the pretest and O_2 is the posttest.

Classic Experiment

O_1 X O_2
O_1 O_2

The top line represents the experimental group and the bottom line represents the control group.

One-Group Posttest Only Design

X O

This design is very weak since there is no control group for comparison and no pretest. The researcher has no way of knowing if the observation is a change in behavior before the introduction of the experimental condition.

One-Group Pretest/Posttest Design

O_1 X O_2

This design gives the researcher a little better idea of the effect of the experimental variable, but it does not tell him or her whether the difference would have occurred without the treatment, for the researcher has no group for purposes of comparison. Any changes could have been due to other elements between O_1 and O_2.

Posttest Only Design

    X   O
         O

This design is almost an experiment for there is a control group for comparison, but even with random assignment for choosing an experimental and control group, without a pretest, one cannot be certain that the groups were equivalent to begin with or to what extent the experimental treatment led to the observed difference between the two groups.

Solomon-Four Design

O_1 X O_2
         X O_2
O_1 O_2
              O_2

This design is perhaps the strongest design to argue a causal relationship between the independent and dependent variables, for not only does it include all of the elements of a classic design but it also controls for the effect of the experimental situation by including an additional control and experimental group not subject to the initial effect of the experiment (that is, the pretest).

See Thomas D. Cook and Donald T. Campbell, *Quasi-Experimentation: Design and Analysis Issues for Field Settings* (Chicago: Rand McNally, 1979), pp. 95–146, for a full discussion of variations in the experimental design and the implications for cause-effect in using these variations.

Assuming all four of the groups are the same in terms of the key dependent variable and there has been no maturation, mortality, or other problem affecting internal validity, the researcher should find similarities between the two experimental groups on the one hand, and similarities between the two control groups on the other. If the two experimental groups are similar to one another but dissimilar to the two control groups, the experimenter is then in a strong position to attribute the differences to the experimental condition. However, if Control Group 1 and Experimental Group 1 are similar in the posttest but different from Control Group 2, the researcher knows that there probably has been some kind of testing effect or other effect of the experiment. The important feature of the Solomon Four-Group design is that the extra two groups allow the researcher to assess the various problems of internal validity.

Other Experimental Designs

While laboratory designs using the Solomon-Four or some similar technique can provide controls and checks for internal validity, the experimental method still has problems with external validity. It may be true in the laboratory, but will it be true in the social world? In certain respects the problem with laboratory research is parallel to the mental patient who successfully adjusts to the institution, but when thrown back into normal social life suffers from mental breakdown. The adjustment is to the institution, not to the real world of social life outside the hospital.

In order to compensate for the problems with external validity, some researchers have devised designs that can be used outside of the laboratory setting in the ongoing social world. Other researchers have found natural ongoing experiments in society and can conduct quasi-experimental research simply by recording what occurs when new programs are introduced. Finally, to redirect the subjects' view from the experimental setting and situation, experimenters have subjects think they are doing one thing while in fact they are being observed for something else. All of these methods will be discussed in this section in order to examine how researchers attempt to control for specific variables while minimizing the overall effect of the experiment itself.

Field Experiments

When researchers introduce an experimental condition into the ongoing flow of social life, such research is referred to as a **field experiment.**[10] In field experiments the researcher does not have the control he or she does in the laboratory experiment; however, the same logic that applies to experiments in general also applies to field experiments. The researcher compares the effect of the experimental variable with situations that do not have the experimental variable.

The variety and creativity of field experiments is wide and broad, and in order to see how they work, we will examine some and discuss how the logic of experiments works in each.

BUMPER STICKERS AND TRAFFIC TICKETS   In a study in 1969, a researcher wanted to find out if the police would harass members of dissident political parties.[11] To test the hypothesis, the researcher recruited a group of 15 students who had exemplary driving records, none having received a ticket in the past 12 months. To control for race, five of the students were black, five were white, and five were Mexican-Americans, with three men and two women in each group. All of the subjects reviewed the California Motor Vehicle regulations and promised to drive especially carefully during the experiment. The experimental variable, political dissidence, was to be in the form of a highly visible bumper sticker reading BLACK PANTHERS. It was hypothesized that if the police did harass political dissidents, then the subjects were likely to be stopped by the police and given traffic citations.

After 17 days, the participants had received a total of 33 citations, which exhausted the $500 fund the researcher had available to pay traffic citations, so that the experiment was suspended. Since none of the students had received tickets in the previous year and began getting them when they placed the bumper sticker on their cars—the first ticket was received one to two hours after the experiment had begun—it was concluded that indeed the police did harass those involved in dissident political organizations.

The logic of the experimental method can be seen in the comparison of the group before (pretest) and after the introduction of the bumper sticker. The introduction of the experimental variable resulted in traffic citations.

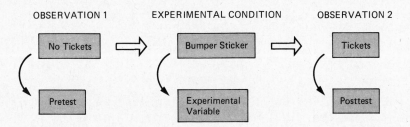

As can be seen, there was no control group, and it could be argued that the police, for some other reason than the bumper sticker, simply increased the number of tickets. Had the researcher matched the group given the bumper stickers with a group not given bumper stickers, the experiment would have been a true one since it would have had both a control and an experimental group. However, given the careful selection of the group and the fact that none had any traffic citations in the pevious year, the dramatic increase in citations is probably sufficient evidence to confirm the hypothesis that the police harassed certain political dissidents.

THE LOST LETTERS In order to examine community orientations toward political groups and other institutions, researchers developed a unique method using "lost letters,"[12] a technique that uses experimental variables with different characteristics. By comparing the reactions to the different experimental characteristics, the researcher is able to assess community values.

The experiment involved addressing letters to different groups, placing them in different locations so that they appeared to be lost, and then seeing if there were any differences in the rate of return. In the experiment, the following groups were listed as addressees:

1. Friends of the Communist Party
2. Friends of the Nazi Party

3. Medical Research Associates
4. Mr. Walter Carnap (a ficticious name repesenting a personal letter)

All letters were addressed to the same address:

P.O. Box 7147
304 Columbus Avenue
New Haven 11, Connecticut

Of course the address was a post office box rented by the researchers so that they could examine the rate of return for the letters. Not surprisingly, letters addressed to the Medical Research Associates and the personal letter were returned at a far greater rate than those to the Communists or Nazis.

Percent of Letters Returned

Group	Percent
Medical Research Associates	72
Personal letter	71
Communists	25
Nazis	25
TOTAL	46

In terms of experimental logic, this field experiment used random assignment in choosing the subjects. Letters addressed to one group were as likely to be found as those addressed to another. Also, we might even consider the personal letter to represent a control group in that the addressee is anonymous and cannot be identified with any group or cohort. There is no pretest, but since there are different assumed characteristics of the different addressees, it is possible to compare the different rates of return as comparative "posttests."

	Posttest	
Experimental Condition	Return	No Return
Medical	High	Low
Communists	Low	High
Nazis	Low	High
Control group		
Personal letter	High	Low

By examining the posttest in terms of the different experimental characteristics, it is possible to determine if the *differences in the experimental condition* resulted in differences in the posttest. Since the "control group" represented by the personal letter can be taken as an estimate of the public's willingness to place a lost letter in the mail, we can see that there is evidence that the "Friends of the Communists" and "Friends of the Nazis" were not generally approved in the community. By the same token, however, because 25 percent of the letters to the Communists and Nazis were returned does *not* mean that 25 percent of the community approved of the groups. Some people simply feel obliged to return lost correspondence, regardless of whom the recipient is.

As can be seen in the lost-letter method, while there is ingenuity in the technique, there is not a lot of control, and in order to assess community attitudes, it would probably be better to use surveys in order to get more detail. However, the method does minimize researcher effect and provides an interesting way of judging attitudes in a community. Other similarly creative field experiment designs have been developed, most of which are designed for a special theoretical problem or issue that could not be adequately handled by other methodologies. Nevertheless, all field experiments employ the same experimental logic, carried out to a greater or lesser degree, by introducing an experimental variable into the world and assessing its effects.

Natural Experiments

Another of the problems with field experiments is that because they take place in an uncontrolled setting, persons not knowingly involved in the experiment can be affected. This is not so much a technical problem, for field experiments were designed to overcome experiment effect and reduce the artificiality of the laboratory, but it can be an ethical problem in that the researcher manipulates people who are unaware of the experiment. Even when people are involved in such an experiment knowingly, as in the experiment with the bumper stickers, the consequences can be a very real problem. The students who received traffic citations (some as many as three in 17 days), may have had their insurance rates increased and their driving records were certainly blemished.

Often, social scientists cannot introduce variables into social life or do not wish to take responsibility for doing so. In such cases, many prefer to use the **natural experiment.** Essentially, a natural experiment is the observation of what some other institution has introduced into society. For example, in a study of the effects of a new law on speeding, the researchers simply measured the accident rate before and after the introduction of the law.[13] The law was the experimental variable. Since the "experiment" was a naturally occurring one, there was not the ethical burden of responsibility, and all the experimentrs really had to do was to examine the records of accidents and citations under the new law. However, more often, the researcher is invited to study the effects of new programs or laws introduced into the community, and in these situations, the researcher can be more than just a passive recorder of data collected by others.

THE CRIME WATCH PROGRAM In a natural experiment involving student researchers, we can see how the logic of experiments works in cases where the experimental variable is introduced by persons other than the experimenter.[14] This also represents an example of evaluation research, since while at the same time the research can be seen as a naturally occurring experiment, the experimental variable was very much being judged evaluatively.

The experiment involved assessing the effects of a community program designed to lessen crime in specified neighborhoods. Basically, the program consisted of organizing people in neighborhoods to keep an eye out for one another. Meeting with a special team of police officers, the neighborhood residents were organized into blocks, with "block captains" acting as coordinators for the people on their block. Eventually, everyone in the neighborhood was instructed by the police on how to protect property, how to spot burglars, and in similar techniques for reducing residential crime. Finally, signs were erected throughout the neighborhood cautioning would-be criminals that the area was a special "Crime Watch Neighborhood."

In order to test the experimental variable of the crime watch program, the researchers took an adjacent area that was not involved in the program that had a similar crime rate the previous year. This second area was the control group. The pretest consisted of comparing crime report data provided by the police. The posttest, however, was going to use a victimization survey, a survey sampling the neighborhoods on the basis of an interview schedule to find the amount of *both* recorded and unrecorded crime. It was necessary to use this instrument since the police rightfully pointed out that they expected a higher reported rate of crime in the Crime Watch Neighborhood since they had instructed the people to report not only all crimes but even suspicious persons. Thus, while the actual crime rate would go down, they believed that because the people were more willing to report crimes in the experimental neighborhood, police records would show an increase in crime in that area.

Having selected random area samples from the control and experimental areas, student interviewers administered the victimization surveys. In addition to the regular random sample, there was a subsample of block captains in the experimental group as well. This was done to control for those who were most actively engaged in the crime watch program. Since it was possible that the people in the crime watch program were not actively involved, and therefore not subject to the "experimental condition" of the program, it was decided to use this subsample for comparative purposes.

The interviewers were instructed to be very careful to ask only about the crimes that did or did not occur during the time the program had been in force. Sometimes, in response to victimization surveys concerning a particular year or other span of time, people will tell researchers about crimes that happened long ago. Since this particular research dealt only with crime during the period the crime watch program had been in effect (to test the effect of the experimental condition), interviewers had to be careful that the respondent specify exactly when the crime had occurred if he or she had been victim.

The results of the experiment, based on the posttest, indicated that the program was a failure. There were no significant differences between the two groups, other than the fact that people in the experimental group were more likely to report cases of "suspicious persons" in the neighborhood. This had been stressed by the police and indicated that people were involved in the program. However, there was actually a slightly higher, but not statistically significant, rate of crime in the experimental neighborhoood; and even though people in the crime watch neighborhood were more likely to report suspicious persons, they were not more likely to report actual crimes than the control group. The students and the police were greatly disappointed in the results, but since the purpose of the research was to *test* the effects of the experimental variable, it was a successful experiment, for the findings suggested that the program did not have an effect. That is, it provided knowledge where only conjecture existed before. The following diagram shows the experimental logic in the research:

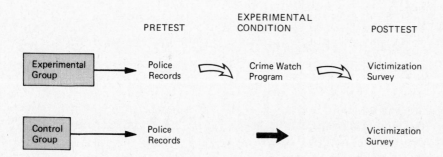

As can be seen, the natural experiment had all the elements of a classic experiment. Two elements that give rise to serious problems of internal validity are the uncertainty of the implementation of the experimental variable and the use of different instruments in pretests and posttests. There was evidence that the people in the experimental group did follow police advice in reporting suspicious persons. We also had data on the block captains, but there was stil other evidence that the experimental condition was less than fully in effect. However, using police records in the pretest and victimization surveys in the posttest was not a serious threat to internal validity since they both measured the same thing. The victimization simply provided a more accurate comparative device.

Misdirected Experiments

In an attempt to reduce testing effect, especially that in which the subjects are trying to "help" the experimenter by changing their behavior along the lines they believe the experimenter wants (such as indicating on posttests that they are now "less prejudiced," since they believe that is what the researchers "wanted"), some experimenters use **misdirected experiments.** Basically, these experiments appear to be concerned with one subject, while, in fact, they are examining something very different. For example, in attempting to see if subjects could "make sense" out of a random set of responses, Harold

Garfinkel set up an experiment that purportedly was testing the effects of a new "counseling computer."[15] The subjects were told that the computer could only answer in "yes" or "no" responses, and so all of their questions would have to be phrased so that they could be answered by "yes" or "no." Then the researcher took a random series of "yes" or "no" responses to the questions asked by the subjects to see if they understood the responses to be sensible replies to their questions. In the posttest, the subjects were asked if they understood the "computer's" replies. As it turned out, all of the subjects made consistent "sense" out of the "responses" by the "computer." The following diagram summarizes the logic of such experiments:

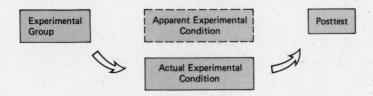

The idea behind misdirected experiments is to minimize testing effect, but depending on the kind of misdirection that is going on, there are ethical questions regarding experiments with human subjects. In Chapter 19, we closely consider the protection of human subjects, especially the issue of subjects giving "informed consent." While subjects in misdirected experiments are informed that they are taking part in *some* kind of experimental research, they obviously do not know exactly what they're getting into. This matter will be discussed more fully in Chapter 19, but for now, it is important to note that in designing misdirected experiments researchers must (and most do) carefully consider the well-being of the subjects. Thus, while it is important to control for testing effect in experiments, it is also important to make certain that there is nothing in the experimental design that may harm the subjects.

Summary

In this chapter we have seen how the basic logic of experimental design is applied to social science research. The most important thing to remember in doing experimental research is the fundamental reasoning behind experiments: *two identical groups are compared, with one of the two groups subjected to the experimental condition, and any differences between the two groups can be attributed to the experimental variable.* With this basic logic in mind, we can see why experiments are considered important research tools—they allow us to isolate key variables to assess the effect of the variable on social behavior.

There are a number of problems in using experiments and for this reason we do not see more experiments in the social sciences. First, there is the problem of doing experiments with human subjects as "guinea pigs" for science. These are ethical problems, which, handled correctly, can be solved. Second, in sociology, anthropology, and political science, the researcher is often dealing with such large groups and long time-frames that it is simply impossible to organize an experiment to find the necessary information. Sometimes a new program or law that will affect an entire society or subgroup will be introduced and the researcher is in a position to conduct a natural experiment, but these opportunities do not allow the researcher to control all of the necessary elements of the "experiment." Third, there are a number of problems with external validity due to the artificiality of the experimental situation. What may be valid in the experiment cannot be generalized to situations outside of the controlled experimental setting. Finally, there are problems with internal validity in that it is often difficult to control all of the variables within experimental situations. Subjects react to the pretest, they change, and they try to "help" the researcher.

Even though there are problems, experimental researches have developed several different variations on the basic classical design to deal with them. Field experiments have overcome some of the problems of artificiality. Various other innovations, such as the Solomon-Four and several misdirected designs, have developed mechanisms for increasing internal validity in experimental research. As for the ethical issues, there is no evidence that experiments in social sciences have led to subject harm over any period of time. While some subjects have been upset during experiments (such as the Milgram experiment in which subjects thought they were administering electric shocks to fellow subjects), post-experiment debriefing of subjects has been sufficient to allay any fears and problems. It is because of researchers' genuine concern for experimental subjects that such problems have been minimized.

Given the basic logic of experiments, we can see the important role they can play in social science research. Moreover, the same logic is applied to other forms of research as well. Therefore, even though we ay not see actual experiments in the classic mold, in all social science research we can see the same reasoning at work. This reasoning focuses on the question—all other things being equal what effect does a single independent variable have on social behavior?

Glossary

artificiality The circumstances of an experimental situation that are rarely or never found in the natural social environment. Such conditions make it difficult to generalize findings to the larger social world. (See *external validity*)

classic experiment An experimental design using an experimental and control group, exposing only the former to the experimental treatment. A pretest and posttest is administered to both groups.

control group A group in experimental

designs which is used for comparison to the group that receives the experimental treatment. Control groups do not receive experimental treatment.

demand characteristics Circumstances in an experiment that influence the subjects to attempt to determine what the researcher "wants" and then to act in a way so as to please the experimenter. Also refers to a willingness to do whatever the experimenter wants even though these actions are not what subjects normally do.

experimental group The group in experimental designs that is exposed to the experimental treatment.

experimental treatment The actual condition that the experimental group is exposed to that is withheld from the control group. The experimental treatment is a condtion repesenting the experimental variable. (Also called *experimental condition*.)

external validity The truth of findings as they can be generalized to other situations. It is the generalizability of findings.

experimental variable The independent variable in an experiment.

field experiment An experimental design applied in a natural social setting.

internal validity The truth value of findings in terms of being actual representations of what was observed in research. Experimental designs have strong internal validity to the extent that they can control variables, but weak internal validity to the extent that the actions of the subjects are due to the demand characteristics of the situation.

laboratory experiment Experiments conducted in specially constructed settings designed to facilitate observations, recordings, and control.

matching Pairing experimental and control groups on the basis of certain characteristics in order to determine the effect of the experimental treatment when comparing posttests.

maturation Changes occurring between the pretest and posttest independent of the experimental condition. The groups "mature" or change naturally, and by minimizing the time between the pre- and posttests, maturation will be minimized.

misdirected experiment An experiment in which the researcher intentionally guides the subjects to believe he or she is testing one thing while, in fact, something else is being tested. Such experiments are designed to reduce the demand effects of experiments.

natural experiment A social experiment set up and admnistered by policy makers and/or programmers but researched by social scientists. Also a naturally occurring change, the effects of which are studied by social researchers.

pretest A measurement of certain characteristics of both experimental and control groups before the introduction of the experimental treatment.

posttest A measurement administered after the introduction of the experimental treatment of both experimental and control group. Posttests are compared to pretests to determine any changes to be attributed to experimental variable.

Solomon Four-Group Design Classic experimental design with an added experimental and control group, which are not pretested. The two added groups are used to determine if there is any effect due to the pretest.

1. Russel Middleton, "Ethnic Prejudice and Susceptibility to Persuasion," *American Sociological Review* 25 (October, 1960): 679–686.

2. Donald T. Campbell and Julian C. Stanley, *Experimental and Quasi-Experimental Designs for Research* (Chicago: Rand McNally, 1963).

3. A. Bandura, D. Ross, and S. A. Ross, "Imitation of Film-Medicated Aggressive Models," *Journal of Abnormal and Social Psychology* 66 (1963): 3–11.

4. Ibid., pp. 8–9.

5. Timothy F. Hartnagel, James J. Teevan, Jr., and Jennie J. McIntyre, "Television Violence and Violent Behavior," *Social Forces* 54 (December 1975): 341–51.

6. Stanley Milgram, "Behavior Study of Obedience," *Journal of Abnormal Social Psychology* 67 (October, 1963): 371–378.

7. This observation was made while one of the authors served as a research assistant in a sociological experiment.

8. Middleton, op. cit., p. 685.

9. R. L. Solomon, "Extension of Control Group Design," *Psychological Bulletin* 46 (1949): 137–150.

10. Paul G. Swingle, ed., *Social Psychology in Natural Settings* (Chicago: Aldine, 1973).

11. F. K. Heussentamn, "Bumper Stickers and the Cops," *Transaction* 8 (1971): 32–33.

12. Stanley Milgram, Leon Mann, and Susan Harter, "The Lost-Letter Technique: A Tool of Social Research," *Public Opinion Quarterly*, 29 (1965): 437–438.

13. H. L. Ross and D. T. Campbell, "The Connecticut Speed Crackdown: A Study of the Effects of Legal Change," in H. L. Ross, ed., *Perspectives on the Social Order*, 2nd ed. (New York: McGraw-Hill, 1968), pp. 30–35.

14. This experiment was directed by one of the authors while teaching a course in research methods at the University of Florida in 1977.

15. Harold Garfinkel, *Studies in Ethnomethodology* (Englewood Cliffs N.J.: Prentice-Hall, 1967).

9

Content and Secondary Analysis

In this chapter we make a departure from the methods we have discussed so far, for here we will deal with methods involving existing data; that is, we will review methods that examine data that has already been recorded in one way or another. Content analysis is a methodology for examining verbal and written materials. For example, in an attempt to study suicide, one researcher conducted a study of suicide notes, using content analysis as his method.[1] In another study using content analysis, the researcher was able to find patterns in rape assaults that could predict the outcome of such assaults by a content analysis of victim statements recorded in police reports.[2] Additionally, social science researchers can reach into the past using content analysis to uncover secrets of societies that no longer exist, through an examination of anything from cave paintings to political speeches. Researchers interested in historical analysis of social behavior have found content analysis to be very useful in this context.

Along with content analysis, we will also look at secondary analysis, which is essentially a method for reexamining existing research data. Whenever researchers collect data, they usually end up with more information than they are really interested in or have tools to analyze it with. For example, in the past, much of the statistical analysis had to be done by hand without the assistance of computers and sophisticated statistical tests. Social science researchers were limited as to what they could do because the sorting, counting, and overall analysis was so time-consuming that only the simplest kinds of relationships could be handled properly. However, the data itself was far more informative than the available techniques for filtering it all out. Introductory research students with a single instruction on a computer card using an SPSS program (see Chapter 16) can analyze thousands of cases in minutes, a process that would have taken an experienced researcher months to do in the precomputer days of social science research. In order to use valuable unanalyzed data, secondary analysis can be employed to squeeze out the last drop of information the data contains. Thus, data collected for the study of one phenomenon can be used through secondary analysis to study other phenomena.

Content Analysis

Content analysis is usually taken to be a quantitative method for the analysis of qualitative data. One definition states that content analysis is a *method for the systematic quantification of verbal and written materials into numeric form for mathematical and statistical analysis.*[3] Importantly, content analysis is a coding procedure and not any kind of statistical test.[4] In other words, content analysis is a methodology for transforming various kinds of documents, speeches, presentations, and other recorded social phenomena into a form that social scientists can analyze by means of statistical tests. The method, though, is the *transformation process* and not the testing process.

As an aside it should be pointed out that there are qualitative applications of content analysis, especially in the study of verbal interaction. In Chapter 11, we will deal separately with a method called "conversation analysis" that employs both qualitative and quantitative techniques, and in some ways resembles content analysis.

Theoretical Problems and Sources of Data

Like all research methods, content analysis begins with a problem or question it would like answered. After examining the various methods, the researcher may choose, not because he or she happens to like it, but rather because it is the best available method to provide an answer to a given question. For example, one student of propaganda was attempting to find out whether there were certain cultural values implicit in television commercials. The question concerned the divergent values of individualism inherent in the Protestant ethic and the other-directed values of the Social Ethic.[5] The student hypothesized that if advertisers believed the public was primarily directed by individualistic values, their commercials would present their clients' products in association with hardworking, unique individuals. However, if they believed the value system to be predominantly guided by the Social Ethic, they would show their wares in the context of cooperation, conformity, and pleasing others. By comparing television commercials on the basis of certain characteristics of both the Protestant and Social Ethics, the student was able to see the extent to which advertisers were attempting to appeal to one or the other value system.

The student chose to examine the content of a sample of television commercials for his study, planning, essentially, to do a content analysis of them. Although he could have conducted a survey of television commercial producers or perhaps even performed an experiment testing the appeal of one value system over another, he chose the content analysis method for several reasons. First, many people are not aware of their own values in terms of either the Protestant or Social Ethics; thus, even if a television commercial producer intuitively or unconsciously felt there was an appeal in terms of one ethic or the other, he or she might not realize or admit it. Second, the researcher would be able to examine a large sample of commercials in a very short period of time—a critical consideration since he was doing the research for a course and did not have the time to conduct a survey using questionnaires or interview schedules. Third, in examining television commercials there would be no researcher effect. Fourth, since it may have been impossible to gather information from other sources, the *availability* of the television commercials allowed for ease in assessment.

There are many different kinds of documents that can be useful for various theoretical problems that social scientists address. To get an idea of what can be used for content analysis, we will examine a sample of types of documents under the headings of (1) written documents, (2) filmed documents, and (3) records. Obviously, there are overlaps in these categories, but they will be used since there are qualitative differences in each.

WRITTEN DOCUMENTS   The most widely available form of preserved document is in the form of the written word. Whether we study the writing on an Egyptian tomb or an entry in a diary, we can gain a wealth of information from the analysis of what people have written down. Literature, newspapers, magazines, diaries, memoirs, letters, and virtually anything else that has been recorded in writing serves as a possible resource for content analysis. Just about any college library contains various collections of documents for examining anything from changing themes in editorials in newspapers during the Vietnam War to special collections of letters written by persons during a period of interest. Documents, such as original letters, are more difficult to obtain and if available at all require special handling and care. However, often a search of one's own attic will reveal a collection of letters or other documents that can be used in content analysis. For example, one student found a collection of letters written by her great-grandfather to her grandfather telling about his experiences in the Civil War. The letters revealed fascinating views of the social situation during that period of American history.

FILMED DOCUMENTS   Content analysis of films, including photographic films and videotapes, provides another, although little-used, resource. By analyzing the contents of films one can pick out themes, issues, and beliefs of the filmmakers. For example, by comparing the content of American and Italian films, it is possible to see the different features of the two cultures. An especially interesting content analysis is possible by analyzing the different content of news stories on television. In one study it was found that television news workers "angled" the news to present a certain point of view.[6] By a content analysis of news stories, especially those from different countries, it would be possible to study the government's or the station owner's biases. The problem, though, is that films and videotapes, except those currently running on television or in theaters, are not as readily available as written documents. However, it may be possible to obtain the use of films or videotapes from local television stations or to borrow from a library collection.

RECORDS   One special type of written document is the official record. Various records have been put into bound collections or special files and are available in most college libraries. Many records from governmental archives are available on micofilm, and so what at one time was restricted to a few select libraries is now at most university facilities.

Depending on what one is researching, records are more or less available. Those interested in, for example, the social history of Civil War will find an incredible collection of every writen order and communication for both Union and Confederate armies in a multivolume collection.[7] The *Congressional Record* contains all the speeches, testimony, and other bits of information (including votes) that occur in the U.S. House of Representatives and Senate. The best thing to do if records are to be used for content analysis is to ask the librarian what records are available in your library to see whether they might be used in your research.

Other kinds of records that may be of great use in research may not be easily available. Those doing organizational research, for instance, may want access to interoffice memos, but unless one has access to a company's files, such records generally are not available. On the other hand, researchers using police and court records have been able to conduct content analysis for testing hypotheses in criminological research. Special permission is required for such access, however, and it can be difficult for students to obtain.

A final kind of record that is highly restrictive but has become widely available is what we might call "leaked" or "purloined" documents. On the publication of the transcript of the Watergate tapes and of the Pentagon Papers, not only researchers but also the general public came into possession of documents that ordinarily might never have been made available or not until long after those involved were dead. Since content analysis is dependent on access to documents, it is doubtful much can be done with these secret records that can tell us a great deal about the inner workings of our government and its institutions. But, when they are available, the analysis done on these records can tell us much about what has not formerly come to light.

It should be pointed out here that the social science research that can be accomplished with the various documents discussed so far can also be achieved through methods other than analysis. To some extent the documents, especially records, are resources for secondary analysis. However, what content analysis is attempting to find is not necessarily the same information the document was intended to communicate. For example, a writer may have intended to present an objective statement and sincerely believed in his or her own unbiased position. Through content analysis, though, it is possible to uncover the hidden, subjective values and beliefs of the individual or of the individual's society and culture that are subtly expressed in the document.

The Process of Content Analysis

As we have seen with other research methods, content analysis begins with a theoretical problem formulated into a research problem. The research design in content analysis involves independent and dependent variables, operational definitions, and all the other general features of social science research. Moreover, content analysis can be employed along with other techniques as well.

To begin the research design, the researcher takes some kind of document as his or her *unit of analysis*, which could be anything from a book, a magazine, or, as one student did, the cover from *Time* magazine.[8] In the student study, the hypothesis dealt with the concept of politicalization, and by analyzing the *Time* covers, the student researcher wanted to find out whether or not the 1960s were more politicized than the 1950s. If during the decade of the 1960s there were more *Time* covers with political themes than in the 1950s, then the hypothesis would be confirmed; otherwise it would be rejected. The unit of analysis, though, was only the cover, not the stories.

Indicators in content analysis can be understood in terms of **scoring units.** Each scoring unit is what the researcher uses to count as an instance of his or her concept. For example, during the Iranian crisis a researcher might have wanted to compare Japanese and American attitudes toward Iran by a content analysis of Japanese and American newspaper articles. Since the Japanese are far more dependent on foreign oil than are the Americans, one might hypothesize that Japanese stories might be *less disfavorable.* Indicators of negative statements about the Iranians' actions could include specific statements, words, phrases, stories, or entire newspaper policies that contained negative references to the Iranians. If the researcher's unit of analysis was the news story, the scoring units might be words, phrases, or sentences in the story. The following illustrates the relationship between scoring units and units of analysis.

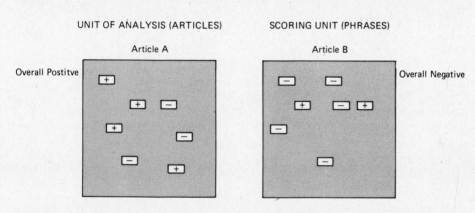

In looking at the illustration, in Article A, there are four positive phrases ⊞ and three negative ones ⊟ while in Article B, there are five negative phrases and only two positive ones.

Overall, we might rate Article A as generally positive and Article B as negative. Since the *unit of analysis is the article,* we would count Article A as one positive unit and Article B as one negative unit. Remember, the phrases are the scoring units, *not* the unit of analysis. The scoring units are used to score the unit of analysis.

Once we have decided on the scoring units that will indicate our concepts, content analysis is very similar to making a survey. In our example, we would take a sample of articles from American and Japanese newspapers, score each article in terms of being positive, negative, or neutral, tally the results, and compare them. The following are hypothetical results:

	Japanese Articles	American Articles
Negative	60	90
Positive	20	5
Neutral	20	5
TOTAL	100	100

In this case the hypothesis would be supported. Even though, overall, both Japanese and American articles on the Iranians' actions were negative, the Japanese were less disfavorable.

Types of Content Analysis

There are several kinds of content analysis, and depending on the kind of information the researcher is seeking, one type may be favored over another. We will discuss five types here, all quantitative and all subject to computer analysis. Each will be discussed in terms of how it can be most usefully employed.

WORD COUNTING   Probably the best known kind of content analysis is word counting: essentially, counting the use of certain key words in different texts. For example, to measure the degree of democratization in the United States, United Kingdom, France, and West Germany, one study counted the words in a sample of elite newspapers in the four nations.[9] They counted words connoting "democracy" and "totalitarianism" in order to determine whether there were any subtle or blatant differences between the nations as represented by elite newspapers. To execute such an undertaking took several months involving numerous coders and analysts. Using far fewer people, another researcher replicated the study using computer analysis.[10]

In a class project, a student took a retirement community's newsletter and conducted a content analysis of it using word counting. By typing the contents of the newsletter on computer cards, the student was able to use a DATATEXT program to provide a frequency/pecentage count of the words. This enabled the research to determine the proportion of integrative words (for example, "friendship," "together") with instrumental words (for example, "status," "duty") to estimate the extent to which the professed "community" was living up to its image.

CONCEPTUAL ANALYSIS   A more sophisticated type of word counting involves words grouped into conceptual clusters (ideas) that constitute variables in a research hypothesis. For example, a conceptual cluster may be formed around the idea of DEVIANCE. Words such as "crime," "delinquency," "fraud," "homosexuals," "corruption," and "embezzlement" could all be clustered around DEVIANCE. Therefore, whenever any of the words were found in the test, they would automatically be counted as an instance of the idea of DEVIANCE.

Using conceptual analysis, a researcher may want to find relationships between public concerns in different sectors of society through the analysis of newspaper articles that attempt to connect one sector with another. For example, in the mid-1960s the economy was booming, but so was crime. During the 1970s the economy cooled and was going downhill into the 1980s, and again crime was increasing. In the 1960s, when the economy was healthy and yet crime was also high, a researcher might hypothesize there to be very few news stories connecting DEVIANCE and ECONOMY, but, rather, the connection was probably between DEVIANCE and VALUES. On the other hand, when the economy cooled and unemployment increased, there were probably more news stories that linked DEVIANCE and ECONOMY. To set up a conceptual analysis, we might develop the following clusters:

DEVIANCE	ECONOMY	VALUES
crime	unemployment	morality
delinquency	inflation	tradition
fraud	recession	authority
homosexuals	devaluation	family
muggers	stagflation	respect

Using articles as the unit of analysis and words as scoring units, texts would be analyzed only in terms of three concepts—DEVIANCE, ECONOMY, and VALUES—even though all of the words that made up the concepts would be counted to determine the weight each concept had. Thus, in an article that mentioned five different words from the same conceptual cluster, the concept would be counted as being in the article five times. The following illustration shows how conceptual analysis counts concepts by counting words in each cluster.

Cluster = ECONOMY

Word	Times Mentioned
Unemployment	5
Inflation	3
Recession	4
Devaluation	0
Stagflation	2
TOTAL OF CONCEPT	14

In the example, even though five different words are used in the counting, conceptual analysis would only count the concept ECONOMY as being in the article 14 times. When using computer programs to do the counting, the programmer includes an instruction that says, in effect, "When you recognize words X, Y, or Z, count them as CONCEPT 1, and when you recognize words D, E, or F, count them as CONCEPT 2. . . ." This speeds up the process considerably, and rather than having hundreds of different words to sift through for the analysis, the researcher only has a few key concepts.

Using our example of a reserch project comparing newspaper articles in the 1960s and 1970s that were centered around the concepts of DEVIANCE, ECONOMY, and VALUES, we might test the following hypothesis using content analysis:

> During periods of high crime and a failing economy, the public will be more likely to relate crime to problems with the economy; however, during periods of high crime and a healthy economy, the public will be more likely to relate high crime to a problem with social values.

Simply by comparing news stories during the decade of the 1960s with those of the 1970s in terms of the concepts DEVIANCE, ECONOMY, and VALUES, it is possible to test the hypothesis. The following illustrates the outline of the research design.

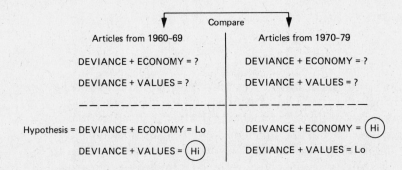

If the hypothesis is correct we would expect more articles connecting the ideas of DEVIANCE and ECONOMY in the 1970s and more articles in the 1960s connecting the ideas of DEVIANCE and VALUES. Table 9.1 shows what the findings might look like if the hypothesis is confirmed.

Thus, we can see from our hypothetical table that values were associated with deviance predominantly in 84 pecent of the articles in the 1960s while in only 30 percent of the articles in the 1970s. Likewise, as the economy got worse in 1970s, there were more likely to be connections between deviance and the economy and less likely to be links between deviance and values.

Using conceptual analysis as a general example of content analysis, we

TABLE 9.1   Economic and Value Explantions of Deviance

Articles Connecting Deviance and	Decade			
	1960s		1970s	
Values	432	(84%)	243	(30%)
Economy	78	(16%)	563	(70%)
	510	(100%)	806	(100%)

will take a step-by-step look at how we went about the research in the example.

Step 1   Beginning with a theoretical position associating viewpoints with the economic situation, we derived an hypothesis.

Step 2   The concepts from our hypothesis, DEVIANCE, VALUES, and ECONOMY, were operationalized in terms of conceptual clusters of certain words.

Step 3   A research design using newspaper articles as units of analysis and words as scoring units (translated into one of the three conceptual clusters) was developed, and a sample of articles was drawn from the decades of the 1960s and 1970s.

Step 4   Articles mentioning the concept of DEVIANCE along with either the concepts of VALUES or ECONOMY were scored as either VALUES or ECONOMY depending on whether more of the former or latter were mentioned in the article also mentioning DEVIANCE.

Step 5   Articles from the two decades were compared on the basis of the predominant concept used with DEVIANCE. (It might be noted that in the table the sample for the 1970s is larger than the sample for the 1960s. This is so because there were more articles in the 1970s that mentioned either or both of the concepts of ECONOMY and VALUES with the concept of DEVIANCE during the period. There would also be a number of articles that mentioned DEVIANCE but not either the concepts of VALUES or ECONOMY.)

SEMANTIC ANALYSIS   In the third type of content analysis, the researcher is not only interested in the number and type of words used, but he or she is also interested in how strong or weak the words are in relation to different dimensions. Essentially, **semantic analysis** is used when the researcher wishes to scale his or her findings.[11] Certain words are given **intensity weights** showing stronger or weaker emphasis. Thus, a word like "love" would be weighted higher than a word like "like." The following is a set of examples of how words in semantic analysis might be weighted on the basis of a weak–strong dimension:

Weak—Strong	
Word	Weight
Love	+3
Like	+1
Adore	+4
Despise	+4
Dislike	+1
Abhor	+3
So-so	0

As we can see, some words imply stronger feelings than others. In studies of public sentiments toward the government, for example, it would be very important to differentiate between the intensity of the sentiments. If there were two opposing camps regarding the government, and one group simply "disliked" the government while the other side "loved" it (as opposed to just "liking" it) then we know that support is strong and opposition is weak. Had we simply compared positive and negative sentiments, we may have found a 50−50 split, but with semantic analysis we can tell the nature of that split.

Taking the same set of words that we weighted in terms of strong and weak, we can also weight them in terms of positive and negative. The positive words are given a plus (+) value and the negative a minus (−) value. On the positive−negative dimension, we also find some words more positive or negative than others. The following is the same set of words we examined on the weak−strong dimension, but weighted now in terms of negative−positive.

Negative—Positive	
Word	Weight
Love	+2
Like	+1
Adore	+2
Despise	−2
Dislike	−1
Abhor	−3
So-so	0

Taking the two dimensions, weak−strong and negative−positive, we can now better measure the qualitative aspects of certain social attitudes and behavior. For example, suppose we use semantic analysis in a study of public support of an incumbent local government based on a random sample of "letters to the editor" that mention local government. The letters will be the unit of analysis and the words the scoring units. Each letter will be given either a positive or negative number, or zero if the positive and negative cancel one another out. The following illustration shows how a single letter is measured.

Dear Editor:

Inasmuch as some of your readers have expressed concern over the city council's
decision to buy land for the purposes of making a public park, I feel obliged
-1(+1) to write and express my feelings. While our city fathers have made decisions
(-1) in the past I have (disliked,) I must say that I (adore) them for having the good
sense to make available park space in the downtown area. We all (abhor) the
crowded, dirty, and thoroughly unlivable area that has been chosen for the park
area, and attempts in the past to even transform that area into a parking lot
+2(+3) have failed. Therefore, even though some of us (dislike) the idea of the added
(+6) cost incurred, we all (love) what the decision will provide us with.

+2 (+4)
(+8)
—NR

-1(+1)
(-1)

In looking at the words that have been weighted, it is important to note that
the weight on the negative–positive scale was multiplied by the weight on the
weak–strong scale. Thus, the word "disliked" has a weight of -1 ($+1$ times -1)
and the word "love" has a weight of $+6$ ($+2$ times $+3$). Also, it should be noted
that the word "abhor" was not rated at all because the word was not used in
connection with what the letter writer felt about the city council. Overall, the
letter is weighted at $+12$ ($+6$ and $+8$ plus -1 and -1).

After weighing the sample of letters in this manner, the researcher, using
semantic analysis, can get a good measure of what the strength of sentiment
toward or against the local government is. Using a small sample of ten letters
for purposes of illustration, we can see what the results might be.

	Positive Letters	Negative Letters
	$+12$	-2
	$+\ 5$	-4
Weight	$+\ 2$ N = 4	-1 N = 6
	$+14$	-7
		-3
		-2
	$+33$ Weighted Score	-17 Weighted
	Weighted Difference = $+16$	Score

Thus, even though there were more negative letters than positive ones,
semantic analysis has shown that, on the whole, the positive letters were far
more supportive than the negative ones were unsupportive. Based on word
counting alone, we would have concluded that the overall feeling in the
community was one of nonsupport, but given the weighted differences
possible through semantic analysis we conclude that the overall picture from
the letters to the editor is more positive than negative.

EVALUATIVE ASSERTION ANALYSIS For a sophisticated technique that uses the
sentence as the unit of analysis, researchers employ **evaluative assertion
analysis.** This method of content analysis classifies sentences in terms of the

grammatical distinctions between words placed in sentences. Essentially, this technique allows the researcher to find how many times X (as subject) did Y (verb) to some (object) A.[12] For example, in a study of the labor movement a researcher might want to find out how often a union paper accused big business of taking unfair advantage of labor. The coding would be done in terms of the relations between the words *big business*, along with associated terms, *labor*, and verbs used to describe how one treated the other. Such an analysis would be very useful in attempting to predict conditions that lead to strikes, slowdowns, or a general dissatisfaction between labor and management. Illustrated, we can understand a possible evaluative assertion analysis counting the following as an instance of union perception of maltreatment by business management:

> By going to 24-hour shifts and hiring parttime workers for a single shift when increased production is necessary, management has effectively taken away the union worker's overtime. All of this is done, they say, for our benefit since most of the parttime help they hire are unemployed teenagers who can earn money honestly instead of hanging around the streetcorners getting into trouble. Further, since many of these kids are the sons and daughters of union members, they tell us we get the added benefits of not only teaching our kids responsibility but also of the savings from not having to finance their leisure-time activities. It looks like they've stuck it to us again, and if we try to stop it, they'll tell our kids they're fired because their old man doesn't want them to work.

In the hypothetical excerpt, it can be seen that evaluative assertion analysis requires more than just identifying the subject, verb, and object in sentences. The first sentence is a complex one, and only the last part deals with what the union perceives management is doing to it. The next two sentences are elaborations and interpretations of management's position from the union viewpoint. And the last sentence, because it is a compound one, is treated as two different units (numbers 44 and 45). From this we get the following:

	Subject	Verb	Object
43	management	taken away	union worker's overtime
44	they've	stuck it	us
45	they'll	tell	our kids, they're
		fired	

From this example it can be seen that a good deal of understanding is required to use this methodology, not the least of which is an understanding of natural language in filtering out interpretations, elaborations, sarcasms, idioms, jokes, and all the rest that is a social skill developed in social interaction. Had we left the entire analysis to a computer, it may have scored the second and third sentences as instances in which a union paper said management was helping them. Obviously, the writer does not believe management is really trying to help labor by hiring parttime workers for overtime that would have gone to union members, even if many of those parttime workers happen to be the children of union members. The sense of those two statements is, *"That's what they say, and we know better than to believe them."* Thus, the two middle sentences cannot be counted as units of analysis reflecting what the union believes to be management's position. In using this methodology, therefore, it is very important to understand the qualitative dimensions of the texts being analyzed.

CONTEXTUAL ANALYSIS   The most sophisticated method of quantitative content analysis is being mentioned here only to provide the student with the information that the method is available. It has been used to predict future verbal behaviors based on the analysis of known word clusters (concepts) and individual words.[13] That is, by establishing scales for known verbal behaviors, it is possible to establish parameters, or contexts, where the parameters are unknown. In this way, it is possible to understand more fully the meaning of various texts and their implications. Based on this method, researchers were able to explain the actions of various African military leaders by an analysis of stated political policies.[14] Because of the complexities required to execute **contextual analysis,** the student is advised to begin with one of the other forms of content analysis, but it is important to know generally what the technique does in order to recognize it when reading research reports that use it. In a more advanced research course, students may wish to employ the method.

Advantages and Limitations of Content Analysis

Throughout this chapter we have seen several uses for content analysis in its many different forms. Depending on the kind of research question, content analysis is more or less useful. Here we will briefly look at some of the ways in which content analysis can be used, as well as point out some of its limitations.

In doing historical analysis, using literature, diaries, and letters from the past, content analysis is often the only way to "interview" people who are no longer available to answer questions. The problem, however, is that in social science research we are interested in a wide spectrum of viewpoints so that we can better see the whole. And since only those who are literate write the texts we analyze, we must realize that such analysis only touches upon a select few. Studying contemporary society, especially in the United States where literacy rates are relatively high, we can have a broader sample, and oftentimes where people write down their thoughts, they are more candid than when confronted by an interviewer or a questionnaire.

Using publicly available documents from the library, this method can take us far and wide with a small research budget and limited resources.

Students interested in a cross section of society rarely have the wherewithal to conduct research outside of their immediate environment. However, by using content analysis, they can compare viewpoints in Seattle, San Diego, Boston, and Miami without ever leaving their hometown. Naturally, there are limitations to what will be possible to study, but content analysis provides a method to examine the macrostructure of society at minimal costs and maximum convenience.

Secondary Analysis

Secondary analysis uses existing data to analyze some social science question not originally posed during the collection of the data, or using new techniques of analysis to reexamine a problem for which the data were originally collected. The techniques of analysis are essentially the same as are used with any of the other kinds of data we have discussed. That is, even though secondary analysis does employ data that was collected either with no particular theoretical and analytical scheme in mind or a vastly different one than may be used for the later analysis, there is no special form for secondary analysis that differs from primary analysis. In fact some truly classic works have emerged from the use of secondary analysis—Durkheim's famous work on suicide, for example. Using data collected for administrative purposes, Durkheim developed vastly different conceptual frameworks for examining the data and was able to show the relationship between anomie and suicide.

Another use of secondary analysis is for the development of new analytic tools in social science. Often the researcher is interested in developing new statistical methods for analyzing data, and rather than collecting vast amounts of data simply to test the statistic, it is far more expedient to use existing data banks for the test. Various techniques can be tested using a single data set to compare the different results. This is especially valuable to students who have sets of computer-coded data. Simply by changing the statistic while maintaining the same variable names in a program, it is possible to inexpensively generate tests of different statistics by making simple program changes. Similarly, in *metaanalysis*—examining several studies using a single analytic tool—secondary analysis is very useful. By taking several individual studies and analyzing their data either in a single statistical test or the same test on each study, secondary metaanalysis allows the researcher to find patterns not seen in any of the individual studies alone or when simply comparing them with each another.

For students, whose resources are limited, secondary analysis is often employed in order to analyze large samples otherwise not available. The first thing, however, is knowing where to obtain all this data.

Sources of Data

Government and private organizations have accumulated so much data that there are many volumes that consist of nothing but listings of different data sources. In order to track down these rich resources, it is best to start with a specific research problem and a specialist in the area of interest. Your professors have spent years in examining a variety of data and sets of data that can help you locate exactly what you want. Sometimes they will have knowledge of little-known sources or they may have data of their own.

If you want to find existing data on your own, the best place to start is the government document room of your library. Many university libraries are "government depositories" for all the data gathered by the federal government, and the document room will have virtually every set of statistical data compiled by the government. Going through every single set of data would take a tremendous amount of time, and so the best thing to do is to begin with general source books for the area of your interest. For instance, if your interest is in studying crime, the Department of Justice has several sets of data concerning the subject. Suppose you are interested in crime in different parts of the country. If your interest is in crimes reported to the police, the Federal Bureau of Investigation publishes a quarterly booklet, *The Uniform Crime Report*, which is a compilation of all crimes reported to and recorded by the police from all over the United States. On the other hand, if your interest is in crime patterns, and not just reported crimes, the Department of Justice publishes reports called "victimization surveys," based on samples of the population who have been asked whether they have been crime victims in terms of several different dimensions. Or, it might be interesting to compare the FBI's *Uniform Crime Report* with various victimization surveys to see the differences between what the police report and what crimes victims report. (In some cases there are ten times the number of crimes occurring than are known to the police!) If your interest in crime is more specific, say a particular type of crime, such as rape, there are many government-sponsored sources of data not only from the Department of Justice but also from the National Institute of Mental Health, a branch of the Department of Health and Human Services. The more specialized data provides the researcher with statistics on more dimensions, over longer periods of time in a single source, and has a fuller collection of further sources available.

The 1980 Census, as the census of every decade, is available with all kinds of demographic data concerning the population of the United States. The United Nations' *Demographic Yearbook* provides similar information for worldwide population patterns. A huge statistical book, *Statistical Abstract of the United States*, has data on just about everything concerning commerce in America, from taxes to water pollution. These sources mentioned here are only a few available in your library or inexpensively from the government. The thing to remember is that since these sources are usually in special places in the library, get the help of a specialist in the field of inquiry or the documents librarian the first time you go looking for them.

Problems of Secondary Analysis

Once the wealth of data available for secondary analysis is discovered, one might wonder why social researchers would bother using anything else. After all, if data on a certain aspect of social behavior is available from a national sample, what can someone with limited resources, especially those as limited as a student's, hope to accomplish with a small sample gathered during a few months? Why not concentrate on more and more sophisticated methods of analysis and let someone else collect all the statistics? Well, secondary analysis depends on statistics being available for the exact kind of information required for the research problem. While the available statistics might be able to tell you something about one dimension of interest, it cannot tell you about all of them. Further, if the researcher wants to find out about the effects of a specific area of theoretical interest but not of general interest, there may not be anything available. Also, there may be something that recently occurred of a unique nature that people know little or nothing about. For instance, when Mt. St. Helen's erupted in May 1980, and sent a cloud of volcanic ash across the country, there was no similar occurrence in the United States for which there were available statistics, and there would be no data available for years from any contemporary government study. Students at Washington State University, right in the path of the cloud, were afforded a rare opportunity to gather data on the social effects of this unusual phenomenon.

Finally, the researcher using available statistics has little knowledge about the actual collection of data. This is especially important in doing comparative studies of different countries. If France and Japan have different methods for gathering the same kinds of statistics, the researcher might end up comparing apples and oranges since he or she is making a comparison of data gathered on the basis of different samples, indicators, and general methodology.

However, we should not throw out existing statistics because of the problems. Such data are useful for comparative purposes, supplementary roles, and on those occasions where just the right combination of data and dimensions are available, for primary theoretical research. It is important, though, to be aware of their limitations.

Summary

This chapter has examined the uses of content and secondary analysis in social research. In many respects, these two methods are essentially forms of "library research," in that most of the materials available are in the campus library. However, the availability of the data sources in no way diminishes the original and useful purposes to which these data can be put. In many ways, content and secondary analysis are like looking at tissue through a micron microscope—anyone can see the tissue with the naked eye, but it takes a special instrument to see the structure of the tissue and the parts that make it up. Similarly, while we can see the various texts and statistics on the shelves of the library, content analysis and secondary analysis allows us to examine features otherwise invisible.

The major limitations of these methods is that the researcher has no control over the selection, compilation, or gathering of the materials, other than choosing from different available texts or statistics. In some cases, especially in content analysis, there is little concern about the compilation, objectivity, or honesty of the text since the research is *studying* the data, not *employing* it as an objective statement. In other cases, namely secondary analysis, the researcher *is employing* the data as an objective statement about social behavior, and so all of the data collection techniques must meet the criteria of validity. Sometimes valid statistics have been gathered and other times not, and unless the researcher knows how the data was collected, he does not know for certain how valid it is.

The extent to which the researcher can learn of the development of data, either as texts or sets of statistics, he or she can know the degree to which the data can be employed in one capacity or another. Therefore, it can be seen why it is vitally important to accurately describe our own methodology. In the future, others may wish to either use our data or to study it (perhaps even as primitive evidence of research activity) in some fashion we had not considered. As long as we can show others our methods, they can intelligently choose whether or not to employ what we ourselves have done, making very similar decisions to those we must make in content and secondary analysis.

Glossary

conceptual analysis Content analysis using conceptual clusters of words for analyzing texts.

conceptual cluster A grouping of similar ideas (concepts) into cohorts (clusters). The groupings are formed around key ideas that constitute research variables.

content analysis Method for the systematic quantification of verbal and written materials into numeric form for mathematical and statistical analysis. It is a coding procedure, not a test. Some qualitative forms of content analysis are available, but the dominant form of content analysis is quantitative.

contextual analysis A form of content analysis used to predict future verbal behaviors based on known verbal behaviors.

evaluative assertion analysis A form of content analysis using the sentence as the unit of analysis, breaking down the sentence into subject, verb, and object.

intensity weights Quantitative values assigned to words in order to differentiate between greater and lesser intensity of the word's meanings.

scoring units Conceptual indicators used to count instances of a concept in a given unit of analysis.

secondary analysis Analysis of data, usually quantitative, that already exists and has been used for other research.

semantic analysis Content analysis using intensity weights for scaling findings.

word counting Content analysis that counts certain conceptually key words in texts.

Notes

1. Jerry Jacobs, "A Phenomenological Study of Suicide Notes," *Social Problems*, 15, 1967.
2. William B. Sanders, *Rape and Woman's Identity* (Beverly Hills, Ca.: Sage, 1980).
3. Charles E. Cleveland and Ellen B. Pirro, "A Review of Contemporary Content Analysis" (Unpublished paper for Consolidated Analysis Centers, Inc., n.d.).
4. Ibid., p. 4.
5. William H. Whyte, Jr., *The Organization Man* (New York: Anchor Books, 1957).
6. David L. Altheide, *Creating Reality: How TV News Distorts Events* (Beverly Hills, Ca.: Sage, 1976).
7. *War of the Rebellion: A Compilation of the Official Records of the Union and Confederate Armies* (Washington, D.C.: U.S. Government Printing Office, 1891–1895). This 128-volume series contains all available communications from both sides in the Civil War. It is interesting to note how the two different sides describe the exact same action in very opposite ways.
8. George Zito, *Methodology and Meaning* (New York: Holt, Rinehart and Winston, 1975), pp. 47–54.
9. Ithiel de Sola *et al.*, *The Prestige Papers* (Cambridge, Mass.: M.I.T. Press, 1970).
10. Cleveland and Pirro, *op. cit.*, p. 7.
11. Ole R. Holsti, *Content Analysis for the Social Sciences and Humanities* (Reading, Mass.: Addison Wesley, 1969).
12. Cleveland and Pirro, *op. cit.*, p. 8.
13. Ibid., p. 10.
14. William Foltz and Ellen B. Pirro, *Black African Leaders Speak* (In press, n.d.).

10

Field Methods

Field methods in social science research are most closely associated with anthropology and sociology. Studies of whole societies on islands in the South Pacific, the headhunters of the Amazon, or nomadic tribes of the Sahara are examples of studies conducted by anthropologists in the field. Sociologists, on the other hand, tend to stay home, observing delinquent gangs, hospital workers, total institutions, and various groups and behavior patterns of interest. Erving Goffman once described such research as a "controlled adventure," since the researcher was able to escape from the mundane everyday world of academia into an excitingly different world of alien beliefs and activities. Without a doubt, field research is an adventure, and we have never met a field researcher who doesn't have exciting tales of field experiences.

However, doing serious research and having a lark, while not mutually contradictory or exclusive, are two very different things. How can field methods be employed to further knowledge in social science? Can two contradictory hypotheses or theories be resolved by field methods? These are the kinds of questions we must examine, for even though field research is a lot of fun (and hard work), we must see how it is also an important tool for the social researcher. In this chapter, we will examine field research in its different forms. However, it is important to keep in mind that while there are a number of common strategies and considerations in doing field research, to a great extent the form of the research is dependent on what is being studied. Unlike the survey researcher, whose work is conducted either through the mail or on subjects' doorsteps, or the experimental researcher working in the social science laboratory, the field researcher has little control over the situation. He or she is in the flow of social events being studied, and depending on what those events are, their organization and routines, the research is conducted in one way or another. For example, one researcher was studying a social welfare office when he encountered hostility from one of the welfare workers. It seemed that the hostile worker was jealous of the researcher since he spent a good deal of time with a woman welfare worker in whom the hostile worker had a romantic interest.[1] At first, the researcher did not understand the hostility, but when he later learned of its cause, he let it be known that the woman welfare worker happened to be a good friend of the researcher's wife, thus solving the problem. Whether hanging around a street corner with a delinquent gang or dealing with doctors and nurses caring for the terminally ill, the field researcher has to make adjustments particular to his or her peculiar set of circumstances. This requires a special sensitivity to the nuances of social behavior, and a good field researcher learns how to handle himself or herself in all different kinds of social situations in all different social strata.

Participant Observation Research

In doing **participant observation** research, the researcher steps into the flow of social behavior he or she wishes to study. There is a continuum of being a participant and an observer. On one end of the continuum, the researcher is fully an observer with no actual participation in the behavior he or she is examining. For example, a researcher might be interested in children's play patterns on a school playground and observes the children at play from a position where he or she is not in interaction with the children. On the other end of the continuum, the researcher fully participates in what he or she observes. In research on pinball players, one investigator learned how to play pinball, becoming an accepted (and surprisingly skilled) member of the pinball group.[2] Most participant observation research, however, falls somewhere in the middle of the continuum so that the researcher participates to some extent in the process or organization under study, but is not a full participant. For instance, in police research a researcher rode along with patrol, accompanying officers in their duties, and occasionally being given some small task. But for the most part the researcher only made observations, asked questions, and took notes about what was seen and heard.[3]

From the vantage point of a participant observer, the researcher can take notes on the behavior transpiring in front of him or her. However, how is that any different from what a reporter for a newspaper does? In other words, what does a social scientist do that a journalist does not? What can be found in a sociological study that cannot be found in a feature story in the Sunday supplement? Like all research in social science, the key is in the use of concepts and theory.

Conceptual Observations

In order to understand the difference between *reporting* and *research* we will begin with Lofland's four principles of how "people do social things."

1. Getting close-up to people actually acting someplace in the real world and developing **intimate familaritity.**
2. Focusing on and delineating the prime or basic **situation** the scrutinized people are dealing with or confronting.
3. Focusing on and delineating the interactional **strategies,** tactics, and so on, by means of which the scrutinized people are dealing with the situation confronted.
4. Assembling and analyzing an abundance of qualitative *episodes* into **disciplined abstractions** about the situation and strategies delineated.[4]

Further on in the book (Chapter 17), we will discuss the process of qualitative analysis, but here it is important to see how qualitative data are set up so that they can be analyzed in a way useful for assessing theoretical problems. Of the four principles Lofland outlined, the most important is the last, that of assembling the qualitative episodes into disciplined abstractions, for it is that kind of procedure, the conceptualization of social life, that sets the social scientist apart from the journalist. However, we will take each principle or step in order so as to best understand each in relation to the other.

INTIMATE FAMILIARITY   In talking about people we speak of them in terms of either "knowing" them or not, in the sense of a continuum from a virtual stranger to an intimate friend. To a close friend, a person's smallest gesture can mean a great deal, while the same gesture, if even noted by a stranger, may mean little or nothing, or even something other than what the gesture signifies. We tell friends our innermost thoughts and feelings, while with strangers we reserve our thoughts and feelings, at least until we get to know them better. It is with the desire to "get to know" a group beyond replies on a questionnaire that researchers conduct participant observation research. The information interviewers or researchers using questionnaires receive is essentially what one stranger will tell another. This is not to say that all interview and questionnaire data is invalid; rather, it can only tell us certain things, only go to a certain depth.

In most participant observation studies, researchers report the process of "getting to know" those whom they are investigating. At first, they are admitted to only certain areas and experiences of the group, but later on they are taken into the group to *see*, for the first time, that part of their life forbidden to outsiders. For example, when one of the authors made a study of rape, he spent a good deal of time with police detectives who investigated cases of rape. For weeks he sat around the office not being allowed to accompany the detectives on their investigations. Slowly, as the investigators came to know the researcher, and he them, they would allow him to accompany them on certain cases, and by the end of the research, he was being taken along on virtually all cases. At this point, they began telling him more and more about rape, its investigations, and other information vital for the study.[5] Moreover, after being accepted in the group of detectives, the researcher came to see how "outsiders" were treated in terms of interviews and information. Interviewers (mainly journalists) were told what the detectives believed the interviewer wanted to hear or what the detectives wanted the interviewer to know. Nothing was volunteered beyond the questions asked, and most interviewers did not know what to ask. None of the subtle complexities of rape or its investigation were learned nor did any of the informal procedures come to light.

A similar feature was discovered by two student researchers, one black and one white. The students were interested in the different responses of blacks to a white interviewer and whites to a black interviewer. They learned that many of the black respondents refused to be interviewed by the white student, but *not* for racist reasons. Many of the blacks in the sample were illiterate and were ashamed to let the fact be known to the white interviewer. On the other hand, the illiterate blacks felt the black student would be sympathetic to their inability to read or write and would understand why. In this case, familiarity with the situation was crucial, for had the black student not been familiar with the circumstances, it would have never been learned why so many blacks refused to be interviewed.

Essentially, then, intimate familiarity with a group entails getting to know more about them than what can be put on most questionnaires and interview schedules. It is coming to know subtleties in the language, customs, norms, meanings, and the whole realm of understanding that is implied in "getting to know" others. The only way to do this is through spending a lot of time with a group or in a particular setting or situation so that one can learn the multitude of nuances that go to make up any patterned behavior.

THE SITUATION The focus on the social situation points to that sphere of behavior where people's actions are geared to other's expectations in a given set of circumstances. Depending on the situation, people will act in one way or another, *the situation determining the appropriate behavior.* One aspect of the situation the field researcher examines includes the various rules or norms governing behavior in a situation. For example, in studying bar behavior, Sherri Cavan found that one situational norm in bars was leaving money on the counter to reserve one's place.[6] If someone sitting at the bar wants to get up and play the jukebox and return to his or her seat at the bar, they can do so by leaving money at their place—invoking the norm that rules a person's place is saved for them as long as their money is left on the counter. Of course, such norms do not exist in all situations, but whatever norms do exist are important to understand, for they tell people how to treat one another in that situation.

There are four dimensions to situations that the field researcher can describe and measure. First, there is the *size* of the situation in terms of the human population toward whom one must direct his or her behavior. Besides sheer numbers, size also refers to the number of social types in a situation: while a social situation may have hundreds or thousands of individuals, the situation may consist of only a few social types. For instance, a factory setting may contain hundreds or even thousands of people, but interaction may be geared to others in terms of only two social types—boss and coworkers. Also, there is what can be called a **phantom population,** an audience for whom subjects are acting but who are not present. For example, if we enter an empty cathedral or church, we may behave *as though* the church were filled with people. Our voices drop, we step quietly, and we observe the other situational norms associated with religious buildings. A second dimension of the situation concerns the kinds of *equipment* or props that accompany it. Papers, pens, pencils, and typewriters are all props of an insurance office situation, while knives, guns, and chains are the equipment of a gang-fight situation. Third, situations can be measured in terms of *space,* varying from an entire country to a corner in a back alley where kids are shooting craps. The same situation can occur in both a small or a large space, as with a small party in an apartment and a ball spread through many rooms in a mansion. The fourth and final dimension of situations is *time.* Bank robbery situations generally occur in less than two minutes, while one may orient himself or herself for years to the situation of medical school training.[7]

By immersing himself or herself in situations, the field researcher is able to delineate each dimension of the situation. Initially, rough measurements are made, but as time passes, the field researcher can finely describe each dimension in terms of the meanings for those involved in the situation and conceptual categories that can be compared to other situations.

STRATEGIES   The ways in which people typically deal with situations constitute both situated strategy and tactics and routines. The focus on these strategies requires the observer to understand not only what is done but why only certain possible moves are made. For example, in situations where we find violent delinquent gangs, a mechanism for dealing with rivals is the *drive-by*, wherein members of one gang get in a car, armed with guns, and then "drive-by" a rival gang's territory and shoot at their houses or at the rivals themselves if they can find them. On the other hand, in a study of middle-class suburban high school students' rivalries between different cliques and clubs, it is unlikely that a researcher will find similar strategies used. What is it, in other words, that would lead to one set of strategies that result in killings and woundings and another set of strategies that do not? Only by understanding the whole situation and examining the strategies and tactics employed, along with those *not* employed (or only rarely so and in opposition to situational norms), can we fully explain such a phenomenon. Moreover, since the researcher does not know what the various strategies are in a situation at the outset of the research, or even the dimensions of the situation itself, it is necessary to employ a field method that will allow observation of the many unknown qualities he or she is seeking to understand.

We might envision different strategies in different situations comparatively as follows:

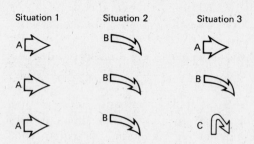

In Situation 1, Strategy A is always employed, in Situation 2, Strategy B is always employed, but in Situation 3, Strategies A, B, and C are present. It is important to remember that a given strategy does not necessarily imply a given situation even though strategies are used to deal with a given situation. As can be seen in the above diagram, for example, even though Strategy A is employed in Situation 1, it is also employed in Situation 3; therefore, just because a given strategy is observed does not mean that a specific situation must be present. Oftentimes inexperienced field researchers confuse a strategy and a situation.

Another problem in dealing with activities within a given situation is in determining the *meaning* of the act in the context of the situation. For example, loud, boisterous laughing and greetings at a party mean one thing, but such behavior at a funeral might be taken to mean that someone has gone mad with grief. Behaviorally, we might be able to describe the two acts as the same, but socially, one is normal, the other insane. Thus, rather than having the *same action* in two different situations, the very situation defines the meaning of the action. In the following illustration, the letter represents the behavior while the different arrows show that even though the behavior is observably similar, the acts are very different.

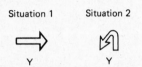

Situation 1   Situation 2

Y   Y

DISCIPLINED ABSTRACTIONS   Perhaps the most important aspect of field research is developing disciplined abstractions. The easiest way to understand disciplined abstractions is to equate them with concepts. In field research, as in all other social science research, there is a reflexive interplay between the concrete and the abstract. Our concepts guide us to look at certain things in certain ways, and at the same time, our observations provide our concepts with a reality that confirms their application.[8] It is a paradox, and in some ways a self-fulfilling prophecy, to say that our concepts and observations elaborate and support one another, but if used properly, instead of reifying themselves, concepts can be used to classify, arrange, and explain our observations.

In the field, researchers are literally swimming in data, and like the fish who may be unaware of the surrounding water, they can be unaware of all the data around them. *The problem is what to look for.* If we record every single bit of possible data, from the ticking of the office clock to the number of words per minute the secretary types, we would quickly become overloaded. On the other hand, we may find that our concepts are woefully inadequate to describe or explain what we observe, or so contrived in their application that we recognize we are forcing square pegs into round holes.

The field researcher must develop an artful and systematic means of going from the abstract to the concrete and back to the abstract. Lofland provides a three-step outline for dealing with this process:

1. Begin with an abstract sense of what a generic situation is and what generic strategies are.

2. Immerse oneself in the concrete items of the actual social life under study.
3. Develop and construct a generically framed analysis of situations and strategies from the organic intertwining of items 1 and 2.[9]

By the term **generic,** Lofland is referring to the more typical, general, common, and universal features of things.[10] For example, suppose we wanted to observe interaction patterns in the student union or commons. We would begin with a general abstract idea of what goes on there in terms of the situation and strategies. By and large the situation involves eating meals, passing time between classes, or socializing with friends. In the context of university life it might be considered a "time-out" situation. Strategies for dealing with the situation involve meeting people you know, eating meals, and reading, usually the school newspaper.

The second step is get into the flow of activities in the student union and observe what takes place in terms of the general parameters we have set up. For instance, let us say we are sitting down at a table with our notebook, observing people in the student union. A student pays the cashier for his lunch, stops, looks around, then walks to a table and sits down at it. After he is seated, he again looks around the room. Then he eats his lunch, occasionally looking around the room and at people passing his table. Finishing lunch, he looks at his watch, looks around the room again, and then picks up a student newspaper and begins reading it, frequently looking up and around. These actions are the *topical* in relation to the generic aspects of a situation. We can put these topical observations into the generic categories as the following table shows:

Generic	Topical
1. Eating	1. Actually sitting down and eating lunch.
2. Passing time	2. Glancing at watch, then reading paper.
3. Socializing	3. Not observed directly, but suggested by constant looking around room.

Finer observations and analyses may tell us more. For instance, we may observe the same person for several days and notice he never sits with anyone or meets anyone in the student union. We might conclude, therefore, that even though he does not socialize with others, he is acting in a way to indicate that he does have friends, but for some reason they are not there at the time. It is a strategy to present himself as a sociable person. The newspaper is an *involvement shield* to hide his solitude from others and a mechanism for passing the time alone.

Access to the Research Setting

Having a clear idea of what is to be observed, the next problem is to gain access to the research setting. In our example of the student union, all one has to do is to walk in, sit down, and start taking notes. However, in other settings or situations, getting in is not so simple and an elaborate entrance ritual is required. For example, in studies of religious cults,[11] television news production,[12] hospitals,[13] or boards of directors,[14] the researchers had to get special permission to enter the situation. In this section, we will discuss some of the ways researchers have gained access to various research settings and the roles they have assumed either to gain access or once access has been obtained.

Known and Unknown Research Roles

As a general tenet we will contend that the best research role is one in which the researcher is known. First, there are the ethics of being an unknown researcher, the implications of which we discuss in full in Chapter 19. Second, there are practical matters involving known and unknown research roles. If one is going to study the police, for example, about the only practical way to do so is to become a known observer. One could get arrested a lot and make notes while his or her hands were uncuffed; not only would such a strategy be absurd and costly but it would also leave the researcher very little time to make the necessary observations. Further, a known researcher can *act* like a researcher in that he or she can ask questions, have good reasons to poke his or her nose into a wide variety of situations, and generally be available for participation at different times of the day. All these actions would otherwise arouse suspicion. There are not the risks of exposure, since as a known researcher there is nothing to expose—everyone knows his or her role as a researcher.

Given the ethical and practical advantages of taking the role of a known researcher, there are still some situations in which the unknown role is either the only alternative or simply more feasible. In her study of bar behavior, Cavan was, for the most part, in the role of an unknown researcher.[15] Because of the high level of sociability in bars, it was easy for her to ask all kinds of questions in the course of a normal bar conversation—for example, "Do you come here often?" Further, because of the sociability of bar behavior, to announce to everyone in the bar that she was a researcher would break the very norms of the situation she was studying. Similarly, in Scott's study of horse racing, not only would it have been very difficult for him to announce to every horse player, trainer, jockey, and other person at the track that he was observing their behavior, but also it would be both ethically and practically unnecessary for the research.[16] Because both Cavan and Scott were studying public settings and behavior in public, there were no special entrance requirements for the researchers different from those subjects they were studying. Essentially, the researchers in the bar and racetrack settings were doing systematically and conceptually what everyone else was doing informally—watching people.

There is a gray area of field research that is often the most attractive and adventuresome: the area in which the group of interest almost certainly does not want its activities monitored by a researcher, yet its activities are so interesting that it is hard to resist attempting the research. For example, the Ku Klux Klan is a facinating group in the area not only of race relations but also of collective behavior and deviance. It is a good bet, however, that if students announced to the Klan that they were sociologists wanting to study them, they would be turned down. On the other hand, it would not be too difficult for a white male researcher to infiltrate the group and learn everything he wanted. If he were caught, there is a good chance of physical harm, even death. Therefore, even though this gray area of research holds the promise of significant knowledge, it is dangerous. Moreover, it is best to remember that one of the most spectacular pieces of research ever done, the uncovering of the Watergate scandal, was accomplished by two *known* researchers, newspaper reporters for the *Washington Post*. Thus, even in this area where unknown infiltration is most attractive, the same ends can be accomplished in the known researcher role.

Roles of the Observer

The known researcher fills the social role of a researcher, but it is not a standard one in field research. Rather, a role is "made," "negotiated," or "constructed."[17] It is important to remember that the role of a researcher within any group is an unusual one, and people are unsure exactly how they are supposed to treat the researcher or be treated in return. Consider what you would do if a researcher decided to study you!

For the most part, the known researcher is a "researcher and. . . ." He or she can be a researcher and friend, researcher and partner, researcher and coworker, or just about any combination of roles we can think of. However, it is essential to remember that the primary role of a researcher is that of a *researcher*, and not the secondary role attached to it. This is especially difficult when the secondary role is that of friend or partner. In his research on the police, Pepinsky reported that he often found himself wanting to help the police in some circumstances, and he even thought of becoming a police officer.[18] Similarly, in a study of detectives, one of the authors became a quasi-partner/"flunky," a job that entailed bagging and labeling recovered property, participating in stake-outs (alone), making administrative judgment on cases to be investigated, and generally any other chore the investigators decided he was useful for. While some of these nonresearch duties certainly took away from the research, they also gave the researcher a great deal of insight into the operations of the detective division under study. To be honest, many of the nonresearch activities were taken on just for the fun of it. It is only when the secondary role reduces the effectiveness of the research role that there is a need for concern. Otherwise, the secondary role allows the researcher to fit into the situation in a way understood by the subjects.

There are a number of standard observation roles in field research, including that of the *researcher and. . . .* Frequently, researchers, especially students who are pressed for time and money, will conduct research from the role of an *employee.* Not only does that role allow access, but the researcher will know many of the nuances of the situation being studied and how to best make observations and take notes. Student research in this area have included studies of a women's shoe store (shoe salesman), restaurant interaction (waitress), singles bar (cocktail waitress), and taxi cab passengers (cab driver). The reverse of the employee role is that of the *patron* or *audience.* Student studies of a pornographic arcade, bars, and a pinball parlor have been conducted in the role of a patron. Likewise, as part of the audience, student researchers have observed rock concerts and religious revivals. The *intern* role has been used by student researchers for observations of probation officers, prisoner-aid societies, and mental health agencies. Since the internships are designed to acquaint students with various aspects of organizations, jobs, and roles, they allow students—indeed, expect them—to ask a lot of questions and poke around in several different areas. As such, the intern role is an ideal one for field research. In the role of the *member,* student researchers have access to all different kinds of groups, organizations, and situations. For example, fraternities and sororities have been researched by student members. There is another type of membership that is less formal than belonging to a club or organization. It is the kind of membership that involves recurrent participation in some kind of activity, usually at a single or limited number of settings. In a study of a nude bathing beach, a team of three researchers became members of the setting simply by showing up frequently in the appropriate attire at the beach.[19]

Rapport

Once a role has been chosen and the researcher has gained access, the next step is establishing **rapport.** In practical research terms, rapport refers to the ability of the researcher to get along with his or her subjects. The extent to which the researcher is trusted and respected, rapport exists. It may take time to develop rapport, or in cases where the researcher is already a normal part of the situation, such as in the role of a member or employee, it may exist at the outset.

Developing rapport should begin at the outset of contact, even before access has been established in some cases. If one is studying an organization, for example, it is necessary to get permission to do the research from those in positions of authority, even though the research may concentrate only on those in lower positions in the hierarchy. In order to plant the seeds of good rapport, though, the researcher should simultaneously seek out permission of those on the lower levels as well. Thus, when the researcher does gain access, not only will the research subjects be somewhat familiar with him or her, but they will also not feel the researcher is someone who has been imposed upon them by "the boss."

Perhaps the best advice in developing rapport is to keep our mouths shut and our eyes and ears open.[20] This does not mean wandering around in a catatonic haze; rather, it suggests we reserve our opinions until we are better known by the subjects and we know them better. As a known researcher, subjects will initially begin their interaction by asking about the research project, and this will provide an opportunity to explain the research and ask questions. The questions provide the *subjects* with an opportunity to say something about themselves, making them feel important and allowing the researcher to present himself or herself as someone who is genuinely interested. (The researcher should be genuinely interested, too.) After a while, the researcher becomes a welcome figure to have around, for he or she is interested in others, is nonjudgmental, and provides good company. That is rapport, and with it the researcher can gather a wealth of information.

There is, however, a tricky aspect to rapport, part of which has to do with the various loyalties and rivalries groups often have. To develop friendship with one group often makes you an enemy of another group; therefore, rapport is not quite the same as becoming a bosom buddy with the subjects. Instead, it is the development of a detached trust and respect with everyone. This problem is somewhat simplified by being a *known* researcher, for it is understood that the person who becomes a companion is there as a researcher and does not want to become involved in petty disputes. The unknown researcher, on the other hand, may be swept into one clique and banned from another, therefore limiting his or her observations to a very narrow range. The other part of the problem with rapport has to do with knowing when to draw the line, especially in studies of crime and deviance. In the study of law-breaking behavior, the *participant observer* had better stress the latter and not the former, for there is no protection—from either side of the law—for the researcher who is caught committing crimes. In at least two cases of research on the lives of convicts, researchers have been employed to hide caches of drugs, albeit only as a last resort, and what rapport was gained by doing so is questionable. Had the researchers been caught, they might have been conducting their studies of convict life as full participants themselves. Likewise, in Whyte's study *Street Corner Society*, the researcher was almost caught attempting to stuff ballots as a favor to his research subjects, an an unnecessarily risky attempt to improve rapport.[21]

The actual mechanics of "gathering" data in field research involves watching and hearing and recording. Usually, notes are jotted down, and from these notes the researcher later makes analytic judgments as to what the social significance of his or her observations have been. The problem is "What to record?"

The most basic guide to what to record are the concepts being employed. As a field researcher it is possible to "sensitize" the concepts to the situation.[22] This involves seeing how the concepts fit a particular situation in terms of the actual behaviors and meanings of that situation. For example, suppose a researcher wants to study role interaction in a restaurant. The primary concepts are (1) status, (2) role, and (3) interaction. Beginning with the concept of *status*, the observer will first look at the different positions. The following illustrates what field notes might look like when the observer is making notes on the different statuses in a restaurant:

Field Notes On Status
There are 3 waitresses, two seem to be "senior" and the other's a "junior." There's a cook and his helper, but the helper also washes dishes and clears the tables in addition to some cooking. So he's a cook, dishwasher, and busboy. There seem to be 3 kinds of customers or maybe even 4. There are the "regulars" who come in almost every day and the "truckers" who come in regularly when they drive through. There are the "occasionals" who seem to be known by the waitresses, but only come in once in a while. Finally, there are the "strangers" who only have been in once.

Breaking down the notes into the distinct statuses, we could see the following list:

Restaurant Statuses
1. senior waitress
2. junior waitress
3. cook
4. assistant cook/dishwasher/busboy
5. regular customer
6. regular trucker
7. occasional customer
8. stranger

Having an understanding of the different statuses, the field reseracher next will want to record the roles of each person and their role performance. Next, he or she will focus attention on the interaction between those occupying different roles. The following notes show the focus on the interaction between the waitresses and the cook and the cook's helper.

A waitress had to return a sandwich since the customer had ordered it on white bread and it was made with rye. The cook's helper had made it and it looked like she was trying to get it changed without the cook seeing her, but he did see her and asked her what was wrong. She explained, and the cook said, "Damnit, Mary, we can't make them right unless we can read the order!" Mary shrugged and walked away. Then the cook turned to the helper and said, "Damnit, Sam, can't you do anything right!" The helper didn't say anything, but made a new sandwich.

The incident described in the field notes may be trivial or significant, and from a single entry, it is impossible to tell. However, by examining the field notes there are a number of possible avenues the researcher might want to explore. Unlike most other methods in which the gathering and analysis of the data are fully separated, in field research the two are intertwined.[23] Using preliminary analysis, or even hunches, the field researcher can refocus his or her observations and questions to locate patterns of interest.

Patterns and Problems

In order to check out a preliminary observation, the field researcher must learn to see things in terms of conceptual patterns. Essentially, a *pattern* is a set of recurrent social actions. For example, in the field notes on the restaurant, one pattern is that of the waitress taking customers' orders, giving them to the cook, and then taking customers' meals back to them—a fairly simple pattern. On the other hand, more complex patterns may exist that are at first invisible because the researcher does not yet fully understand the social situation. In going over the field notes on restaurant interaction, there are possible patterns of subordination and superordination. The cook appears superordinate to both the waitress and cook's helper, indicated by his shouting at them and their lack of retaliatory measures. Also, the cook's helper seems to be a notch above the status of the waitress, for while the cook waited for the waitress to leave before turning on his helper, he shouted at the waitress in front of his helper. Whether these dominating behaviors were part of a pattern or not is determined by continued observations. If after further observations the same dominant-subordinate relationship is observed, it can then be considered a **standing pattern of behavior** in the situation. If not, and at other times the waitress berates the cook with the same vigor, and he humbly takes the abuse, then the initial observation was simply an incidental flux. Further complexities enter the picture when we find that the cook's helper is the cook's son, the "junior waitress" is the son's girlfriend, and one of the regular customers is having an affair with one of the waitresses who is married to a trucker.

Besides looking for patterns by examining the same activity as it occurs again and again, another way to find what "fits" a situation is by looking at what causes problems. If someone says, "You can't do that!" he or she is enforcing the norms of the situation. By examining what was accorded *negative sanctions* we see patterns of behavior in negative relief. Stating what cannot be done implies what can be or must be. In his study of the convict code in halfway houses, D. Lawrence Wieder noted the sense of the code when one of the residents of the halfway house answered, "You know I can't do that," when asked by a staff member to organize a baseball game. What the convict resident was saying was that the convict code states that inmates should not cooperate with the guards (or staff in the case of halfway houses), and by agreeing to help organize a baseball game he would be breaking the code.[24] Thus, by implication, we can see that the pattern of behavior for the residents of the halfway house is noncooperation with the staff. Careful observation, though, would be necessary to see whether such norms are followed or merely voiced for the benefit of significant others.

Elaborating Notes

In the field it is often difficult to take full and complete notes. Sometimes only fragments of events can be recorded, jotted down on scraps of paper. The purpose of field notes in these cases is to jog the memory so that the field researcher can expand on the notes later, usually the same day, into a full and complete description of his or her observations. The following example shows notes quickly written in the field and later elaborated:

Notes Written in Field

Possible fight over Chico's "girlfriend"

Notes Elaborated from Those Taken in Field
Chico was trying to get the Los Lobos to take on the El Loco gang because of an alleged insult to one of the girls in the barrio. Chico had dated the girl a couple of times, and even though he wasn't going steadily with her, he was trying to get something started between the two gangs by referring to her as "my girlfriend" and "my woman." Ramon said, "Hey man, she ain't your girl, we've all been with her." To this Chico retorted that even if she had been with a lot of the Lobos that didn't make her a *puta* (what the Loco gang had called her). He used that point to claim that she was indeed a homegirl, and since she took care of the Lobos, they should take care of her (by attacking the Locos). When they went home for the night, Ramon said they'd decide what to do the next day.

As can be seen from the above example, just a few notes taken in the field hold a lot of material. It is necessary, however, to elaborate the sketchy field notes as soon as possible, preferably the same day they were taken. If elaborate notes can be taken in the field, so much the better. In studies of organizations where "doing the paperwork" is part of the daily routine, field researchers can do their own paperwork while the research subjects are doing theirs. It is even better if the notes are typed in their elaboration, for not only is it simpler to make multiple copies of notes for later analysis, cross-indexing, and sharing with fellow researchers, but they are much easier to read, ensuring that none of the data are lost.

The Observation Schedule

With the observer in the field literally swimming in data, it is often difficult to record everything important. In order to use a large number of observers in a field research project and still maintain consistency, Albert Reiss, Jr., developed an instrument very much like an interview schedule.[25] Instead of having questions to be answered by *talk*, the questions are answered by *observations*. Thus, instead of becoming lost in a sea of data and possible data, the observers were able to organize their observations in terms of the **observation schedule.**

In order to employ the observation schedule, there must be a clear unit of analysis. With interviews, each interviewee or household typically constitutes the unit of analysis, but in the field things may not be quite as tidy. In Reiss's study, the unit of analysis was the encounter between police and citizens. Each time the police would stop and interact with citizens, whether it resulted in an arrest or simply taking information from a crime victim, an observation form was filled out for the encounter.[6] Included on the form were questions as to how the encounter was initiated, what kind of crime was involved, whether or not the police and citizens were civil to one another, plus several other variables of interest. All of these "questions" could be answered by observations. The following illustrates items on the observation schedule and shows how it was filled out:

| | DEMEANOR | |
Officer	Citizen 1	Citizen 2
_____ deferential	_____ deferential	_____ deferential
✓ civil	✓ civil	_____ civil
_____ antagonistic	_____ antagonistic	✓ antagonistic

In the example, all the observer had to do was to make three check marks (✓) to indicate the interaction demeanor of the three people involved in the interaction. Elsewhere on the observation schedule, Citizen 1 is identified as a crime victim and Citizen 2 is identified as a suspect, each indicated by a simple check. In the same manner, all other types of information can be systematically recorded on observation schedules in field research situations. Sometimes, the observation schedule includes an "open" section for field notes that summarize the events observed. This allows the researcher to examine the context of the other data that has been recorded. In situations where the "objective" observations that have been checked off include apparent contradictions, the researcher can read the summary of the recorded situation to see if the context can explain the other observations.

Informants

In addition to making observations, a crucial part of field research is asking questions. The most important function of questions is to determine the **social meanings** the subjects have for their actions. In some cases this means learning a new language, either one that is totally alien, as is the case in much anthropological research, or a special form of a known language, as is the case with various forms of jargon and slang such as that used by real estate salespeople or the radio code used by police.

To gather this kind of information, along with various historical and other nonobservational data, field researchers depend on **informants,** people who explain the meaning and history of events. An informant may be one key person or several. In anthropological research, sometimes a village may have only one person who speaks English, for example, and so that person becomes the primary informant until the researcher has learned the language. In other situations, any single informant will provide only a single perspective—their side—and so it is important to have a number of informants in order to determine the various viewpoints and structure of the group generating them.

One advantage in field research is that one can check out what an informant has told him or her. If a certain pattern or meaning has been learned from an informant, the observer can either try using an action or meaning to see if it is appropriate by means of a small field experiment, or simply watch to see whether what the informant said was correct or not.

In some cases what informants say will not conform with observations, yet the researcher will find a high consensus among all informants that a given pattern or meaning is true. This situation can be one of two things. First, it can be a *belief,* which while objectively false, is still believed to be true. For example, for years it was believed, and perhaps still is, that women were inferior drivers. Several studies showed that women were involved in fewer accidents than men, but men and women informants would have claimed women were involved in more. Second, the problem can lie in the application of meanings. In a study of detectives, a researcher was told that the criterion used in deciding whether or not to investigate a case was the seriousness of the crime.[27] Among the serious crimes detectives claimed they always investigated was attempted murder. One day the researcher saw an attempted murder case in a pile of cases not to be investigated, so he asked the sergeant why it was not being worked. By way of explanation, the sergeant said, "This is nothing but a glorified domestic." The term *domestic* referred to a "domestic disturbance" such as a family fight. Therefore, even though the patrol officer who took the original report logged the case as an "attempted murder," the detectives reformulated it as a "domestic disturbance," and because the detectives did not waste time with petty cases (such as domestic disturbance) the case was not investigated. Thus, to everyone involved, the action was perfectly consistent with their policy of only investigating serious crimes. Thus, in all use of information by informants, it is necessary to check out exactly how a piece of information is used and the effects of different contexts on both meanings and actions.

Summary

Field methods consist of many techniques used simultaneously to systematically collect observational data on social action. An important aspect of social action is the component of meaning in that action, and so while field methods allow direct observation of social behavior patterns, they also allow assessment of the meanings in the observed action. The real key, however, is in the ability of the field researcher to make conceptual observations for the development and testing of theory. By identifying the generic features of social patterns of behavior in a conceptual framework, field research allows virtually every aspect of social behavior to be studied.

The techniques of field research are a combination of learned skills, patience, and a willingness to explore the depths of social life. For the most part, observations in the field are best made in the role of a known researcher, and access to specialized or forbidden niches of social life must be negotiated. Once in, the researcher develops a combination role, while stressing that of researcher. This also requires that other roles and quasi-roles be played out, while one develops and maintains rapport. In this situation, the field researcher collects and elaborates notes of his or her observations and at the same time probes the actors' understanding through the use of informants.

In Chapter 17, we will discuss how all of this data can be analyzed, but even while collecting data, the field researcher engages in preliminary analysis by comparing applications of different concepts, small field experiments, and multiple observations to test the validity of an initial one. There is a total immersion into the fabric of social life, constantly seeking a coherent understanding of the maze that makes up that life. To be sure, such research is a controlled adventure, as was suggested by Goffman, but it is an adventure nevertheless, extracting far more from the research than just the rich data to be analyzed.

disciplined abstractions Conceptualizing qualitative observations into coherent social science categories.

generic forms The more typical, general, common, and universal features of things. Showing how observations of a given type display features common to a certain form.

informants Trusted subjects who give researchers insight into the beliefs, values, and meanings of the informant's group and culture.

intimate familiarity Field relationships with research subjects that allows access to a group's innermost feelings, meanings, and understandings of their world.

observation schedule A device used by field researchers to systematically record observations. Similar to interview schedules and questionnaires except it employs observations instead of verbal questions.

participant observation Research method where the researcher involves himself or herself in the setting and group life of research subjects.

phantom population An audience for whom the research subjects are acting but who are not present.

rapport A relationship of trust and understanding between the researcher and research subjects.

situation A structural concept referring to the roles, activities, meanings, and involvements expected under a given set of circumstances.

social meanings Shared understandings of how certain events, roles, situations, and other phenomena are to be treated by a given group in any context of social interaction.

standing pattern of behavior Recurrent observable activities and actions in a given setting or social situation.

strategies The ways in which people typically deal with situations.

Notes

1. John Johnson, *Doing Field Research* (New York: Free Press, 1975).
2. William B. Sanders, "Pinball Occasions," in Edward Sagarin and Arnold Birenbaum, eds., *People in Places: The Sociology of the Familiar* (New York: Praeger, 1973).
3. Peter K. Manning and John Van Maanen, eds., *Policing: A View from the Street* (Santa Monica, Ca.: Goodyear, 1978).
4. John Lofland, *Doing Social Life* (New York: Wiley, 1976), p. 3.
5. William B. Sanders, *Rape and Woman's Identity* (Beverly Hills, Ca.: Sage, 1980).
6. Sherri Cavan, *Liquor License* (Chicago: Aldine, 1966).
7. Lofland, op. cit., pp. 26–27.
8. Kenneth Leiter, *A Primer on Ethnomethodology* (New York: Oxford, 1980); Howard Schwartz and Jerry Jacobs, *Qualitative Sociology: A Method to the Madness* (New York: Free Press, 1979).
9. Lofland, op. cit., p. 66.
10. Ibid., p. 31.
11. John Lofland, *Doomsday Cult* (Englewood Cliffs, N.J.: Prentice-Hall, 1966).
12. David Altheide, *Creating Reality: How TV News Distorts Events* (Beverly Hills, Ca.: Sage, 1976).

13. David Sudnow, *Passing On: The Social Organization of Dying* (Englewood Cliffs, N.J.: Prentice-Hall, 1969).

14. William B. Shaffir, Robert A. Stebbins, and Allen Turowetz, *Fieldwork Experience* (New York: St. Martin's Press, 1980), pp. 45–56.

15. Cavan, op. cit., p. 45.

16. Marvin B. Scott, *The Racing Game* (Chicago: Aldine, 1968).

17. Myron Glazer, *The Research Adventure: Promise and Problems of Field Work* (New York: Random House, 1972), pp. 11–13.

18. Harold E. Pepinsky, "A Sociologist on Police Patrol" in William B. Shaffir, Robert A. Stebbins, and Allen Turowetz, eds., *Fieldwork Experience* (New York: St. Martin's Press, 1980), pp. 223–234.

19. Jack D. Douglas and Paul K. Rasmussen with Carol Ann Flanagan, *The Nude Beach* (Beverly Hills, Ca.: Sage, 1977).

20. Ned Polsky, *Hustlers, Beats, and Others* (New York: Doubleday, 1969), p. 121.

21. William F. Whyte, *Street Corner Society* (Chicago: University of Chicago Press, 1943).

22. Norman K. Denzin, *The Research Act* (Chicago: Aldine, 1970), p. 14.

23. John Lofland, *Analyzing Social Settings: A Guide to Qualitative Observation and Analysis* (Belmont, Ca.: Wadsworth, 1971).

24. D. Lawrence Wieder, *Language and Social Reality: The Case of Telling the Convict Code* (The Hague: Mouton, 1974).

25. Albert J. Reiss, Jr., "Stuff and Nonsense About Social Surveys and Observation," in Howard S. Becker, Blanche Geer, David Reisman, and A. S. Weiss, eds., *Institutions and the Person* (Chicago: Aldine, 1968).

26. Ibid.

27. William B. Sanders, *Detective Work: A Study of Criminal Investigations* (New York: Free Press, 1977).

11

Special Techniques in Research

In this chapter we will examine three methodological procedures that are put to unique and interesting use in social science. They are presented to provide a brief look at some methods that deal with specific kinds of research problems and assumptions about social life. These techniques are often used as supplements to other methods discussed in this book.

First, we will discuss *investigative social research*,[1] a methodology emphasizing the "backstage" of social life and the strategies for uncovering that side of life people do not want others to know about. Basically, it is the social science version of investigative reporting as made famous during the Watergate scandal and weekly on television's "60 Minutes." Second, we are going to examine *unobtrusive measures*.[2] These measures are geared to capture the candid side of social life, those activities that are nonreactive to social science measuring techniques. We might look at unobtrusive measures in the same way we think of "clues" used by detectives, especially physical evidence. Such measures are used easily with investigative social research methods. Finally, we will look at *conversation analysis*,[3] a method for analyzing the structure of conversations, one of the most typical forms of social interaction. Several interesting findings have come out of this method, which is one of the more refined methodologies for understanding the nuances of social intercourse.

Investigative Social Research

Like most methods, investigative social research takes as its primary goal the uncovering of the truth in social situations, groups, and organizations. The method's basic assumption is that people tell others what they think others want to hear or what they want them to know. In other words, people say one thing and do something else. What they tell researchers is even less candid and accurate, for researchers are considered outside snoops to whom one does not owe loyalty or honesty, and to believe otherwise is either wishful thinking or self-deception. As Goffman noted, "I rarely believe what people say, and in interview situations, I hardly believe them at all."[4] The problem, then, is to overcome the obstacles to the truth and maneuver to get at it. Investigative social research, while not alone in seeking the truth in research, uses exhaustive measures to get behind the facades of social life.

Consensus versus Conflict

In his work on investigative social research, Douglas compared the classical (cooperative) paradigm of field research with that of the conflict paradigm. To summarize the viewpoints, Douglas drew from two very different conceptions of what people are like, using the following two quotes:

> It is surprising how quickly the average person will respond to the genuinely scientific attitude of an investigator and make an effort to give accurate, revealing statements.[5]

It took me a long time to discover that the key thing in acting is honesty. Once you know how to fake that, you've got it made.[6]

In the first quote, people are assumed to be friendly, open, and honest, while the opposite is assumed for the second. Given the extent to which people are proud of their actions and unsuspicious of the motives of others in a research situation, there is little reason to assume they will be anything other than honest and open. However, Douglas argues that at the heart of the social order there is conflict and distrust, and except for inquiries about the more innocuous aspects of social life (such as what one watched on television the night before), people are suspiciously dishonest toward research inquiries. Moreover, in a number of studies it has been found that people will say one thing but do something else.[7] This is especially true regarding sensitive areas of social life such as sex, politics, and racial attitudes.

Conflict Assumptions

Taking the conflict point of view, the investigative researcher is confronted with a number of different types of invalid information. The first problem is to recognize that what one is told is not the truth or at least not the entire truth. We will examine each of the four problems envisioned by the investigative researchers.

MISINFORMATION   The first problem one encounters is **misinformation** or information that is considered truthful but is simply wrong.[8] Often this can be from an informant who thinks he or she knows the truth and is willing to share it with the researchers. Sometimes an entire group is misinformed about something, but the group mythology maintains a *belief* as a *fact*, and the researcher must be able to distinguish one from the other. For example, Douglas pointed out that those people who worked in "massage" parlors were wholly misinformed about the nature of vice laws, and in explaining how the massage parlor workers used word games to protect themselves from arrest and conviction, the researchers at first believed their explanation as the truth about the law. Later, however, the researchers learned that the group was not well-informed about the vice laws, and was subject to arrest even with the word games they used to protect themselves.[9] However, since the massage parlor workers believed what they said, the problem was one of misinformation and not of lies.

EVASIONS   A second problem assumed by the investigative researcher involves **evasions,** which are partial lies that are known to be untrue by research subjects but are not flat lies.[10] The essence of an evasion is *not* revealing information or redirecting the researcher down a false path. Unlike misinformation, however, the use of evasions is an intentional move to mislead the researcher. Four common types of evasions include the following: (1) *silence*, (2) *avoiding the situation*, (3) *turning aside questions*, and (4) *loopholing*.[11]

First, silence is simply not responding to questions in certain areas. When a girl asks a boy, "Do you love me?" the following silence evades the issue—not requiring the boy to deny his love or affirm it or to tell a lie. Similarly, when a researcher asks a politician if he is influenced by the lobby of a chemical company, the stony silence signals evasion. A second kind of evasion is avoiding the situation. If one doesn't allow oneself to be in a situation to be interviewed, it is possible to keep silent about an issue and not reveal anything. A third evasion, turning aside questions, maneuvers the questions away from what the researcher wants. For example, if a researcher asks a religious group leader about the amount of money he has been able to accumulate for himself, the question can be turned aside by saying something such as, "Well, that's not what's important. I don't care a whit for the money except for our mission in Mongolia. Now you wouldn't believe what it costs to run a mission. Our mission is important to us; let me tell you about it." Thus, the religious leader has turned the question from his *personal finances* to the mission and its finances. A final type of evasion is called loopholing. Since all meanings can be subject to more than a single interpretation, loopholing is evasion by focusing on a "literal" but not generally shared meaning of a statement or question. For example, if a researcher asks a politician if he takes "kickbacks," the politician may huff and puff in the negative, but if later caught taking bribes, the same politician may piously state, "You asked about *kickbacks*, not a thing about *bribes*."

LIES People lie to investigative researchers all the time, regardless of class, sex, race, or just about any other variable. Lies are simply false statements intentionally designed to mislead. There are "good lies," such as telling lies to set someone up for a surprise party or to relieve the grief of a surviving widow by telling her that her husband died peacefully while in reality he suffered terribly before his death. In fact, people are expected to tell good lies in many situations and would be considered boorish, rude, and stupid not to. Then there are "bad lies" or those kinds of lies we tell to mislead others about something shameful we have done. Of course, even bad lies are rationalized or neutralized[11] so that to the teller they are really not so bad. But the point is not whether the lies are good or bad, routine or extraordinary, but rather that people tell lies frequently for all kinds of reasons. The important thing is to recognize lies and find the truth behind them.

FRONTS The use of the term **fronts** by investigative researchers refers to socially shared and learned lies.[12] In the corporate world, various businesses are fronts for behind-the-scenes financial dealings; ownership under relatives' names are fronts for the principal owner for tax purposes; and a flower shop can be the front for a mob-controlled business. In horse racing, people called "beards" make bets for jockeys, trainers, and others whose special knowledge of a horse's chances to win a race may be followed by others, thereby upsetting the odds.[13] Massage parlors are common fronts for prostitution operations as are bars for bookie joints. One of the more ingenious fronts was an ice-cream truck whose jingling bells signaled not the availability of frozen treats but rather of slightly cooled marijuana. A well-known nude beach, where the sunbathers claimed a sexless interest in the "natural" benefits of nude bathing, was in fact a front for meeting others who enjoyed orgies, both straight and gay, at another location.[14]

The existence of a front is of research interest *per se*, but it is equally important to understand a setting as a front and not the essential social focal point. A researcher who understands massage parlors as a place to have one's muscles relaxed and nothing more, even though most of those who used the place did so to have sex, misses the essential character of the setting. The problem for the researcher is to get to the inside behind the front, identifying the outside as a front, and learning what the front shields.

Investigative Strategies and Tactics

Given all of the obstacles to the truth seen by investigative researchers, one might resign oneself to researching superficiality. However, there are a number of ways to confront the problems of falsehood and get at the truth.

Direct Experience

The most basic proposition of investigative research is to gain knowledge through direct experience rather than relying on what others say. Clearly this entails a form of participant observation discussed in Chapter 10. The emphasis in investigative research is on total immersion in the research setting, situation, and group, the *participant* side of participant observation. In this way, the researcher is able to obtain access behind the fronts, to get around the evasions and through the lies to the reality that these obstacles to validity cover up. Not only can the researcher uncover that which is intentionally or unwittingly hidden; he or she can also come to terms with the subtle meanings and nuances understood only by insiders. The problem of "going native" is considered minimal in that as long as the researcher maintains his or her identity *as a researcher*, the analytical process of interpreting the data will pull the researcher out of any native mind set.

Friendly and Trusting Relations

Since people are more likely to tell those whom they trust and consider friends the truth, it is important to develop these relationships in research. This does not imply that one must be an unknown researcher, and there is no reason that a fully known researcher cannot develop such relationships. Acting detached and aloof from those whom we study may look or sound more scientific, but in fact it places the researcher in a position of being an outsider, a stranger who cannot be fully taken into confidence. This does *not* mean totally committing oneself to the life-style of the subjects or even necessarily engaging in all of a group's habits. For example, in studying delinquent gangs, researchers have developed trusting and friendly relations with gang members but have never participated in a gang fight or other delinquent gang activities. One observer, a Catholic priest, who developed such relations with a delinquent Mexican-American gang openly disapproved of the majority of the gang's activities and did everything he could to change their behavior, but he was able to maintain friendly and trusting relations with them.[15] They would tell him many things they would never tell outsiders, especially whites. Obviously, there are problems in intentionally developing such relationships purely for research purposes, and no researcher is immune from developing loyalties and not wishing to reveal the dark side of a group's behavior. But even if such loyalties come to exist and secret knowledge is kept so by the researcher, he or she can still impart better information than those who do not have inside information in the first place. This is so because such researchers can put the meaning and actions in the proper context based on their knowledge of what's going on behind the scenes.

Independent Confirmations and Retests

In research situations of all sorts, whether it is one in which all of the subjects are trusted or all suspected, it is important to have **independent confirmations** and double checks of observed behaviors. On the one hand, independent confirmations allow others to confirm what one observer has seen and understood. On the other hand, such confirmations tell researchers to what extent personal biases, if any, enter into their observations. For the investigative researcher such independent confirmations are especially important, for it is assumed that something may be hidden, and if one researcher does find a hidden side to a group, it is necessary to have it confirmed independently so that the findings will be convincing.

Likewise, it is important to have **retests,** especially in cases where something seem to be highly unusual or significant. If one does find something behind the shield of lies, evasions, and fronts, if the backstage really does exist, it should be possible to have repeated observations and tests of it.

Appearances and Realities

One way we can see how an investigative researcher works is to look at a transcript of an interview with a research subject and to read the researcher's comments, which were added later. The following excerpt is from a study of nude beach members and sexual swinging. The person referred to as "Doc" is the subject.

DOC   My first wife and I slowly grew apart. One day, after we had been married fourteen years, she told them (our nudist camp) she was resigning her membership and, consequently, as a result of doing this, that I would not be allowed to come, nor would the children be allowed to come anymore. And I went out and filed for a divorce the next day.

RESEARCHER'S COMMENTS   Actually what happened was that Doc and Denise (his second and present wife) got caught having an affair by Doc's first wife. Both Denise and Lola (a close friend of both) saw Doc's present actions, playing around and all, as a repeat of the same thing. First, he would start playing around and then he would leave her.

DOC   My present wife and I lived together for about a year and have now been married about seven years. And we've been avid nudists before and since our marriage. I think truthfully that probably there are two things, and I'll put them in order, that my wife and I share in common that keeps our marriage together: (1) sex, we are very compatible, and (2) our love for nudism.

RESEARCHER'S COMMENTS   At this point in time, Doc's and Denise's marriage was anything but together. She had just returned from a six-month vacation with her boyfriend and there had been doubt that she would ever return. In fact, Doc was so certain that she would not return that he had given some of her clothes to Lola, which was a source of conflict between them when Denise returned.

DOC   I think that swinging will destroy a weak relationship, whether it be marriage or whatever. I think that it will strengthen a strong relationship. I think that swinging in many cases will revitalize the marriage as far as your sexual interests and desire [goes]. I think that everything is comparative. I think that in order to know how much you enjoy each other physically or sexually that it is absolutely necessary sometimes to compare. I think that variety truly is the spice of life. And I think we accept this in everything other than sex.

RESEARCHER'S COMMENTS   Doc may or may not have believed this at the time, but in later private statements to me Doc explained that Denise had failed to keep up with other people and had let herself go. That he looked at swinging as a way to get rid of her without telling her flat out to leave. Further, after we'd been studying him for about eight months, Doc fell in love with a beautiful 19-year-old, Darlene. He was terribly possessive of her and jealously guarded his "rights." He would hardly even share her conversation with the young men; he most definitely had no intention of "sharing" her so they could "compare." Doc also gave up his free sex life and played it 100 percent straight. No parties and no cheating.[16]

To summarize, investigative social research assumes everybody's got something to hide, either individually or collectively. In order to get through to the behind-the-scenes action, the researcher must first understand there is a backstage to social life, and then using both cooperative and conflict modes of interaction, gain access to it. Much of investigative social research is based on the cooperative paradigm in which friendship and trust are recognized criteria for sharing experiences. In fact, most of the investigative strategies discussed have been cooperative ones. On the other hand, a conflict mode is adopted when the researcher is faced with continual lies, evasions, and fronts. Usually this simply is a confrontation with evidence of intentionally misleading statements, not to be escalated into a fight, but rather to show that the information is not going to be used to harm, simply to understand and grasp the situation better. It is not the purpose of investigative social research to expose and embarrass, but rather to provide an accurate social science picture of a given researched phenomenon. If researchers cannot get behind the scenes, they cannot fully understand what is presented for all to see nor the meanings of group and situated activities. Thus, rather than being a seamy tactic of exposé, investigative research is simply a method for maximizing validity.

Unobtrusive Measures

A major concern of all social science researchers has been the problem of **reactivity.** Reactivity refers to the ability and even propensity of social actors to *react* to the fact of being researched. Thus, rather than studying natural social interaction, researchers study people performing for researchers. In the preceding section, we saw how investigative techniques were employed to break through misleading information; in this section, we will examine measurements that do not cause people to react.

Detective Work

In a study of detectives, an investigator was observed examining two license plates that had been recovered in a burglary case. The detective declared one to be the front plate and the other the rear plate, and the researcher, a sociologist, asked him how he knew which was which. The detective explained that the plates on the front of a car always had more bugs splattered on them than the rear ones.[17] Similarly, in an interview with two Scotland Yard detective inspectors, it was shown how they could tell whether an amateur or professional burglar had hit a house. Where professionals had operated, all the drawers were left open; in amateur cases, only the bottom drawer was open. When the researcher asked how that told them anything, the detectives explained that amateurs always began with the top drawer and worked their way to the bottom. As they went through each drawer, they had to close the one above until they came to the bottom drawer, which they left open. The professional, on the other hand, knew it was faster to start with the bottom drawer, opening each as he went *up* to the top drawer. In this way, he would not have to take the time to close each drawer after rummaging through it.[18]

In both of the above examples, the detectives used *unobtrusive measures.* Without interviewing any subjects or even seeing the actual behavior, researchers can measure what kind of social behavior occurred.[9] Since there were no social actors present during these observations, the measures were *nonreactive*—that is, social actors were not reacting to the presence of a researcher. The value of such measures, of course, is that what is measured is not influenced by the measuring itself—such as can be the case in interviews, experiments, and participant observation. Because these measures do not intrude on the subjects, we refer to them as "unobtrusive measures."

There are three categories of unobtrusive measures we will discuss: (1) physical traces, (2) archives, and (3) observation.[20] **Physical traces** consist of different kinds of matter people create, change, or destroy by their presence. We know, for example, that people have been camping in the woods by the presence of campfire remains. **Archives** are various kinds of records of transactions, anything from voting records to tombstones, all telling more than intended. Finally, **observations** refer to those kinds of viewings of social behavior that are not noticed by those being observed. Often, by knowing what to look for in people's behavior—the way they walk, dress, and generally look—one can see a great deal more than meets the casual eye. We can tell, for instance, by the way a person eats his or her meals whether the person is likely to be American or European. Americans cut their food with the knife in their right hand, and once they have cut it, place the knife down, take the fork from their left hand and place it in their right, and eat with their right hand. Europeans, though, keep their eating utensils in the hands they use for cutting, not making the exchange from one hand to the other.

PHYSICAL TRACES

HOLMES "Your neighbor is a doctor?"
WATSON "Yes. He bought a practice, as I did."
HOLMES "An old-established one?"
WATSON "Just the same as mine. Both have been ever since the houses were built."
HOLMES "Ah, then you got hold of the better of the two."
WATSON "I think I did. But how do you know?"
HOLMES "By the steps, my boy. Yours are worn three inches deeper than his."

(The Stockbroker's Clerk)

Sherlock Holmes fans through the years have always been thrilled by the great detective's ability to see something and make connections between it and an underlying behavior pattern. Most of the observations are very simple inferences (usually *not* deductions, as Holmes claimed), and once explained by Holmes become obvious to the mystified Dr. Watson and the reader. However, as Holmes pointed out, "The world is full of obvious things which nobody by any chance ever observes."[21]

Unfortunately, social science researchers make little use of the massive physical evidence that surrounds them. The one exception is the archeologist. By sifting through the unearthed remains of a civilization, the archeologist is able to tell us a great deal about a society—its structure, family life, beliefs, and many of its norms and values. If we look at our own society in the same way an archeologist would, we can begin to see all of the various physical signs of social behavior that tell us about society.

We can distinguish between two basic kinds of physical traces, *erosion measures* and *accretion measures*.[22] Erosion measures refers to the selective wear on some materials, as in the example of the stairs to Dr. Watson's office. Accretion measures are evidences of some deposit of materials. People's trash is a common accretion measure, both quantitatively and qualitatively.

Erosion Measures. By examining natural erosion, it is possible to tell something about people's interests, values, beliefs, and general behavior. For example, by noting the amount of wear on books in libraries, it is possible to get a general idea of which books people are interested in. In college libraries, some books show a great deal of wear but have only a few stamps in them, indicating they have been checked out infrequently. It's a good bet these books are used as texts in classes, and were checked out at the beginning of the term each semester by thrifty students saving on the cost of the text.

Traffic patterns also leave distinct erosion measures. Across campus, there are probably all sorts of shortcuts through the lawns, shrubbery, and elsewhere not paved by cement walks. The wear on tiles to different degrees will tell the researcher something about the interest people have in a display or exhibit. In one study of pinball, the researcher determined the most popular pinball machines by examining the wear of tiles in front of the machines.[23] All other kinds of erosion measures exist, and the use of them depends on the creativity of the researcher. It is only because of the failure to notice them that they have not been used to greater advantage.

Accretion Measures. Past behavior is indicated by what we leave behind as well as what we damage and erode. One of the more interesting accretion measures is the radio station dial. Dial settings tell us what kind of music people like and something about the people themselves. Younger listeners leave their dials on rock stations, while folks from rural areas may be more likely to tune in to country-western music. By noting the dial setting, we can determine a little about what people favor and, therefore, a little about them. (One enterprising auto repair shop owner had his mechanics note radio dial settings in cars to determine which stations he would use for advertising.)[23]

By close observation of what is around us, we can tell a great deal from both what *is* and *is not* present. For instance, smokers will usually notice the presence or absence of ashtrays, not only because they want a place to put their ashes, but also because the lack of ashtrays is a signal that smoking is not allowed or appreciated. Likewise, in rooms displaying "no smoking" signs, the presence of ashtrays belies the enforcement of the norm. The disappearance of spittoons signaled the end of indoor spitting, and perhaps the decline of chewing tobacco. The *lack* of locks on bicycles tells us of a low theft rate in the same way that the presence of such locks reminds us that there is a good chance of theft.

Finally, litter and trash tell us a great deal about what people have done. The lack of aluminum cans, both in trash cans and littering the roadsides, tell us such items have some value, while the presence of tin and steel cans, along with nonreturnable bottles, tells us they are of little or no value. We might be able to make predictions about the economy by the sheer amount of litter and trash. The less of both suggests less waste, fewer car trips, and lower consumption, indicating hard economic times, while more points to better times. However, we must be careful here, for changes in the amount of litter, for instance, can indicate an antilitter campaign or tougher laws for littering.

ARCHIVES

"The *Times* is a paper which is seldom found in any hands but those of the highly educated." *(The Hound of the Baskervilles)*

Having discussed archives in some detail in Chapter 9, we will only briefly review them here, emphasizing their unobtrusive aspects. First, we can distinguish between the *running record* and the *episodic* and *private record.*[24] Running records refer to those kept on a routine, ongoing basis. Actuarial records, such as birth, marriage, and death records are maintained by most societies, resulting in a demographic profile for researchers to investigate. An interesting instance of such records are tombstones, their size, inscription, and placement telling us about the status of the deceased. Other running records include various types of government records, such as crime records, the *Congressional Record*, and all kinds of mass media records. Since these records are public, we can assume that they are reactive—to journalists, the public-at-large, or some other audience. The trick is to locate unintended or nonreactive consequences from examining these archives, such as identifying a newspaper's political bias even though it proclaims itself to be neutral.

Episodic and private records are not as easy to obtain as are the more public running records, but they can be quite valuable. One of the more useful private records are those recording sales. The study of popular culture by sociologists can be greatly enhanced by knowing which items are "hot" at a given time. Records of roller skate sales and rentals, for instance, show the popularity of that fad rising in the late 1970s, as do earlier sales of jogging shoes and clothes. As with sales records, sales tags themselves document the social value placed on various items. Declining prices document the demise of a fad or fashion, while an increase heralds the opposite. One interesting example of a fad revealed by price tags was the rapid increase in the price of "depression glass" or "green glass" during the 1970s. Made during the 1930s and given away as a bonus for buying tanks of gasoline or sold by the set for a few dollars, depression glass became a collector's item during the late 1960s and throughout the 1970s. A plate that sold originally for a nickel could bring a price of twenty dollars or more once the collection of the glass became popular.

All other kinds of private archives, from suicide notes to consumer complaints, can be unobtrusive measures of social behavior. The decline in numbers of credit card applications, building permits, and similar financially related documents are a measure of the decline in the economy in the late 1970s and early 1980s. Refund slips could be used to document the degree of consumer awareness and willingness to act when sold flawed goods. Notes from teachers, showing atrocious grammar and spelling, were used to document the failing ability of teachers in our public school system.[25] Just by thinking about possible private archives available, the researcher adds another possible source of information to his or her arsenal.

OBSERVATION

"It was easier to know it than to explain why I know it. If you were asked to prove that two and two made four, you might find some difficulty, and yet you are quite sure of the fact. Even across the street I could see a great blue anchor tattooed on the back of the fellow's hand. That smacked of the sea. He had a military carriage, however, and regulation side-whiskers. There we have the marine. He was a man with some amount of self-importance and a certain air of command. You must have observed the way in which he held his head and swung his cane. A steady, respectable, middle-aged man, too, on the face of him—all facts which led me to believe that he had been a sergeant." (Sherlock Holmes explaining to Watson how he knew the identity of a man he had only just observed and not yet met, in *A Study in Scarlet*)

All of us probably know a great deal more about others from simple observation than we think we do. By and large, though, we do not use our "powers of observation" and are quite timid in making pronouncements lest we "jump to conclusions" or "prejudice" our views. Making judgments from observations is hardly a matter of stereotyping, and even though every judgment based on observation is not accurate, most are.

Beginning with the obvious kinds of observational judgments, we can move to the more subtle. For instance, if you walk by a classroom and see an older person standing and talking to a group of younger persons, you *assume* from your observations that the older person is the professor. Such a judgment would not be unwarranted, but it is possible that the older person is a student making a class presentation. However, we would not consider it "jumping to conclusions" if anyone suggested that the older person was the professor. Similarly, if we are walking down the street and see a group of youths wearing denim vests with the inscription "Savage Nomads" on the back, we might assume the group to be a delinquent gang and make a detour around them. However, they could be a bowling team, but it is doubtful and we'd rather not take a chance. (If we are "street-wise," we may well know the group is a street gang from smaller details of the group's dress, their way of standing, and their location.)

The more we learn how to read details and observe the same, we are able to tell more and more about others, just as we know how to read the larger signs. People's hands tell us whether they engage in manual labor or not, and their clothes are also a sign of their occupation. Certain occupations in which uniforms are worn, such as police work, signal clearly what a person does, but even out of uniform there are signs of a police or military career. Haircuts are usually shorter, there is a military bearing, and rarely do we find beards, except in the case of the Navy, and then the beard is accompanied by short hair.

We also can observe with our ears. Accents tell us something about the part of the country a person is from, but more subtle clues tell us something about social class. For instance, in differentiating upper class from middle class, we find the following nuances in choice of words:

Middle Class	Upper Class
bathroom	toilet
drapes	curtains
home	house

The use of idioms and slang, whether technical or cultural, provide further clues to a person's background. A novice skier, for instance, may know about "snow" and "slopes," but he or she may not be able to differentiate between the various kinds of snow and slopes—not to mention descriptive terms for equipment. When skiers meet, they can test each other's knowledge (and expertise) by simply listening to how each uses the language.

We can also glean states of mind by close observation—states the actor may be attempting to conceal. People's hands may be twisting below the table while aboveboard they are the very picture of composure. In one situation in which a young woman was presenting a paper to the class, she was the image of cosmopolitian sophistication in her upper body, while her foot kicked wildly below the desk—an outlet for her state of nerves. Chinese jade dealers used to closely observe the pupils of their customers' eyes to judge their interest and adjusted the asking price of the jade accordingly. If the pupils were dilated, this indicated a good deal of interest and a better bargaining position for the jade seller.

In short, observation is a matter of really looking and asking "What does that mean?" and "What can that tell me about those people?" The best place to begin is with yourself. Stand in front of a mirror and ask what a person who looked very closely at you could infer. Your clothes, the way you wear your hair, your hands, face and all the rest tell a story that someone can discern without even knowing your name.

To summarize, in this section we have examined different kinds of unobtrusive measures. The main idea behind such measures is that they are nonreactive ways of finding out about social behavior so that what data we gather is not a reflection of the research process itself. But, there is much more to the technique, for it forces the researcher to think critically and look closely at social behavior. So much of the social world we live in is taken for granted and therefore overlooked. Americans cannot see their "Americanness" until they are in a foreign country. Similarly, people from the Midwest may not realize that they have a "Yankee accent" until they spend time in the South. For the most part we cannot see all of the social characteristics of ourselves and others simply because we do not look, and because unobtrusive measures make us look at a lot of things we never thought of before, they are an added valuable tool for social science research.

Conversation Analysis

When we think of analyzing language and talk, gramatical structures usually come to mind; we think of diagraming sentences in high school. Moreover, we may think the language of conversation is structured very much like our written language, except that it is in the form of dialogue. However, when we examine the way in which people actually talk to one another, we find many ungrammatical forms, sentence fragments, interjections, grunts, other sounds, and even pauses, all of which make speech different from written language. Since conversations of one sort or another are the heart of verbal interaction, it is extremely important that we understand the structure of conversations and how people go about this most common form of social interaction.

Capturing Conversations

In order to analyze conversations, we must first put them into some kind of format that can be studied. We can listen to people talking and learn something about how conversations are structured, but in order to closely scrutinize them it is necessary to make special transcripts.

The first step in capturing a conversation is to make a *recording* of a conversation between two or more people. Usually the recordings are made unobtrusively so that there is no researcher effect, but there are a number of ways in which normal conversations of certain types can be overheard and recorded with the knowledge of the participants. For example, one conversation study used a transcript of a police interrogation.[27] Since all of the interrogations were recorded with the criminal suspect's knowledge, as well as that of the police interviewer, all parties to the conversation were aware of the recording. Likewise, it is possible to make recordings of classroom discussions, club meetings, and other get-togethers with the full knowledge of those involved. At first there may be some shyness in front of the tape recorder, but as time passes, the instrument is forgotten. Also, even though people may be careful of what they say when they know they are being recorded, this usually

TABLE 11.1 Transcript Conventions

Symbol	Meaning
(x)	Hitch or stutter by speaker.
//	Point where one speaker interrupts other speaker.
::::	Syllable is prolonged.
=	One speaker "latches" talk on end of other speaker, with no gap between them.
<u>word</u>	Heavy emphasis.
(?), (!), (,)	Punctuation marks for intonation, not grammar.
(word)	Word believed to be uttered, but researcher is unsure.
((description))	Indicates a description of conversation, not utterance.
(*)	Pause of less than a second.
(#)	Pause of about a second.
(3)	Pause of indicated number of seconds.
CAPS	Very heavy emphasis.[28]

has little or no effect on the structure of the conversation, but only on the content.

The second step in making a conversation available to analysis is to make a *transcript*. This is the heart of data recording in conversation analysis, for the transcript of a conversation captures not just what we hear in a conversation but literally every utterance. Similarly, conversation transcripts capture the silences—the little pauses and gaps—in talk. In order to see how transcripts are made, we will first look at the transcript conventions, and then at some examples of transcribed conversations.

TRANSCRIPT CONVENTIONS The signs and marks used to signify the various utterances in conversations are called *transcript conventions* or *symbols*. These conventions work very much in the same way as the grammatical marks in written language—commas, periods, and colons—do, except that they indicate what is uttered rather than what is written. The following symbols constitute a partial list of conventions used to reproduce to the fullest extent what transpired in a conversation.

Using these symbols, we will look at some transcripts and discuss briefly some concepts used in conversation analysis.

The first transcript is an excerpt from a conversation between a man and a woman. The letter "B" represents the female speaker and "A" the male, and the numbers to the side indicate the line number, used as a reference in analysis.

Male—Female Conversation

1		B	It's a funny thing about my father (#) I never really
2			<u>knew</u> him or even like saw him except for in pictures
3			but I still feel//
4		A	That you're more his did
5 (4)			
6		B	I guess so (*) I just I can't understand how he could
7			never even want to find out y'know what I turned out like
8			an'//I
9		A	[Ya'] mean how you developed or if you're still
10			alive or what[29]

Often the meaning of a line in a transcript will not make sense. For instance, line 4 does not seem to have any connection with the discussion and the sense of it is unclear, but most conversations, when closely transcribed, are full of what is apparently nonsense. Also, there are interruptions and both speakers talking at the same time. The bracketed portion of line 9, for instance, shows Speaker A talking at the same time as Speaker B.

The primary concepts used by conversation analysts are **sequences** and **talk turns.** *Sequences* refers to a chain of utterances in relation to some structure. For example, a simple sequence found in conversations is the "question-answer" sequence, abbreviated to QA sequence. When a question is posed, we expect the next utterance by the other speaker to be in relation to the question—an answer, a clarification, or another question.[30] Using this conceptual sequence structure, a study of police interrogations in which the police ask the questions and the suspect provides the answers, it was found that the structure of the QA sequence itself forced talk.[31] Other sequences discovered by conversation analysts have begun to map the structure of conversations in a way that provides some prediction and a good deal of insight into how conversations are organized.[31] The following excerpt is from a transcript of an interrogation, showing the suspect "stuck" with talking.

Police Interrogation

1		Q	Do you want to tell me about the weapon? Where you got it?
2			When you got it?
3 (#)		A	Ah (7) it was just about two weeks//
4		Q	[Uh huh]
5 (3)		A	Before Christmas (4) and I bought it from this at the
6			gun shop (#) ah (3) Whew :::: six, six-hundred block I can't
7			remember the exact address. Six (4) six something ah (4)
8			Parksburg.
9 (#)		Q	Six-hundred block Parksburg?
10 (#)		A	I think that's it.
11 (#)		Q	Do you know the name of the shop?

As can be seen in the excerpt, the police officer, "Q," always poses a question forcing the suspect, "A," to provide some kind of talk. The nature of the sequence obliges some kind of talk from the person questioned. In classrooms it might be noted that the instructor often uses this kind of sequence to start a general classroom discussion, obliging students to say something in reference to a question.

Finally, the concept of "talk turns" simply refers to the fact that people take turns talking. Ideally, while one speaker talks, the other(s) remain silent; then, at the appropriate time, others take their turns talking. One of the most interesting aspects of talk turns in conversation analysis is the artful manner in which people know exactly when to take their turn. Commonsensically, it is not difficult to know when it is one's turn to talk, but upon analyzing conversations, it is a tricky maneuver and the very essence of successful social interaction. Another aspect of interest in talk turns is when people interrupt and overlap another speaker. In the first excerpt we examined, it can be seen that the male speaker overlapped and interrupted the female speaker, but the female speaker never did the same to the male speaker. In her studies of interruptions, West found that sex and status roles played an important part of who was interrupted and who was not.[33] Those of a higher social standing routinely interrupted those of a lower standing, and while men often interrupted and overlapped women, they themselves did not typically suffer the same indignities at the hands of women. Such findings showed the falsity of stereotyping women as being the more talkative gender.

To summarize, conversation analysis is a relatively new methodology, but its application has been most useful in understanding the structure of conversations and thereby social interaction. In part, it has been an added tool in the area of sociolinguistics, but the primary contribution of the methodology is in examining microstructurss and processes in social intercourse. At the same time, conversation analysis has been used in some more traditional concerns in sociology, such as examining social status and roles, and as such it can be incorporated as a primary or adjunct method in many different kinds of social science research.

Summary

All three of the methodological areas discussed in this chapter—investigative social research, unobtrusive measures, and conversation analysis—provide the researcher with added tools for uncovering and analyzing social data. Each method has its strengths and limitations, but the real purposes of examining them is because each offers a somewhat different angle on the process of social research. Both investigative social research and unobtrusive measures given research the aura of a Sherlock Holmes case, a mystery to be solved.

Conversation analysis, on the other hand, takes mundane conversations and shows them to be full of an intricate structure under the surface of talk. Each method shows how research can uncover more than meets the uncritical eye, bringing to the surface new insights into social life.

archives Refers, in its broadest sense, to any record of social life that can be examined as data.

evasions Not providing information by redirecting the researcher down a false path.

fronts Collective lies that a group uses to hide information from outsiders. (The concept of *front* is used differently here than the conventional meaning developed by Erving Goffman.)

independent confirmation Having another researcher examine a finding to see if he or she can see the same thing. Sometimes independent confirmations use researchers of different sexes or races to determine if the researcher's gender or ethnic background affect an observation.

misinformation Information an informant believes to be accurate, but which is not.

observations In the context of unobtrusive measures, it refers to direct sighting or hearing of natural social behavior. (The term is also used in all other forms of research to indicate some kind of recordable data.)

physical traces Any physical artifact that can tell the researcher something about the social use of an area. Two major types of physical traces are *erosion* (wear on something) and *accretion* (what has been left behind).

reactivity The influence that a research methodology has on normal social behavior causing people to "react" to the method and not to independent variables of interest.

retest Refers to repeated observations by researchers to determine whether an initial observation was correct.

sequences Concept in conversational analysis referring to a chain of utterances in relation to some structure.

talk turns Refers to the turn a given person has talking in a conversation.

Notes

1. Jack Douglas, *Investigative Social Research: Individual and Team Field Research* (Beverly Hills, Ca.: Sage, 1976).
2. Eugene J. Webb, Donald T. Campbell, Richard D. Schwartz and Lee Sechrest, *Unobtrusive Measures: Nonreactive Research in the Social Sciences*, (Chicago: Rand McNally, 1966).
3. David Sudnow, ed., *Studies in Social Interaction* (New York: Free Press, 1972).
4. Erving Goffman, "Interpersonal Persuasion," pp. 117–193 in Bertram Schaffner, ed., *Group Processes: Transactions of the Third Conference* (1957).
5. Vivien Palmer, *Field Studies in Sociology: A Student's Manual* (Chicago: University of Chicago Press, 1928).
6. John Leonard (1970) quoted in Douglas, op. cit., p. 55.
7. Irwin Deutscher, *What We Say/What We Do* (Glenview, Ill.: Scott, Foresman, 1973).
8. Douglas, op. cit., pp. 57–59.
9. Ibid., p. 58.
10. Ibid., p. 59.
11. Gresham Sykes and David Matza, "Techniques of Neutralization: A Theory of Delinquency," *American Sociological Review* 22 (December 1957): 664–70.
12. Douglas, op. cit., p. 73.
13. Marvin B. Scott, *The Racing Game* (Chicago: Aldine, 1968).

14. Jack D. Douglas and Paul K. Rasmussen with Carol Ann Flanagan, *The Nude Beach* (Beverly Hills, Ca.: Sage, 1977).

15. Hilary McGuire, *Hopie and the Los Homes Gang* (Canfield, Ohio: Alba House Communications, 1979).

16. Douglas, op. cit., pp. 157−159.

17. Observation by one of the authors during research on detectives, 1973.

18. Related to one of the authors by a Scotland Yard detective during an interview, July, 1973.

19. Webb, op. cit., pp. 13−16.

20. Ibid., p. 3.

21. Sir Authur Conan Doyle, "The Hound of the Baskervilles," in *The Annotated Sherlock Holmes*, Vol. II, William S. Baring-Gould, ed. (New York: Clarkson N. Potter, 1967), pp. 3−113.

22. Webb., et al., op. cit., p. 36.

23. Ibid., p. 39.

24. Ibid., pp. 53−111.

25. *Time*, June 16, 1980, p. 59.

26. Webb, op. cit., p. 2.

27. William B. Sanders, "Pumps and Pauses: Strategic Use of Conversational Structure in Interrogations," in William B. Sanders, ed., *The Sociologist as Detective*, 2nd ed. (New York: Holt, Rinehart and Winston, 1976), pp. 274−281.

28. Emanuel A. Schegloff, "Notes on a Conversational Practice: Formulating Place," in David Sudnow, ed., *Studies in Social Interaction* (New York: Free Press, 1972), pp. 75−119.

29. Candace West, "Sexism and Conversation" (University of California, Santa Barbara: Unpublished Master's Paper, June, 1973). See also by Candace West, "Sex Roles, Interruptions and Silences in Conversation" in Barrie Thorne and Nancy Henley, eds., *Language and Sex: Difference and Dominance* (Rowley, Mass.: Newbury House, 1975); "Women's Place in Everyday Talk: Reflections on Parent−Child Interaction," *Social Problems* 24, No. 5 (June, 1977); and "Against Our Will: Male Interruptions of Females in Cross-Sex Conversation" *Annals of the New York Academy of Sciences* 327 (June, 1979).

30. Emanuel Schegloff, "Sequencing in Conversational Openings," *American Anthropologist*, Vol. 70, pp. 1075−95.

31. Harvey Sacks, "An Initial Investigation of the Usability of Conversational Data for Doing Sociology," in David Sudnow, ed., *Studies in Social Interaction* (New York: Free Press, 1972), pp. 31−74.

32. Sanders, op. cit., p. 276.

33. West, 1973.

12

Quantification and Data Reduction

Imagine a mailed questionnaire has been returned to you at the rate of 75 percent or that your trained and tired interviewers have just returned from the field—with 600 completed interviews. There are interview schedules stacked around the office, under the desk, and on top of filing cabinets. What now? Now that the data have been collected, now that all our questions have been asked and recorded, what happens next?

The beginning researcher is usually very concerned about what to do with data after it has been collected. Generally, there appears to be so much of it that it is almost frightening. Because there can be so much data, it is often difficult to conceive of a way to report it. Intuitively, we realize the information we have gathered must be boiled down to a workable form; it must be somehow reduced so it can be reported in an understandable way. At this point in the research process it becomes necessary to transform our data into a language understood by a computer. From the mountain of data described above, we can plainly see reducing it by hand is out of the question. It would be far too costly because of the time and labor involved. So we transform data into another language and let computers reduce and analyze it for us. How this is done is the topic of this chapter. We will discuss the various methods used in the process of quantifying and reducing vast amounts of data into neat summaries to fit into research reports. We will begin with a discussion of **computer cards,** and turn to the **coding** process and related topics later in the chapter. These discussions will include the keypunch process, the **precoding** of questionnaires and other research instruments, and the **post-coding** of research schedules as well. Also discussed are **edge coding** and **codebook** preparation, problems associated with **nonresponses,** and methods of **cleaning data** after they have been transferred to computer cards.

Computer Cards

There are several ways to "talk" to a computer. For example, one way is to type data directly into the computer using a console that looks like a television set with a keyboard. In some cases it is possible to simply *talk* to the computer, using standard English. Usually, however, the conversations begin when the researcher feeds a series of computer cards into the machine. If we understand the language written on the cards, and the computer does too, all we have to do is tell the machine what it is we want done with our data, and it will comply. It turns out there are several very basic and similar languages that can be written on computer cards, and it also turns out that most computers understand most of the languages available. For the time being we will forget about any specific language and discuss only the very basic dialects we will need to know. In later chapters we will talk about a specific language called SPSS, and when you find yourself in the company of hardcore "computer jockeys" or "**number crunchers**" (as they are sometimes called), be warned they will often speak about and talk in languages such as SAS, OSIRIS, Data Text, Fortran, and other strange tongues. But again, almost all of these languages begin with a conversation of computer cards.

A Description of Computer Cards

Many of us are already familiar with the standard computer card. They are used for paying bills and for class registration on most college campuses among other things. As indicated in Figure 12.1, they contain 80 columns upon which information can be stored. As can also be seen, each column is composed of a series of numbers, from zero through nine, running from the top of the card to the bottom. These numbers will be the means by which we will talk to the computer. It turns out that the data gathered from a survey or by some other data gathering technique can be stored on computer cards, and it will be helpful to begin thinking of each card as an *individual respondent* because all of the characteristics and answers respondents give are stored on these cards in much the same way they might be stored in any other recordkeeping system. For example, if our data had been transferred from questionnaires to computer cards, we could consult a particular card to find out how an individual respondent had answered our questions. However, the trick is to learn how to understand it when the computer begins to analyze them.

The Keypunch Machine

A **keypunch machine** is used to punch holes in computer cards, and this is how we store data on them. A keypunch machine has a keyboard very similar to that of a typewriter, but rather than simply typing letters or numbers on the cards, it actually perforates them, leaving a hole over a particular number in a specific column. This is how the computer will read our message, by finding and understanding what each particular hole is supposed to mean. Data are now considered *machine readable*. That is, by assigning one or more columns of a computer card to a specific variable from a data set, and assigning punches or holes within that column to the various values a variable can assume, the computer will be able to read and understand each of the cards. For example, suppose the sex variable was to be a part of our data set, and one of our questions asked respondents, "What is your sex? Are you a male or a female?" The response categories for such a question would look like this:

1. Male .... (   )
2. Female ... (✓)

Notice that before each of the response categories there is a number, which is called a *code* because we will assign either a 1 or 2 to each of our respondents, depending upon how they answer the question.[1] If the answer indicates a person is a male, he will be "coded" as a 1, if a person is female, she will be "coded" as a 2, and so on for questions that have more than only two possible responses. Now, if we had a completed questionnaire in front of us, and if we were sitting at a keypunch machine, for the respondent in our example we would punch a 2 on the card. The 2 indicates that that particular respondent is a female. It is necessary, of course, to know which column of the card will be set aside for this particular response. As we indicated earlier, researchers must assign a number (or code) for each value a variable can assume. If we look at Figure 12.1, we can again note that it has 80 columns; which of these columns is assigned the sex variable? This decision is left to the researcher, and the only really important thing to remember about assigning columns to variables is that *they be the same column for each respondent*. That is, if you were to assign the first column the sex variable, that column would be used to indicate each respondent's sex, *for all respondents*, on *all* of the cards used.

Let's explore another example. Suppose we had also included an age question on our questionnaire. The age of most respondents will take up two spaces or two columns on a computer card. Let's assign columns two and three to the age variable. On our questionnaire the age item might look like this:

"What was your age on your last birthday?"   26

As can be seen in the example, the respondent has indicated her age to be 26 years. We would now simply punch the numbers 2 and 6 in columns 2 and 3, respectively, of the card. Now the card would read 226, taking up columns 1, 2, and 3. Notice that for this question we didn't need a specific code to stand for the respondent's age because the response was recorded in actual years.

The main idea here is that each of our questionnaires or interview schedules represents a respondent, and each of the computer cards stands for a questionnaire, and each column on the card represents a single variable. Each variable takes on a different value which we have assigned to it, and the

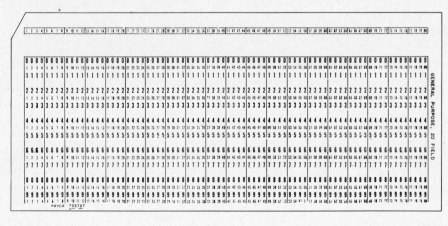

**FIGURE 12.1
The Computer
Card**

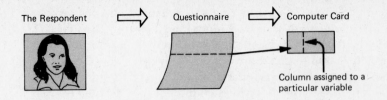

The Respondent → Questionnaire → Computer Card

Column assigned to a particular variable

value has been punched into its proper column. If we understand the "code" for our variables, we can pick up a card, and by inspecting the appropriate columns, understand the answers a particular respondent gave to our questions. Of course, the idea is to have the computer read the cards, and not us.

Coding Questionnaires

Precoding

Given that most of the data we gather is eventually *quantified* in the manner described above and placed on computer cards for computer analysis, it is a good idea to **precode** items on questionnaires, interview schedules, or observation instruments. That is, it is wise to assign codes before actually going to the field when we are constructing our research instrument. If the codes for each of the values a variable can take on are included on the instrument, it will make the process of transferring information to cards that much easier. Here is an example of how a precoded question would look:

> Should divorce in this country be easier to obtain, more difficult to obtain, or stay as it is now? Circle the number corresponding with the appropriate answer:
> Easier   1
> More difficult   2
> Stay as is   ③
> Don't know   9

In this example, the respondent circled 3, so we would simply punch a 3 in the column we had assigned for this particular question.[2] Precoding can save time, and time is money, so it is often better to precode questionnaires rather than to **postcode** them, that is, rather than wait until all the data has been gathered before deciding how to handle responses.

Postcoding

The term *postcoding* refers to the practice of coding questionnaires after they have been completed rather than while they are being constructed.[3] An example of an item that would require postcoding would look like this:

Should divorce in this country be easier to obtain, more difficult to obtain, or stay as it is now? Check the appropriate answer:

Easier   ( )

More difficult   ( )

Stay as is   (✓)

Don't know   ( )

A keypuncher would have to have memorized all the codes for this particular question before entering this response or he or she would have to go through each of the questionnaires before they were keypunched, and then assign the codes. This would require a good deal of work even if a sample were only a small one, and the extra step could increase the probability of **coding error.**

There are times, however, when it is impossible to avoid postcoding. For example, a few open-ended questions almost always appear on a research instrument, and they are impossible to precode because each respondent gives his or her own answer. What is done in cases where open-ended questions are used? Coders must first read each answer, and then place them in categories as they emerge from the responses. Each time a different answer is encountered, a new code is provided. After all the answers have been read, and after all appropriate codes have been assigned, then the keypunching can take place just as if the items had been precoded. We note again, however, that this requires additional work, an additional step, and the consumption of time that might otherwise be devoted to a different aspect of the research process.

Edge Coding

Edge coding is a method of precoding research instruments, making it very easy to keypunch directly from the original data.[4] To edge code, the outside margin of each page of a research instrument is marked to correspond with the codes we have assigned to our variables. After going through each questionnaire, each of the codes for the variables is placed in its designated spot in the margin, and this makes it easy for keypunchers to work directly from the edge-coded instrument. Edge coding eliminates the need for transferring data to **code sheets,** which are also called *transfer sheets*. Code sheets are very much like large computer cards, having 80 columns that correspond to the columns on a computer card. When data have been transferred from the original data-gathering instrument to the code sheets, the sheets themselves are given to keypunchers, who then transfer the data to cards. As we illustrate later in this chapter, there are times when it is impossible to avoid transferring data to code sheets, and there are times when this extra step in the coding process will actually be the most economical route for the researcher to take.

Codebook Preparation

We have used the term *coding* and we have mentioned *coders*, but we have not yet explained how it is that a coder knows what the codes mean or how they have been used. The preparation of a *codebook* prior to actually starting the coding process will provide coders a means for understanding each of the "numbers" assigned to the variables in a study. A codebook contains the definitions of the numerical codes used, and it also indicates the location of a variable on the computer card(s). Let us take a look at a sample page from a codebook:

Column	Variable Description	Codes
1–3	Q1 Respondent identification number	1 – n
4	Q2 Sex of respondent	1 = male 2 = female 9 = no answer
5–6	Q3 Respondent's age	Coded in years 99 = no answer
7	Q4 Marital status	1 = married 2 = widowed 3 = divorced 4 = separated 5 = never married 9 = no answer

In the codebook example, we can see that across the top of the first page are several headings provided to indicate (1) which columns are to be assigned to a particular variable, (2) a brief description of each of the variables, (3) the number of the question on the questionnaire from which the variable was derived, and (4) the actual codes to be assigned to the various values the variable can assume. The first three columns are reserved for respondents' ID (identification) numbers. Each returned questionnaire or interview schedule should be assigned its own ID number as soon as it is completed or returned by a respondent. The ID number is assigned by the researcher, of course, and not by the respondent. However, we have listed ID numbers as question 1 of the questionnaire. Under the "codes" heading we have indicated the code to be assigned. This "variable" will run from 1 to as high a number as there are questionnaires returned. The small "n" instructs coders to code ID numbers until there are no more respondents left to code. If there were 500 respondents, the first code would be "001" and the last coded ID number would be "500."

For question number 2 in our example, we asked respondents to indicate their sex. This will take up only a single column because there are only two values the sex variable can take: 1 for male and 2 for female, as shown under the "codes" heading. However, you can see we have decided to use the number 9 for the code to be used when respondents fail to check this item. The number 9 is often used in coding procedures to indicate no answer was given to a particular question, and you will find researchers across the country understand that 9 means no data were obtained for a question.

The third question asked respondents to indicate their age. This consumed two columns, since it was believed none of the respondents would be over 99 years old. Ages could theoretically run from 01 to 99 years, and because they were given in *actual years* on the questionnaire, they can be considered precoded. The instructions under the "codes" column tell coders that "age" is to be recorded on the computer cards just as it appears on the questionnaire. If respondents fail to respond to the age question, the code of 99 is used. Again, this is a standard practice among coders, using 9 or a combination of 9s to indicate no data or "no answer" was given for this question by the respondent.

The final question used in the example asks respondents to indicate their marital status. Six possible responses could be given to this question, ranging from 1 through 5 for the possible marital arrangements, with a 9 for no answer. This variable takes up only a single column but a variable could take up three, four, five, or more columns on a card. For instance, suppose our sample included 1,500 persons, and we wanted to include an ID number for each of them (which we would certainly want to do). The ID numbers for our data would range from 0001 to 1,500, and would take up four columns. If for some reason we had no ID number for a respondent (we can think of no good reason for not having one for every respondent, however, since we assign them the number no matter what they answer on a questionnaire), you would assign them a "no answer" or "no data" code of 9999.

A few final notes: Keep codebooks with data sets so you and the others you are working with can see just what it is that makes up the data that have been placed on the cards. Keep several codebooks on the same data set in a few different places in case one or more of them is lost or destroyed. If we have data but no codebooks, our information can be permanently lost, since we won't know what the codes mean without the book. Imagine what would happen if we didn't have a codebook and we wanted to reanalyze our data set five years after it had been gathered. Without a codebook we would be helpless.

A Note on Nonresponses

As we have suggested, the number 9 or a combination of 9s should always be used when there have been no answers given to an item. However, we must be careful to keep these nonresponse codes straight. For example, if a nonresponse code of 9 could be confused with an actual response code, that is, if one of the possible true responses could also be a 9, use 00 or some other numeral as your missing code value.[5] Later we will indicate how to tell the computer that 9s mean there is no data present, and the machine will handle this for us automatically. In our example of "age" we could have used 00 as our nonresponse code since there was no one in the sample who could have responded if he or she was "zero" years old! However, for some variables a zero could be a legitimate response, just as a 9 could be a legitimate response for some questions.

In summary, when a 9 or some combination of them (99,999, and so forth) can be an actual code for a value of a variable, use 0 or some combination of them (00, 000, and so forth) as a nonresponse code. Keep these nonresponse codes in mind when preparing codebooks and don't confuse them with codes indicating an actual response.

Coding

There are really several ways in which to handle the coding process.[6] So far we have suggested it is possible to precode questionnaires or interview schedules, and then keypunch directly from them. Because some of the items on our research schedule will be open-ended, we will have to postcode them, which means we have to go through each of our returned questionnaires or interview schedules and create the proper categories and codes for each open-ended item. This is often unavoidable even though it is an extra step, requiring additional time. Some researchers prefer not to keypunch directly from the questionnaire, and because they are usually going to have to go through each of the questionnaires anyway, to edit them and to see that they are complete, they prefer to transfer the data from the questionnaires to *code sheets*, which are simply large pieces of paper that look just like a very big computer card. These sheets have 80 columns just like computer cards but each line on a code sheet represents the individual respondent. As we have shown, every respondent is represented by a computer card. In this case every line on a code sheet represents a single computer card. This adds an additional step to the coding process when working with questionnaires and interview schedules. We will later see this is not always the case when coding other kinds of data. In any event, when using code sheets in this way, data are transferred to the code sheets from questionnaires, and then from the sheets to computer cards. Coders go over each of the questionnaires and write the appropriate code for each variable into the assigned column and space on the code sheet. Later, a keypuncher is given the sheets with the recorded codes. The keypuncher then transfers the information from the code sheets to the computer cards. Because each line on a code sheet represents an individual respondent, which means each line represents one questionnaire, there is usually less paper for the keypuncher to handle, making the job easier and quicker. But there are several additional reasons for following this kind of coding procedure, and we will elaborate on this below.

Coding Noninterview Data

Not all data come from interviews, and there are several additional sources of data used by social researchers often requiring quantification for computer analysis. For example, suppose we had an interest in conducting a content analysis to see which sociologists were publishing the most research.[7] We could answer this question by counting the number of articles and research notes appearing in professional sociology journals. No interviews are used to conduct this research, so how will we code it? We will have no precoded questionnaire to follow or to give to a keypuncher. What will we do?

Working from the Data Source

In this situation, researchers generally train coders to work directly from the data source, using code sheets to record the codes assigned to the variables in the study. Specifically, for the example above, we would go over our data (that is, professional sociology journals) and prepare a codebook for our coders to follow. The codebook would be constructed in the exact same way as if our data had been derived from interviews, except that there would be no precoded questions. Then, using the codebook as a guide, coders would transfer the data directly from the source to code sheets that would later be used to keypunch the information onto computer cards.

The same technique could be used if we wanted to analyze census data or for content analyses of all kinds (for letters, comic books, and so forth). The steps we would follow to code almost any form of data are basically the same:

Step 1 Review the data source; if it is from precoded interview schedules or questionnaires, it can be keypunched directly from the source; if it is not from a precoded questionnaire, we'll have to use code sheets before going to the keypuncher.

Step 2 Prepare a codebook for coders to follow; this step must be done no matter what our source of data because we will always want a codebook for future reference.

Step 3 Code the data following the codebook; transfer data to code sheets for sources other than precoded schedules.

Step 4 Check data codes and begin keypunching onto computer cards.

After our data have been transferred and stored on computer cards, we will be ready to begin our analysis. In later chapters we illustrate how simple it is to use computers in the analysis of sociological data.

Cleaning the Data

No matter how carefully we go about the coding and transferring of data, there are always errors that come about during the process. We often find, for example, that codes have been misread by the coders who were transferring data to code sheets or to the margins of the edge-coded documents. Keypunchers can also misread data, and in some cases codes will have been miswritten by interviewers in the field. Our task is to make our data as *clean* as possible, that is as free from error as we can possibly make it. When we clean our data, we begin with our finished **deck** of keypunched cards. There are two basic methods used to clean a data set; the **possible-punch technique** and **contingency cleaning.**[8]

THE POSSIBLE-PUNCH TECHNIQUE There are two different ways to use the possible-punch technique to clean data. First, we can have a computer program that will let us tell the computer to look for the specified "punches" associated with each card column. We can also use a **card sorter** to accomplish the same task. All that is required is to determine whether there are any incorrect punches in the columns. Of course, we know what punches should appear because we prepared the codebook and know what values each of the variables can have. For example, if the column for our marital status question had an 8-punch in it, we would know it contained an error. If the column we had assigned for the sex variable had an 8-punch in it, we would know there had been an error made because there are only three *possible punches* that column can contain: a 1 for males, a 2 for females, and a 9 for no answer. For the marital status column all possible punches would include 1 for married, 2 for widowed, 3 for divorced, 4 for separated, 5 for never married, and, finally, 9 for no answer. Any departure from all the possible punches appearing in a column constitute errors that must be corrected before analysis begins. To correct the error, simply locate the cards containing them, and check them against the information appearing on the questionnaire that is represented by an individual computer card. Because each card has an ID number corresponding to each questionnaire, there should be no problem matching cards to questionnaires and making the appropriate corrections.

CONTINGENCY CLEANING This method of cleaning data is somewhat more complex than the possible-punch technique but can still be used to accomplish the job. If we recall the contingency questions discussed in Chapter 7, we will better understand the strategy behind the contingency cleaning method. Remember that not all persons could respond to the second part of a contingency question because they had been "screened" by an earlier question, and the answer to the second part of the question was "contingent" upon their answer to the first. For example, if we had asked a question about actually experiencing an abortion, we would expect no male respondents would have been able to reply unless they used a "no response" category. Males just don't get abortions, and the fact that we found one who claims he did means an error has been committed somewhere in the coding process. Another example would be finding males in a data set who had answers listed for a question about the number of children they had given birth to. Again, giving birth to children is contingent upon being female, and if we find males responding to this kind of question, we can safely bet we have located an error.

A Note on Card Sorting

We have made reference to card sorting and card sorters throughout this chapter. We should note *card sorters* are machines that can be programmed to "sort" out cards according to any of the 80 columns of a computer card. The sorter separates the computer cards into piles depending on what punch appears in a column. The punches, of course, correspond to the codes we have assigned to our variables. For example, if we used a card sorter to check out a deck that included the sex variable, we would set it to sort on all possible punches for that item. The outcome would be three piles of cards, one for males, one for females, and one for "no response." If a fourth pile of cards were to emerge from the sorter, we would have detected an error. The card sorter is a handy tool we can use for cleaning data sets. If our sample is not too large, we can simply run the deck through a counter-sorter machine and sort out all the possible punches that are supposed to appear. When additional stacks of computer cards emerge from the machine, simply follow the same steps outlined above: match the card with the questionnaire using the ID number and make whatever corrections are necessary. And remember, if we leave our data dirty, we'll end up with misleading analyses, or as is often said around computer terminals, "Garbage in, garbage out."

Terminology

Before turning to our next topic, we should formally introduce some of the terms often used around computer centers, where most of our data-cleaning activities will take place. Some of these terms have already been used in this chapter, and you have probably gained some idea about their meaning. However, there are several additional terms you might encounter, which are described below.

Deck

When you hear the term **deck** used around a computer terminal, it will refer to a set of computer cards containing the same information for all the subjects or respondents in a study. Usually, a deck will contain a single computer card for each unit of analysis under investigation but in some cases records can be kept for individuals on several cards. At times, then, we will hear people refer to "deck number one" or "deck number two," and so on. This means the number of variables in their data set take up more room than is provided on a single 80-column card, and records must be stored on additional cards to make the data set complete. Therefore, a single respondent in a survey study could have as many as five cards, for example, containing his or her responses. Each set of cards is referred to as a deck, and a number is attached to each one to ensure it remains in the proper sequence for analysis.

Code

As we have seen, this term refers to the process whereby numbers are assigned to the various values that a variable can assume. *Coders* are the persons who are trained to go through questionnaires or interview schedules or some other data source and transfer responses from these documents onto *code sheets*, which are then used by *keypunchers* to store the data on computer cards.[9]

Codebook

A **codebook** is compiled by the researcher to tell the meaning of each code for all of the questions on a questionnaire or interview schedule.[10] Codebooks can also be prepared for other data sources, to include census data and information gathered for content analysis of all kinds.

Case

The term **case** refers to the units of analysis of a study.[11] In a survey study, each individual respondent would be a case. The number of cases in a study simply means the number of respondents in the study. You will also hear the term n used to indicate the number of cases, and n is symbolically used to indicate the same meaning. For example, people may ask, "What's your n?" meaning how many cases are in your study.

File

The term **file** refers to the data gathered for a given case or respondent.[12] For example, all the data gathered on respondent x would be considered his or her data file. Remember, a case does not have to be an individual human being; hence, the term *file* could be used to refer to all the data gathered for any given unit of analysis.

Record

A file can be composed of one or more **records.** In most instances, a record refers to a computer card that contains data for a single case.[13] However, as we have seen, there can be several records for a single case, and several cards may be necessary to store data for a single respondent.

Byte

When we hear the term **byte** used around the computer center, it will generally be in reference to a column on a computer card. It indicates the location of data within a record. When you hear the term byte, then, think of it as being a column on a computer card.[14]

Tapes and Discs

Not all data are stored on cards; sometimes they are stored on magnetic **tapes** or on **discs.** When this occurs the method of analysis is usually somewhat different than when using computer cards. Rather than store data on cards, information is transferred to tapes, which are mounted on special machines when researchers begin to analyze their data. In this text we do not specifically discuss tapes or discs because in most cases data will have to be placed on cards *before* it can be stored on one of these additional forms of datakeeping devices. When we hear people talk about *disc drives* or *mounting tapes*, they will be talking about another form of storing data similar to storing information on cards. If you stay around computer centers for awhile, you will probably begin to store data on tapes too, but until that time just think of the method as being similar to storing data on cards.

Number Cruncher

A **number cruncher** is a person who spends most of his or her time at the computer center analyzing data by means of the most sophisticated techniques available. Such persons are usually very interested in statistical analyses of data, and generally don't involve themselves in participant observational studies or studies that don't include the quantification of data. We often hear people say, "She's a real number cruncher," or "Let's go crunch some numbers." Number crunchers are also called "computer jockeys."

There are several additional terms you will hear when beginning to clean and analyze your data. The few we have listed should help you understand enough of the general "lingo" to get you started. After you have been at it for awhile, however, you will undoubtedly pick up several more terms than the ones we have listed here.

Summary

After data have been collected using an instrument such as a questionnaire (but not restricted to questionnaires alone), researchers who wish to do a quantitative analyses with a computer must code their data in such a way as to represent it easily on computer cards. Additionally, the coding must take into account conventions that will make the cards readily acceptable to the computer. A code is simply a value assigned to represent the various values a response can have. Some variables, like income or age, have natural numeric values and no special codes are required for them. However, other items have no numeric value and codes must be assigned. For example, a question might be answered with a simple "yes" or "no" and codes might be the numbers 1 and 2 to represent "yes" and "no," respectively. In some cases data will have to be transferred to coding sheets, while in other cases they will not. For instance, if questionnaires have been edge coded, they will not have to be reproduced on transfer sheets. On the other hand, if there are several open-ended questions on an instrument or if data are gathered from a source like the U.S. Census, or a content analysis has been conducted, we will have to transfer data to coding sheets before they can be keypunched. After data have been placed on the cards and the deck is complete, it is time to "clean" the data. Two methods were discussed to accomplish this part of the data-management process: contingency cleaning and the possible-punch technique. Our coders will know what codes should appear in which columns because our codebook will describe all of the variables in the study and list their locations. Remember, if data are left dirty, analyses can be misleading, and misleading analyses will add little to our understanding of social behavior. By thoroughly cleaning our data sets we will avoid the garbage-in-garbage-out epitaph and we will become full-fledged number crunchers. In the following chapter we describe some of the elementary analyses that can be conducted to discover relationships among the variables in our data. Some of these techniques will require that our data be stored on cards, and some will not. Given that survey studies are generally large ones, however, it is usually the case that their results are generated from conversations with computers. These conversations require quantified data placed on computer cards before the real talking can begin.

---

byte A column on a computer card.

card sorter A machine that sorts computer cards according to the assigned values that are to appear in a column; used in cleaning data.

case The units of analysis for a study; in survey research this is always the individual human being.

cleaning data The process of eliminating errors that may have come about through the coding process (see *possible-punch* and *contingency cleaning techniques*).

code sheets Also called *transfer sheets;* used to transfer data from original source to cards.

codebook A book containing the definitions of the numerical codes used in a research project; indicates the location of a variable on computer cards.

coding The assignment of numerical values to the various categories of a variable to be used in the analysis of data.

coding error The errors coders can make while transferring data from questionnaires to transfer sheets, or by keypunchers who can punch the wrong code onto a computer card; the possible errors that can be made during the coding process.

computer card An 80-column card used for storing data; it is used to "talk" to computers.

contingency cleaning A method of cleaning data; the researcher inspects data to see that only those who are supposed to have answered a question have answered it.

deck A set of computer cards containing the same information for all of the respondents in a study.

edge coding A method of precoding instruments making them very easy to keypunch directly from original data; uses the outside margin of each page of a research instrument as place to put codes corresponding with variables.

file The data gathered for a given case; each respondent would have his or her own file.

keypunch machine A machine used to punch holes in computer cards as a way of storing quantitative data.

nonresponse When respondents fail to reply to a question; usually coded with a "9" or a series of "9s" or some other numerical value.

number crunchers Persons who spend most of their time around computer centers quantitatively analyzing data; also called *computer jockeys.*

possible-punch technique A method of cleaning data; researcher looks for only the punches that should be in a column, if some other punch is present, it is corrected on the computer card.

postcoding The practice of coding research instruments after they have been completed instead of before going to the field.

precoding The assignment of codes prior to going to the field with a research project, and placing those codes on the research instrument itself; this can make coding and processing a much simpler process.

record A file can be composed on one or more records; a computer card might contain data for a single case and this would be a record.

tapes and discs Recordkeeping devices similar to cards.

1. William J. Goode and Paul K. Hatt, *Methods in Social Research* (New York: McGraw-Hill, 1952), pp. 315−325, offer a detailed discussion of the coding process and some of the problems associated with it. Fred N. Kerlinger, *Foundations of Behavioral Research*, 2nd ed. (New York: Holt, Rinehart and Winston, 1973), p. 417, also suggests detailed discussions and instructional materials are available at small cost from the Institute For Social Research, University of Michigan, Ann Arbor, Mich. 48104.

2. The question used in this example was taken from *General Social Surveys, 1972−1978: Cumulative Codebook* (Roper Public Opinion Center, New Haven: Yale University), p. 136.

3. Kenneth D. Bailey, *Methods of Social Research* (New York: Free Press, 1978), pp. 312−313, offers an excellent introduction to the postcoding process.

4. See Earl R. Babbie, *The Practice of Social Research*, 2nd ed. (Belmont, Ca.: Wadsworth, 1979), p. 370.

5. Bailey, op. cit. pp. 314−315, points out that leaving blanks for nonresponses should be avoided at all costs because different computer programs handle blank spaces in different ways. Earl R. Babbie, *The Practice Of Social Research* (Belmont, Ca.,

Notes

Wadsworth, 1973) p. 194, also strongly recommends assigning a numerical code for nonresponses.

6. David J. Armor and Arthur S. Couch, *An Introduction to Computerized Social Data Analysis: Data-Text Primer* (New York: Free Press, 1972), pp. 13–23, offer an excellent introduction to the conventions of data coding.

7. This example draws fram a research experience of one of the authors. See Michael D. Grimes, Thomas K. Pinhey, and June Phifer, "Departmental Prestige in Rural Sociology: Its Measurement and Comparison with General Sociology Prestige Hierarchies," *Rural Sociology* 43, No. 1 (1978): 7–16.

8. See Babbie, op. cit., pp. 372–373, and Bailey, op. cit., pp. 317–319. Both discuss this topic.

9. Armor and Couch, op. cit., p. 13.

10. See also ibid., pp. 20–21, and Bailey, op cit., p. 430.

11. See also Babbie, op. cit., p. 362.

12. Compare with ibid., p. 362.

13. See also Armor and Couch, op. cit., p. 141.

14. See Babbie, op. cit., p. 363.

13

Analysis of Relationships

After our data have been stored on computer cards and cleaned or after they have been put in condition for analysis, it is time to begin thinking about *how* we will analyze and present them. Of course, long before we had gone to the field with our project, we should have made some decisions about which variables in our study would be related to others. More specifically, researchers should state their hypotheses of the nature of the relationships to be found among certain variables prior to constructing research instruments, drawing samples, and so forth. Toward the end of a study, when analyses are started, theories consulted at the very beginning return to center stage. Specifically, researchers know what relationships to look for because the theory that guided their work tells them which associations and relationships they should find. This is what guides them in the preparation of questionaire items and tells them which variables from the census data—or some additional data source—are the important ones to look at, and, therefore, how to begin their analyses.

Types of Analysis

With the introduction of the computer in the early 1950s, sociologists began to rely more and more upon the **multivariate analysis** of data.[1] When the term *multivariate analysis* is used, it is intended to mean an analysis of several variables at one time. When researchers simultaneously examine relationships among several indicators, for example, when they attempt to examine status attainment by focusing on education, income, occupation, and parents' income, they are conducting a multivariate analysis. There are several ways in which to conduct a multivariate analysis, and this form of data analysis is not a single method. Instead, we could select from several multivariate techniques, depending upon the nature of the relationships our hypotheses indicate we should look for. Status attainment researchers have often turned to *path analysis* as their primary multivariate analysis method, but several additional multivariate techniques are available: factor analysis, multiple classification analysis, multivariate nominal scale analysis, multiple regression, and multiple correlation are examples of techniques a researcher might select. However, it is best that we learn to walk before we try to run so we will put the multivariate techniques aside for more advanced presentations and will introduce here only the basic analysis techniques. To understand how multivariate techniques work we will first have to understand how the basics of all statistical manipulations operate. First, we will examine *univariate* analysis, and then turn to **bivariate analysis** (see Table 13.1). Toward the end of this chapter we will look at trivariate analysis, a very basic multivariate technique we might wish to use to begin our data analysis. However, we will move slowly, and pick up speed only after the groundwork has been laid.

Table 13.1   Types of Analyses

Univariate Analysis	=	Single Variable
Bivariate Analysis	=	Two Variables
Multivariate Analysis	=	Several Variables

Univariate Analyses

When we examine a univariate distribution, we are examining a *single variable*. Although **univariate analysis** is at the bottom of the scale when compared with the more complex multivariate techniques, it is a very useful descriptive tool to have in our analysis kit. For example, imagine we wanted to describe a sample in terms of its marital status. We could begin by simply listing all the persons in your sample and beside their ID (identification) number indicate if they have ever been married, widowed, divorced, and so on. Such a method would consume a great deal of space in a research report, especially if our sample were a large one, and although it would provide its readers with the most detailed description of the marital status of the sample, it would hardly be a practical method for presenting the data. What is needed is a method to present this information without providing so much detail that our readers are overwhelmed with individual figures for each member of the sample. These data must be reduced so that readers will know at a glance, without being confused, what the distribution of marital status is for the sample. A simple frequency distribution can solve our problem.

FREQUENCY DISTRIBUTIONS   A **frequency distribution** is a count of the number of cases within the categories of a variable.[2] Let us look at an example to help us better understand how frequency distributions work. Suppose we have listed the suicide rates for the twenty-five largest cities in the United States:

3	2	3	6	7
2	7	9	8	6
5	9	2	9	6
9	3	5	1	4
7	9	2	3	8

Even a very careful examination of these figures will leave most readers unclear about the incidence of suicide in large cities, even though there is all the "detail" possible in the data presented. In fact, there is too much detail and this generally confuses readers rather than enlightens them. If we group these data and then list the frequency of suicides for each group, the presentation will be better organized and much clearer to readers. Below we have listed some possible ways in which these data could be grouped:

Class Interval = 1		Class Interval = 2		Class Interval = 5	
Suicide Rate	**Frequency**	**Suicide Rate**	**Frequency**	**Suicide Rate**	**Frequency**
1	1	1−2	5	1−5	12
2	4	3−4	5	6−10	13
3	4	5−6	5	TOTAL =	25
4	1	7−8	5		
5	2	9−10	5		
6	3	TOTAL =	25		
7	3				
8	2				
9	5				
TOTAL =	25				

An examination of the various intervals we have selected for this example indicate that when intervals are too narrow, as in the case where we used a class interval of 1, there is still too much data for readers to make sense of. On the other hand, when intervals are too broad, as in the case of the 5-interval example, too much information is lost and the distribution of suicide rates is still unclear. The example using class intervals of 2, however, provides readers with a much clearer picture of the suicide rates in the twenty-five largest cities in the United States. The construction of the class intervals themselves is a very important aspect of the frequency distribution. As Malec suggests, there are actually two basic operations associated with constructing frequency distributions.[3] First, researchers must decide the appropriate number of categories or class intervals into which they will group their data; and second, the data must be sorted and counted and placed into the categories selected. The first task is the most crucial, and there are four rules that should be followed when attempting to determine class intervals.[4]

Rule One. Use at least six and not more than fifteen classes. When too few classes are used, as in the example of class intervals of 5, *homogenation* of the data will result, and the distinction between classes will become "blurred." On the other hand, too many classes will result in a picture that is not much different from ungrouped data.

Rule Two. Define classes so that each case will be included. If there are extremely low or high scores in our sample, we will have to make sure they are included in a class also. For example, if we added a suicide rate of 25 to our example, we would have to add additional classes to ensure that it was also included in the distribution of scores. In this case our "2-interval" example would have to take on 8 additional classes beyond what it has in the illustration, and 7 of these class intervals would report a frequency of zero. It would be possible, under certain circumstances, to simply add an interval labeled "11 and above" to the categories. This would solve the problem of having 7 class intervals listed with nothing in them, but it would make impossible certain statistical operations that might become necessary later, and would also not make clear just how many cases fit into the "11 and above" class. That is, a reader would never really know what the highest score for that interval was. Another possible solution that is *not* recommended would be to create class intervals that had "gaps" between them. For instance, we could rewrite the 2-interval illustration to finish off as 7−8, 9−10, and then 25−26. However, there should never be any gaps between classes, and in this case we would have jumped over about 7 intervals!

Rule Three. Each case should fit into only one class. We have heard this rule several times before as it follows the rules associated with the nominal scale of measurement. Stated somewhat differently, classes should not overlap one another. We should never include classes such as 1−2, 2−3, and so forth. If we did, where would we place a city that had a score of 2? Remember, a single score can't be placed in two categories at the same time.

Rule Four. Whenever possible, class intervals should be of equal size. Each class should cover the same range of scores as every other class. If the boundaries of the intervals change from one class to another, it becomes very difficult to make comparisons between them, and this could make further analyses misleading, difficult, and in most cases, impossible. Stated differently, we should not begin a distribution with a range running from 1−2 and then switch to a range that was three units wide: 3−5. *Each interval should be the same width.*

When data are put into categories or class intervals as illustrated here, there is always a loss of detail that goes with the process. However, if proper precautions are taken, as indicated here, the result is usually a much clearer and more understandable picture than would be the case if data were left in raw form.

PERCENTAGES Before moving to an illustration of bivariate distributions, we should note that most sociological data are often presented in percentages. By converting data into **percents** it becomes possible to make meaningful comparisons between various groups of data. For example, suppose we had two communities represented in a data set and we wanted to compare them on a key variable. We could begin by constructing appropriate class intervals for the variable of interest for both communities:

Raw Data

Community 1		Community 2	
White	29	White	34
Black	22	Black	69
Others	241	Others	541
TOTAL	292	TOTAL	644

Which of our communities has the larger relative number of white respondents? To calculate the various percentages to answer that question, simply divide the number that appears in each separate category by the total, then multiply by 100. It turns out that *per cent* means *per hundred* and thus remembering these calculations is an easy thing to do. In our example, we could begin by dividing Community 1's first category (White) by the total: 29/292 = .10; we would then multiply the resultant figure by 100. This turns out to be 10 percent, after rounding to the higher number. Progressing through the data we would finish with the following:

Percents

Community 1			Community 2		
White	(29)	10.0%	White	(34)	5.2%
Black	(22)	7.5%	Black	(69)	10.8%
Others	(241)	82.5%	Others	(541)	84.0%
TOTAL	(292)	100.0%	TOTAL	(694)	100.0%

In our example we have included the raw data from which these percentages were calculated, and when we are preparing a table for presentation in a research paper, we will always want to include these individual figures for each category so that readers would be able to follow our work and recalculate the percentages themselves.

Note that at first glance Community 1 appears to have fewer whites than Community 2 (see "raw data" table). This is the case when we examine the raw data before they have been transformed into percentages. After percentage calculations have been made, however, we can see that the larger relative number of white respondents actually live in the first community and not the second (see "percents" table). If we had drawn conclusions based on our first presentation of data, they would have been misleading. We would have concluded that more white respondents lived in Community 2. By using percentages we are *standardizing* for the size of each community by calculating the number of individuals who would be in a given category if the total number of cases were 100 and if the proportion in each class remained unchanged. This is why percentages always sum to 100.[5]

RULES OF THUMB There are some rules of thumb associated with calculating percentages. First, always report the number of cases along with the percents calculated (as mentioned above). Second, never compute percentages unless the total number of cases is at least 50 or more.[6] Otherwise, comparisons will be misleading.

WHAT ABOUT NONRESPONSES? As illustrated in Chapter 12, each nonresponse should be given a code so it can be identified the same way as any other variable. However, in our examples we failed to list a nonresponse category. It is possible the data we used for our community descriptions came from survey responses, and that some of the respondents didn't indicate their race. What happens to these persons in the calculation of percentages? There are essentially two ways to handle nonresponses when reporting data: (1) we can subtract the total number of nonresponses from the sample for a given variable and use this smaller total for the calculation of percentages, or (2) we can use the total sample size *including* nonresponses, and indicate a category for them with a percentage just as if they comprised any other category. There are some advantages and disadvantages associated with both methods. For example, one of the major benefits of retaining nonresponses in the data set is that this makes the base figure a constant from one analysis to the next. One reason for excluding nonresponses is that they don't represent a substantive category of the variable being analyzed. Rather, nonresponses are more like error or residual categories. Our decision to include or exclude nonresponses will depend upon the focus of our study and the importance we give them.

There are also statistical techniques available that will help describe the "average" or "central tendency" of a univariate distribution. Three measures of central tendency are commonly used: the **mode,** the **median,** and the **mean.**[7]

THE MODE The mode refers to the most frequently occurring value of a variable in a distribution. The mode is actually the name (or number) of the class interval possessing the largest frequency. As such, it is our *best guess* of the average characteristic under analysis for the entire sample. For example, suppose we had data describing the various classes at a university, and that we wished to know from these data the *average* class standing at that particular school. Because the mode is a summary statistic for the entire distribution when data are measured on a nominal scale, we will simply look for the category with the greatest frequency:

Class Standings at State University	Frequency
Freshman	1,800
Sophomore	2,000
Junior	1,500
Senior	1,200
Graduate	900

In the illustration the modal category is sophomore because this is the most frequently occurring value of the "class" variable being analyzed.

THE MEDIAN The median is the value in a distribution with the property of having the same number of scores with smaller values as there are scores with larger values on either side of it. The median, then, is that point in a distribution which divides an ordered set of scores into equal parts. Let us look at an example. Suppose we were able to rank a group of students by socioeconomic (SES) background:

Student	Rank
A	5
B	4
C	4
D	④
E	3
F	2
G	1

The students are placed in an *array* from the highest score to the lowest, and, as can be seen, several students have "tied" on the social class measure. For our illustration the middle case or the median is the fourth score from either the bottom or the top of the distribution. This case is represented by Student D, whose rank is 4, and this is the median rank for the data because there are the same number of cases with smaller scores as there are scores with larger values on either side of it. What is the modal score for this distribution, by the way? It is the most frequent score, so in this sample the mode would be 4 also.

It was very easy to locate the middle case in this example because there were an odd number of students. What would have happened if there had been an even number of cases? Let us rewrite our example for this contingency:

Student	Rank
A	5
B	4
C	4 ⎫
D	3 ⎬ 3.5
E	3
F	2

Now we have an even number of ranks and there is no middle case to select for the median. The actual middle case is located somewhere between Students D and C, who have scores of 4 and 3. In this case both scores would technically qualify for the median because they divide the distribution into parts with equal numbers falling both above and below these points. However, we can't have two medians. In this case, convention dictates that we locate the median halfway between these two ranks. This is accomplished by summing the two scores and dividing by the number of scores that were summed. Thus, 4 + 3 = 7/2 = 3.5, which for this example is the median.

Note, also, that in the present example there are two sets of scores that qualify for the modal category of the distribution, represented by the ranks 3 and 4. What then is the mode for these data? Because there are essentially two modes, this is called a *bimodal* distribution. When we encounter this type of distribution in our analyses, we will not be able to place as much confidence in our measure of central tendency because there will be two averages rather than one.

In summary, to calculate the median first arrange the scores of a distribution in an *array*, from the highest to the lowest scores. Then determine whether N, the number of cases, is odd or even. If N is odd, the middle case will be the median. However, if N is even, the two middle cases must be used to calculate the median. If these two scores are the same, if they are tied, the median takes that value. If they differ from one another, the median will be located halfway between the two.

THE MEAN The mean is a single-number summary of the total distribution when scores are measured at the interval level. Like the mode and the median, it is an average or measure of central tendency. To find the mean of a set of scores, simply add them together and divide their sum by the number of scores in the set. For example, suppose we wished to know the average age of a group and we had gathered the following data:

The Age of 25 Persons				
22	23	17	19	25
25	18	19	32	15
19	18	26	15	31
20	19	22	16	19
16	26	30	26	44

To calculate the average score for these data, we would simply sum them and divide the total by the number of cases we are analyzing. The sum for these data is 562, and the total number of cases is 25. To find the mean, we would simply divide 562 by 25 and obtain 22.48 (562/25 = 22.48).

A Comparison of Measures of Central Tendency: The Mean, Median, and Mode

One group of basic statistics involves assessing the central tendencies of distributions. The mean, median, and the mode are examples of this type of statistic, and we have given examples of each measure. As indicated, these statistics are used to locate center points and are used for comparisons and in determining change. Using the following data as an example, each are reviewed and explained.

Monthly Income

	Group 1		Group 2		Group 3
1.	$1,000	1.	$2,000	1.	$700
2.	900	2.	1,800	2.	700
3.	800	3.	1,000	3.	700
4.	700	4.	100	4.	700
5.	700	5.	100	5.	700
6.	500	6.	100	6.	700
7.	400	7.	100	7.	700
8.	200	8.	100	8.	700
9.	200	9.	100	9.	700
	$5,400		$5,400		$6,300

Each group has 9 members, and they have been arranged in descending order according to monthly income. To find the *mean* income of any of the groups, simply divide the total of all incomes by the number of cases. Group 1 has 9 cases totaling $5,400, and by dividing $5,400 by 9 we find the mean of $600. Group 2 also has a mean of $600, and Group 3 has a mean of $700. Thus, based on mean income, Groups 1 and 2 are the same.

A *median* is the value of the middle item when the items have been arranged in increasing or decreasing order (an array). In the three groups presented, item 5 is the median, since it is midway between the first and last items. Thus, Groups 1 and 3 have a median income of $700, and Group 2 has a median income of $100. Now, based on medians, Groups 1 and 3 are the same.

A final measure of location is the *mode,* and it is based on the category with the highest frequency. In Group 2, $100 is the modal income, since it is more frequent than any other income figure. That is, more members earn $100 than any other amount. Group 1 has two modes, since there are an equal number of members who earn $700 and $200. Finally, since all of the items in Group 3 are $700, its mode is $700. Note also that the mean, median, and mode in Group 3 are all $700.

Before making comparisons using any one of these statistics, the researcher is cautioned to first look at the distribution. For example, even though Groups 1 and 2 have the same mean, the groups are different in that they are differently distributed. Similarly, Groups 1 and 3 have the same median, but Group 3 has an equal distribution, whereas Group 1 has an unequal distribution. In making comparisons or in looking for changes, the analysis will be much better if more than one statistic is employed.

When data are thoroughly examined, and when all three measures of central tendency are used by the researcher to describe a data set, it is often discovered that there is a wide difference between the mean, median, and mode. However, when all the observations in a data set are very similar, when scores do not differ from one respondent to the next, the mean, median, and mode will be very close to one another. Whether these measures are similar or not depends on the distribution itself. The additional examples of these statistics presented in the box on p. 268 provide a comparison of these three measures, and from these examples we can see it is both a good idea to examine each measure as a researcher as well as from a consumer's point of view.[8] That is, if we are not sure what kind of an "average" a person is talking about, we can be misled.

Bivariate Analyses

Bivariate analyses examine two variables together in a single table and allow researchers to explore the relationships between the two. When bivariate tables are constructed they are called *cross-tabulations* or **contingency tables.** When the variables in a bivariate presentation have only two values (like the sex variable), that is, when our variables are *dichotomous*, the resultant table is called a **two-by-two table** or a *fourfold table.* For the sake of clarity, we will use only the simplest of contingency tables in our presentations, those with only four **cells** (fourfold tables).[9]

Convention dictates that one variable in a bivariate table be labeled the *column variable*, which is placed at the top of the table so its columns run vertically down the page. The second variable, called the *row variable*, is placed to the lefthand side of the table so its rows will run across the page horizontally. The column variable is generally the independent variable in the analysis, while the dependent variable is generally the row variable. Thus researchers can compute percentages to add to 100 down the page, making comparisons among the values across the cells at the top of the table.

SETTING UP AND EXAMINING TABLES   To demonstrate how a table is constructed we will use a data set containing fifteen sets of scores. One score is an environmental concern score and the other indicates the sex of respondents. The table is set up as shown, and because the environmental concern score is the dependent variable in this study, it is placed on the left side of the table. Respondents could score an "H" for high on this variable, or an "L" for low. The sex variable is placed at the top of the table because it is the independent variable for the analysis.

Because it has two columns and two rows, making four cells in the **body of the table,** this is a fourfold or two-by-two table. The actual mechanics of setting it up include counting the number of males with high or low scores and placing the number in the proper cells, then counting the females with high or low scores and placing that number in the appropriate cell. Each of the boxes in our illustration is called a *cell*, although researchers do not outline cells as we have in the example:

Key	Respondent ID	Environmental Concern Score	Sex Score
M = male	A	L	F
F = female	B	L	F
H = high	C	H	M
L = low	D	H	M
	E	H	M
	F	L	F
	G	L	M
	H	H	M
	I	H	M
	J	L	F
	K	H	F
	L	H	F
	M	L	M
	N	H	M
	O	H	F

Environmental Concern By Sex

Environmental Concern	Sex		Row Totals
	Male	Female	
High	╫╫╫╫ l 6	l l l 3	9
Low	l l 2	l l l l 4	6
Column Totals	8	7	15

The frequency placed in each of the cells is called a **cell frequency.**

TABLE TERMINOLOGY A more detailed example of a two-by-two table illustrates both proper table construction as well as the terminology associated with it (see Figure 13.1). As can be seen, the far lefthand column of a table is called the **stub,** and this is where the dependent variable should be listed. The "rule" of placing the dependent variable in this location, however, is not always adhered to by every researcher, so it is wise to be certain of how others have set up their tables before attempting to interpret them.

The independent variable is placed at the top of a table so its categories or values run across it horizontally. This is called the **heading,** and in our illustration this variable is represented by a measure called "Value of Natural Areas." The **title** of the table should also appear at the top of it, and should be written so readers will clearly understand what data the table contains. We should include in a title the dependent variable, whether the table contains frequencies or percentages or some other measure, the independent variable(s), and the kind of case upon which the measurements were taken. As

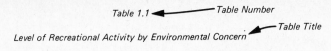

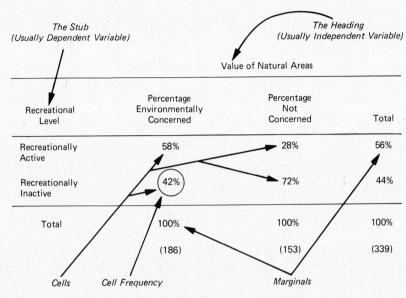

**FIGURE 13.1
Example of Table
Construction
and Terms**

Loether and McTavish point out, if a table is a percentage table it is important to indicate the base upon which the percentage was computed.[10] This is usually placed in brackets at the bottom by the total percentages. Otherwise, cell frequencies are omitted from percentage tables, as in the example.

The totals listed on the righthand side of the table and across the bottom of the page are called *marginals*. These are actually no more than the univariate distribution of each separate variable.

The *body* of a table is composed of *cells*. In the example, because we are illustrating a two-by-two table, there are four cells making up the body of the table. Each cell contains a *cell frequency*, which is the number or percentage that corresponds to the cross-tabulation of responses making up that particular cell. For example, all those persons who were considered recreationally active in our sample (Figure 13.1), and who were also described as being environmentally concerned, are placed in the upper lefthand cell of the table. Those who were active but not concerned are placed in the upper righthand cell, and so on until the table is filled. It should be noted that tables can be much larger than simple fourfold tables, and the number of cells can become numerous. The same methods for table construction work just as well, however, for variables that have more than two values. That is, three-by-three tables, four-by-four tables, and so on can each be constructed using the rules presented here.

Before we conclude our discussion of bivariate analyses, we must consider one additional point. Notice in our examples that the *low* categories of the independent variable, where there are low categories on that variable, are listed at the left and the high category at the right. For the dependent variable the highest categories should be at the top of the table and the low categories at the bottom. This procedure is not unlike the labeling practices used to construct graphs and other charts, although, as Loether and McTavish note, this convention is not always rigidly adhered to, and researchers should be careful to check the layout of a table before beginning to make interpretations.

Trivariate Analyses

So far we have looked at ways to examine a single variable (univariate analyses) and two variables (bivariate analyses). We now turn to trivariate analyses, the examination of three variables simultaneously, which is the basic way of conducting a multivariate analysis. Indeed, there can be several occasions when it is desirable to analyze variables in a *two-by-two-by-two* table. Suppose, for example, we had gathered data containing these three variables: sex, race, and attitudes toward premarital sex. Suppose, further, we believe there is a relationship between these measures. We believe the effects of one's sex will have a different effect on one's attitudes because of one's racial group. An example of how we might begin to analyze this relationship is presented below:

Attitudes toward Premarital Sex by Race and Sex

Black			White		
Attitude Toward P-M-Sex	Sex		Attitude Toward P-M-Sex	Sex	
	Male	Female		Male	Female
Favor	a	b	Favor	e	f
Disfavor	c	d	Disfavor	g	h

As seen in the illustration, a **trivariate table** consists of two two-by-two tables, one for each race. In our example, race would be called a *control* variable because we are controlling the data to see how race influences respondents' answers to our question on premarital sex. If black males have a significantly different attitude toward premarital sex than white males, this technique of table construction will let the relationship be seen. To construct this type of table, simply follow the same procedures outlined earlier in the chapter.

DETECTING RELATIONSHIPS How do we know when there is a relationship between two variables in a table? How do we interpret data once it is in tabular form? Let us go back to our earlier example of the data on sex and environmental concern. In the following illustrations we have presented the same data in four different ways. In the first table we have listed only the frequency distribution of these variables, while in the next three we have calculated the percentages for the grand total, for the columns, and with the rows of the table as the base:

TABLE 13.2A   Environmental Concern by Sex

Environmental Concern	Sex		Row Totals
	Male	Female	
High	6	3	9
Low	2	4	6
Column Totals	8	7	15

TABLE 13.2B   Environmental Concern by Sex (Percents of Total)

Environmental Concern	Sex		Row Totals
	Male	Female	
High	40%	20%	60%
Low	13%	27%	40%
Column Totals	53%	47%	100%

TABLE 13.2C   Environmental Concern by Sex (Percents of Column)

Environmental Concern	Sex		Row Totals
	Male	Female	
High	75%	43%	60%
Low	25%	57%	40%
Column Totals	100%	100%	100%

TABLE 13.2D   Environmental Concern by Sex (Percents of Rows)

Environmental Concern	Sex		Row Totals
	Male	Female	
High	67%	33%	100%
Low	33%	66%	100%
Column Totals	54%	46%	100%

Both Loether and McTavish[11] and Blalock[12] strongly suggest that when researchers set up percentage tables, they always compute percentages in the direction of the independent variable. This means our percentages should always sum to 100 percent for each *category* of the independent variable. If we follow convention and always place the dependent variable at the stub of our tables, we will always calculate percentages to sum to 100 percent down the columns, so comparisons can be made across the columns. In our example of percentages calculated with column totals as the base (Table 13.2C), we can see by following convention we have made it possible to compare the differences between males and females on their attitudes toward environmental issues. If we look back at the first table, which presents the actual number of cases, it is obvious one cannot compare the numerical frequencies in such a table. The fact that only 3 females demonstrated a high concern for the natural environment compared with 6 males does not mean males are more likely to be environmentally concerned than females. The marginals indicate there are really "more" males than females in the sample; 8 males compared to 7 females. This means there are actually fewer females to indicate their attitudes about the environment than there are males. Although in our illustration the difference may not at first appear great, to control for this inequality of Ns, it is necessary to compute percentages. Because one of the variables in the example is an independent variable, and the other designated the dependent variable, we follow convention and use the base of the independent variable total to calculate percentages. In this case, 8 males represent 100 percent of the males in the sample, and we wish to see what percent of these 8 persons score high on environmental concern, and which score low. Similarly, 7 females form 100 percent of all females in the illustration, and we wish to see how they scored on the environmental concern variable as well. In Table 2C the percentages sum to 100 percent down the columns for male and female categories.

When we're reading another researcher's table, our first task is to determine in which direction the percentages have been calculated. Have the percents been computed down the columns, across the rows, or on the basis of the entire table? The direction is determined by observing where the researcher has placed the 100 percent for the total number of cases. For example, in Table 13.2C the percentages have been calculated to sum to 100 percent down the columns. As can be seen now, 75 percent of the males demonstrated a "high" concern for the environment in contrast to only 43 percent of the females. It turns out that males *are* somewhat more likely to be environmentally concerned than females.

Note the way in which the comparisons were made. If the percentages have been computed *across* the rows, as in Table 13.2D, then we should compare percentages *down* the columns. The percentage of those with "high" environmental scores is compared with those who had "low" environmental scores. We can see the percentage of "low" scores for male respondents is the same for females who scored "high" on the same variable, and that the same percentages emerge also for the "high" scoring males and "low" scoring females.

If a researcher does not begin comparing the cells in the same direction in which the percentages have been computed, he or she can "misread" a table and provide faulty interpretations. By following convention when setting up tables, and when examining them, we can save a great deal of trouble for ourselves and for our readers.

However, is there a relationship between sex and concern for the environment? Do females demonstrate less concern than males? How would we know if they did from examining a two-by-two table? When constructing tables remember to place the low categories of the independent variable at the left and the high categories at the right, and for dependent variables the high category is at the top and the low at the bottom of the stub. By following this convention we will be better able to detect relationships among variables and easily indicate the direction of the relationship.

POSITIVE RELATIONSHIPS For example, let us suppose we were looking at the relationship between educational level and income. What kind of relationship should exist between these two variables? Most would agree the relationship would be a *positive* one. That is, the higher one's education, the higher we would expect incomes to be. Stated differently, as one variable increases in its magnitude (education) so does the other (income). Let us consider income the dependent variable, and take a look at an example of a **positive relationship.**[13]

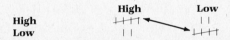

If we expected a positive relationship between a respondent's education and income, we would expect to find high income scores and high education scores located in the same cell. Also, we would expect low income scores and low educational scores to be located in the same cell. As can be seen in our illustration, this is the case. What we find, however, is that the majority of respondents with higher educational levels also had higher income scores, and that persons with lower educational levels had lower income scores. Because we followed convention and listed the independent variable with high categories on the left and low categories on the right of the heading, and the dependent variable from low at the bottom of the stub to high at the top, we would expect to find a *pattern* of responses running from the top lefthand side of the table to the bottom righthand corner. The arrow in our example indicates the pattern of the direction we would expect, which is the pattern we have actually "found."

NEGATIVE RELATIONSHIPS What if we had hypothesized that as the level of education went up, the level of income would go down? Although this doesn't seem a logical hypothesis, for the sake of example let us see what it would look like:

As can be seen in the illustration, the pattern of the relationship has reversed, and now we find the majority of scores in the upper righthand corner of the table and in the bottom lefthand cell of the table. This pattern is called a **negative** or *inverse* **relationship.** When we expect an inverse relationship to be found in our data, we expect high scores on one variable to coincide with low scores on the other. A better example of variables that might actually distribute themselves in this pattern would be the relationship between the educational level of women and the number of children they desire. The relationship found is one where, as the level of education increases, the number of children desired decreases. As noted above, this is called a negative or inverse relationship, and it can be detected by looking for a pattern that runs from the upper righthand cell to the lower lefthand cell of a table.

NO RELATIONSHIP   But what if there is no relationship to be found in our data? What does a "no relationship" look like? First, let us consider how we might define association or relationship from a statistical point of view. Generally, an *association or relationship between two variables is said to exist whenever a position on one variable is conjoined with a position on the other variable in a disproportionate number of cases.*[14] This is what we found in our examples for both a positive and a negative relationship. However, what kind of relationship is demonstrated in the illustration below?

	High	Low
High	⊔⊤⊤⊤	⊔⊤⊤⊤
Low	⏐ ⏐	⏐ ⏐

In this example the original pattern of the distribution of the variables is the same for both their univariate and bivariate distributions. There is no disproportionate number of cases in the cells that would indicate either a positive or negative association. Rather, the pattern of variation in income persists among both highly educated members of the sample as well as for those with lower levels of education. According to Watson and McGaw, in a bivariate distribution *statistical independence* is said to exist whenever the original pattern of variation in a variable persists for that variable when examined within the categories of another variable.[15] When we find that there is **statistical independence** in a bivariate distribution, we can consider the condition as one denoting an absence of association between two variables. As can be seen, the patterns of either positive or negative associations cannot be found in the above data.

A Note On Figuring Rate of Increase

We have discussed the methods and techniques needed to calculate simple percentages when constructing tables of both the univariate and bivariate variety. One useful technique is the method of calculating the rates of change that might be noted between two distributions representing variables measured at two different points in time. For example, in computing this kind of rate a researcher would take the actual increase during the period covered and divide that by the original measure at the beginning of the period. Suppose we had an interest in examining the population of a community, and we found there was a population increase from 45,000 to 70,000 between the years 1970 and 1980. The rate of increase for that period would be calculated as follows:

$$\frac{70,000 - 45,000}{45,000} = .56$$

Of course, .56 can be understood as indicating an increase or percentage change of 56 percent. Blalock notes percentages can go over 100 percent when calculating change in this manner, and figures can be negative if there is an actual decrease in size from one point in time to another.[16]

In a similar way we can calculate differences in percentages between categories in a table. For example, the difference between percentage high on environmental concern among males and females in Table 13.2C is 32 percent (75% − 43% = 32%). This value is called *epsilon*, and it is the percentage difference in a table. When tables become bigger than two-by-two there can be a large number of epsilons computed to aid researchers in their interpretations.

Summary

This chapter was devoted to the discussion of the elementary analyses of relationships among variables in sociological data. We first explained univariate distributions, where only a single variable was examined and presented, and we then turned to bivariate presentations. We found it was necessary to place data in frequency distributions before readers were able to easily make sense of them, and we summarized a univariate distribution with three different measures of central tendency: the mode, the median, and the mean. Percentages were also discussed, and we illustrated how it was possible to make meaningful comparisons between groups of data by converting raw scores into percents. Bivariate analyses consist of the exploration and presentation of two variables at a single time. Tables of this kind are called cross-tabulations or contingency tables. When the variables used in the table are dichotomous, the resultant table is called a two-by-two or a fourfold table. Tables are made up of several parts, including a stub, a heading, marginals, cells, and a title. By following the conventions of table construction, we will always be able to present data in a clear and understandable way. By being sure the tables we are interpreting were constructed following the basic conventions of table preparation, we can avoid making misleading interpretations of other researchers' data.

Trivariate tables contain three variables and can be considered a type of multivariate analysis. However, no matter how large or small a table or the number of variables used, we will have to know how percentages were calculated before being able to properly read them. Were the percentages calculated as percents of the total, or for rows or for columns? We can tell by finding where the totals sum to 100 percent. We have also illustrated the patterns that emerge when relationships are positive, negative, and when there is no relationship between variables. And, finally, we noted that *epsilon* is the name given to the percentage differences found in a table, and that researchers could easily calculate rates of increase or decrease when such rates were needed.

The main objective of this chapter has been to acquaint you with the "table manners" associated with the analysis of tabular data.[17] If we mind our manners, we'll have far fewer problems both with preparing tables and consuming them. *Bon appétit!*

Glossary

association An association or relationship between two variables is said to exist whenever a position on one variable is conjoined with a position on the other variable in a disproportionate number of cases.

bivariate analysis The analysis of two variables in a single table.

body of the table That portion of the table that is comprised of the cells.

cell Portion of a table containing a frequency.

cell frequency The number or percents found in a cell.

contingency table A table is that shows how the value in any cell is dependent upon the value of a score in a corresponding cell.

epsilon The percentage difference between variable scores in a table.

frequency distribution The count of the number of cases within the categories of a variable.

heading The top portion of a table; usually the title of the independent variable categories.

mean A single number summarizing a total distribution when scores are measured at the interval level; to calculate the mean, sum the scores and divide by the number of cases in the distribution (see *median* and *mode*).

median The value in a distribution that has the property of having the same number of scores with smaller values as there are scores with larger values on either side of it; the point in an ordered distribution that divides it into two equal parts (see *mode* and *mean*).

mode The most frequently occurring value of a variable in a distribution; a measure of central tendency; an average (see *mean* and *median*).

multivariate analysis An analysis of several variables at the same time.

negative relationship Also called an *inverse relationship*; when a high score on one variable corresponds to a low score on another. The association between a woman's educational level has been found to be inversely related to the number of children she desires. As her education increases, the number of children desired decreases (see *positive relationship*).

percent Means per one hundred; a means of controlling for the size of a sample when conducting analyses; dividing a category total by the total number of cases in a sample.

positive relationship The relationship that emerges when a high score on one variable corresponds to a high score on another.

The typical relationship between educational level and income is a positive one; as education increases, so does income (see *negative relationship*).

statistical independence Whenever the original pattern of variation in a variable persists for that variable when examined within the categories of another variable; when no relationship exists.

stub The lefthand column of a table; usually contains headings for the dependent variable.

title The name of the table; usually contains a description of the dependent variable, whether the table contains frequencies or percents or some other measures, the independent variable and the type of case upon which the measurements were taken.

trivariate analysis Analysis of three variables in a single table.

trivariate table A table made up of three variables; a two-by-two-by-two table.

two-by-two table Also called a fourfold table; when two dichotomous variables are examined in a single table; has four cells.

univariate analysis The examination of a single variable in a univariate distribution.

1. Herman J. Loether and Donald G. McTavish, *Descriptive and Inferential Statistics* (Boston: Allyn and Bacon, 1976), p. 584.
2. Hubert M. Blalock, Jr., *Social Statistics*, rev. 2nd ed. (New York: McGraw-Hill, 1979), pp. 41–52.
3. See Michael A. Malec, *Essential Statistics for Social Research* (Philadelphia: Lippincott, 1977), pp. 12–15.
4. See John E. Freund, *Modern Elementary Statistics*, 4th ed. (Englewood Cliffs, N.J.: Prentice-Hall, 1973), p. 11.
5. Blalock, op. cit., p. 33.
6. Ibid., p. 34.
7. Ibid., pp. 55–71.
8. William B. Sanders, *The Sociologist as Detective: An Introduction to Social Research Methods*, 2nd ed. (New York: Holt, Rinehart and Winston, 1976), pp. 16–17.
9. Morris Rosenberg, *The Logic of Survey Analysis* (New York: Basic Books, 1968), pp. 251–258, provides an excellent introduction to bivariate analysis and table con-

Notes

struction. See also Thelma F. Batten, *A Guide for Social Science Methods: Reasoning and Research* (Boston: Little, Brown, 1971), pp. 47−62.

10. Loether and McTavish, op. cit., pp. 174−185.
11. Ibid., p. 177.
12. Blalock, op. cit., p. 36.
13. George Watson and Dickinson McGaw, *Statistical Inquiry* (New York: Wiley, 1980), pp. 153−156, provide an excellent introduction to understanding relationships in fourfold tables.
14. Ibid., p. 154.
15. Ibid.
16. Blalock, op. cit., p.38.
17. Watson and McGaw, op. cit., p.141.

14

Scale and Index Construction

In Chapters 4 and 5 we introduced some of the basic concepts associated with measurement. In this chapter we take an additional step by illustrating the actual construction of various measurement instruments. We introduce here the methods and techniques needed to build our own measurement devices: **scales** and **indexes.** As pointed out in earlier chapters, measurement is the assignment of numerals to objects or events according to rules.[1] It turns out that measurement is much easier for some variables than for others. For example, it is generally not difficult to measure a respondent's sex, but problems do arise when we attempt to measure abstract concepts like alienation, racial prejudice, and attitudes in general. We often find a single indicator isn't enough and turn from simple indexes to composite or multiple-factor indexes or to scales of one variety or another. Because attitudes are not directly observable, researchers prefer to use as many indicators as possible to measure them. Remember, an index is used to measure phenomena that cannot be observed directly and that are comprised of several dimensions, whereas a scale is used to quantitatively measure the intensity with which an attitude is held. Because attitudes can have several dimensions, we generally try to measure as many of these dimensions as possible, and because attitudes are very difficult to observe, we create indexes to stand for them and use these as our measures. In this chapter we discuss the scales and indexes most common to sociological analyses. We present illustrations of the **Guttman** scaling technique, **Thurstone** scales, **Likert** scales, the **semantic differential,** and others. However, before we turn to the construction of these scales and indexes, let us examine the differences between them.

Scales and Indexes Reviewed

Even sociologists will often use the terms *scale* and *index* in an improper way, which is not too surprising since the two techniques have so much in common. For example, both are usually ordinal indicators of the variables they seek to measure. That is, both an index and a scale will place an individual respondent in a rank-ordered position on a continuum, and show where that person is *relative* to the others on the index or the scale. Both are constructed using *multiple factors* rather than a single indicator. Specifically, scales and indexes are generally comprised of several indicators of the concept or attitude being studied. A respondent's socioeconomic status (SES), for example, is usually a multiple-factor measurement consisting of his or her educational level, occupational status, and income. Because each of these factors is thought to be related to a person's social class, each is used to capture the multiple dimensions of the SES concept.

Although there are similarities between indexes and scales, there are also important differences. A scale, for example, can be one of three kinds: a **summated ratings scale,** an equal-appearing interval scale, or a cumulative scale (or Guttman scale).[2] A summated scale is a set of attitude items, all of which are considered as being of approximately the same value, and to each of which respondents answer with various degrees of agreement or disagreement. The scores of the items of such a scale are summed, or summed and averaged, to give an individual's score. As in all attitude scales, the purpose of the summated rating scale is to place an individual somewhere on an agreement–disagreement continuum. The summated scale, however, appears to be very much like an index, although there are differences. The index is simply the sum of scores from a list of items while the scale assumes that the items from which the measure was derived also have a structure, that they too are scaled. In our discussion of the summated scale, the items were answered "with various degrees of agreement or disagreement," but for an index the final score is derived from the simple summation of items not necessarily structured along a continuum from "highly agree" to "highly disagree."

An Example

Suppose we wanted to measure the intensity with which individuals participated in their leisure-time activities. We could go about this in several ways. Using survey techniques, we might ask which activities they had participated in during the year before our survey was conducted: (1) fishing, (2) hunting, (3) picnicking, (4) hiking, (5) running, and so forth.[3] Then for every activity they checked we could assign a single point and the sum of these points would be their score. The assumption would be that the more activities an individual participated in, the more intense his or her recreational attitude. Of course, some respondents would check all the items and others would check none and the items themselves would not assume any rank or structure of their own. This would be *an index*.

The same problem could be approached in another way. We could assume certain types of activities were more physically demanding than others; for example, certain items themselves could demonstrate the intensity of a respondent's recreational attitude: (1) playing roller ball, (2) playing football, (3) shooting marbles. This set of items is structured from high to low (roller ball to marbles) according to the physical requirements of each of the individual activities. We would assume a person who played roller ball would certainly be able to handle marbles. The sum or average of a series of items of this variety would constitute *a scale*.

Building an Index or Scale

Constructing an index or scale can involve several steps, the first of which is the selection of the items used to build it.

Item Selection

Each item selected to indicate an attitude should appear to have an epistemic correspondence to the concept being measured. Specifically, each item selected should appear to have a definite relationship to the attitude being measured. For example, if we wanted to measure recreational intensity, each item considered should indicate some aspect of "recreational intensity," such as the examples given above. If we wanted to measure religiosity, items to be considered might include church attendance, strength of belief, and so forth. Put another way, the items we select should demonstrate a certain degree of *face validity*.[4] That is, on the face of it, each should appear to have a valid reason for being on our list—because each should appear as if it was measuring the topic we are interested in.

If we were planning to use several indicators of the attitude under study, we would attempt to keep our items **unidimensional.** That is, all of the items taken together should measure only the one attitude or a single dimension of the variable being studied. We should not include items dealing with recreation on an alienation scale or on an index designed to measure political liberalism. Similarly, we should not include items focusing on religion in an index constructed to measure *anomie*.

Not only should items possess face validity and unidimensionality, they should also be related to one another in a statistical sense. For example, if all the items appear to measure the concept *powerlessness*, then all of those items should demonstrate a clear bivariate relationship to one another. Items demonstrating a correspondence to one another should then be retained for our final scale or index, and those not meeting our criterion for a "strong" relationship should be discarded.[5]

So far we have considered the first three steps needed when constructing an index or scale:

Step 1 Select items that appear to have an epistemic correspondence to the concept being studied; items should demonstrate face validity.

Step 2 Items should be selected to represent a unidimensional pool of measures; they should focus on a single dimension.

Step 3 Items should be checked to see if they are actually *related* to one another; this ensures that the items are unidimensional and provides confidence in the validity of those selected.

Now let us turn to the other steps required to finish the job. It turns out there are several kinds of scales and indexes, and each type has its own particular methodology. We will begin with the simplest of all: typologies.

The Construction of Typologies

Typologies are simply classificatory schema composed of two or more ideal or constructed types.[6] Ideal types provide abstract categories in terms of which individual or group phenomena are analyzed. The differences between ideal-type categories can be conceptualized as a gradual continuum or as discrete. The distinction between introvert and extrovert, *Gemeinschaft* and *Gesellschaft*, rural and urban, or the fourfold classification of ecclesia, denomination, sect, and cult are examples of typologies commonly used in sociology. Typologies are used to organize data, and can also be used as a conceptual model for guiding research and building theory.

Recall that scales and indexes are built to provide an ordinal measure of a variable. However, researchers often want to summarize two or more dimensions of a set of variables, and this is where typologies are used. For example, we might wish to examine residence in terms of location at time of socialization and current location of residence:

Current Residence and Residence at Age 16

| | Current Residence | |
Residence at Age 16	Rural	Urban
Rural	A	B
Urban	C	D

As can be seen in the illustration, the respondents in cell A are rural both in place of current residence and in place of residence at age 16, which is used to operationalize area of residence at time of socialization. Cell D, however, is at the other end of the continuum, with both place of current residence and residence at age 16 being urban. The respondents in cells B and C are urban on one measure and rural on the other. It is now possible to code each respondent according to where he or she fits into this new typology, giving those in cell A a code of 1, those in cell B a code of 2, those in C a code of 3, and the respondents in cell D a code of 4. This coding would allow us to further examine the relationship between this new variable and other variables in our data set. However, because typologies are comprised of mutually exclusive categories taken from an exhaustive list, they are nominally scaled measurements.This means certain statistical analyses using typologies are impossible. Before constructing a typology researchers should carefully consider the analyses they plan for their data. If typologies can be analyzed in the manner desired, they are useful tools from both a methodological and a theoretical perspective.[7]

The Summated Ratings Scale

Bailey argues that attitude scales serve three functions: (1) measurement, (2) as aids in defining concepts by providing operational definitions for them, and (3) to prevent bias by covertly measuring a sensitive topic so respondents do not realize they are being measured on an attitude, and thus cannot manipulate their answers.[8] Keep these three functions in mind as we discuss the various types of scaling techniques used. We begin with the summated ratings scale.

The first objective or function of an attitude scale can be met by simply scaling a question:

> On a scale of 1 to 10, how would you rate the attractiveness of the parks in our community? (Please circle one): 1   2   3   4   5   ⑥   7   8   9   10

To meet the other two objectives of attitude scales it is necessary to construct a scale from an entire series of questions, even though only a single variable or dimension is being measured. Because there are generally a large number of items, a respondent's score can vary, depending upon how many questions were answered and the manner in which he or she responded (that is, either in a positive or negative manner). Higher scores represent a higher level for the concept being measured, and lower scores a lower level. Because a respondent's score is determined by summing up the number of questions answered in a certain way, this type of scale is called a **summated ratings scale.** Let us take a look at another example.

Suppose we were interested in examining the general morale and adjustment of a population. We could develop a set of items like the following:[9]

	Agree	Disagree
1. Times are getting better.	1	0
2. Any person with ability and willingness to work hard has a good chance of being successful.	1	0
3. Most people can be trusted.	1	0
4. A person can plan his or her future so that everything will come out in the long run.	1	0
5. A man does not have to pretend he is smarter than he really is.	1	0
6. One seldom worries so much as to become very miserable.	1	0
7. Real friends are as easy to find as ever.	1	0
8. It does not take long to get over feeling gloomy.	1	0
9. The young person of today can expect much from the future.	1	0
10. It is great living in these exciting times.	1	0

For this scale a respondent's agreement to an item is scored as a 1 and disagreement with a 0. If each item appeared agreeable to a respondent, the total score would be 10. If none of the items were agreeable to a respondent, the final summated score would be 0. It is noteworthy to mention that there are several ways a respondent could come up with the same score other than a 10 and 0 for complete agreement or complete disagreement. There are any number of ways to score a 2. For example, one respondent could agree with questions 1 and 2 and disagree with all of the others; another respondent could agree with items 7 and 10 and disagree with all of the others; another respondent could agree with items 5 and 6 but not with any of the others; and so on. This kind of scoring is fine if we are positive the scale is unidimensional and that each item is measuring *the exact same aspect of morale*. It could be, however, that each of these scores (the 2s) had a slightly different meaning because each combination of questions was tapping a somewhat different concept. Thus, the final scores could represent concepts not intended as part of our study. Of course, by checking all the items to see how strongly they are related to one another, and by being certain they demonstrate strong relationships, we can have more confidence in the final summated ratings scale.

The Likert-Type Scale

The summated scale most frequently employed by sociologists follows the pattern devised by Rensis Likert, and is called the *Likert-type* scale.[14] In fact, according to Selltiz and her associates, most scales currently used in the social sciences are Likert-type scales.[15] this kind of scale consists of a series of items to which respondents are asked to indicate their agreement or disagreement with each item on an intensity scale of its own. This scale is highly reliable when it comes to a rough ordering of respondents with regard to a particular attitude. The final score includes a measure of intensity as expressed by each statement. Specifically, Likert has developed a technique for helping to solve the problem of questionable items appearing on a scale by increasing the variation in the possible scores a respondent can receive by coding responses from "strongly agree" to "strongly disagree" instead of simply "agree" or "disagree." Let us look at the steps required to construct this kind of scale.[16]

Step 1 Assemble a large number of items considered relevant to the attitude being investigated that indicate either a clear favorableness or unfavorableness toward it.

Step 2 Administer the items to a group of respondents who are representative of those with whom the final questionnaire will be given.

Step 3 Score the responses to the various items in such a way that a response indicative of the most favorable attitude is given the highest score.

Step 4 Compute each individual's score by simply adding his or her item scores.

Step 5 Analyze responses to determine which items differentiate most clearly between the highest and lowest quartiles of total scores.

Step 6 Use the items found to differentiate best to form a scale of at least six statements.

Researchers can divide the respondents into quartiles and compute the median score on each item for the highest and lowest 25 percent of the scores.

If any item has the same median score for both the high and low groups, it is eliminated from consideration. Only those questions revealing widely different median scores for the highest and lowest groups will be retained. Each item can also be correlated with the total score or with other highly discriminate items, and items that do not appear to be highly associated with them can be eliminated from the scale. Let us look at an example of some items that might appear on a Likert-type scale.[17]

1. The future is too uncertain for a person to plan on marrying. Strongly agree ( ); Agree ( ); Undecided ( ); Disagree ( ); Strongly Disagree ( ).
2. After being caught in a mistake, it is hard to do good work for awhile. Strongly agree ( ); Agree ( ); Undecided ( ); Disagree ( ); Strongly disagree ( ).
3. Home is the most pleasant place in the world. Strongly agree ( ); Agree ( ); Undecided ( ); Disagree ( ); Strongly Disagree ( ).

Each response category would be assigned a weight from 1 to 5, the highest score representing strong agreement with an item. A scale score is computed for each respondent. If respondent 1 makes a very high score and respondent 2 a low score, their answers can be compared to see if there are any particular items that both respondents answered in the same way. These questions would be eliminated from the scale because they obviously do not discriminate between the widely diverse scores described above. For example, if one respondent had a score of 100 and another had a score of 12, but both respondents had the same answer to item number 15 of the scale, that item would be dropped.

The Thurstone Equal-Appearing Interval Scale

The Thurstone-type scale consists of a number of items whose position on the scale has been determined by a ranking operation performed by a group of judges.[10] Miller has outlined the steps required to construct this particular type of scale.[11]

Step 1 Gather together several hundred statements conceived to be related to the attitude being studied.

Step 2 Have a large number of judges (50−300) independently classify the statements in eleven groups ranging from most favorable to neutral to least favorable.

Step 3 The scale value of an item is computed as the median position to which it is assigned by the judges.

Step 4 Items that have too broad a spread are discarded.

Step 5 The final scale is formed by selecting items that are evenly spread along the scale from one extreme to the other.

The resulting Thurstone-type scale should be a series of about twenty statements. Respondents are asked either to check each item with which they agree or to check the two or three items that are closest to their position. An illustration of some items from a Thurstone-type scale are presented below. These items were taken from an early study of attitudes toward natives in South Africa.[12]

Scale Value	Item Number	Statement
0.8	11	I would rather see the white people lose their position in this country than keep it at the expense of injustice to the native.
3.1	3	It seems to me the white man, by placing restrictions such as the "Colour Bar" upon the native, is really trying to exploit him economically.
3.8	22	I consider that the white community in this country owes a real debt of gratitude to the missionaries for the way in which they have tried to uplift the native.
10.2	2	The idea of contact with the black or dark skin of the native excites horror and disgust in me.
10.3	1	I consider that the native is only fit to do the "dirty" work of the white community.

Of course, scale values are not shown on the questionnaire, and the various items are arranged in a random order rather than in the order of their value. The median of the scale values of the items the respondent checks is interpreted as that person's position on a scale of favorable—unfavorable attitudes toward the concept being studied.

There are several objections that can be made against the Thurstone-type scale. First, the amount of work and time required to construct such a scale can be prohibitive, one of the reasons the technique is not as widely used as it once was. A second objection is that, like the summated ratings scale, different attitudinal patterns may be expressed by the same score. For example, a respondent could check two moderately negative statements and receive a scale score of 7, which would represent the median value of the two items. Another respondent could theoretically check several items, including some indicating a positive position, and also receive 7 for a score. The two respondents would be rated as having the same degree of prejudice even though the second respondent checked the most favorable items in the scale and the first did not.[13]

Guttman Scaling

The Guttman technique of scale construction, named after its developer Louis Guttman, focuses on the unidimensionality of a scale.[18] Only those items meeting the criterion of **reproducibility** are acceptable for the scale. If a scale is unidimensional, then a respondent who has a more favorable attitude than another respondent should respond to each statement with equal or greater favorableness than one with a less favorable attitude. Let us look at the steps that are required to construct this scale before discussing them in more detail.[19]

Step 1   Select a group of statements that apply to the measurable objective.

Step 2   Test statements on a sample of the population (about 100).

Step 3   Discard statements with more than 80 percent agreement or disagreement.

Step 4   Order *respondents* from most favorable responses to fewest favorable responses; order from top to bottom (see Table 14.1).

Step 5   Order *statements* from most favorable responses to fewest favorable responses; order them left to right (see Table 14.1).

Step 6   Discard statements that fail to discriminate between favorable respondents and unfavorable respondents.

Step 7   Calculate coefficient of reproducibility:

    a.   Calculate the number of errors (favorable responses that don't fit the pattern).

    b.   Reproducibility $= 1 \dfrac{\text{Number of errors}}{\text{Number of responses}}$

    c.   If reproducibility equals .90, a undimensional scale is said to exist.

Step 8   Score each respondent by the number of favorable responses.

This method of scale construction, also called *scalogram analysis*, ensures there is only one combination of responses for each different scale. A sample of items appearing on a Guttman scale would be the following:

1. How many of your best friends who live in your neighborhood did you get to know since you or they moved into the neighborhood?
   Two or more (greater neighborliness); one or more (less neighborliness).
2. Do you and any of your neighbors go to the movies, picnics, or other things like that together?
   Often or sometimes (greater neighborliness); rarely or never (less neighborliness).
3. Do you and your neighbors entertain one another?
   Often or sometimes (greater neighborliness); rarely or never (less neighborliness).

The above items are taken from a neighborliness scale developed by Wallin during the early 1950s.[20] The coefficient of reproducibility for the entire series of items from two samples of women was .92 and .924.

The key to understanding the Guttman scale is realizing that some items are more indicative of an attitude than others. For example, in our illustration of items taken from the Wallin scale, we might find item number 2 is a much

TABLE 14.1 Example of Guttman Scaling

Respondent	7	5	1	8	2	4	6	3	Score
				Items					
7	yes	yes	yes	yes	yes	yes	yes	—	7
9	yes	yes	yes	yes	yes	yes	yes	—	7
10	yes	yes	yes	yes	yes	yes	—	—	6
1	yes	yes	yes	—	yes	yes	—	yes	6
13	yes	yes	yes	yes	yes	yes	—	—	6
3	yes	yes	yes	yes	yes	—	—	—	5
2	yes	yes	yes	yes	—	—	—	—	4
6	yes	yes	yes	yes	—	—	—	—	4
8	yes	yes	yes	—	—	yes	—	—	4
14	yes	yes	yes	yes	—	—	—	—	4
5	yes	yes	yes	—	—	—	—	—	3
4	yes	yes	—	—	—	—	—	—	2
11	—	—	—	—	yes	—	—	—	1
12	yes	—	—	—	—	—	—	—	1

better indicator of neighborliness than the other two items. However, if this particular item actually does measure the neighborliness of respondents, and if a respondent is very neighborly, then you would expect him or her to score highly on the other two items as well. In other words, if an item is truly measuring an attitude or object, and if a respondent agrees with that item, then he or she should also agree with other items that also indicate that attitude but to some lesser degree. For example, if you would let your son or daughter come home at 12:00 P.M., you would certainly allow him or her to stay out until 11:30, and if you would let your child come home at 11:30 we might expect that you would agree to let him or her come home at 10:15. On the other hand, if you wouldn't let your daughter stay out until 11:30 because it was too late, we wouldn't expect you to agree with the statement, "Would you let your daughter stay out until 12:30?" This is the logic behind the Guttman scale: *If a scale is unidimensional, then a person who has a more favorable attitude than another should respond to each statement with equal or greater favorableness than the other.*

To see if a scale structure exists among the responses to all the items in a scale, the response patterns must be examined. In our illustration, we have presented an example of how such patterns might appear (see Table 14.1). For each of the numbered items we have indicated "agreement" with the word "yes" and "less neighborliness" with a dash (—). Following the steps listed earlier (steps 4 and 5), we have ordered respondents from most favorable responses to fewest favorable responses to all the items, and listed them on the lefthand side of the table from top to bottom. Respondent 7 agreed with 7 of the items, as did respondent 9, with the others having scores descending to only 1 favorable response from respondent 12. Following step 5, we have ordered the individual items themselves across the top of the table from left to right. We can see that all of the respondents in our example except for a very few agreed with items 7, 5, and 1. Responses to the remaining items appear to be mixed to a certain degree, but a general pattern can be seen. Specifically, if a respondent agrees with item 6, we can almost bet he or she will agree with items 4, 2, 8, 1, 5, and 7. Item 6 might be thought of as the "witching hour," the latest time parents would let their daughter or son stay out at night. If item 6 were 1:00, then the other items (4, 2, 8, 1, 5, and 7) must each be times that come before 1:00 such as 12:30, 12:00, 11:30, and so on. If respondents agree to let their children stay out until 1:00, we can be positive they will agree to let them stay out until 12:00.

However, on further inspection we can see there are some responses that do not fit this pattern at all. In some cases there are respondents who agreed with an item indicating they would let their child stay out until 12:00 P.M., and then disagreed with another indicating they could stay out until 11:30. For example, both respondents 1 and 8 reveal this pattern. According to the steps outlined above, these favorable responses that do not fit the pattern are *errors*. These errors figure importantly into the calculation of the coefficient of reproducibility. Following the formula presented in step 7, and using the number of "yes" responses that are out of the "pattern" as errors, we arrive at the following:

$$\text{Reproducibility} \quad = \quad 1 - \frac{3 \text{ (Number of errors)}}{112 \text{ (Number of responses)}} \quad = .97$$

Note that the number of responses is 112. To arrive at this figure we simply multiply the number of items by the number of respondents, and divide the number of errors by the result (112). When this is subtracted from 1, we see that our scale has a coefficient of reproducibility of .97. We would conclude, at this point, that our scale is unidimensional. The higher the coefficient of reproducibility, the higher the researchers' ability to reproduce scores accurately. That is, the better the ability to predict that if a respondent has answered one item in a certain way, usually by agreeing with a statement such as those illustrated earlier, he or she will agree with all the other items less indicative of the attitude being measured. Stated differently, if we agree to let our children stay out until 12:00 P.M., we can *reproduce* our responses for questions asking if the children can stay out until 11:30, 11:00, and 10:30. By knowing what a respondent said about 12:00 we can be positive about what he or she said about earlier times.

In summary, we have introduced five different scaling techniques: simple typologies, summated scales, the Thurstone scale, the Likert scale, and Guttman scaling. Each of these methods of scale construction are somewhat different but each attempts to measure or weigh attitudes. The summated ratings scale appeared to be the easiest to construct while the Thurstone scale required the assistance of several judges and took a great deal of time and effort to prepare. In several cases, the pooled items for a scale had to be given to a representative sample of the population for whom the final questionnaire was to be given. As becomes clear, then, scaling can be a costly and time-consuming research activity. As a consequence, most researchers use some variation of the summated scale when preparing research instruments. Remember, however, that all research instruments must be pretested. This means that all of the scaling techniques described above could be used if adequate pretesting was conducted. Now, let us take a look at the construction of an index under actual research conditions to get a better feel for the preparation of measurement devices.

Environmental Concern and the Social Maturity Index: An Illustration

Lowe and his associates recently examined the relationship between respondents' age and their concern for the natural environment.[22] Previous studies had reported a negative association between these two variables; younger people were generally more concerned with environmental issues than older people. Therefore, as part of their study, these researchers developed what they called a *social maturity index*. Two general hypotheses were examined by these investigators, one of which stated that the exposure of younger age groups to the "youth movements" of the sixties and early seventies aided in explaining their greater concern with environmental issues. The researchers discovered that some writers and commentators believed the involvement of youth with the environmental movement represented an extension of their highly organized efforts focusing on civil rights and the Vietnam War. On the one hand, antiwar proponents protested the military aspects of the "military-industrial complex" while the environmental movement represented a protest against the "industrial" aspects of the system. One corollary to this explanation was the hypothesis that those who favor environmental controls will oppose the military-industrial complex (this was found to be true). Because of the influence of past events in the history of the environmental movement, this explanation was called the *historical* hypothesis.

However, an additional hypothesis suggests young people demonstrated a greater concern, not because of past historical events, but because they were less strongly tied to the larger social system of which they were a part. This *maturation* explanation of the age-environmental relationship focused on the aging process itself and not on the occurrence of specific historical events. From this perspective it was argued that young persons are less integrated into the larger societal system. Because solutions to environmental problems are often seen as "threatening to the dominant order," it followed that younger persons would more often support environmental reforms and ideologies than would older persons. Stated somewhat differently, younger persons tend initially to be more idealistic in response to questions concerned with social change, but as age and social responsibilities accumulate, these same individuals tend largely to become more pragmatic in their approach to social issues.[23] There are a number of ways in which commitment to existing institutions tends to mount during the aging process, and consequently the older the person, the more likely the integration of the individual into the roles associated with the basic institutions (for example, the family, religion, and political and economic subsystems).

The Problem

The researchers had two measurement problems: (1) the measurement of environmental concern and (2) social maturity. Since Lowe and his associates were conducting a secondary analysis (see Chapter 9), they were restricted to only the variables available from the General Social Surveys, which had been conducted for the National Data Program for the Social Sciences at the National Opinion Research Center of the University of Chicago. Let us see how they measured these two variables.[24]

MEASURING ENVIRONMENTAL CONCERN   First, the environmental concern measure: From the NORC data, a question dealing with several problem areas was located. The question asked respondents was, "We are faced with many problems in this country, none of which can be solved easily or inexpensively. I'm going to name some of these problems, and for each one I'd like you to tell me whether you think we are spending too much money on it, too little money, or about the right amount." The problem areas listed were:

1. Space exploration program.
2. Improving and protecting the environment.
3. Improving and protecting the nation's health.
4. Solving the problems of the big cities.
5. Halting the rising crime rate.
6. Dealing with drug addiction.
7. Improving the nation's education system.
8. Improving the conditions of blacks.
9. The military, armaments, and defense.
10. Foreign aid.
11. Welfare.

The following weights were assigned to each of the response categories for each problem area: "too little" = 3; "about right" = 2; and "too much" = 1. Now, the final environmental concern score was the weight of each respondent's answer on the environmental item minus his or her average weight (the "mean" score) for the other ten problem areas. Scores on this "scale" that are below zero indicate the respondent scored lower on environmental concern than his or her average attitude or opinion about spending money on the other problems. A respondent who thought we were spending too much on everything would score zero—as would respondents who thought we should spend more across the board. This final score was their measure of concern with the environment.

THE MATURITY INDEX   Next, the researchers explored all of the items available in the NORC data to see which of them had a correspondence to maturity. Eight items were found that were thought to have face validity, and one point was given for each of the following: if a respondent (1) was working full time; (2) was married; (3) had children at home; (4) had voted in a national election; (5) had paid income tax; (6) attended church; (7) was a member of some voluntary organization; or (8) had one or more children born alive; and zero for each "no" response. The final index was a respondent's score on all of the items.

As can be seen from this illustration not all researchers begin a research effort with the intention of gathering new data. Generally, data that had previously been gathered are used several times before being put to rest. When a new problem emerges that can be studied using the secondary analysis of existing data, measurement problems are not impossible to overcome. As in the illustration, it is possible to examine the codebooks of existing studies to see which items have face validity for the measures needed, and then conduct the analysis. By the way, the maturity hypothesis proved to be the best explanation!

Now let us turn to two additional scaling techniques sometimes used in social research: the **semantic differential** and the **Bogardus Social-Distance Scale.**

The Semantic Differential Technique

Osgood and his associates have developed a technique for investigating the connotational dimensions of respondents' inner worlds by means of a systematic interviewing procedure.[25] Osgood states:

> In the typical semantic differential task, a subject judges a series of concepts (e.g., *my mother, Chinese, modern art,* etc.) against a series of bipolar, seven-step scales defined by verbal opposites (e.g., *good-bad, hot-cold, fair-unfair,* etc.). The concept is given at the top of each sheet, and the subject judges it against each successive scale by putting his checkmark in the appropriate positions, e.g., + 3 *extremely good,* +2 *quite good,* +1 *slightly good,* 0 *equally good and bad or neither,* −1 *slightly bad,* −2 *quite bad,* and −3 *extremely bad.*

According to Osgood and his associates, this measuring instrument is not greatly affected by the kind of object being measured or by the type of respondent using the scale.

Four steps are required to construct this type of measurement device:[26]

Step 1 Prepare a list of concepts appropriate to the theory guiding the variable to be measured.

Step 2 Then select pairs of polar adjectives.

Step 3 Selection of adjectives is determined empirically by asking different groups to take prescribed orientations in responding to an adjective-rating task. One group of respondents might be asked to rate as it believes a person would rate the concept if he or she held a positive attitude; another group as it believes a person would rate the concept if he or she held a strong negative attitude; analyze data and select adjective pairs that distinguish clearly between the groups.

Step 4 Select new groups of respondents who take prescribed orientations in rating concepts; analyze data.

Let's suppose we wanted to study the impact of the women's movement on perceptions of the female role. We would begin by preparing a list of items thought to be descriptions of that role. For example, mother, sister, daughter, girlfriend, and so forth. Next, following step 2, we would determine the dimensions along which each selection should be judged by our respondents. Following step 3, we would next select pairs of polar adjectives representing the extremes of each dimension. Our format might look like this:

Sister

Valuable	Worthless
Clean	Dirty
Tasty	Distasteful
Large	Small
Strong	Weak
Deep	Shallow
Fast	Slow
Active	Passive
Hot	Cold
Tense	Relaxed

On each line of the rating instrument, respondents would indicate how they felt about each of the concepts or terms listed at the top. Specifically, each respondent would rate the term "sister" along each of the adjective continuums from "valuable" to "worthless" through "tense" to "relaxed." The adjective pairs that distinguished most clearly between the positive and negative raters would be used in our final study.

The Bogardus Social-Distance Scale

This type of scale is used to measure the social distance or acceptance that exists for certain groups of persons.[27] The method is often applied, for example, to racial distance, regional distance, class distance, occupational distance, and religious distance. Suppose we wished to examine the extent to which people are willing to associate with a certain occupational group: social scientists. The following questions and format could be used for such an instrument:

	Sociologist	Anthropologist	Other
1. To close kinship by marriage.	_____	_____	_____
2. To my club as personal friends.	_____	_____	_____
3. To my street as neighbors.	_____	_____	_____
4. To employment in my occupation.	_____	_____	_____
5. To citizenship in my country.	_____	_____	_____
6. As visitors only to my country.	_____	_____	_____
7. Would exclude from my country.	_____	_____	_____

The following instructions might also be used:

1. Give your *first feeling reactions* in every case.
2. Give your reactions to each occupation as a *group.* Do not give your reactions to the best or to the worst members you have known, but think of the picture or stereotype you have of the entire occupational category.
3. Put a cross after each occupation in as many of the seven rows as your feelings dictate.

Note that each of the items indicates an increased closeness of contact which the respondent may or may not want with sociologists or other occupations. What we have done is to develop several questions that indicate differing degrees of intensity for this variable. This suggests a pattern similar to the Guttman technique. Presumably, if a respondent is willing to accept a given kind of association, he or she would be willing to accept all those following it. For example, a person who is willing to become close "kin" by marriage to a sociologist or anthropologist would certainly be willing to keep them in the country as citizens.

Summary

In this chapter we returned to the questions of measurement introduced in earlier chapters; however, here we moved into the actual building of scales and indexes. First, we reviewed the differences and similarities between the two types of measurement techniques. We discovered an index simply sums the scores from a list of items, but a scale contains items that are themselves scaled from positive to negative. The first step in building either a scale or an index involves the selection of items that appear to be related to the concept or attitude being measured. Items should be selected to represent an unidimensional pool of measures, all focusing on a single dimension. It is best to see if items are statistically related using the techniques discussed in Chapter 13.

We next turned to a discussion of typologies, and showed how variables can be created through the use of fourfold or larger tables. We also discussed and gave illustrations of the summated ratings scale, one of the easiest scales to construct and therefore one of the most widely used techniques in the social sciences. Next we turned to the Thurstone Equal-Appearing Interval Scale, which takes a great deal of time and effort to construct and therefore it is not used as often as the summated ratings scale or the Likert scale, another popular measurement technique, which was the next topic we discussed. Finally, we illustrated the techniques necessary for the construction of the Guttman scale, which focuses primarily upon the unidimensionality and reproducibility of measurement.

Examples of two problems of measurement were given, and we showed how some researchers went about building scales and indexes from existing data sources. We then turned to some other well-known and commonly used measurement devices: the semantic differential and the Bogardus Social-Distance Scale.

If we follow the guidelines provided here, we should be able to adequately measure any concept we become interested in. There are several scaling techniques to select from and, as a result, our problems will be fewer because of the numerous options that are "tried and true" and readily available.

Glossary

Bogardus Social-Distance Scale A scaling technique designed to measure social distances or acceptance that exists for certain groups of persons.

Guttman scale This scale focuses on the unidimensionality and reproducibility of the measure; also called *scalogram analysis*; a composite measure used to summarize several discrete observations to reflect a more general construct (see *reproducibility*).

index Used to measure phenomena that cannot be observed directly and that are comprised of several dimensions.

Likert scale A summated scale developed by Rensis Likert where respondents are asked to respond to a series of items by indicating their agreement or disagreement.

reproducibility When the response to one item will allow us to accurately predict a response to another item; reproducibility can be computed for the Guttman scale as follows:

$$\text{Reproducibility} = 1 - \frac{\text{Number of errors}}{\text{Number of responses}}$$

scale Produced from items that are themselves scaled; provides a quantitative measure of a respondent's position on an attitude continuum (see *index*).

semantic differential A method for investigating the connotational dimensions of a respondent's inner worlds by means of a systematic interview procedure.

summated ratings scale Measurement of attitudes is determined by summing the number of questions answered; the questions themselves are scaled from high to low.

Thurstone Equal-Appearing Interval Scale Consists of a number of items whose position on the scale has been determined by a ranking operation performed by a group of judges.

typology Classificatory schema composed of two or more ideal or constructed types.

unidimensional When only one concept is being measured, as contrasted with *multidimensional*, where several concepts would be measured.

Notes

1. S. S. Steven, "On The Theory of Measurement," *Science* 103 (1946): 677–680.
2. Gene F. Summers, *Attitude Measurement* (Chicago: Rand McNally, 1970), pp. 1–17.
3. See Thomas K. Pinhey and Michael D. Grimes, "Outdoor Recreation and Environmental Concern: A Reexamination of the Dunlap-Heffernan Thesis," *Leisure Sciences* 2 No. 1 (1979): 1–11.
4. Fred N. Kerlinger, *Foundations of Behavioral Research*, 2nd ed. (New York: Holt, Rinehart and Winston, 1973), pp. 456–476.
5. The techniques discussed in Chapter 13 would be appropriate for this type of analysis. In Chapter 15 we illustrate several additional techniques that are also appropriate for this task.
6. George A. Theodorson and Achilles G. Theodorson, *Modern Dictionary of Sociology* (New York: Thomas Y. Crowell, 1969), p. 445.
7. See Kenneth D. Bailey, *Methods of Social Research* (New York: Free Press, 1978), 355, and Earl R. Babbie, *The Practice of Social Research*, 2nd ed., (Belmont, Cal.: Wadsworth, 1979), pp. 417–418, for additional discussions of typology construction.
8. Bailey, op. cit., p. 356.
9. These items derived from Delbert C. Miller, *Handbook of Research and Social Measurement*, 3rd ed. (New York: David McKay, 1977), pp. 343–357.
10. See L. L. Thurstone, "Attitudes Can Be Measured," *American Journal of Sociology* 33 (January 1928): 529–554, and L. L. Thurstone and E. J. Chave, *The Measurement of Attitudes* (Chicago: University of Chicago Press, 1929), for additional discussions of this technique.
11. Miller, op. cit., p. 88.
12. I. D. Macrone, *Race Attitudes in South Africa* (Oxford: Oxford University Press, 1937).
13. See Claire Selltiz, L. S. Wrightsman, and Stuart W. Cook, *Research Methods in Social Relations*, 3rd ed. (New York: Holt, Rinehart and Winston, 1976), pp. 416–417, for additional discussions of this particular scale and problem.
14. See Rensis Likert, "A Technique for the Measurement of Attitudes," *Archives of Psychology* 22 (1932): 1–55 for a discussion of this technique.

15. Selltiz et al., op. cit., p. 418.

16. Miller, op. cit., p. 89.

17. These items were taken from ibid., pp. 346–357.

18. Louis Guttman, "A Basis for Scaling Qualitative Data," *American Sociological Review* 9 (1944): 139–150; Louis Guttman, "The Cornell Technique for Scale and Intensity Analysis," *Educational and Psychological Measurement* 7 (1947): 247–280. Portions of these articles are also reproduced in Summers, op. cit.

19. Miller, op. cit., p. 91.

20. Paul Wallin, "A Guttman Scale for Measuring Women's Neighborliness," *American Journal of Sociology* 59 (1953): 243–246.

21. This illustration was adapted from Miller, op. cit., p. 90.

22. This example was taken from an unpublished paper written by George D. Lowe and Thomas K. Pinhey.

23. Thomas K. Pinhey and Michael D. Grimes, "Comment on the Decline in Public Support for Environmental Protection," *Rural Sociology* 44, No. 1 (1979): 201–203.

24. National Opinion Research Center, *General Social Surveys, 1972–1978: Cumulative Codebook.* Roper Public Opinion Research Center, Yale University, New Haven, was the source of data used by these researchers.

25. Charles Osgood, "Semantic Differential Technique in the Comparative Study of Cultures," *Transcultural Studies in Cognition*, ed. A. K. Romney and R. G. D'Andrade, *American Anthropologist*, special number. See also, Pertti J. Pelto, *Anthropological Research: The Structure of Inquiry* (New York: Harper & Row, 1970), pp. 109–110, and Charles E. Osgood, George J. Suci, and Percy H. Tannenbaum, *The Measurement of Meaning* (Urbana: University of Illinois Press, 1957).

26. Miller, op. cit., p. 95.

27. See Emory S. Bogardus, *Social Distance* (Yellow Springs, Ohio: Antioch Press, 1959): Emory S. Bogardus, *Immigration and Race Attitudes* (Boston: Heath, 1928); and Emory S. Bogardus, "A Social Distance Scale," *Sociology and Social Research* 17 (January–February 1933): 265–271.

15

Basic Statistics

Many students treat empirical research in much the same manner as they might an emergency visit to the dentist. On the one hand, they want their toothache to stop as rapidly as possible, but on the other hand, it is the kind of trip they often put off again and again or try to avoid altogether. The reason for this approach-avoidance behavior usually centers around a concern about mathematics and statistics. Most of the sociology students we know claim to have selected sociology as a major because of their interests in the sociology of the family, criminology, studies of delinquency, and so on. But few of them express an interest in statistics as the primary reason for their turning to the study of society. However, it turns out there is really no good reason to be afraid of a few numbers, particularly since most of what is done by way of complex statistical analysis is done with computers anyway. Nevertheless, it is a good idea to understand what it is the computer does with our data so we will understand the kinds of analyses that should be conducted, and how to interpret the results. Let us take a look at an example of what "statistics" really are before turning to a more complete discussion of how they are used.

Statistics as a Language

Statistics are simply a language, and right now all of us probably understand most of its "rules" and how to read it. For instance, we understand the rules of addition, subtraction, multiplication, and division. We can "read" the language as well, and we understand the meaning of $+$, $-$, and so forth. To understand statistics we will have to add a few additional symbols and signs to our vocabulary, but for the time being that will be a rather simple task. Given what we already know, let us see how we would calculate the *mean* for a group of data. As recalled from earlier discussion (see Chapter 13), the mean is a *measure of central tendency*; that is, the mean describes the *average* score from among our data. This is really no more than the "average" we learned to compute when we were in grade school. To compute the mean average of a series of scores, we simply add all the scores together, and then divide the total by the number of scores in the series. If we had five scores, 3, 5, 8, 9, and 12, the mean would be found by first summing

$$3 + 5 + 8 + 9 + 12 = 37$$

and then dividing this sum by the number of items:

$$\bar{x} = \frac{37}{5} = 7.4$$

That's all there is to it. Later, we will discover there are specific symbols used to represent the mean ($\bar{x}$) as well as symbols for instructing us in how to compute it. For example, the Greek letter sigma (Σ) is used to indicate that a series of numbers should be "summed" or added together, and a radical ($\sqrt{\ }$) tells us to take the square root of a number. These symbols, as we shall see, are grouped together into a set of instructions called a *formula*.

It is impossible to present *all* the statistics available to us in a single chapter, and, indeed, a statistics course generally takes an entire semester or more to complete. What we can do here, though, is provide an introduction to some of the techniques available so we will be better prepared when it is time to advance to more detailed statistical discussions. There are two general areas of statistics presented in this chapter: **descriptive statistics** and **inferential statistics**.[1] Descriptive statistics are used to describe data sets, to provide a picture of what the data look like. The mean, median, and mode are descriptive statistics, and we will discuss several measures that describe associations in this chapter. Inferential statistics are used to estimate parameters and for hypothesis testing. Later in this chapter we describe a statistic called *chi-square*, which is used to test hypotheses, and finally we review the standard deviation and the standard error that were discussed in Chapter 6.

Descriptive Statistics

As the phrase implies, descriptive statistics give us a *picture* of our data. Often they provide us with a single summary figure, which acts to describe an entire series of scores. We have just seen the arithmetic mean used to do just that with only five scores, but the same could have been done to describe a much larger series of numbers. Descriptive statistics are also used to describe the relationships or associations occurring among variables. We have already illustrated how to detect associations using tabular presentations. Now, with the use of descriptive measures, we will be able to more accurately describe these associations. Let us begin our discussion of descriptive statistics with a review of data reduction procedures, and then move into the calculation of measures of association.

Data Reduction Reviewed

In Chapter 13 we demonstrated the appropriate methods for "boiling" data down to neat summaries and frequency distributions that would give readers an understandable picture of a data set at a single glance. We pointed out that each individual respondent was represented somewhat differently at each step of the data reduction process. Specifically, we moved from the respondent, to the questionnaire, to the computer card, with additional stops along the way when transfer sheets were needed. Transfer sheets, it turns out, provide us with a way to introduce the idea of a **data matrix.** Let us take a look at a matrix and then see what can be done to describe some of the relationships among the variables it contains.

TABLE 15.1 A Data Matrix

Cases	V1	V2	V3	V4	V5	V6	V7	V8	.	.	.	Vn
	Variables											
Case 1	6	5	1	4	7	8	5	8				5
Case 2	2	1	2	1	1	9	2	1				2
Case 3	1	2	3	2	4	3	1	1				2
Case 4	8	7	6	5	3	1	7	6				5
Case 5	3	4	8	9	1	2	9	7				6
.												
.												
.												
Case n	1	3	4	7	1	1	8	5				4

THE DATA MATRIX In Table 15.1 we can see the different variables as they are listed across the top of the matrix with each individual case listed down the lefthand column. This is exactly what a transfer sheet would look like if our data had been processed using this procedure. Each variable is identified by its own unique number, just as each case has an ID number of its own. For example, variable 1 (V1) could be "marital status" and variable 2 a measure of some attitude. A raw data matrix contains all of the data in our data set, and because it is in "raw" form, it has yet to be boiled down for presentation. When we last discussed data reduction, we illustrated how we could place data into various intervals and distributions so readers could easily understand them. What we will demonstrate here is a way to present the *relationships* or *associations* between variables using a *single summary number* similar to an arithmetic mean, median, or mode. Keep in mind, however, the trade-off between raw scores and grouped data: When data are grouped together for presentation, information is inevitably lost. However, by grouping data or performing some other statistical manipulation on them, we can make them more meaningful and easy to understand.

Measuring Associations

As we discovered in Chapter 13, the relationships among variables can be detected in a data matrix of their own called a *contingency table.* If we recall our "table manners," we can remember how we simply *cross-tabulated* variables to see what associations could be found: positive, negative, and so forth. Let us look at some data in a matrix to see how it compares to tabular presentations:

	Variable x			
Variable y	**x1**	**x2**	**x3**	**x4**
y1	15	10	11	12
y2	10	16	12	10
y3	11	13	18	11
y4	10	12	10	20

In the table we have used raw data rather than data placed in categories, but these data still provide us with a way to examine the relationships between the variables we are studying. The column headings in our table represent the values of variable x (the independent variable), the row headings represent the values of variable y (the dependent variable), and the numbers in the body of the table represent the number of cases having a particular score and pattern of attributes. For instance, 15 cases have the pattern $x1$ $y1$, 18 cases $x3$ $y3$, and so on. We can even see what may be a positive association between the two variables when we note there is an increase in the number of scores falling in the diagonal of the matrix (or table). Specifically, as the values of x increase so do the values of the y variable. We can clearly see this pattern because the largest numbers in the matrix appear in the diagonal and run in the direction to indicate a positive association (that is, 15, 16, 18, and 20). However, there is still too much data in this presentation; we must think of a way to summarize it even further to provide readers with a clearer picture of what is going on. We can do this by turning to the descriptive statistics that are appropriate for the level of measurement of the variables in the matrix. In this case we are dealing with a fictitious data set so we can illustrate several of the possible statistics we could select from. We will begin at the lowest level of measurement and proceed to the highest. Our first statistic will therefore be appropriate for nominally scaled variables, and from that we will proceed to ordinal associations, and finally to associations between two variables measured at the interval level.

Measuring Associations Between Two Nominally Scaled Variables

For our first example we will deal with measuring relationships when both the independent and dependent variables are measured at the nominal level. Let us suppose, for example, that we are interested in seeing what relationships emerge between respondents' sex and their voting behavior. **Lambda** (λ), a **proportional reduction in error** measure (PRE), will allow us to do just that.[2] What is a PRE measure? It is the basic model behind several different statistics, and we will illustrate how it works before we continue with our explanation of the lambda statistic.

AN EXAMPLE   Let us suppose we had a sample of 100 individuals, and we know 60 of them had voted for the Republican ticket in the previous election while 40 of them voted for the Democrats. If we knew nothing else about this sample, if we had no further information, and if we were asked to predict for *each* indiviual in the sample whether they had voted Republican or Democrat, what would be our best strategy? Let us suppose further that for each correct guess we would be given a dollar. Because our information is so limited, our best strategy would be to determine the modal category of voting behavior for the entire sample, and for each individual, use the mode as our "best guess" or prediction of how they voted. The mode, of course, is Republican, and by guessing that each respondent had voted the Republican ticket, we would be correct 60 times and earn $60.00. We would have been incorrect, however, with 40 of our guesses. This illustration provides us with the first of two rules we will have to keep in mind when dealing with similar problems: *to predict the dependent variable, when measures are at the nominal level, use its own mode.* By doing so in the example, our errors in prediction were 40, and the error rate is 40/100 = 40 percent. Suppose we could have had some additional information other than simply how the 100 respondents voted? Could we reduce our error rate and collect more than $60.00? Let us look at our data when the sex of each respondent is also included:

	Male	Female	Totals
Democrats	8	32	40
Republicans	44	16	60
	52	48	100

With this additional information what will our guessing strategy be? Can we earn extra dollars by knowing the sex of each of our respondents in addition to their voting preferences? Let us use the mode again as our basis for guessing, but not the overall mode. This time we will predict *within-category modes.* For the 52 males in our sample the within-category mode is Republican (44), and when we use this as our "best guess" we will make 8 errors for an error rate of 8/52 = 15 percent. Of the 48 females in our sample of voters, the modal category is Democrat (32), and we would have guessed wrong 16 times and had an error rate of 16/48 = 33 percent. Our total errors are now 8 + 16 = 24, and our error rate is (8 + 16)/(52 + 48) = 24/100 = 24 percent. We have reduced our error rate from 40 percent to 24 percent simply by knowing the sex of our respondents! We would also have increased our earnings because we would have increased our correct guesses by the same margin (see additional example of PRE model)!

From the above example we can begin to understand the logic of lambda: lambda provides us with the number of *reduced errors* in guessing when we move from one guessing rule to the other, that is, when we move from guessing the overall mode to guessing within category modes. Lambda can be calculated using the following formula:

$$\text{Lambda} = \frac{\Sigma \max f_i - \max F_d}{N - \max F_d}$$

where $\max f_i$ = the maximum frequency within a subclass of the *independent* variable, and $\max F_d$ = the modal frequency of the *dependent* variable. For our illustration, $N = 100$ and $\max F_d$ is 60. There are two categories of the independent variable (the sex of our respondents), and the maximum frequencies within these categories are 44 and 32. Using the above formula we arrive at the following:

$$\text{Lambda}_r = \frac{(44 + 32) - 60}{100 - 60} = \frac{16}{40} = .40.$$

Note that we have used the subscript r in the above formula. This designates the *row* variable as the *dependent variable*. We do this because we are predicting voting behavior (the row variable) from our knowledge of the respondents' sex (the column variable). We could simply compute a value for lambda$_c$ (for column variable as the dependent variable) by guessing a respondent's sex from our knowledge of his or her voting activities.

Rationale for PRE Measures

If we had the following data, what would be our *best guess* about the typical student who had taken an exam?

Passed	30
Failed	20
Total	50

Because our data are at the nominal level, we would select the mode as our best indicator of the average student and we would guess "passed" as the most typical case. We would be correct 30 times in 50 guesses, and we would be in error 20 times. If we had additional information about our group of students we might be able to reduce our guessing errors below 20. Suppose we had the following additional information:

	Passed	Failed	Total
Experienced	22	3	25
No Experience	8	17	25
	30	20	50

Now we know whether or not the students had previous experience with the type of exam we had given them and we can now reduce our guessing error. First we could take only those students who had experience in taking exams, and we see that 22 of this 25 passed, so our error would be 3 in 25 if we again guessed the mode. Students without experience indicate that 8 of 25 passed, and if we again guessed the mode, we would guess "failed." Our original error was 20, and if we sum the errors made by guessing the within category modes, we would have made only 11 errors (3 + 8 = 11). This is the way PRE measures work and the basic model is presented below:

$$\frac{\text{Amount of Reduction in Error}}{\text{Amount of Original Error}}$$

Or as in our example above:

$$\frac{20 \text{ (original error)} - 11 \text{ (error with new knowledge)}}{20 \text{ (original error)}} = \frac{9}{20} = .45$$

But what does a lambda of .40 tell us? It tells us the proportional reduction in error that is achieved when we move from one guessing rule to another. In the case of lambda, the first rule is: *to predict the dependent variable, use its own mode.* When the only information we had was the voting activity of our sample, our best guess of how all of them voted was the mode. This is so because, as we pointed out in Chapter 13, the mode is the *average* for a variable measured at the nominal level. This means the average vote would have been the mode, which in this example was Republican. As we discovered, the second guessing rule is: *within categories of the independent variable, predict the dependent variable by using the within category modes.*

INTERPRETING LAMBDA   Lambda will vary from 0.0 to 1.0, and it will never be a negative number. When we compute a lambda of 1.0, this means knowledge of the independent variable enables a perfect prediction of the dependent variable. Although a lambda of zero can indicate the within-category modes are the same, both to each other and the overall mode, it generally means knowledge of the independent variable is of no help in predicting the dependent variable. Anything between 0.0 and 1.0 indicates the *proportional reduction in error.* Thus, a value of .40 means that, in moving from guessing rule 1 to rule 2, we reduce the amount of prediction error by 40 percent. There is a moderate association between these variables, and we can predict voting behavior *40 percent better* when we know the sex of our respondents.

There are several additional ways in which to utilize the basic logic of lambda, and we have presented only a few aspects of the statistic here. Malec,[3] Freeman,[4] and others provide more detailed accounts of its use.

Measuring Associations Between Two Ordinally Scaled Variables

Suppose we wished to explore the relationship between two variables measured at the ordinal level. For instance, let us see what the association is between income and education when these variables are in general categories ranging from "high" to "low" rather than measured in actual years or dollars. We will again use a PRE measure: Goodman and Kruskal's coefficient of ordinal association, simply called **gamma.**[5] As with our example of lambda, gamma uses knowledge about one variable to tell us something about a second variable. Gamma, however, is a **symmetric measure** because any contingency table yields only one value of this statistic regardless of whether the row variable or column variable is considered independent or dependent. Let us look at the formula for gamma and work some example problems with it:

$$G = \frac{f_a - f_i}{f_a + f_i}$$

where f_a = the *frequency of agreements* and f_i the *frequency of inversions*. Remember that this statistic is calculated when variables have been measured at the ordinal level, and by ordinal we mean a general *ranking* of data from high to low. This means that the way in which we will "guess" an association will differ somewhat from what we did at the nominal level. We are no longer interested in guessing membership in a specific category (that is, Democrat or Republican); instead we are concerned with guessing *order*. The problem here is the degree to which an individual's relative rank or position on one ordinal scale is predictable from his or her rank on another ordinal scale.

PREDICTING RANKS   Freeman points out there are two conditions under which rankings are completely predictable from each other.[6] First, if all the respondents are ranked in exactly the same order on two ordinal scales, the scales are in perfect *agreement*. Second, if all the respondents are ranked in exactly the opposite order on two ordinal scales—if there is an inverse or perfect negative association—the scales are in perfect *inversion*. In both cases we can guess a person's rank on one scale from his or her rank on the other without making any errors at all.

Let us assume, for example, we had two judges rank-order a number of persons according to their singing ability. If there were perfect agreement between the judges, the rankings they would give would look like this:

Singer	Judge 1	Judge 2
A	1	1
B	2	2
C	3	3
D	4	4
E	5	5

It is obvious from the rankings that Judges 1 and 2 agreed perfectly on how the singers in our example should be rated, and if we know the ranking provided by Judge 1, we can always predict the ranking provided by Judge 2. Knowledge of an individual's ranking on one scale predicts his or her ranking on the other ordinal scale perfectly in each and every case. But what if the judges didn't agree? How might that look?

Singer	Judge 1	Judge 2
A	1	5
B	2	4
C	3	3
D	4	2
E	5	1

Our judges have obviously not agreed in the above example, and there is a perfect *inverse* relationship between their ratings. That is, as one judge's rankings go up, the other's go down. However, because the rankings are an example of a **perfect inverse relationship,** we can still predict one ranking perfectly from the other. Specifically, if we know Judge 1 ranked a singer as being 5 on his singing quality scale, we know Judge 2 ranked that individual as being 1 on hers. But we can still perfectly predict a respondent's rank on one scale from his or her position on another ordinal scale.

But what if the judges had ranked our sample of singers in a manner that *didn't* allow a perfect relationship? The result would be more difficult to interpret, and it might look like this:

Singer	Judge 1	Judge 2
A	4	5
B	1	2
C	3	3
D	2	1
E	5	4

Remember that both perfect inversions and perfect agreement are *complete associations*, which means both arrangements could produce a coefficient of association of 1.0. However, we can make our coefficient more useful by making it possible to distinguish between a value of 1.0 on perfect agreement and one based on perfect inversion. This is done using a plus or minus sign, with the sign indicating whether the relationship is based primarily on agreements or inversions. When two sets of ranks are in perfect inversion, gamma is −1; when they are in perfect agreement, the result is +1. However, the plus sign is not reported, and when no sign is given, we simply assume the relationship is a positive one. In any event, our final coefficient of association could thus lie between −1 and +1. Let us rearrange the data above into a table that will let us compute the inversions and agreements that are present:

Singer	Judge 1	Judge 2	Inversions	Agreements
E	5	4	0	0
A	4	5	1	0
C	3	3	0	2
D	2	1	0	3
B	1	2	1	3
			2	8

We have rearranged the data so the ranks of Judge 1 are in their natural order: *no smaller number lies above a larger number.* Now when we inspect the rankings of Judge 2, we see a tendency toward agreement but the arrangement is not a perfect one. If we start at the bottom of the rankings of the second judge, we see the first number or rank assigned is a 2. However, Judge 1 has given this individual the rank of 1. Rank 1 is above rank 2, so we do not have agreement between the judges. Because rank 1 lies above rank 2, there is a departure from perfect agreement—*an inversion*—which we record under the inversions heading at the top of the table. There are no inversions for ranks 1 or 3, but when we encounter 5, there is an inversion because 4 (the rank given that singer by Judge 1) lies above the rank of 5 (or of being fifth as opposed to fourth). Agreements are calculated in the same way; whenever a larger number lies above a smaller one in the rankings of Judge 2, her rankings are in the same *order* as those of Judge 1. Let us calculate inversions and agreements for our data when the judges provide us with perfect associations:

Singer	Judge 1	Judge 2	Inversions	Agreements
A	5	5	0	0
B	4	4	0	1
C	3	3	0	2
D	2	2	0	3
E	1	1	0	4
			0	10

If we begin at the bottom of the table, we see that whenever there is a larger number above a smaller one in the rankings of Judge 2, her rankings are in the same order as those of Judge 1. How many rankings are above Judge 2's first ranking? Because the first rank is 1, there are no rankings above it. We would thus have zero inversions. How many scores lie below number 1? There are 4, so we enter this number for singer E under the "Agreements" heading of our table. Moving to the next ranking in Judge 2's column, we see a 2. How many *rankings* are above this number? There are none, so we place a zero under the inversions column. There are, however, 3 scores below the rank of 2 (3, 4, and 5), so we place a 3 under the "Agreements" heading and continue this way through the data. Finally, we see there are 10 agreements and zero inversions when we arrange the data in this manner. There is a **perfect positive relationship** between the judges' rankings. If we place these figures in the formula for gamma, we obtain the following:

$$\frac{10 - 0}{10 + 0} = 1.0$$

Now let us look at the data when they are rearranged to depict a perfect inverse relationship:

Singer	Judge 1	Judge 2	Inversions	Agreements
A	5	1	0	0
B	4	2	1	0
C	3	3	2	0
D	2	4	3	0
E	1	5	4	0
			10	0

In this illustration, we have arranged Judge 1's rankings in natural order such that *no smaller number lies above a larger one*. Now we begin by inspecting the ranks of Judge 2. Our first question is how many numbers smaller than 5 now lie above it in Judge 2's rankings? We can clearly see there are 4 such numbers, and this is indicated under the inversions column. There are zero numbers or ranks below this figure, so we indicate a zero under the agreements column of our table. We then move to the next ranking and find Judge 2 has ranked this singer fourth. How many ranks are ahead of this number? There are 3 of them, and this is indicated under the inversions heading, and we continue through the data in this manner until we have filled the inversions and agreements columns of the table. In this illustration we find there is a perfect agreement between Judges 1 and 2, and we thus have 10 inversions because the agreement represents an *inverse relationship*. If we place these figures in the formula for gamma, we obtain the following:

$$\frac{0 - 10}{0 + 10} = -1.0$$

It turns out that very little of our data are arranged in ranks as neatly as presented in our examples. Rather, most data are placed in contingency tables. How do we compute gamma from a contingency table? This is accomplished using the formula we gave earlier in this chapter. Let us look at some new data and see how the formula works:

Rank on Variable Y	Rank on Variable X		
	1	2	3
1	10 (a)	10 (b)	20 (c)
2	10 (d)	20 (e)	10 (f)
3	20 (g)	10 (h)	10 (i)

Suppose the data here represent the measurement of respondents' income and education at the ordinal level, and we wish to more closely examine any association existing between these two variables. How will we go about calculating agreements and inversions for these data? Note we have placed a letter in each cell, which we will use to help us work through the formula for gamma.

CALCULATING GAMMA   To calculate agreements and inversions from grouped data, think of each cell as containing a number of respondents who are *tied* on both the independent and dependent variables. When paired with anyone else in the same row, each is tied on the ranking of the income variable (the dependent variable), and when paired with anyone else in the same column, each is tied in rank on the education variable (the independent variable). These variables are represented by variables X and Y in our example, respectively. If we think of the 10 individuals in cell a, we can think of them as being tied on the ranking by the two judges. *We didn't have any ties in our earlier examples, but the formula for gamma takes ties into account automatically.* Because the members of cell a are at the "low" end of both measurement continuums, we can think of them as being ranked "less than" each member of the remaining cells on both variables. Now, we obtain the frequency of agreement (f_a) for our table *by multiplying each cell frequency by the sum of the cells below and to the right, and summing all the products.* For our table we would begin by multiplying cell a by the sum of cells e, f, h, and i, because each of these cells is below and to the right of cell a, as our rule states. Next we would move to cell b and multiply the frequency of that cell by the sum of the frequencies in cells f and i. We would continue on to cell c, where we see there are *no cells* below and to its right. Therefore, we simply move to the next row and continue with cell d $\times$ h + i; then cell e $\times$ i. For our illustration the calculations would look like this:

F_a = a (e + f + h + i) + b (f + i) + d (h + i) + e (i) = 1,100
F_a = 10 (20 + 10 + 10 + 10) + 10(10 + 10) + 10(10 + 10) + 20(10) = 1,100

To calculate frequencies of inversion (F_i), *multiply each cell frequency by the sum of the cells below and to the left, and sum all the products.* For our example it would look like this:

F_i = c(e + d + h + g) + b (d + g) + f (h + g) + e (g) = 2,200
F_i = 20 (20+10+10+20) + 10 (10+20) + 10(10+20) + 20(20) = 2,200

The Calculation of Gamma from Grouped Data: An Illustration

A

10		
	20	10
	10	10

B

	10	
		10
		10

C

10		
	10	10

D

	20	
		10

E

		20
10	20	
20	10	

F

	10	
10		
20		

G

		10
20	10	

H

	20	
20		

A = 10(20 + 10 + 10 + 10)   B = 10(10 + 10)   C = 10(10 + 10)   D = 20(10) = 1,100 (F_a)

E = 20(20 + 10 + 10 + 20)   F = 10(10 + 20)   G = 10(10 + 20)   H = 20(20) = 2,200 (F_i)

Now we simply place the calculated f_a and f_i into the formula given earlier, and we obtain the following:

$$\text{Gamma} = \frac{1{,}100 - 2{,}200}{1{,}100 + 2{,}200} = \frac{-1{,}100}{3{,}300} - .33$$

Note the gamma we have calculated is negatively signed, which means there is an inverse association between the variables in our example. From these data there appears to be a decrease in the amount of money a member of our sample earns as his or her educational level increases. This is certainly not the relationship we would expect to exist between these variables, and indeed, we have used this example to illustrate the point that gamma, unlike lambda, can be negatively signed, indicating the *direction* of the relationship among our variables. From this figure $(-.33)$ we know that there is a moderate association between the two variables, that we can increase our ability to guess the rank of one variable based on information about another variable by 33 percent, and that the association is an inverse one. Let us review the steps required to calculate gamma:[7]

Step 1 Arrange the two rankings in an ordered contingency table.
Step 2 Tabulate the frequency of occurrence for each cell in the table.
Step 3 Determine the values of f_a and f_i from these frequencies.
Step 4 Determine the value of gamma by using the formula given earlier.

If our data are simply ranked, if they are not in a contingency table, and if there are no ties, we can follow these steps to calculate gamma:

Step 1 Order observations on the x variable from 1 to the highest rank; order observations on the y variable in the same way.
Step 2 Determine whether two or more cases are tied for a single rank either in x or y.
Step 3 If there are no ties, follow these steps:
   (a) Arrange the list of respondents so their ranks on the x variable are in their *natural order.*
   (b) Determine the values of f_a and f_i from the order of the y rankings.
   (c) Determine the value of gamma by using the formula given here.

Measuring Associations Between Two Intervally Scaled Variables

If variables are measured at the interval level, there is only one appropriate statistic to use: Pearson's product-moment correlation coefficient (r).[8] The computation of this statistic is rather complex and a complete illustration of its derivation is beyond the scope of this book. However, we can provide the appropriate formula and an illustration of its use. Remember that **Pearson's r** is calculated from data expressed in two *interval* scales, and that it is necessary to assume a *linear* relationship between variables. Here is the formula for Pearson's r:

$$r = \frac{\Sigma xy - \dfrac{(\Sigma x)(\Sigma y)}{N}}{\sqrt{\left[\Sigma x^2 - \dfrac{(\Sigma x)^2}{N}\right]\left[\Sigma x^2 - \dfrac{(\Sigma y)^2}{N}\right]}}$$

It really isn't as confusing as it looks, and almost anyone can calculate Pearson's r if he or she gives it a try. Let us illustrate a problem to see how it works. Suppose we want to examine the relationship of respondents' scores on two attitudinal items and suppose the items are measures of (1) concern for the natural environment and (2) support for the military-industrial complex.

Because concern for the natural environment is to be considered our dependent variable, we will assign it the letter Y, leaving the X to represent our independent variable, support for the military-industrial complex. Our data would look like this:

	X	X²	Y	Y²	XY	
	2	4	5	25	10	
	2	4	4	16	8	
	3	9	4	16	12	
	3	9	3	9	9	
	4	16	1	1	4	N = 9
	4	16	1	1	4	
	4	16	0	0	0	
	6	36	0	0	0	
	8	64	0	0	0	
$\Sigma =$	36	174	18	68	47	

If we carefully reexamine the formula for Pearson's r, we can see why the data were arranged as they are. Remember, the X variable is a measure of support for the military, and the Y variable represents scores on an item mesuring concern for the environment. As we can see in the formula, both the X and Y scores will be needed in various forms. For example, each score will have to be *squared* (multiplied by itself) as well as multiplied by the corresponding variable (XY). We have already calculated these scores. First, we simply listed all the scores on the X variable, and then squared each score (X^2). We then listed all the Y variables, keeping them in order with the X scores for each individual respondent, and we then squared them (Y^2). Next, we multiplied X times Y for each case, and listed the result in the XY column of our illustration. Note that our sample size is 9, and we have summed each of the columns. Each of these calculations is called for in the formula. Now we place each figure in its place in the formula and calculate through. Here is what the formula looks like after all the proper numbers are in the right place:

$$ r = \frac{47 - \dfrac{(36)(18)}{9}}{\sqrt{\left[174 - \dfrac{(36)^2}{9}\right]\left[68 - \dfrac{(18)^2}{9}\right]}} $$

$$ = \frac{47 - 72}{\sqrt{(174-144)\,(68-36)}} $$

$$ = \frac{-25}{\sqrt{(30)(32)}} $$

$$= \frac{-25}{\sqrt{960}}$$

$$= \frac{-25}{30.98}$$

$$= -.81$$

As can be seen in our illustration, we begin by placing the sum of XY in the formula, then subtract from that figure the sum of X times the sum of Y divided by N (N = the number of cases in our example). When we work through the top portion of the formula, the result is a negatively signed number (-25). The lower portion of the formula consists of the sums of X^2 and Y^2 and the sums of X squared and Y squared divided by N, and then multiplied together. The result, after we have taken the square root, is 30.98. When we divide, we arrive at an r of $-.81$. How do we interpret this figure?

INTERPRETING PEARSON'S r A Pearson's r of $-.81$ tells us the relationship between our two measures is an inverse one; as the scores on one variable increase, the scores on the other decrease. That is, as one becomes more concerned with the natural environment, one is less likely to support the military, and vice versa. A Pearson's r of $-.81$ also tells us the association we have found is rather strong because r runs from -1 (for a perfect inverse relationship) to 1 (a perfect positive association), and .81 is very close to 1, meaning there is a strong association between these two variables.

An easier way to interpret r, however, is to square it, making it an $\mathbf{r^2}$ (read as r square). If we square $-.81$ we obtain an r^2 of .66, which means we can explain 66 percent of the *variation* in the dependent variable in our analysis. The Pearson's product-moment r is a measure of the extent to which a change in another intervally measured variable is associated with change in another intervally measured variable, and when the number is squared, it tells us the amount of variation we can account for in the dependent scores we have measured.

What the formula is doing is this: suppose we had two interval measures of items we would like to examine:

Respondent	Item 1	Item 2
A	1	1
B	2	2
C	3	3
D	4	4
E	5	5

Suppose further we assumed there was a *linear* relationship between the two variables, and if we plotted the two variables, they would *vary* together in a linear fashion. To illustrate this point, the above data will be used to plot the association between items 1 and 2 for the data set above. First, we place the variables on an *X* and *Y* axis. Because we have not designated which item is what, we really don't know the dependent variable from the independent variable but we will assume item 1 is the dependent variable. Of course, we are sure you have already noticed the scores on item 2 are identical to those on item 1, and that this designation is only for instructive purposes. Also, from what we have already discussed, you probably realize that whatever association we find will be a positive and perfect one. This is because of the configuration of the data we are using in the illustration. Each respondent has the same score on each variable.

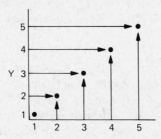

In our illustration we have placed a dot at each intersection of the two item scores. That is, after we have placed all the possible scores on an *X* or *Y* axis, we can then see how a score on one variable corresponds to a score on the other. To begin, respondent A has a score of 1 on both measures, so we place that score at the point in our graph where these two measures would coincide. The next score, for B, is 2, and we have placed a dot where these scores come together on our graph. We continue this procedure through the data until we have plotted each of the five scores. Now, if we draw a line connecting all the dots we have plotted on the graph, we obtain a "picture" of the relationship found among our variables. When we find a pattern such as this, with the scores running up and to the righthand side of the graph, we call the association a *positive linear* one. There are several forms an association can take, however, and not all of them are as neat as the one we have used in our example. Indeed, if we calculated a Pearson's *r* for the data we have used here, we would arrive at a perfect and positive *r* of 1. The formula we have given is actually drawing the best line it can between the data points we have generated or between the points generated from other data. The closer the actual points approach the patterns illustrated, the stronger and greater the magnitude of the statistic we will calculate. That is what the formula is doing, except it is doing it with much more data and with data points that are not so neatly arranged (Figure 15.1).

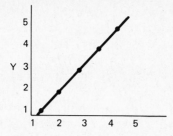

FIGURE 15.1

Figure 15.2 contains examples of the types of relationships we might discover when using Pearson's *r* with two intervally measured variables. The illustrations indicate the data points in four different arrangements. The first represents a positive linear relationship similar to the association we found in our earlier example. The second represents the data points as they might emerge if a relationship were an inverse or linear negative association. The third kind of relationship, a curvilinear one, is often difficult to identify when using Pearson's *r*, and other types of statistics are used to describe this kind of pattern.[9] When no association exists between the two variables, the pattern of data points would look like those in the fourth illustration. Remember, the formula for Pearson's *r* is actually drawing a mathematical line through the data points created by the two variables. The line is constructed so as to be as close to each of the data points as possible without bending it. For this reason it is generally easier to identify a linear positive or negative pattern, while the others are more difficult to detect. The greater the magnitude of our final statistic (Pearson's *r*), the closer and more easily detectable the relationship between the variables being examined.

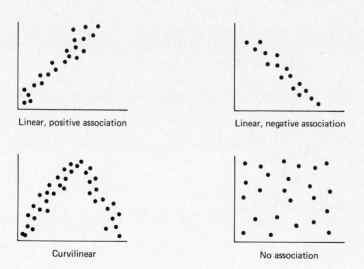

Linear, positive association

Linear, negative association

Curvilinear

No association

FIGURE 15.2

Measuring Associations

In summary, this chapter started by introducing some general measures that can be used at three different times during the analysis of data: (1) when variables are measured at the nominal level, (2) when both measures are at the ordinal level, and (3) when both measures are intervally scaled. For each level of measurement there was one statistic presented that could be used to describe the association between two variables. Lambda represented a way of moving from one guessing rule to another to improve powers of predictability. The rules were to guess the mode when only one variable was under consideration, and to guess within category modes when information on a second variable was available. The general type of statistical model upon which the lambda statistic was based is called the proportional reduction in error (PRE) model. The general idea behind the PRE model is to arrive at a statistic (lambda, gamma, and others) that will summarize the association between two variables by giving us some indication of how much better we can predict a person's membership in one category based on knowledge of membership in another category. In our example, the categories were the sex of the respondents and their political parties. We found that by knowing a respondent's sex, we could better predict voting behavior by 40 percent.

When we moved to the ordinal level, we turned to gamma as our measure of association. This statistic is also a PRE measure, but we used it to predict a respondent's rank on one variable from his or her position or rank on another variable. We found that unlike lambda, which could vary from 0 to 1, gamma could attain a value anywhere from -1 to $+1$. This allowed us to examine the direction of the relationship as well as the strength of the association between two ordinally measured variables. In our illustration we discovered that by knowing a person's rank on an educational measure, we could improve our prediction on that person's rank on an income measure by 33 percent. In our example we illustrated how gamma can indicate a negative association. There were two ways in which we could calculate gamma: when there were no ties between judges and when data were in a contingency table. The same formula worked for both situations.

Finally, we examined Pearson's r, a statistic designed to measure the level of association between two intervally measured variables. This staistic also indicated both the strength of associations and the directon the relationship took. We discovered that this statistic was easier to interpret when it was squared. This allowed us to see how much variation in one score could be accounted for by knowledge of an additional variable. An examination of several of the ways in which data of this type can be related indicated four general patterns of association: positive linear, negative linear, curvilinear, and no association at all.

We turn now to one additional statistic that is often used in the social sciences: *chi-square*. We then review the standard deviation and standard error.

At the beginning of this chapter we made a distinction between descriptive and inferential statistics, noting that inferential statistics were used to provide estimates of parameters and for testing hypotheses. In this section we introduce **chi-square,** a test of statistical independence, which is used for hypothesis testing when variables have been measured at the nominal level.

The statistics we have discussed so far have been used to indicate the strength of association between variables, and the direction relationships can take. We turn now to a statistic that can be used to see if two nominally scaled variables are statistically independent of one anoher. Chi-square, an inferential statistic and one of the most frequently used tests in the sociological literature, will let us do just that.[10] Before we illustrate the computation of chi-square, let us first discuss the logic behind this statistic.

The Logic of Chi-Square

Suppose we had two *fair* coins, not biased, not "weighted" in any way, not subject to controls other than chance, and *independent* of one another. If we tossed these coins fifty times, we might expect them to result in a twenty-five heads and twenty-five tails split. From our discussion of probability in Chapter 6, we learned that there were several combinations these coins could take, and that we might not always come up with a perfect 25-25 split. We could obtain, for example, a 30-20 split or a 35-15 outcome, and several other combinations of heads and tails from the two coins. What we can say when this happens is that the coins have departed from the model of statistical independence. The question is, is the departure we have witnessed significantly large enough to be meaningful? Is it possible that the combination of heads and tails we observed could have occurred by chance alone? Is the difference between what we have observed and what we would expect to have observed large enough to really make a difference? Are both coins statistically independent or is one or both of them biased? To help illustrate the use of chi-square, we have placed data based on a number of coin tosses in a contingency table:

	Coin 1	Coin 2	Totals
Heads	31	21	52
Tails	19	29	48
TOTALS	50	50	100

As can be seen, we have tossed two coins one hundred times, and we have recorded each flip for each coin. When we compare what we have found by actually tossing the coins with what we would have expected by chance alone, we see that the figures in our illustration depart from a model of statistical independence. There is a difference between what we have *observed* empirically and what we would have *expected* theoretically. Is what we have observed *significantly* different from what we would expect by chance alone? We will see when we can compute the expected frequencies for the data in our table of coin tosses.

Testing Hypotheses

Before we turn to our discussion of computing expected frequencies, we should note that we are actually testing the hypothesis that one coin is different from the other. However, when sociologists test hypotheses, they begin by stating that there is no difference between the objects under investigation. Such a statement is called the **null hypothesis** (H_0), also called the hypothesis of no difference. When we test hypotheses we do not prove them right as much as we reject other alternatives. If "nothing is going on" with the two coins we are flipping, we would expect that the outcome of their flips would be roughly the same, given our knowledge of probability (see Chapter 6). If, however, there is something going on with the coins, there will be a difference that is significant. Our null hypothesis is then, "There is no difference between the two coins when they are flipped one hundred times." Our **alternate hypothesis**, also called the **research hypothesis** (H_1) is, "There is a difference between the two coins when they are flipped one hundred times." Our objective is to try to reject the null hypothesis, thus giving weight to our decision to accept the alternative. If we reject the hypothesis that the coins are the same (that is, the null), we will have an easier time accepting that they are indeed different. The value of the chi-square statistic will help us in making this decision. If it is greater than what we would expect by chance alone, we will reject the null hypotheses of no difference, and conclude that there is a significant difference in the two coins we are tossing, and that one is coming up heads more often than we would expect according to chance alone. We now turn to the calculation of expected frequencies, which are the cell values we would expect under the null hypothesis.

Computing Expected Frequencies

Given our knowledge of probability, we would expect our coins to have distributed themselves equally between heads and tails for each of the cells of the table. If we flipped the coins one hundred times, we could expect to obtain twenty-five heads and twenty-five tails for each coin, resulting in a frequency of 25 in each of the cells. This is what we would expect from a pure chance model, assuming that there was nothing wrong with the coins we were tossing. There is another way to figure expected frequencies, however. We can, for example, take full advantage of the data we have in our table and examine the

marginals (that is, the totals) as well as the cells. If chance factors are the only thing operating, we would expect to find no differences in outcome within the two categories of coins. We would also not expect to find any differences between the heads and tails that emerged when we tossed the coins. Using this information and the marginals, we can compute the **expected frequencies,** what we would expect by chance alone, by multiplying the marginals associated with a cell and dividing that product by the total (N). For the cell in the upper lefthand corner of our illustration, for coin 1 and heads, we multiply 50 times 52 and divide that by 100. For the cell containing the results of coin 2 for heads, we multiply 50 times 52 and divide the result by 100. For the cell with the outcomes of coin 31 for tails, we multiply 50 times 48 and divide the result by 100 and so forth until we had finished the calculations for the entire table. We have calculated the expected frequencies for our illustrations, and we have placed them in a table with the observed frequencies:

	Coin 1	Coin 2	Totals
Heads	31 (26)	21 (26)	52
Tails	19 (34)	29 (24)	48
TOTALS	50	50	100

Computing Chi-Square

To compute chi-square, we will need the following formula:

$$\chi^2 = \frac{(f_o - f_e)^2}{f_e}$$

where f_o is an observed frequency and f_e is the corresponding expected frequency. Chi-square (χ^2) is equal to the sum of the squares of all differences, each divided by its corresponding expected frequency. We will place these data into a form that makes chi-square a very workable formula:

f_o	f_e	$f_o - f_e$	$(f_o - f_e)^2$	$(f_o - f_e)^2/f_e$
31	26	5	25	.96
21	26	−5	25	.96
19	24	−5	25	1.04
29	24	5	25	1.04
				$\chi^2 = 4.00$

In the table above we have simply listed the observed frequency (f_o) for each cell of our table. With the observed frequency, we have also listed the expected frequency for each cell (f_e). An inspection of the chi-square formula indicates that we will need to subtract the expected frequencies from what we have observed $(f_o - f_e)$, square the result $(f_o - f_e$ squared), and then divide that figure by the corresponding expected frequency as we have indicated in the last column of the illustration. The sum of this final column is chi-square, which for our data is equal to 4.0. What does this chi-square mean? How do we interpret this statistic?

Interpreting Chi-Square

It is impossible to interpret chi-square independently; we will need one additional number before we can see if what we have found is significantly different from what we might find by chance alone. We will have to calculate the *degrees of freedom* for our table, a very easy operation to do because degrees of freedom are calculated simply by multiplying the number of rows in a table, minus one, times the number of columns in a table, minus one:

$$df = (r - 1)(c - 1)$$

In our example, there are two columns and two rows, so the degrees of freedom for our table are $(2-1)(2-1) = (1)(1) = 1$.[11] Next it is necessary to turn to Appendix B to see how large a chi-square is needed with df = 1 to tell us if there is a significant difference between what we expected by chance alone when we flipped the coins in the example or if what we got was what could be expected to occur if there was a biased coin used. In Appendix B, we find that the various degrees of freedom for tables of all sizes have been previously calculated and listed in the lefthand column. We begin by locating our degree of freedom, which is 1. Next, we look across the top of the listing of chi-square values to see if we can find the value of the statistic we have calculated. The top row of the table lists the probabilities or levels of significance for observing a given value of chi-square. As we have noted, the first column of figures indicates the degrees of freedom. If we have df = 1, and a calculated chi-square of 4, our statistic is significant at the .05 level because our chi-square is larger than the one listed in the table for that position (3.841). When inspecting this appendix, always look for a value *larger* than the one calculated for the appropriate degrees of freedom, and when we have calculated such a chi-square we can conclude that there is a significant difference among the data being analyzed. For our illustration, we can conclude that there is a significant difference between the two coins we have tossed based on the numbers of heads and tails that emerged. One of the coins is not a fair one, or there is something going on that is influencing the outcomes of our tosses. What we can't tell from the chi-square is the strength of the relationship between these variables. All we can tell is that there is a statistically significant difference between the coins. To find the strength of the association, we would have to return to lambda, a measure of association between two nominally scaled variables. Let us review the procedures necessary for calculating chi-square:[12]

Step 1   Place the observed frequencies in a contingency table.

Step 2   Determine the number of degrees of freedom (df) for the table.

Step 3   Determine the expected frequencies for each cell and compute chi-square using the formula given here.

Step 4   Determine the significance of the computed X^2 by referring to the table in Appendix B; if chi-square is equal to or greater than the tabulated value for the appropriate df and significance level, conclude that there is a difference between the variables being studied (reject the null hypothesis).

As pointed out earlier, the derivation of the statistics we are presenting and an in-depth discussion of them are beyond the scope of this book. We can, however, introduce the general methods and techniques associated with the most often-used statistics in sociology. If we carefully follow what is presented here, we should have a much better understanding of basic social statistics when they are introduced in a more formal way. Before closing our discussion of basic statistics, we must turn to one additional measure: **the standard deviation.**

The Standard Deviation Reviewed

Suppose we were getting ready for a trip to New Orelans, Louisiana. What kinds of preparations might we make for such a trip? We could be concerned with the weather in New Orleans, and we would probably check to see how "hot" or "cold" it got in that city before we made a decision about what clothes to take with us. To get a better understanding of the weather in New Orleans, we might ask people about the city's *average temperature.* Suppose we discovered that the average temperature was 82 degrees. That sounds nice, and we would probably take some light, spring-type clothes with us on our trip. However, we could get off the airplane in New Orleans and discover that the temperature was a scorching 120 degrees! This is far from the balmy 82 degrees we had expected, and even the light clothing we packed would be too warm for such weather. What happened? Did someone lie to us about the weather in New Orleans? It turns out that an average of 82 degrees can be calculated in several ways:

	Temperature in New Orleans 1	**Temperature in New Orleans 2**
Time 1 =	120 Degrees	82 Degrees
Time 2 =	110 Degrees	82 Degrees
Time 3 =	70 Degrees	82 Degrees
Time 4 =	60 Degrees	82 Degrees
Time 5 =	50 Degrees	82 Degrees
	$\overline{X} = 82$	$\overline{X} = 82$

We can see that the two measures of temperature above each yield the same average of 82 degrees. However, measurements taken in column 1 *vary* significantly from the average, while those taken in column 2 do not vary at all. If we actually believed the figures in the first column we would have to take not only very light clothing, but we would also have to pack some fairly warm clothes as well because the temperature can drop down to around 50 degrees. If we stay with the temperatures in the second column, we would not have to vary our clothing at all because there is apparently no variation in the temperature. What all this means is that we really can't understand the mean temperature without having an understanding of the *variation* temperatures take. Just as there is a formula for the arithmetic mean, and for the median, there is a formula that can be applied to our data that will give us an indication of the *dispersion* of the scores we are examining. The statistic this formula yields is called the *standard deviation*, which is based on the squared deviations whose mean is then unsquared. This is what the formula looks like:[13]

$$s = \sqrt{\frac{\Sigma x^2}{(N-1)}}$$

When reading this formula, notice that the x is a *small* x and not a large one. This means that the figure is the result after subtracting the average score from it $(x = X - \overline{X})$. What the formula is telling us is to take the deviation of each score from the mean score, square each difference, sum the results, divide by the number of cases minus 1, and take the square root. Here's an example:

Temperatures in New Orleans 1 (X)	$X - \overline{X}$	$(X - \overline{X})^2$
120	38	1,444
110	28	784
70	−12	144
60	−22	484
50	−32	1,024
410/5 = 82	0	3,880/5−1 = 970

$$s = \sqrt{970} = 31$$

We have returned to our trip to New Orleans and calculated the standard deviation *(s)* for the five temperatures that appeared to vary so much. We have arrived at a standard deviation of 31. What does this mean? How is it interpreted? *The greater the spread about the mean score, the greater the standard deviation.* If we had used the second column of New Orleans temperatures where all the scores were the same, the deviation from the mean would have been *zero*, and the standard deviation would have been *zero*. We can thus view the standard deviation as an index of variation. Simply put, as the variation among scores increases, so does the standard deviation. With a mean of 82 and a standard deviation of 31 degrees, we can see that simple spring clothes will be out of the question for New Orleans. To calculate the standard deviation, data will have to be measured at the interval level. The formula we have given here can be applied to any series of ungrouped scores, and the characteristics of the standard deviation will always be as follows:

1. It is always a positive number.
2. It measures variability in the same units as those of the original observations.
3. No matter how the original observations are distributed the mean plus or minus two standard deviations will include at least 75 percent of the observations.
4. No matter how the original observations are distributed the mean plus or minus three standard deviations will include 89 percent of the observations or more.

With this information and our understanding of the standard deviation, we can return to a problem we discussed in our chapter on sampling: the **standard error.** If we recall Chapter 6, we will remember that we described the standard error in detail, and that we indicated how it was used. It turns out that the standard error is simply the standard deviation of the theoretical distribution of the sampling means discussed in Chapter 6, and that the standard error is directly related to the sample size and standard deviation in the following way:

$$\text{Standard Error} \quad = \quad \frac{S}{\sqrt{n-1}}$$

where s is the standard deviation, and n is the sample size. From this information we can compute a standard error for a single sample and easily set confidence intervals around the standard error. The standard error for our illustration of temperatures in New Orleans would be:

$$\text{Standard Error} \quad = \quad \frac{31}{\sqrt{5-1}}$$

$$= \quad \frac{31}{2}$$

$$= \quad 15.5$$

For these data there is a mean of 82 and a standard error of 15.5. Because the standard error is a standard deviation, it can be interpreted using the normal curve. Specifically, the distance from the mean to + or − one standard error will include the true population mean 68 percent of the time. In other words, 68 percent of all sample means lie within one standard error of the population mean (parameter), and the mean + or − two standard errors will include the mean of the population 95 pecent of the time, and three standard errors will include the population mean 99 percent of the time. Using this information, it is possible for researchers to determine how closely sample means approximate the population mean.

Summary

This chapter has focused on the basic statistics available to us for the analysis of data. Although we have been able to only introduce these statistics, and while we haven't been able to include in this single chapter everything we would need to know about social statistics, we have given a general idea of the kinds of things that could be done. We have found, for example, that there are certain statistics appropriate for certain levels of measurement, and that when variables are not measured at a specific level, we have to find the appropriate statistic for discovering the association between them. Lambda was given as an example of a measure for nominally scaled variables; gamma was used to illustrate techniques for examining associations at the ordinal level; Pearson's r was used to measure at the interval level. Chi-square, one of the most often-used statistics in sociology, was also applied at the nominal level, but was used to see if there was statistical independence rather than associations among variables. Finally, we again illustrated the use of the standard deviation, and found that only knowing the mean of a distribution wasn't enough, that we needed an index of dispersion before we could make a decision about the distribution of a variable. We also reviewed how the standard deviation was related to the standard error, a statistic introduced in an earlier chapter. The standard error gives us an idea of how closely our sample approximates the population from which it was taken.

Given the large samples that sociologists now work with, it is often the case that the statistics presented here are left to the computer. In the following chapter we illustrate how the same statistics we have been working with here can be computed using the computer and a language called SPSS.

Glossary

alternate hypothesis The research hypothesis or the hypothesis that states the differences we expect to find.

chi-square A statistic that tells us if there is a significant difference between two nominally scaled variables; one of the most often-used statistics in sociology.

data matrix The raw data from a study before it is "boiled" down to summary numbers or distributions.

descriptive statistics Statistics that give us a picture of our data, and provide a single summary number to describe an entire data set or series of scores. scores.

expected frequencies The values we would

expect if no relationship existed between variables; used in the calculation of chi-square.

gamma A PRE meaure of association for ordinally measured variables.

inferential statistics Statistics used to test hypotheses and estimate parameters; chi-square was used in this chapter to test the hypothesis that two coins were fair coins.

lambda A PRE measure of association for nominally scaled variables.

marginals The totals in a table for its categories.

null hypothesis The hypothesis of no difference; we attempt to reject the null so we can accept the alternative.

Pearson's *r* Measure of association for intervally measured variables; indicates strength and direction of relationships.

perfect inverse relationship When knowledge of one variable allows prediction of another variable perfectly as one increases and the other decreases.

perfect positive relationship When knowledge of one variable allows prediction of another perfectly as one increases and the other also increases.

PRE Proportional reduction in error; the model for several statistics used in the social sciences.

r^2 An easier method of interpreting Pearson's *r*; simply square *r* and interpret as the amount of variance accounted for in *y* by knowledge of *x*.

standard deviation A measure of dispersion (see also Chapter 6).

standard error A statistic used to indicate the degree to which a statistic represents a parameter (see also Chapter 6).

symmetric measure When a continency table yields only one value of a statistic regardless of whether the row or column variable is the independent or dependent measure in a study; gamma is such a measure, lambda is not.

Notes

1. Linton C. Freeman, *Elementary Applied Statistics* (New York: Wiley, 1965), and Michael A. Malec, *Essential Statistics For Social Research* (New York: Lippincott, 1977), offer excellent introductions to beginning statistics. We suggest these texts to students who are interested in doing further study in this area, and we have followed their lead often in this chapter. For more advanced treatments see Hubert M. Blalock, Jr., *Social Statistics*, 2nd ed. (New York: McGraw-Hill, 1979), and John H. Mueller, Karl F. Schuessler, and Herbert L. Costner, *Statistical Reasoning in Sociology* (Boston: Houghton Mifflin, 1977).

2. See for further examples, Blalock, op. cit., pp. 310−311; Freeman, op. cit., pp. 71−78; Malec, op. cit., pp. 124−131, and Herman J. Loether and Donald G. McTavish, *Descriptive and Inferential Statistics: An Introduction* (Boston: Allyn and Bacon, 1974), pp. 214−218.

3. Malec, op. cit., pp. 124−130.

4. Freeman, op. cit., pp. 71−78.

5. Leo A. Goodman and William H. Kruskal, "Measures of Association for Cross Classification," *Journal of the American Statistical Association* 49 (December 1954): 732−764; and Leo A. Goodman and William H. Kruskal, "Measures of Association for Cross Classification II: Further Discussion and References," in the *Journal of the American Statistical Association* 58 (June 1959): 123−163.

6. Freeman, op. cit., pp. 79−88.

7. Ibid., p. 87.

8. Ibid., pp. 89−107; Malec, op. cit., pp. 161−182.

9. See Freeman, op. cit., pp. 120–130, and Malec, op. cit., pp. 180–182 for discussions of *eta*.

10. Freeman op. cit., pp. 215–227, and Malec, op. cit., pp. 108–119.

11. With tables having df = 1 or simply 2 × 2 tables, Yates's correction should be used. For instructive purposes, we have not included this correction here. See Malec, op. cit., pp. 119–120.

12. Freeman, op. cit., p. 226.

13. Ibid. pp. 59–67; Malec, op. cit., pp. 47–55; Loether and McTavish, op. cit., pp. 146–150; Mueller, Schuessler, and Costner, op. cit., p. 161; and Blalock, op. cit., pp. 78–85.

16

Calculators and Computers: Tools of the Trade

Sociologists have recently come to rely more and more on two essential research tools: the **pocket calculator** and the **computer.** Without these tools the analysis of quantitative data would be far more difficult and much less precise than it is. The purpose of this chapter is to familiarize you with pocket calculators, and to introduce the computer and one of the several languages it can speak and understand—the *Statistical Package for the Social Sciences*, or SPSS. As we have seen throughout this text, much of the data gathered by sociologists are quantitative, and these kinds of data require basic statistical analyses. In the previous chapter we demonstrated several statistics we might use in various research situations, assuming they would be calculated *by hand*, and that we would use a calculator to compute only the statistics illustrated. In this chapter we provide information about the means that make it possible to analyze very large data sets, data sets that contain so many respondents or units of analysis that it would be impossible to analyze them without the help of a computer and calculator. However, before we begin with the pocket calculator and an introduction to SPSS, some brief comments should be made about two additional research tools sociologists often use in the field: the *tape recorder* and the *camera*.

The Tape Recorder

During recent years tape recorders have become very compact and portable, and thus have become handy tools to take to the field when we are conducting ethnographies or unstructured interviews. We note here that it is generally an easy task to record portions of interviews when compared to taking notes with a pad and pencil. Thus, the use of the tape recorder can help cut down on the time spent writing and rewriting field notes. However, it is not wise to record everything an informant tells us while in the field because the typing and editing of recorded interviews is a costly and time-consuming process. Fieldworkers should therefore use tape recorders with a degree of discretion, and should in every case attempt to reduce the intrusive effects of mechanical recordings. Before going to the field with a tape recorder, interviewers should become familiar enough with the machine to make its use as unobtrusive as possible. Fumbling with the device could possibly influence an informant in a negative way, and he or she could refuse an interview because of it. As in the training of interviewers for survey research, fieldworkers who plan to use a tape recorder should practice using it before going to the field. When they become proficient in using the device for taking "recorded notes," it can become a useful research tool.

The Camera

A fieldworker seldom goes to the field without a camera. A camera can be used in many ways to aid in a research effort. It can be used to visually record complex events that would otherwise be difficult to describe, such as celebrations or rituals. Photographs can also be used to "jog" a researcher's memory, helping to recall more vividly a particular research setting and the objects present in that context. However, like the tape recorder, the camera should be used with discretion. If informants are sensitive to having their picture taken, the appearance of a camera during an interview might cause them to cut off the conversation. Be careful, when using a camera, to have the permission of those you are working with or they might not provide the information being sought. Slide presentations can also be compiled using the camera, and as is often said, a picture is worth a thousand words.

The Pocket Calculator

The illustration below depicts a pocket calculator. Most of us are already familiar with this particular research tool. Over the years, almost everybody has at one time or another had occasion to operate a pocket calculator similar to the one pictured below. In our daily lives we use them to balance checkbooks and to calculate the mileage of our cars when we are on long trips. When we are conducting research we use pocket calculators to compute statistics for contingency tables that may have already been constructed using a computer program similar to the one we will introduce later. Pocket calculators are also used to "check" the work of other social scientists, to see if the statistics they are reporting are correct. There are times, for example, when we will believe that the statistic selected by a writer is the wrong one for that situation, and we will want to calculate another statistic on the same data to gain a better understanding of the relationships that are there. Specifically, suppose we have found an article with a contingency table containing two variables measured at the nominal level, and the researcher who has written the article has calculated a chi-square to see if there are significant differences between two categories of respondents. We might wish to calculate a PRE measure to get a better understanding of the strength of the relationship he or she is

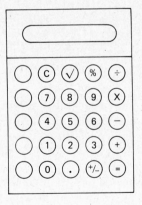

reporting (see Chapter 15). We could use our calculator to compute lambda or one of several additional statistics that can be computed from the chi-square statistic.[1] In another situation we might use a pocket calculator to compute the percentage differences that occur among the cells of tables we have constructed or tables that others have built and published in an article. Once data are in tabular form, it is easy to check and rearrange them using a pocket calculator, and the uses a sociologist can find for this very essential tool are almost too numerous to list here, but the building and reconstruction of tabular presentations is perhaps the most useful. Let us take a detailed look at the calculator.

Most calculators display up to 8 digits in their window—7 digits to the right of the decimal—and can indicate both positive and negative values by displaying a minus sign to the left of any negative number that appears in the display window. The key marked "C" clears the window of any display that is there, and if we turn the machine off, the display will automatically be cleared of any digits that may have been there. Let us look at the basic functions of the machine to gain a better "feel" for it.

Addition and Subtraction

The algebraic entry system of most calculators allows a problem to be entered in the same order it is written. For example, suppose we wished to simply add and subtract a few numbers for a formula. Here is how it would be done:

$$8 + 2 - 13 = -3$$
$$8 \oplus 2 \ominus 13 \ominus{=} -3$$

Multiplication and Division

Multiplication and division are almost always necessary when computing a statistical formula. Here is an example of how these functions operate using the calculator:

$$\frac{6 \times 6.5}{3} = 13$$

$$6 \otimes 6.5 \oslash 3 \ominus{=} 13$$

Square Root Calculations

As we discovered in the previous chapter, there are also several occasions when it is necessary to find the square root of a portion of a statistical formula. Here is an illustration of this function:

$$36 = 6$$

$$36 \ \sqrt{}{} \ominus{=} 6$$

Powers and Roots

Often a displayed number can be raised to an integer power by pressing the $\otimes$ key, then pressing the $\ominus$ key one less time than the integer power desired:

$$5^6 = 15625$$

$$5 \; \otimes \; = \; = \; = \; = \; = \; 15625$$

The $\sqrt{}$ key can also be used to solve for roots that are a power of two:

To find $\sqrt[4]{N}$ enter N, press $\sqrt{}\sqrt{}$
To find $\sqrt[8]{N}$ enter N, press $\sqrt{}\sqrt{}\sqrt{}$
To find $\sqrt[16]{N}$ enter N, press $\sqrt{}\sqrt{}\sqrt{}$

$$6561 = 3$$
$$6561 \; \sqrt{}\sqrt{}\sqrt{} = 3$$

That is about all there is to knowing a pocket calculator. Of course, as we continue to use it, and as we begin to actually work some of the formulas given in this book, we will become even more proficient in its use. Let us turn now to a much larger research tool—the computer—and one of the languages it understands—SPSS.

Using the Statistical Package for the Social Sciences (SPSS)

This section is devoted to introducing you to the *Statistical Package for the Social Sciences* (SPSS).[2] SPSS is one of many computer languages available for our use, and along the way you may learn several of these statistical "packages" while conducting research. We have selected SPSS for presentations here because it is so widely used in both the business world and on college and university campuses. We will provide the information needed to run a very simple computer job using SPSS. Some of the information that is required to do computer analyses at your own school will have to come from an instructor, however, and he or she will have to make the special codes and procedures that are particular to your college or university available before you will be able to "get on line."

The Data

For our examples we will be using a fictitious data set and suggest you use the same one so that you will be able to check your work against the results presented in the book. We strongly encourage you to do this. We also suggest you go back into the book and convert some of the examples we have given into "data sets" and rework the problems illustrated using a calculator and computer rather than just your pencil. Here is the data that we will be using; you may wish to punch these figures on computer cards before continuing:

| | Column Number | | | | |
Card Number	1	2	3	4	5
Card 1	1	1	1	4	6
Card 2	1	2	1	7	5
Card 3	2	1	1	3	6
Card 4	2	2	1	7	4
Card 5	3	1	1	5	5
Card 6	3	2	1	6	4
Card 7	4	1	1	5	3
Card 8	4	2	1	6	3
Card 9	5	1	1	4	7
Card 10	5	2	1	8	3
Card 11	1	1	2	4	5
Card 12	1	2	2	4	5
Card 13	2	1	2	4	5
Card 14	2	2	2	4	5
Card 15	3	1	2	6	5
Card 16	3	2	2	6	5
Card 17	4	1	2	5	4
Card 18	4	2	2	5	4
Card 19	5	1	2	4	7
Card 20	5	2	2	4	7

We have listed the column numbers across the top of the page, and the computer cards that will represent each respondent down the lefthand side of the page. Our N is therefore 20 cases, and we have measured 5 variables for each respondent in the data set.

Setting Up a Job

Now that we have punched the cards that we will use as our data for this illustration, we can move to the mechanics of setting up the computer "run" or "job" that will be conducted. Keep in mind that we will be "talking" to a computer, and that we will be speaking with the help of computer cards and a language called SPSS. One of the first things we will have to do is tell the computer *who we are* and that it is all right for us to be running a job. To do this we will need Job Control Language (**JCL**).

JOB CONTROL LANGUAGE Every computer job begins and ends with a series of cards written in Job Control Language. These cards tell the computer who we are, who should be charged for the computer time that is about to be used, the kind of job that will be run, and how long we believe the job will take to be completed. The JCL is different from one computer installation to another so we can't give the appropriate instructions for your computer here. Your instructor or the personnel at your school's computer center should be able to provide the instructions needed to prepare the appropriate JCL cards. Once we have done that, we will be ready to start talking in SPSS. It turns out that

SPSS is not a great deal different from English so all we will have to do is write the desired steps we want the computer to take with the data and submit them to the computer. The various steps are written on computer cards but they are written in a specific way. The first part of our instructions that are punched onto the computer cards are called the **commands** and are punched into the **control field** of the card, which runs through the first 15 columns of the card. The second part of the instructions is called the **specifications field,** which is written beginning in column 16 and runs through the last column of the card (column 80). If the specifications we are writing run beyond the last column, if they take up more than 64 places, we will have to move to another card to continue writing. Remember to start the second card in column 16, and don't repeat the first portion of the instructions that are punched into the control field on the first card. Let us set up a simple job that you can run:

```
1               16

Run Name        An Example of SPSS

Comment         These examples are for Sanders and Pinhey
```

After we have finished punching the JCL for a job, our first card should be a *run name* instruction. This card's control words ("Run Name") provide a heading label at the top of each of the pages of our job as it comes off the computer. In the example, the run name instruction will ensure that the words "an example of SPSS" will appear at the upper left corner of each page of the run. Notice that our command is punched in the first 15 columns and the specification begins in column 16.

Beneath our run name card, we have placed a *comment card,* a handy tool we can use for bookkeeping with our data. The word "comment" is placed in the first part of the card, and is followed (beginning in column 16) with whatever comments we might want to include in the job. If we are running a series of jobs with each job in the series being slightly different from all the others then we can use the run name or comment options to keep our records straight. This way we would know exactly what we did with a particular run, and we won't confuse one type of analysis with another. A comment card can be placed in the deck *anytime* we wish to write a note to ourselves about the analysis we are conducting. We could have had a comment card that looked like this:

```
1               16

Comment         This run is for male respondents only
```

This comment tells us that we have modified our data especially for this run, that only the males in our sample were examined. If we didn't have this comment appearing in the deck, we could become confused about what we had done during this portion of the analysis.

VARIABLE LIST CARD Our next card, the *variable list card*, simply lists the variables that appear in our data set. In our illustration we are working with five variables, so our variable list card might look like this:

```
1               16

Variable List    S  G  T  X1  X2
```

We have just told the computer, in SPSS, that we are dealing with five variables, and that they are labeled S, G, T, X1, and X2. These variable "names" become permanently associated with the corresponding variables in our data set, and all future processing is accomplished by reference to these names. In our illustration we have used letters and numbers to "name" the variables in our set, but we could have written out the actual names of the variables as follows:

```
1               16

Variable List    Sex, Grade, Time, Skill, Sanity
```

In this example, each data case would consist of five variables (the sex, grades, time measures, skill measures, and sanity measures), and therefore the order of the variable names must be the same as the order in which the values of the variables are read off the raw-input-data-set. Specifically, the SPSS system matches the names with the values read in the corresponding order. A maximum of 500 variables may be defined for any given file. If our variable names run over on the first card, remember to move to a second card:

```
1               16

Variable List    Tom, George, Teddi, Brent, Paul, Bill,

                 Sidney, Stephanie, Holly, Fred, Bubba,

                 Frank
```

INPUT FORMAT CARD We will next have to tell the computer the type and location of the variables on the cases we are studying. We do this with an *input format card.*[3] Here is an example:

Input format   Fixed {5F1.0}

The word "fixed" means that the values of the variables are located on the same card and in the same column(s) for every case in the data set. Following the word "fixed" comes a series of elements that should be read *Fw.d*, where *F* indicates that the variable is numeric, *w* indicates the column width of the variable (including signs and decimal points if we have punched them onto our cards), and *d* is the number of digits or columns to the right of the decimal point. F1.0 would define a single-column numeric variable in which the decimal point had not been punched. F2.0 could either be a single column integer variable in which the decimal had been punched or a two-column variable in which the decimal had not been punched. If a decimal had been punched on the cards, its position would take priority over the number specified by *d*. The following table illustrates the rules and conventions used in defining numeric variables:[4]

Format Element	Value Appearing On Data Card	Value Read and Stored
F3.0	100	100
F3.1	100	10.0
F3.1	.10	0.10
F3.1	010	01.0
F3.2	1.0	1.00

What we have told the computer in our example is that there are five variables, they are numbers (and not letters), they each take up only one column, and there are no decimal points used in our data. On the print-out we receive when this job is completed, we will find that the SPSS system has listed each variable separately, giving the name we have assigned it, its individual format, number of records used to store it, and the columns each variable appears in. According to our input format statement, the variables are to be read as follows:

Variable	Format	Record	Columns	
S	F1.0	1	1–	1
G	F1.0	1	2–	2
T	F1.0	1	3–	3
X1	F1.0	1	4–	4
X2	F1.0	1	5–	5

INPUT MEDIUM CARD The next instruction we will have to give the computer deals with the actual input medium we are using. In this case we are working with computer cards, so we must inform the SPSS system of this fact. In some cases data are stored on tapes or discs similar to the tapes we play in a cassette or the records we play on a stereo. However, we are using *cards:*

```
1                       16

Input medium       Card
```

Now the computer knows that our medium of communication is through cards, that our raw data will be entered into the system on cards, not on tape or disc. This statement should be followed by an instruction telling the system the number of cases it will be dealing with. In our illustration we are working with an *N* of 20; that is, 20 respondents make up our data set. The instruction to the SPSS system would look like this:

NUMBER OF CASES CARD

```
1                       16

N of cases         20
```

If our data set contained 500 cases, we would have punched "500" instead of "20" on this card:

```
1                       16

N of cases         500
```

Labeling

VARIABLE LABELS CARDS   At this point in the job it is possible to provide each of the variables with an *extended label*, something more than the letters we used with the variable list card. Whenever a variable having one of these extended labels is used in a calculation, the label is printed on the output from that calculation. The card used to enter these extended variables labels, called a variable labels card, contains the control words "Var Labels" followed by a single variable name. The variable name is then followed by a label of up to 40 characters in length. A slash follows the label, which is succeeded by a second variable name and its associated label. Here is an example of a variable labels card:

```
1                       16

Var Labels          S, subject/T, time/G, grade/X1, computer/

                    skill/X2, sanity/
```

As can be seen in our illustration, when we reach the end of a card while doing a variable labels statement, we simply continue on a second card beginning in column 16. A variable label may apply to only one variable, and a variable must have been previously defined before a label can be assigned to it.

VALUE LABEL CARDS   SPSS also allows us to label the various values a variable can assume. Whenever used, the *value labels card* automatically lists the values assigned for each category of a variable. These labels are particularly useful when documenting output for cross-tabulations. Here is an example of a value labels card:

```
1                   16

Value Labels        T {1} Pretest {2} Posttest / G {1}

                    Exp {2} Cntl
```

What we have done with this statement is label the various values of the variables named "T" and "G." The first variable (T) can now take on two values, which will be labeled (1) "Pretest" and (2) "Posttest." When SPSS sees these values associated with these variables, it will print out the value labels we have assigned for values "1" and "2." We have also labeled the values for the variable "G," assigning the abbreviation "Exp" for the value of 1, and "Cntl" for the value of 2. These abbreviations stand for *experimental* and *control* groups, but we could have written them out in just that way. However, when preparing value labels to be processed through the *crosstabs* program, be aware that only the first 16 characters of the value labels are printed by SPSS. Moreover, the value labels for column variables are printed on two lines. The first line contains the first 8 characters, the following line the second 8 characters, and characters 17 to 20 are ignored. As with the other cards we have illustrated here, if we run out of room on the first card, we go to a second card and continue, starting in column 16.

CALCULATING SIMPLE STATISTICS   The next card used in our example tells the computer to calculate some statistics on our data set. When the *condescriptive all card* is used, SPSS prints out ten different statistics for each of our variables. It calculates the mean, the variance, the range, the sum, the standard error, kurtosis, the minimum value for that particular variable, the standard deviation, a measure of skewness, and the maximum value of the variable. Here is an example of a condescriptive statement:

```
1                   16

Condescriptive      all
```

Finally, we instruct the SPSS system to read out data. The key words "Read Input Data" are simply placed in the first 15 columns of a card, and this card is followed by the data cards. If we summarize the job we are about to run, it looks like this:

```
1                       16

JCL Cards {Get these from your instructor}

Run Name        An example of SPSS

Comment         These examples are for Sanders and Pinhey

Variable list   S  G  T  X1  X2

Input Format    Fixed {5F1.0}

Input Medium    Card

N of Cases      20

Var Labels      S, Subject/T, Time/G, Group/X1, Computer

                Skill/X2, Sanity/

Value Labels    T {1} Pretest {2} Posttest/G {1} Exp {2}

                Cntl

Condescriptive  All

Read Input Data

{Your data cards go here}

JCL {Get these from your instructor}
```

Using what we have given thus far, we should be able to run a simple SPSS job. This example provides you with only an introduction to many of the statements and keywords that are commonly used when preparing to analyze social scientific data. What you will receive by way of a print-out will look something like this:

File Noname {Creation date = -----}

Variable S   Subject

Mean	3.000	Std Error	0.324	Std Dev	1.451
Variance	2.105	Kurtosis	-1.323	Skewness	0.000
Range	4.000	Minimum	1.000	Maximum	5.000
Sum	60.000				

Valid Observations - 20   Missing Observations   - 0

The above print-out is only for one of the variables (S) in our data set, but our print-out will contain the same information for all the variables (G, T, X1, and X2).

Table Building

One of the central concerns of earlier chapters was illustrating the procedures to be used when constructing a table. We also suggested several statistics that can be computed when data are in a contingency table. Let us see what must be done to have SPSS do this work for us.

Crosstabs

Beginning at the end of the data deck, behind the cards containing the raw data, place the following cards:

1	16
Task Name	Experimental Design
Crosstabs	Tables = T by G
Statistics	All

We have just instructed the computer to cross-tabulate variables T and G. Because we have placed T before G in our request, T will be the dependent variable and will be listed down the lefthand side of the table. G will become the independent variable and will appear at the top of the table. The *task name card* is another recordkeeping device that simply tells us what it is we are doing with the data. The "Statistics All" statement asks SPSS to compute every statistic it can on the table we have asked it to build. Remember, these cards are to be placed at the end of the raw data deck, before any JCL that is supposed to "end" a computer job. The print-out would look like this:

	Count		G		
			Cntl		Row
	Row Pct	Exp	1.	2.	Totals
	Col Pct				
	Tot Pct				
T	1.		5	5	10
Pretest			50.00	50.00	50.00
			50.00	50.00	
			25.00	25.00	
	2.		5	5	10
Posttest			50.00	50.00	50.00
			50.00	50.00	
			25.00	25.00	
	Column				
	Total		10	10	20
			50.00	50.00	100.00

Several statistics will be listed and presented just below the table, including lambda, gamma, Pearson's r, and chi-square. There are requests other than "all" for the statistics statement, and we can call up almost any statistic we would care to compute using the crosstabs program. The numbers that can be used to call out a specific statistic are listed below:

1.—Chi-square
2.—Phi for 2 × 2 tables, Cramer's V for larger tables
3.—Contingency coefficient

4.—Lambda, symmetric and asymmetric
5.—Uncertainty coefficient, symmetric and assymmetric
6.—Kendall's tau b
7.—Kendall's tau c
8.—Gamma; Partial and zero-order gamma for three to n-variable tables
9.—Somer's D, symmetric and asymmetric
10.—Eta

There are also ways to create multiple-variable tables using this type of SPSS statement. For example, suppose we wrote a "tables" statement as follows:

```
1              16

     Tables = Party by Sex
```

This would produce a simple two-way frequency table using the variables "party" and "sex."

```
1              16

     Tables = Party by Sex by Age
```

This statement will yield several tables for "party" and "sex," one for each value of the "age" variable.

```
1              16

     Tables = Party by Sex by Age by Income
```

This command will result in party by sex tables for all possible combinations of the values of "age" and "income." For example, if there were three categories for income (low, medium, and high), and two age categories (old and young), six subtables would be produced. The following would be a multiple table request:

```
1              16

     Tables = Party, Sex, Age by Income
```

This command would result in "party" becoming a row variable that would be cross-tabulated with "income." Next, "sex" would become the row variable, and it would be cross-tabulated with "income." Finally, "age" would become the row variable, and it too would be cross-tabulated with the "income" measure. In other words, through this type of command with the keyword *by* properly placed, we can run a series of tables from a single statement.

Suppose we wished to conduct a *regression analysis* on our data. We might suspect a relationship between our two variables, X1 and X2 (computer skill and sanity measures). There are several options available. For example, we could run a *scattergram* program to obtain a picture of the suspected association. This is the same as asking SPSS to print-out a picture of the data points that Pearson's *r* uses to draw its straight line. Our request would look like this:

```
1                16

Task Name        Regression analysis

Scattergram      X2 with X1

Options          6

Statistics       All
```

We have again used a task name card to help with our bookkeeping. The scattergram statement is like the others we have discussed in that it starts in column 1 and runs no further than column 16. Starting in column 16, we instruct SPSS to compute a scattergram using the X2 and X1 variables. We have also instructed SPSS that we would like a special *option* of the scattergram program. This particular option (6) will see that a test of significance is made for the variables being plotted. Eight options are available:

Option 1 All missing values are included in the graphs and in the statistical calculations specified on the statistic card.

Option 2 Missing values are excluded from the graph and from the statistics also, meaning a case is deleted if any of the variables in the *scattergram* variable list have a missing value.

Option 3 The variable labels will not be printed if this option is selected.

Option 4 The plot grid lines are suppressed using this option.

Option 5 SPSS prints diagonal grids when this option is used.

Option 6 A two-tailed test of significance is made if statistic 3 is selected by the user.

Option 7 *Automatic scaling*. This option produces integer plot labels. The lowest scale value is set to the largest which is less than or equal to the lowest value found in the data; the highest value is set to the smallest integer which is (1) larger than or equal to the highest value encountered in the data, and (2) will produce integer scale values all along the axis.

Option 8 If there is not enough *core* (computer storage space) available to process all of the cases in your data set, the plots will be run nevertheless and will include the first "n" cases, where "n" is the maximum number that may be produced.

The statistics that are available include the following:

Statistic 1 Pearson's r will be computed when "1" is selected
Statistic 2 r^2 is computed
Statistic 3 The significance of r is computed
Statistic 4 Standard error of the estimate
Statistic 5 Intercept with vertical lines
Statistic 6 Slope

In the illustration here we are requesting that all of these statistics be computed on our data along with the scattergram showing the plots of our data points. If we include this request in our own program, we should experiment with a few of these options and statistics to see the differences that emerge in the print-outs obtained.

Doing Pearson's r

When we discussed statistics in the previous chapter, we showed how to use Pearson's r to see what the correlations were between two intervally measured variables. We can also show a way to have SPSS compute Pearson's r:

```
1                    16

Pearson corr         X1 X2 T G

Options              3

Statistics           All
```

To have Pearson's r computed, simply instruct SPSS using the card illustrated above. In the illustration we have instructed SPSS to compute Pearson's r using four variables (X1, X2, T, and G), which means there will be a correlation run for every possible combination of these four variables. We have also requested a special option that is available with the Pearson correlation program, and we have also instructed SPSS to compute all the statistics that go with this request. We will list the various options and statistics that SPSS computes in this situation, and then give an example of the print-out we will receive from the above request.

Option 1 Inclusion of missing data regardless of any missing-value data that may be defined.
Option 2 Listwise deletion of missing data. This means that cases containing missing data will be deleted from the run, and that n will be slightly reduced when there is missing data in a data set.
Option 3 Causes a two-tailed test of statistical significance to be applied to each coefficient request rather than the normal one-tailed test.

Option 4 Punching or writing matrices for future access.

Option 5 Omission of number of cases and significance. This means the correlation coefficients will be printed in matrix form, but the number of cases and the significance for each coefficient will not be printed. This means that when using this option, many more coefficients may be printed per page of print-out (11 columns and 43 rows may be printed per page).

Option 6 Printing only nonredundant coefficients in a serial-string format. This option causes only nonredundant coefficients, with their associated number of cases and significance levels, to be printed.

Two statistical options are available when using the Pearson Correlations program. We have listed these statistics below:

Statistic 1 Causes the means and standard deviations for each of the variables referenced on the *Pearson Corr card* to be computed and printed. Means and standard deviations are based on all cases containing valid or nonmissing data for a particular variable unless Option 1 is selected.

Statistic 2 Causes the cross-product deviations and the covariance to be printed for each pair of variables for which correlation coefficients were requested.

In our example of the Pearson Corr procedure we have requested option 3 and all of the statistics that are available using this statement and request. The output from the computer looks like this:

Variable	Cases	Mean	Std Dev
X1	20	5.1500	1.2680
X2	20	4.8000	1.2814
T	20	1.5000	0.5130
G	20	1.5000	0.5130

Variables		Cases	Cross-prod Dev	Variance Covar	variables		Cases
X1	X2	20	-19.4000	-1.0211	X1	T	20
X1	G	20	-3.5000	-0.1842	X2	T	20
X2	G	20	2.0000	0.1053	T	G	20

Cross-Prod Dev	Variance-Covar
6.5000	0.3421
-4.0000	-0.2105
0.0	0.0

	X1	X2	T	G
X1	1.0000	-0.6284	0.5259	-0.2832
	{ 0}	{ 20}	{ 20}	{ 20}
	S=0.001	S=0.003	S=0.017	S=0.226
X2	-0.6284	1.0000	-0.3203	0.1601
	{ 20}	{ 0}	{ 20}	{ 20}
	S=0.003	S=0.001	S=0.169	S=0.500
T	0.5259	-0.3203	1.0000	0.0
	{ 20}	{ 20}	{ 0}	{ 20}
	S=0.017	S=0.169	S-0.001	S=1.000
G	-0.2832	0.1601	0.0	1.0000
	{ 20}	{ 20}	{ 20}	{ 0}
	S=0.226	S=0.500	S=1.000	S=0.001

The first portion of our computer return contains the means and standard deviations and the number of cases these statistics were computed on. The second portion of the print-out provides an even more sophisticated analysis of these data. Finally, the last section of the program gives us a correlation matrix of the coefficients we have asked to have calculated. The figure at the very top of the print-out, 1.000, is the correlation between variables X1 and X1. These are, of course, the same scores so you would expect a perfect association. When we move across the top of the matrix from left to right, the next coefficient is −0.6284, and below the figure is "20," which is the *n* used for computing this particular coefficient. The correlation between items X1 and X2 is therefore an inverse one because it is negatively signed. What's the correlation between variable T and X2? Simply locate T at the top of the matrix and then locate X2 at the side of the matrix. Where these two variables intersect you will find a Pearson's *r* has been computed. In this case, the correlation between T and X2 is −0.3203, meaning the association is an inverse one of a moderate magnitude. The figure at the very bottom of each listing of association, the figure preceeded by the *S*, is the significance level for the association.

Convention suggests that this number should be a .05 or lower before we can consider the association between variables a significant one. The association between T and X1 is .017, and this indicates the relationship is statistically significant. Finally, note that the lower half of the matrix is the mirror of the upper half. In other words, there are two parts to the matrix and we can locate associations between variables at two points in the print-out. Note also that the matrix is dissected by a series of figures representing perfect associations (1.0000). This divides the matrix into its two separate parts.

WRITE CASES CARD There is one additional SPSS statement that may be of importance for the beginning computer analyst. We may wish to print the actual raw data from our data set to inspect it for errors. This is done with the following statement:

```
1                  16

Task Name          Raw Output

Write cases        {5 {f1.0,2X}} S T G X1 X2
```

This command will have SPSS print all of the data from our data set in its raw form. We may wish to do this to check our data against the data listed here in the text. If we discover some values in our individual data set that do not correspond to what is listed here, we can change a few cards and rerun the program. The general format of the "write cases" procedure is simply the control phrase *Write cases* followed by a parenthesized format statement and then the variables you wish to have listed. The print-out you will receive will look just like the listing of variables and data we presented earlier in the chapter.

Summary and Recode Cards

Let us look at a summary of the way the cards should be placed in a deck for making computer runs:

```
JCL {get these cards from your instructor}

data definition cards {for example, variable list}

▮

▮

▮
```

```
data modification cards {for example, recode}

∎

∎

∎

documentation cards {for example, var labels}

∎

∎

∎

data processing card{s} {for example, crosstabs

Read Input Data

actual data cards go here

∎

∎

∎

data processing cards {for example, crosstabs}

∎

∎

∎

Finish

//
```

From this illustration of the general pattern of setting up an SPSS job we can see that there are several different types of cards that go in different places in the deck. We have already introduced most of these cards and statements.

After we have completed our JCL cards, they are followed by cards that are used to modify the original data in some way. For example, this is where we would place a card if we had to "recode" data such that it could be used to build a table. The format of the *recode card* is simply:

```
1                    16

Recode               X1 {8=7}
```

If we inspect the data we are using here, we will find that under the variable X1 there is one score of "8." This number has been mispunched, and should actually be a "7." Using the recode statement, we have simply asked SPSS to read that number as a 7 rather than as it was punched onto the card. To recode variables, prepare a recode card and list in parentheses, after punching in the variable you want changed, the modifications desired. If we wanted to modify the variable *S*, our recode statement would look like this:

```
1                    16

Recode               S {0 thru 1 = 1} {2 thru 4 = 2} {5 thru 6 = 3}
```

This statement would regroup our data into three general categories or intervals running from 0 through scores of 1 as one category, 2 through scores of 4 for the second general category, and 5 through 6 for the final category.

The second group of cards are called *processing cards* and they follow any modifications we have made. An example of a data-processing card would be a crosstabs request. This would be followed by a "Read Input Data" statement and then the raw data cards. After the data deck, we can again return to the processing cards and conduct a series of analyses. Here we could place another tables request card or compute Pearson's *r* for another series of variables. Finally, we will have to "finish" our job with the JCL that is required at our computer installation.

Although we have not been able to provide, in this chapter, all the information that is available on computers, pocket calculators, or the SPSS language, with the introduction we have given here, you should be able to complete a successful computer run on your own.

Glossary

commands Several commands are available in the SPSS package and examples would be comment cards, run name cards, crosstabs statements, and the like. Each of the cards described in this chapter is a form of command statement.

command field The first 15 columns of a computer card when using SPSS.

JCL (Job Control Language) Every computer job begins and ends with a JCL that is unique to every installation.

pocket calculator Used to rearrange tables and compute statistics when samples are small or when computers are impractical or unavailable.

specification field Runs from column 16 through column 80 of a computer card; this is where we specify what we want done with our data when speaking SPSS.

1. See Michael A. Malec, *Essential Statistics for Social Research* (New York: Lippincott, 1977), pp. 121–123, for a presentation of the various statistics that can be computed with chi square.
2. Norman H. Nie, C. Hadla Hull, Jean G. Jenkins, Karlin Steinbrenner, and Dale H. Bent, *SPSS: Statistical Package for the Social Sciences*, 2nd ed. (New York: McGraw-Hill, 1975), and William R. Klecka, Norman H. Nie, and C. Hadla Hull, *SPSS Primer* (New York: McGraw-Hill, 1975), are two sources students should consult when preparing to conduct research with the SPSS system. We have based our discussions of the SPSS package on these two sources.
3. See N. Nie et al., op cit., pp. 41–49, for a discussion of the use of this statement.
4. This table was adapted from ibid., p. 43.

Notes

17

Qualitative Analysis

One of the greatest advantages of dealing with data that have been transformed into numbers is that they lend themselves to some kind of mathematical or statistical analysis. As we saw in Chapters 12 through 16, there are many ways we can check our data to see if there are significant relationships, by the application of tests using the numbers generated in the data. But what about the kinds of data gathered that have not been quantified? How do we analyze them? We noted in Chapter 10, when discussing field methods, that the researcher can gather a rich array of data with far more depth than through many other methods, but unless we have a way to analyze that data, they will do us little good.

Perhaps the best way to begin our discussion of qualitative analysis is to point out that all methodology, even quantitative methods, involves some kind of qualitative work. In setting up the different categories and questions for survey research, for instance, the investigator must first make several *qualitative* judgments. He or she must state what *qualities* go to make up a particular category. In differentiating between upper class and upper-middle class, for example, the researcher describes the qualities of each to be differentiated and counted in separated categories. Even if the researcher uses income to differentiate social class, it still involves an essentially qualitative judgment, for no matter what figure is chosen to be the drawing line between one social class and another, that decision is based on the qualitative value of income in society at a particular time.

The main difference between quantitative and qualitative methods is that most of the qualitative decisions in quantitative research are made at the *outset* of the research project, whereas, in the more qualitative types of research, those same decisions are made *during* and *after* the data have been collected. However, there are many kinds of qualitative decisions in the analysis of quantified data after all of the data have been collected—for instance, what statistical tests to use, what variables to run cross-tabs on, and what a particular quantitative finding means in relation to another.

The question still remains, though, "How do we analyze qualitative data?" In this chapter we will look at the analytical process in determining the meaning of qualitative data. We should also bear in mind our methodological counterpart in crime detection, the detective, for in all of the great cases solved, in both fiction and real life, the analysis of clues was done without a single statistical test but rather through qualitative analysis of the evidence.

Gathering and Analyzing Data Simultaneously

Since most of the data we will be discussing is that gathered in field research, we will be using examples from participant observation and ethnographic studies. However, other kinds of qualitative data, such as that from the analysis of written documents, can also be analyzed using the same procedures.

A unique aspect of qualitative methods is the conscious interplay between gathering and analyzing data. In most quantitative studies, there are three steps: (1) setting up analytic categories; (2) gathering the data; and (3) analyzing the data. Each of the steps is separate and without overlaps, unless the researcher conducts pilot studies or finds an obviously invalidating error in the categories during the data-gathering process. In qualitative research, on the other hand, data gathering and data analysis go hand in hand.[1] There is more analysis after all of the data have been collected, but even with initial observations, the researcher begins analysis—deciding what the data mean. The two parts of Figure 17.1 compare the difference in quantitative and qualitative methods.

In order to combine analysis with observations, it is necessary, as in all research, to have some initial conceptual scheme—a theoretical guide. As data are collected, the researcher can look at them conceptually to see whether the conceptual scheme can account for what is observed. If there is no fit between the observations and the framework, one of two things can be wrong. First, the conceptual application may be inappropriate or simply false. By redefining conceptual categories or conceptual meanings, the researcher may find that the theory will fit the observations, and his or her initial observations and analysis was nothing more than "sensitizing the concepts."[2] For example, the concept of "stigma" refers to "discrediting marks"—the opposite of a status symbol.[3] If a researcher studying delinquent gangs takes a delinquent record to be a stigma, based on the larger societal views, he may find that his observations and the concept of stigma as indicated by a delinquent record do not correspond. This is so because among certain delinquent gangs, a delinquent record is considered a status symbol, not a stigma. A record shows others they have "heart" or bravery because they are not afraid of the police and the courts. Now, there is nothing wrong with the concept of stigma, but

QUANTITATIVE METHOD

Organize Categories	Observation (Collect Data)	Analysis
1	2	3

QUALITATIVE METHODS

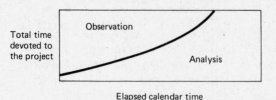

Elapsed calendar time

FIGURE 17.1

From John Lofland *Analyzing Social Settings* (Belmont, Ca: Wadsworth, 1971), p. 118.

rather it has been inappropriately applied in this case. In further observations and analysis, the researcher will find other stigmatizing behaviors for a gang member—such as running from a fight or having his "colors" (jacket, vest, or sweater with the gang's name on it) taken from him. In order to find the appropriate application of concepts, it is necessary to mix analysis with observations. A second problem that can arise when theory and observations do not correspond is that the observer does not have access to the relevant data. The theoretical assumptions are correct, but the researcher has been unable to make the necessary observations. For example, in a study of massage parlors, the researcher was operating under the assumption that the parlors were fronts for prostitution activities. In his initial observations he learned that those who worked in the massage parlors did little to dissuade others from believing that it was a prostitution operation since such a belief was good for business. However, all they did was to give massages. At this point, the researcher was about to reconceptualize his observations, but he began seeing evidence that the massage parlor was indeed a front for a prostitution ring. Upon further observation, he learned that in fact it was a prostitution ring, but this information had been intentionally kept from him. Thus, with the correct data, he was able to bring the theoretical and the observed into correspondence.[4]

Observational, Theoretical, and Methodological Notes

In order to simultaneously gather and analyze data in qualitative research, it is necessary to have special kinds of data records so that analysis is possible during and after all of the data have been gathered. Some notes are recorded on the basis of observations that may or may not be important to analysis, others are gathered on the basis that some observation *at the time it is made* seems theoretically relevant, and still other notes are comments on the methodology itself and how it may affect the quality of the data.[5]

OBSERVATIONAL NOTES The first kind of notes are those gathered simply by watching and listening—the who, what, when, where, and how of social action.[6] They stand by themselves as data, and at the time they are made, it is unknown of what analytical use they will be. They may prove to be support for a proposition during later analysis, but at the time they are recorded, they are simply indicated by ON (for **Observational Note**) without analytic comment. The following examples are observational notes, one from a study of a county psychiatric inpatient unit, the other, a study of a detective unit:

Psychiatric Unit
ON   Asked the tech, "What kinds of patients do you usually get on the ward?" "Mainly schizy ones," she says, then proceeded to categorize them by sex and age. But most of her answer contained a string of categories more descriptive of behavior or personality: "angry ones," "noisy," "withdrawn," and "real crazy

ones." Then, without my asking, she said, "You have to control them or they give you a hard time."[7]

Detective Division

ON   Andy got a Patrol Report on a 459 which said "Inactive pending further investigative leads." This surprised me and I asked him about it. He said that the patrolman saw no possible leads and inactivated it—it was not a too uncommon practice. I had thought only detectives could inactivate a case.[8]

As can be seen in the above two examples, the researchers were looking at events and meanings using a combination of observations and questions. There is no analysis *per se*, either theoretically or methodologically at this point, only notes as to what was observed and said.

THEORETICAL NOTES   The second kind of note is directly analytical. **Theoretical notes** (TN) are not necessarily out-and-out propositions and hypotheses, but rather self-conscious, controlled attempts to derive meaning from any one of several observational notes.[9] These are particularly important, for the hunches, insights, conjectures, and hypotheses gathered in the field may turn out to be major analytical statements later on, and unless the researcher makes TNs, they are apt to be lost later on. Using our examples from the study of a psychiatric unit and of detectives we can see what theoretical notes look like:

Psychiatric Unit

TN   This tells us a little more about how the techs think; about their level of thinking relative to the pros. But we can't say all the techs think this way (see Monday's notes, Nov. 15, on the conversation with the tech who is a college grad). Maybe can classify the techs on levels of comprehension? Is this worth a memo? Right now it doesn't excite me.[10]

Detective Division

TN   An idea I've been kicking around is the notion of an "Organizational Net" set up by the police. The organization is set up so that it maximizes their chances of catching someone, while at the same time it reflects their idea of what constitutes social organization. Their sense of social organization is reflected in the structure of their organization and organizational practices. This, in turn, leads to the organization of experience any members of the organization will encounter, depending on what part of the net they are in. From a purely practical viewpoint the flow of information between the parts of the net will enhance the effectiveness of the total net. To wit—today there was a discussion between the narcs and burg concerning a big rip [arrest] in the making. The narcs figured to bust a heroin dealer and the burglary detail figured to recover stolen property since it is generally believed that hypes steal stuff to feed their habit.[11]

In the example of the TN for the psychiatric unit, the researcher pointed out a possible relationship between the tech's viewpoint and educational level and a general pattern that may be emerging. The TN in the detective study, though, is somewhat more elaborate and constitutes a major analytical statement in the middle of other field notes. What is important to understand is that no matter how minor or major a TN is, it must be recorded, for even though it may not be used later when more evidence is available, it might prove to be a significant insight.

METHODOLOGICAL NOTES   The third kind of note is the **methodological note** (MN), and even though it may be argued that such notes have an indirect bearing on the analysis of data, their major purpose is to remind the researcher of some feature of the methodological process. When the findings are presented to others, usually in the form of a publication, the MNs can be employed to explain research tactics.[12] The following examples illustrate the use of methodological notes:

> *Psychiatric Unit*
> **MN**   It all sounds kind of cynical but the more I think about those patients who are kept and those shipped off to state hosp., the more valid it seems. So: 1. scan all data to date for evidence on both professional patient and calculus; 2. interview chief, social worker, head nurse; 3. prepare memo if either or both pan out. Maybe link both concepts around "mutual selection process."[13]

> *Detective Division*
> **MN**   Sort of a note to myself here about change in the research procedure. I've been taking fewer notes, using tape [recording] more and focusing on certain specific things. Before, I put down all sorts of things and would stay around all day. Now, however, because of a change in my work schedule as well as an understanding as to what is worth getting into, I've been able to get at some central issues. When I get back to juvenile and maybe checks [check fraud], I'll be able to focus better and ask questions more to the point.[14]

Both of the above notes are methodological ones, but they are very different. The MN from the psychiatric unit is set up to test out a supposition and, as such, is very analytical even though it points out three research activities to be carried out by the investigator. The MN from the detective study, though, is more of a self-conscious statement about the way the research is being done. Less time is being spent with the detectives, and at that particular stage of the research, the researcher has a very clear focus, developed after an unclear focus typical of initial observations. As a result, he is taking fewer notes. This is a signal for analysis in that it states that notes in that section are more concise and relevant to theoretical concerns than earlier notes when the researcher was not as sure of what was going on or of the meaning of the various activities he observed.

Analytic Files

A simple yet effective way to carry on the simultaneous processes of observation and analysis is to start **analytic files.** In order to do this the researcher needs more than one copy of field notes, or texts in the case of qualitative content analysis. By typing notes on a duplication master or simply machine-copying the original set of elaborate notes, it is possible to have copies for as many different categories as desired. By labeling file folders in terms of the appropriate analytic categories, all the researcher has to do is to place relevant notes in the corresponding file. As the information and categories grow, the file system can grow with them. Beginning with broad general categories, the researcher can narrow them down as he or she gathers more data. Having multiple copies of notes, the researcher can put the same notes in different files if a single note page has information pertaining to more than a single category. Figure 17.2 shows a general file system to begin with that is reorganized into a more specific one:

Using multiple copies of notes, it is possible to make the filing system as simple or as complex as necessary. Often it is a good idea to cross-index materials, so that the same thing is in more than a single file. For example, a certain role might be filed under both "roles" and another file for its specific place within the organization. Then the same notes can be used in explaining both roles and organizational features.

In order to organize the notes to go into the files, especially where cross-indexing is used, the relevant portions of the field notes are bracketed. Where there are several dimensions to consider, it is helpful to use different colored pens to bracket the excerpts to be filed. In this way, both a master set of notes along with the notes for the separate files can be maintained. In the master set, the different colors show what file each portion is in, but the notes for the separate file are only bracketed for the relevant excerpt for that file. The following example shows how a single page of notes was categorized so that the notes would be placed in four different files:

Log   38 Pg. 1
Saturday about 2:30 Mike called me and said there had been a 187 at the Biltmore Hotel. My wife was gone with the car so I had a neighbor drive me over to my sister's to get her car to go to the S.O. (Mike had called back and said that Sgt. R. was at the office.) When I got to the office, the Sheriff, Under-sheriff and everyone from Major Crimes was there. WB was in the interrogation room with the suspect—a 77-year-old Armenian. At the time there were conflicting reports as to what had happened, and it wasn't until later that I was able to put it all together.

The first report from patrol (CL 68) was written in pencil and on Sgt. R's desk. It listed the crime as 187/217 (murder and attempted murder). The murders took place at noon, and at the time the report was written one of the victims was still alive and in surgery, but at 4:00 they called and said he had died. It'll be interesting to see if the report is typed as just 187 or a 187/217.

Sgt. R. showed me the names of the victims and told me that one was the Turkish consul and the other guy was the vice consul, and I thought the suspect's name sounded Turkish as well. However, it was an Armenian name, and right away I thought it might have something to do with the fact that the Armenians hated the Turks, and as it turned out that was what the motive seemed to be.[15]

R

E C

E

L

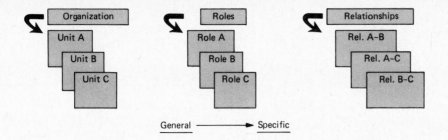

General ──────▶ Specific

FIGURE 17.2
An Analytic File

The red bracket (R) indicated a research problem, essentially the same as a methodological note. The green bracket (E) pointed to work in establishing a case, and the brown line (C) indicated investigative work in attempting to get a confession from the suspect. Finally, the blue line (L) showed what was construed as a lead. It should be noted that the section with double brackets of E and C pointed to notes dealing with both detective work in establishing a case *and* getting a confession.

Using the duplicate set of notes, that page was put into four different files. Only those portions relevant to the particular file were bracketed. Thus, while the master set of notes has multicolored brackets and multiple brackets for the same portion, what goes into the individual files only has the excerpts marked that correspond with the file name. For example, in the file marked "Leads," only the last paragraph of that page of notes was bracketed since that was the only portion pertaining to leads. In a similar manner, the researcher would place copies of that page of notes in files for "Research," "Confessions," and "Establishing Cases."

Analytical Procedures

Keeping in mind that analysis accompanies data collection as well as taking place after all of the data are collected, we will now examine the analytic process in dealing with qualitative data. To begin, it will be helpful to take a simple, yet very accurate, notion of analysis. Expressed in its most elemental form, analysis refers to the *working of thought processes.*[16] The process involves what we do all the time more or less unwittingly. Consider, for example, how we might look at a messy room that has been a mess for some time. We might think to ourselves, "I've got to get organized." The problem is to take a disorganized jumble and make some kind of organized sense out of it. We might begin by thinking, "What goes together?" and a first step we might take is to decide to put our shoes in one place in the closet. A little at a time, we create an order from chaos. Once we get everything organized and we want to find something, we do a bit of analysis by asking, "What category did I put my pen in?" In our organization, it might be under "desk items" kept in the top drawer of the desk, and by looking in the top desk drawer, we locate the pen.

If we compare qualitative data with items in a messy room, the analysis would be the organization of items and relocating them, but slightly more involved. Nevertheless, the same thought process is operating, and by extending the analogy, we can get into the analytic process.

Classes

The first step in analysis is to identify significant *classes*.[17] Like organizing a messy room, we start by seeing what goes together, or what has common properties.[18] For example, in a study of an office, we might begin with classes based on duties of the office workers. The classes in an insurance office might include (1) secretaries, (2) accountants, (3) salespeople, (4) claims adjusters, and (5) supervisors. The properties of the classes would be made up of the duties or job of each position. In this example, the classes were simply statuses and the properties were the role behaviors. Other concepts suggest other kinds of classes, and the research setting and situation will offer their own unique set of classes.

The kinds of classes available and developed in research are not all the same. We can identify three main kinds of classes, plus two subclasses:

1. Common Classes
2. Special Classes
   a. collegial classes
   b. host classes
3. Theoretical Classes

COMMON CLASSES Those classes that are part of the culture are called **common classes.** They help people in society distinguish between and among the varieties of things, persons, and events.[19] For example, in looking at social settings, just about everyone can distinguish among a grocery store, a bar, a bank, a park, and a shoe store. In analysis of data collected in one's home culture, common classses are recognized and understood at the outset, but for anthropological studies in foreign societies, such classes must be discovered.

SPECIAL CLASSES The next set of **special classes** are of two types, both referring to selected areas of interest and used to distinguish among the things, persons, and events in this area.[20] The classes of things, persons, and events brought by the researcher are called *collegial classes*, referring to the researcher's cohort. Basically, collegial classes are made of various concepts the researcher employs in differentiating between phenomena. A political scientist might be interested in distinguishing groups on the basis of the type of political power they use, while a sociologist might use concepts of role and status to mark differences in the same group.

On the other side of the coin, those studied by the researcher have what we call *host classes*. These are the special classes that a group has for itself but that are not commonly recognized by the rest of society. For example, in his study of prisons, John Irwin identified the following host classes of inmates:

1. thief
2. hustler
3. dope fiend
4. head
5. disorganized criminal
6. state-raised youth
7. lower class "man"
8. square john[21]

Likewise, events and settings can have special classes understood by the research subjects. Homicide detectives differentiated between "walk-throughs" and "whodunits" in distinguishing between murders that were easily solved and ones that took a great deal of investigative work.[22] Cavan identified different classes of bars based on how patrons saw and used them.[23]

THEORETICAL CLASSES The final and most important kind of class is the **theoretical class.** These are classes discovered by the researcher in the course of his or her observations and analysis.[24] For the researcher there is nothing more gratifying than this kind of discovery, for it stands as a previously unseen state of affairs. Beginning with common and special classes, the researcher finds an order that needs a classification different from what was expected. For example, in attempting to account for the class of activities employed in distributing patients in a hospital, the researchers developed a theoretical class called "calculus of patienthood."[25] Such a class was not employed by anyone prior to the research, and yet it explained certain categories of action better than anything else did.

Linkages

Having established classes, the next step in analysis is to identify **linkages** or how classes are related to one another.[26] The process begins by linking one class to another, and as the linkages increase in density, the researcher develops *sets*. The initial linkages are posed as simple propositions, stating how one class is related to the next. Figure 17.3 shows this process of moving from simple linkages to sets:

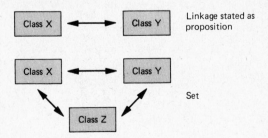

Linkage stated as proposition

Set

**FIGURE 17.3
From Linkage
to Set**

A simple way to think about linkages is in terms of roles, role sectors, and role sets.[27] Each role constitutes a class, and the connection between roles are linkages within the organization. A group of roles that "go together" make up a set. Take, for instance, a small diner that is run by a single cook and waitress. We can imagine at least three roles: the cook, the waitress, and the patron. The waitress and cook are linked directly, and the patron and waitress are linked directly. Indirectly, the patron is linked to the cook, since the cook prepares the customer's meals. Based on common knowledge, we could establish the linkages and set, along with propositions establishing the connections, as indicated in Figure 17.4.

Figure 17.4 shows a fairly simple description, describing how things work in the diner based on classes (roles) and linkages (the role sectors and sets) that are common. More interesting and complex relationships discovered in qualitative research depend on the researcher's skill and creativity in seeing unexpected linkages and sets in theoretical classes. In one interesting finding, the researcher found a linkage between how well a group of boys did in bowling and their status in the group.[28] The interesting aspect of the finding was *not* that their status was derived from the bowling scores; rather, their standing in the group determined their bowling ability with their group. For instance, one of the boys who was a very good bowler and scored higher than other members of his group when playing outside of the group, scored much lower when playing with members of the clique to which he belonged. In other words, he played according to his status in the group. Similarly, a study of pinball players revealed that pinball was more than a test of skill or a means to pass the time. For the regular players, their actions playing pinball were linked to a demonstration of character. Many players who had the necessary coordination skills to win pinball games lacked an inner self-control to perform. When they were close to winning, they became nervous and shaky—losing their "cool"—and lost the game. This indicated to others that they lacked social character—the inner self—placing them in a low status

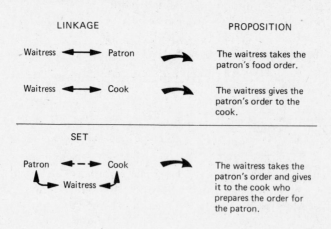

FIGURE 17.4
From Linkages
to Propositions

relative to players who could keep their head and composure and make the last final points to win a game.[28]

A final aspect of linkages involves the key linkage.[29] Such linkages serve as an overall theme, model, or organizing scheme that ties everything together and makes sense out of diverse data. Usually the key linkage is a theoretical framework from the body of social science theory, but it can be "grounded theory" that is discovered in the process of the research.[30] In the example of the study of pinball players, the key linkage was from Erving Goffman's theory of "action," wherein the development of social character is described.[31] Other key linkages can be found in different social science theories, and as we have stressed throughout the book, theoretical constructs and concepts greatly simplify the methodological process. It is also important to understand that theories, in the form of key linkages, can be tested in qualitative analysis. If the key linkage suggested by the theory is not reflected in the data, the data can be used to disprove that theory and either support another one or be used to develop an entirely new theory.

Patterns

Throughout the analytical process, the researcher attempts to locate social patterns. The problem is to differentiate between patterns of social behavior and all sorts of other actions that are either wholly irrelevant to the research interests or are somehow idiosyncratic actions that are not part of a pattern. In order to find social patterns in data and to confirm their status as patterns, it is necessary to have guidelines or criteria for locating them. To some extent patterns are the same as the classes we discussed above, but they have a more general character and refer to somewhat larger segments of social action.

TYPICALITY   The first indication of a pattern is that the behavior involved is *typical;* that is, the activities occur in a certain way and are not idiosyncratic. For example, in studies of marijuana use, a typical action was found to be "passing the joint." One person would roll and light a marijuana cigarette, take a puff, and then pass it on to the next person. In numerous observations of marijuana smoking, the pattern occurred in the same way and the participants all felt that "passing the joint" was *typically* how groups smoked the stuff. Therefore, it is safe to say that the activity met the criterion of **typicality.**

PERSISTENCE   A second feature of patterns is that they last over a period of time or are *persistent.* With our example of "passing the joint," we know from earlier studies of marijuana use that the pattern has been around for a long time. In Becker's classic study, "Becoming a Marijuana User," based on observations made in the 1950s, he found the same pattern back then as can be found in the 1980s.[32] Another persistent "passing" pattern can be seen in the behavior of hobos—homeless men. In his study shortly after the turn of the century, Anderson found that, when drinking, hobos "passed the bottle" as a standard practice,[33] and, in 1970, Jacqueline Wiseman found the same pattern in her study of homeless derelicts.[34] Thus, the fact that, in different studies over a long period of time, the same social practice was observed points to the **persistence** of a pattern. However, in a single study, besides reviewing the relevant literature, all a researcher really needs to do is to check to see if a behavior pattern is persistent over the period of observations.

TRANSSITUATIONALITY   The third criterion for a pattern is that it is **transsituational,** which means that the observed practice is seen in more than a single situation. In the pattern of "passing a joint," the observer can see the same pattern in all kinds of different situations. From Maine to Southern California and from the state of Washington to Florida, in situations where marijuana smokers gather, one can observe marijuana cigarettes being passed from one user to the next. Of course, a researcher need not go all over the country to determine such a pattern, and in analyzing one's notes, as long as the same patterned behavior can be observed in several situations, the criterion has been met.

TRANSPERSONALITY   The final feature to examine in determining the status of a pattern is its **transpersonality.** Some activities are peculiar to a certain group or cohort, and as such do not constitute a true social pattern. On the other hand, patterns that transcend any single cohort are transpersonal. For example, in looking at the pattern of "passing a joint," we find that it is transpersonal in that it is not peculiar to any single cohort of marijuana smokers. That is, the activity is not restricted to the personal practices of a few people, but rather it is a pattern of behavior that just about any group involved in marijuana smoking employs when using the drug. In the analysis of qualitative data, it is important to check and see whether a conjectured pattern is carried out by just certain people or whether it is generally engaged in by all.

Negative Cases

One of the best ways to see social patterns is in their violation. We are all involved in numerous social patterns ourselves, but if we were asked, "What's normal?" we would be hard-pressed to state the "normal" or "routine" without explaining what is "incorrect" or "abnormal." In observing others' behavior, when something goes wrong, people usually say something or do something to let others know that they are not acting correctly. When such an outburst occurs, the researcher can "see" the normal pattern. For example, we may never "see" the pattern of "passing a joint" because it is so taken-for-granted. However, if in observing others smoke marijuana we hear someone say, "Hey, what are you doing?" to someone who *does not* pass on a marijuana cigarette, we can then *see* the pattern in its violation. Therefore, in analyzing our data, including the process of collection/analysis, it is critically important to note those instances in which someone invokes a negative sanction or fails to do so. If what we believe to be a pattern is negatively sanctioned because of its violation, we have evidence that it is indeed a pattern. On the other hand, if what we consider to be a pattern is broken and there is *no* negative sanction, we had better start asking questions or look at our other data. This is so because a social pattern represents a socially supported and expected manner of behavior, and if it is not followed and its violation is not negatively sanctioned, either the practice is not a strong pattern or there is a special situation in which the pattern is not in effect. If the latter is the case, we should note the nature of the situation so that we can explain the action appropriately. For example, if a woman runs up and kisses a man she has never met, we might be surprised, for kissing is usually not done between unacquainted men and women. However, during parties where there is a lot of drinking or on special occasions, such as New Year's Eve, it would not be unusual to see a woman run up and kiss a strange man.

Another type of **negative case** has to do with what the observer believed to be part of a sequence or theoretical pattern. Figure 17.5 shows the expected and the negative case. For example, in studies of police decisions whether or not to make an arrest, one of the criteria that seems to play an important role is demeanor.[35] If a person is polite and civil he or she is far less likely to be arrested than if he or she is antagonistic and impolite. However, there have been numerous observations where people were very antagonistic but were not arrested in situations where the police had every legal right to do so. When negative cases like this occur, it is important to see why the predicted pattern was broken. Usually, it is because there is another pattern or process working. The following list shows why police might not make an arrest when the person known to have broken the law is antagonistic:

1. Crime was too petty to make arrest.
2. Antagonism was directed at situation and not police officer.
3. Officer's shift was about over, and he didn't want to take time to process suspect.
4. Complainant did not want arrest made.

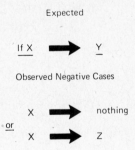

Expected

If X ➡ Y

Observed Negative Cases

X ➡ nothing

or

X ➡ Z

**FIGURE 17.5
The Expected
and the
Negative Case**

For the purposes of analysis, negative cases do not disprove a pattern so much as they show the interrelationship between a complex of patterns and processes. In the example of police decision-making, the pattern of taking into account a suspected law violator's demeanor was only a *single* pattern interwoven into several other patterns. The listed explanations for nonarrest constitute four other patterns that are necessary to take into consideration, and so negative cases themselves can actually be patterns.

Finally, negative cases can simply be quirks in behavior. As pointed out above, some negative cases are due to special situations, but they can also result from unusual circumstances on personalities. Therefore, when examining negative cases, it is not only important to see whether they are patterns of another sort themselves but also whether they are exceptional and unusual.

Social Processes

The concept of social process is used in various discussions of social science, but it is a concept that is difficult to operationalize and fully understand in the context of qualitative analysis. In part, this is due to the vague status it has in the social sciences, and so we social scientists are as responsible for its misunderstanding as anyone else.

Actually, though, the idea and concept of *social process* is quite simple. Take, for instance, the concept of *socialization*. For both sociologists and anthropologists, socialization refers to learning the ways of one's society. It is a process that we can understand intuitively. Similarly, take the process of "getting to know" somebody. We all go through this process at one time or another and are familiar with it. In dating behavior, a boy and girl first make contact, then go out together, and eventually get to know one another as friends and/or lovers. Since these processes are quite common, why all the mystery about the analysis of social processes?

The best way to think about social processes in research and analysis is in terms of *sequences*. There is a step-by-step *order* to a sequence, one step being necessary before the other. In the analysis of data, the task is to uncover the sequence and show how each step is linked to the next. For instance, in the socialization process, we can see the sequence in terms of parents teaching their children the basic skills of communication in language acquisition, the norms and values of society, and so on through the educational institutions to the point where an individual is fully socialized. Before a child learns to write, he or she must first learn to read, and so in the socialization process, the Reading Step precedes the Writing Step. Likewise, in dating behavior the Introduction Step comes before the Kissing Step, and the process of getting to know someone in dating requires a fine sequence to be followed.

In locating and explaining social processes in qualitative analysis, the researcher does very much the same thing as in pattern analysis except that the key is in the sequence. Finding the sequence is a matter of first hypothesizing a process, based either on grounded observations or available theory, and then seeing what events repeat themselves in the process. Having located the events, see if they have an order or sequence. Once the sequence is determined, examine the data to see how the steps in the sequence are interrelated. Broken down, the *process* of analyzing a process looks like this:

Step 1 Hypothesize process (imagine a possible process that may be taking place).

Step 2 Look for recurrent events within the parameters of hypothesized process.

Step 3 Determine sequence (if any) of events that make up hypothesized process.

Step 4 Determine interrelationship of sequential steps to explain process.

Using an example from a study of rape assaults, we will see how this kind of analysis takes place. To show how the analytical procedure was done, we will start by looking at the sequence in the rape process.

1. Contact with victim through innocent presentation.
2. Isolation of victim.
3. Revelation of rape intentions.
4. Rape assault.[36]

In order to see how this sequence was determined, we will explain the steps taken by the analyst. The first thing the researcher did was to hypothesize that some typical process occurred in rape, beginning with the rapist contacting

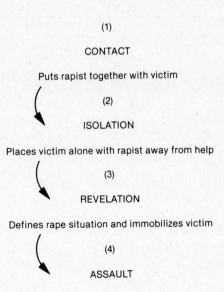

(1)

CONTACT

Puts rapist together with victim

(2)

ISOLATION

Places victim alone with rapist away from help

(3)

REVELATION

Defines rape situation and immobilizes victim

(4)

ASSAULT

Previous steps designed to maximize rape completion

the victim and ending with the rape assault. Thus, the parameters were established for the process between *contact* and *assault.* In going over the data, the researcher determined that the first step was in the nature of the contact, usually a contact that did not scare off the victim. This could be anything from offering the victim a ride to presenting himself as a door-to-door salesman. The next step was to isolate the victim from others who might come to her aid. Having isolated the victim, the rapist would reveal his intentions to rape her, a direct or implicit threat of harm accompanying the revelation. This threat would usually put the victim in fear of her life, immobilizing her so that the rapist could sexually assault her, the final step in the sequence.

In diagraming the sequence we can begin to see how the parts are all interrelated. (See diagram on page 369.)

In the example of the rape sequence, we can see how qualitative data can be analyzed to draw out and explain a social process. Not all rapes exactly followed the sequence, but it represents a typical rape. Some rapes collapsed the sequence, such as those in which the rapist appeared in the victim's bedroom in the middle of the night—Steps 1 through 3 being crushed together as soon as the victim became aware of the rapist. However, even though the sequence was collapsed, the same process could be seen operating. Likewise, in the analysis of other social processes, there may be a stretching or condensing of the sequence, but the important aspect of such analysis is to see what events occur within the parameters of the process no matter what temporal frame is involved. Later, once the process has been determined, a time-frame can be worked out if necessary.

Meanings

A final feature of qualitative analysis, whether determining classes, linkages, patterns, or processes, is establishing *social meanings.* Unlike analysis of physical data, social data has all kinds of meanings before the researcher comes on the scene, and in order to analyze such data it is a prerequisite to understand what meanings the observed actions have to the social actors.

For the most part, we can assume meanings in observed actions since we are part of the social reality under observation. That is to say, we understand social action in the same way as those who engage in the action. However, even though our assumptions will probably be correct, especially if we employ commonsense ones, we must test out as many as possible. This is especially true if we are observing a group or situation outside of our own normal experience. If we assume one meaning for an action and the actors are assuming a totally different one, then our observations and analysis will be invalid.

The determination of meaning requires simultaneous observation and analysis, asking a lot of questions as to what a particular pattern means. In establishing social meaning for data already collected, the researcher must look to see what other activities are occurring and determine the context of the action. If the same observed behaviors have different contexts and different reactions to them, it is a good bet that the actions have different meanings. For example, observations of children on school playgrounds will reveal instances of hitting behavior. The following is a partial list of what a "hit" can mean:

1. a fight
2. revenge
3. flirting
4. play
5. contest
6. tag

Usually, we can tell the meaning of a "hit" as well as the children can. There are misunderstandings, and boys who are hit by flirting girls may mistake the sign of affection for something else, leading to a fight or tears. By and large, however, in a strictly behavioralistic sense, one hit looks very much like another, and unless the meaning of the action is taken into account, it is possible to misconstrue the entire observation.

Summary

To many, qualitative analysis looks more like an art than a science. However, when we break it down into its component parts, we can see a logical procedure similar to quantitative analysis, the only difference being that the latter relies heavily on statistical tests. The "art" in qualitative analysis is the creativity of the researcher in making linkages and discovering new classes, patterns, and processes, but a quantitative analyst who does the same thing is no less creative.

A key feature of qualitative analysis is that it begins early in the research process and occurs simultaneously with the collection of data. This allows the researcher to check the data as he or she goes along and increases chances for new discoveries. Various kinds of observational, theoretical, and methodological notes play back on initial observations and guide subsequent ones. Classes and linkages are developed while observations are being made and then reanalyzed once all the data are collected. Similarly, patterns and processes, along with their meanings, are analyzed while the researcher collects the data and then are subjected to further analysis once all the observations have been completed.

As in all analysis, the key to good qualitative analysis is organization. The organizational framework is social science theory, whether it is abstract or grounded. This framework pulls all of the pieces together and allows the researcher to draw both descriptive and analytic conclusions regarding a theory's validity. Because of such analysis, social science research using qualitative data is significantly different from simple journalistic accounts and idiosyncratic diaries.

analytic files Field-note files that are divided into categories reflecting relevant research interests. Multiple copies of field notes allow researchers to make multiple categories for a single page of notes.

common classes Categories or classes of events, people, and things that are part of a culture being studied.

key linkage Linkages that serve as an overall theme, model, or organizing scheme that ties everything together. Usually a key linkage is a theoretical framework.

linkages Simple propositions stating how one class is related to another.

methodological notes Field notes commenting on some methodological aspect of the research.

negative cases Observed cases that do not conform to an established pattern. They are used to "see" patterns.

observational notes Field notes recording observations made by the researcher. Such notes reflect "raw data" without any theoretical interpretation.

persistence An analytical feature of social patterns pointing to the recurrence of a pattern over a period of time.

special classes Categories or classes that are not part of the larger culture under study. *Collegial classes* are made up of various concepts the researcher employs, and *host classes* are group-specific categories under study but not part of the larger culture.

theoretical classes Classes discovered by the researcher in the course of observation and analysis, which were previously unknown about the culture.

theoretical notes Field notes that comment on possible theoretical properties or relationships.

transpersonality Analytic feature of social patterns indicating that the behavior is independent of a single cohort.

transsituationality Analytic feature of social patterns indicating the behavior is independent of a single situation.

typicality Analytic feature of social patterns indicating that the behavior happens in a certain fashion indicative of the pattern.

Notes

1. John Lofland, *Analyzing Social Settings* (Belmont, Ca.: Wadsworth, 1971), pp. 117–118.
2. Norman Denzin, *The Research Act* (Chicago: Aldine, 1970), pp. 14, 257–258.
3. Erving Goffman, *Stigma* (Englewood Cliffs, N.J.: Prentice-Hall, 1963).
4. Paul Rasmussen conducted a study on massage parlors mentioned in Jack Douglas, *Investigative Social Research* (Beverly Hills, Ca.: Sage, 1976), pp. 142–145.
6. Ibid., p. 100.
7. Ibid., p. 99.
8. Unpublished field notes. See William B. Sanders, *Detective Work: A Study of Criminal Investigations* (New York: Free Press, 1977) for results of study based on these notes.
9. Schatzman and Strauss, op. cit., p. 101.

10. Ibid., p. 99.
11. Unpublished field notes, William B. Sanders. See note 8.
12. Schatzman and Strauss, op. cit., p. 101.
13. Ibid., p. 100.
14. Unpublished field notes, William B. Sanders. See note 8.
15. Ibid.
16. Schatzman and Strauss, op. cit., p. 109.
17. Ibid., p. 110.
18. Ibid.
19. Ibid., p. 112.
20. Ibid.
21. John Irwin, *The Felon* (Englewood Cliffs, N.J.: Prentice-Hall, 1970), p. 34.
22. Sanders, op. cit., p. 174.
23. Sherri Cavan, *Liquor License* (Chicago: Aldine, 1966).
24. Schatzman and Strauss, op. cit., p. 112.
25. Ibid., p. 112.
26. Ibid., p. 110−111.
27. Erving Goffman, *Encounters* (Indianapolis: Bobbs-Merrill, 1961), pp. 85−91.
28. William B. Sanders, "Pinball Occasions" in Arnold Birenbaum and Edward Sagarin, eds., *People in Places* (New York: Praeger, 1973).
29. Schatzman and Strauss, op. cit., p. 111.
30. Barney G. Glaswer and Anselm L. Strauss, *The Discovery of Ground Theory* (Chicago: Aldine, 1967).
31. Erving Goffman, *Interaction Ritual* (New York: Doubleday, 1967), p. 185.
32. Howard S. Becker, *Outsiders* (New York: Free Press, 1963). See chapter titled "Becoming a Marijuana User," pp. 41−58.
33. Nels Anderson, *The Hobo* (Chicago: University of Chicago Press, 1923).
34. Jacqueline Wiseman, *Stations of the Lost* (Englewood Cliffs, N.J.: Prentice-Hall, 1970).
35. Irving Piliavin and Scott Briar, "Police Encounters with Juveniles," *American Journal of Sociology* 70 (September, 1964): 206−214.
36. William B. Sanders, *Rape and Woman's Identity* (Beverly Hills, Ca.: Sage, 1980), p. 68.

18

Evaluation Research

$\mathbf{A}$t the heart of social science research is the testing and development of theory. Throughout this book we have emphasized the importance of organizing propositions and concepts linked to theory before setting out to do research, with the key question always being, "How is this methodology related to a theoretical problem?" However, there is another use of research methods, one that has taken on an increasingly important role over the last several years, and that is the use of social science methods to evaluate social programs. Basically, the purpose of **evaluation** research is to determine whether or not a program works—that is, does it accomplish the goal it sets out to accomplish?[1]

The best way to understand how evaluation research works is to consider our own behavior when we are attempting to improve in some area of endeavor. For instance, let us say that we would like to improve our grades and we devise a study program to that end. After using the new program for a semester, we compare our grades with those received the previous semester. If the grades are better, we evaluate the program a success, but if the grades are the same or lower, we evaluate the new study program a failure and either go back to our old habits or try another program.

On the face of it, such "evaluation research" as determining the success or failure of a study program appears fairly simple, and in most respects it is. There is a clear logic to the method of evaluation and we can see the results plainly at the end of the semester. However, there could be some snags. First of all, we have to be sure that the results are connected to the program. If the grades improve at the end of the term as compared to the previous term, it is possible that the courses we took were easier during the evaluation period. Thus, the improved grades would not be due to the program, but instead to having simpler courses. Or it could be due to better instructors, more interesting courses, or even a change in grading policies. Likewise, if the program appeared to fail based on lower grades, the change could be due to more difficult courses, a "get tough" grading policy, or uninspiring instructors. So, in evaluating any study program, we would have to consider the nature of the courses, instructors, and any policies implemented by the university during the evaluation period. A second question we must consider has to do with the implementation of the program itself. We could plan and even set up a new study program, but that does not mean it was actually implemented. Perhaps we promised ourselves we would diligently follow the program, but when we review our actual behavior during the evaluation period, we might find we widely deviated from the plan—for better or worse. So before deciding what effect the program had, we had better make sure that it was operating in the first place. Finally, we might want to know exactly why a program succeeded or failed. That is, what was the basic logic and conceptual framework in our program that made it work or fail? If determined a success, we would want to know what general principles were involved in the program, so that we learned more and our grades improved. Once this question is posed, we are right back to theory, for the general principles imply some theory as to the mechanics of human behavior.

Having an idea of what is involved in evaluation research, we can see that it is considered the most "practical" of uses to which social science research can be employed. Often called "applied research," evaluation research examines factors that make a difference in social behavior. If a program leads to an improvement in the human condition, whether it is improved educational techniques, better health services, or effective crime reduction, it is of practical importance to know if and why a program works. Evaluation research provides this kind of knowledge.

Theories and Programs

There has always been a split between "pure" and "applied" research. The former is often considered to be the true and proper use of social science research since it tests theory, while the latter is thought of as almost a prostitution of the profession because it does not. This split between applied and pure research is not only unfortunate, since it dissuades many researchers from using their skills in a manner that can be of great social importance and help to people, but it is also an inaccurate characterization of evaluation research. The basic assumption that gives rise to this misunderstanding is that *social programs have absolutely no theory*. Therefore, the first thing we must do is examine the grounds for such an assumption.

In the so-called "practical world of action," theory has always taken a back seat—at least in rhetoric. We might hear statements to the effect, "We've wasted enough time with theory. Let's do something practical for a change." To this kind of charge, the audience nods "amen" and everyone rolls up their sleeves and gets to work. However, the *really practical* question is, "What are the goals and how do we know the plan will work?" Again, for the "practical" person of action, the reply is in terms of, "We won't know unless we try," and the goals are assumed to emerge out of hard work and good intentions. Breaking this discussion down into conceptual parts, we can see that a highly practical approach is very much a matter of theory and research. First, let us take a look at "getting something done." The activity and hustle and bustle of action constitute the *means*, and what is hoped to be accomplished is the *end.*

PRACTICAL ACTION

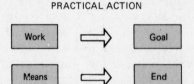

Depending on the desired goal, the work will be of one sort or another. That is, depending on the nature of the end, different means will be used. The question then becomes, "What is the best way to accomplish the goal?" Such a question is essentially one of cause and effect. Stated differently, the question would become, "What are the *causes* for the desired *effect?*" In this context, we can clearly see that the elementary question in the most practical of endeavors is a theoretical one, for it brings up the issue of cause and effect. In a budget-minded world of accomplishing practical ends, the theoretical question looms even larger, for not only must the theory state cause and effect, it must do so in terms of **efficiency** and **effectiveness.**[2] That is, it must show what causes are the least expensive and does the best job in terms of achieving the desired effect. The relationship, then, between the theoretical and practical can be seen in terms of the progression shown in Figure 18.1.

By now, it should be clear that the more practical a program is, the more it relies on theory. Even the most energetic person of action realizes that a house put together with rubber cement will not last very long, for the adhesive does not cause the materials to stay together as well as nails. It may not appear to be a theoretical judgment to understand that nails hold wood together better than rubber cement, but since we are dealing with cause and effect, it can be understood as a theoretical proposition just as any other such statement is.

Perhaps the most persistent misunderstanding that exists between theory and practical action is that the former is not as certain and observable as the latter. That is, we can *see* the results of practical action, but we cannot do the same with theory. To the reader such a statement may seem absurd, for throughout this entire book all we have been talking about is empirical research that will provide us with observable evidence that will test the validity of theory. To use an untested theory for a social program is certainly naive and highly impractical. However, since we are assuming that any theory a programmer would even think of using has been thoroughly researched and tested, the untried program, not the theory, is really the set of conditions that has not been *shown* to work. To use an untested theory for a social program is doubly dangerous, for at the outset neither the theory or the program has any empirical proof. Therefore, in discussing evaluation research we would expect that the *tested* aspect of the research is the theory and the *untested* is the program, not the other way around.

Now the great irony with so many "practical" programs is that they are not based on tested theory. In fact, many programs are grounded in only the most rudimentary of all theories—the "hunch," or "idea"—most of which are

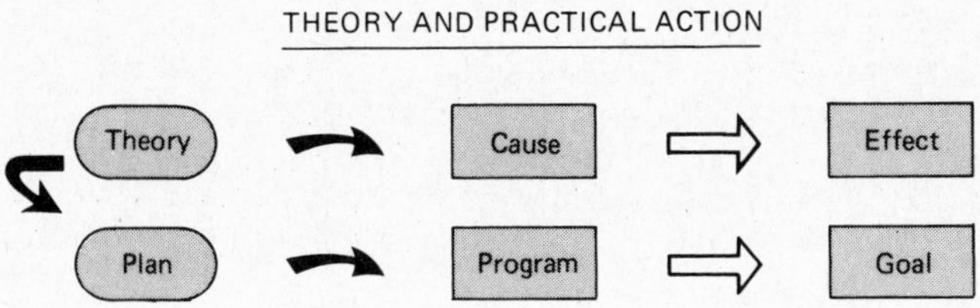

THEORY AND PRACTICAL ACTION

**FIGURE 18.1
Theory and
Practical Action**

nothing more than commonsense prejudices whose validity rests on the fact that they have been stated so many times that they are believed to be true. Of course, it is highly probable that programs launched under such procedures will fail and success will be random. It would also seem that given a history of failure that it would become clear for the need of tested theory to be used with programs, and to some extent this has been realized, but far too often, the only "theory" behind social programs is an argument based on little or no systematically collected evidence.

Linking Programs and Tested Theory

Given the need to link social programs with some kind of tested theory, the question becomes, "How can theory be used for social intervention programs?" To answer this question we must decide (1) what the program hopes to accomplish and (2) what theory shows a relationship between variables leading to the program's goal? The more specific the goal, the easier it will be to identify a theory that can be used to develop a program to meet the goal.[3] For example, if a goal is "to make the world a better place to live," there are so many different directions one could go to achieve this goal that it would be impossible to focus on any single theory. On the other hand, if the goal were "to provide better medical care to the elderly," we can begin looking at theories dealing with health-care delivery and problems of the elderly. More general theories dealing with community and organizational change would also be consulted for setting up a program to implement procedures to better serve the elderly.

To see how this linkage is possible, we will examine a program that used tested social science theory to implement a set of conditions that would reduce delinquency. Basically, the program was grounded in labeling and differential association theory, but it also included counseling theory as well. We will concentrate on the application of labeling and differential association theory to simplify the example.

The general problem being addressed was juvenile delinquency, especially juvenile status offenders—those offenders who have violated no law for which an adult could be arrested, such as running away from home and truancy.[4] Labeling theory has shown that juveniles who are stigmatized as delinquent are more likely to be forced into a delinquent role and to commit further delinquency.[5] Differential association theory has shown that juveniles learn delinquency from associations with other delinquents.[6] From these two theories a program based on the concept of "diversion" emerged.[7] The idea is that if juveniles are diverted from the juvenile justice system, especially the courts and correctional system, they are less likely to (1) be labeled delinquent and thrust into the delinquent role, and (2) come into sustained contact with other delinquents and learn delinquent behavior. The first point was based on labeling theory, the second on differential association theory.

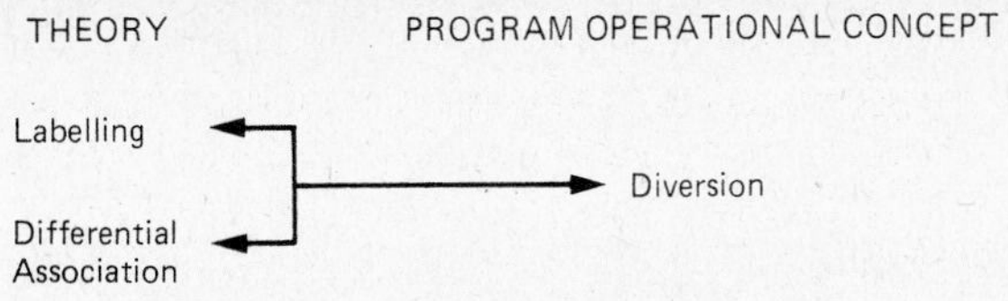

FIGURE 18.2
Theory–Program
Connection

As we can see, there is a direct relationship between tested theory and the program. To the extent that the program operationalized the theoretical concepts, we would expect the program to work. In order to test the operational concept (that is, the program) specific goals were stated, and if accomplished, the operation would be considered successful. The following goals were established:

1. Reduce the number of cases going to court.
2. Decrease overnight detentions.
3. Reduce the number of repeat offenses.
4. Accomplish these goals at a cost no greater than that required for regular processing of cases.

Put in terms of theoretical linkages, we can see the goals as follows:

Goal 1   Reduce *labeling* by reducing delinquent records generated in court.
Goal 2   Reduce *associations* with other delinquents in detention.

In turn, accomplishing the first two goals would lead to:

Goal 3   Remove the *causes* of delinquency and thereby reduce repeated delinquency.

The fourth goal was simply a fiscal one and did not relate at all to the theory.

Obviously, we cannot claim too much by way of theoretical testing under such circumstances, since more than a single theory was employed. However, we can see exactly what theoretical constructs were involved and tell in a general way whether or not the theories were applied in the right direction. If a single theory is employed in guiding a social program, it is possible to have a test of the theory's validity in addition to a program's success. Also, if a highly tested and proven theory does not work in an applied program, we can suspect the application of the concepts rather than the idea itself, and instead of throwing out the entire theory, we look for operations that reflect the theory. A program without theory, though, has no guidelines or points of reference to examine or further apply, and so even if such a program is successful, we do not know why or how to use it elsewhere.

Pilot Programs and Evaluation Design

In pure social science research, the investigator will often conduct a *pilot study* in order to sensitize concepts and work out any bugs in the instruments and procedures. Similarly, in applied social science, programmers usually start off with a *pilot program* to see whether the ideas work before going into a full-fledged general application. This allows the programmer to see whether the plan works, what adjustments need to be made, and what will be required for the program to be run efficiently and effectively.

In our example of the juvenile delinquency program, we were looking at a pilot program, a forerunner to the general diversion programs that later came into being. Like most good pilot programs, it was set up as an experiment, using a comparative control group to see whether the new procedures really made any difference. The control group used the old procedure of sending juveniles to court and detention, and the new program diverted the juveniles in the **project group** as part of the pilot project. Unlike the classic experiment where *nothing* is done to the control group, in pilot programs, usually the old program is used as a "control."

If there are any differences at Time 2, the differences can be attributed to the different programs. In cases where no "old program" exists, the pilot project is introjected very much in the same way as the experimental condition in a field experiment, with the control group being a random sample of a comparable cohort.

In making the comparisons it is important to make certain that the pilot project has been implemented in comparison to the control group. Since some programs are fairly complex in their application, this may be no small feat, but in others it is merely a matter of making sure that all the subjects who are part of the pilot project (project group) have been exposed to the program. Likewise, when using an old program for a control group, it is important to make sure that the old program is still working the way it always has and doing so consistently. Any attempt to "improve" the old program during the pilot project will only serve to confuse any differences that may appear after being exposed to one program or the other. For example, in the delinquent diversion program, one of the measured comparisons made was between overnight detention in the control and project groups as seen in Table 18.1.

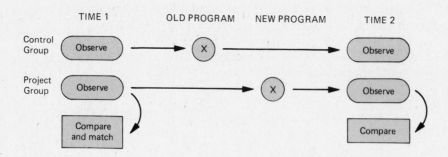

FIGURE 18.3

Table 18.1   Overnight Detention in Juvenile Hall as a Result of Initial Referral

	Control (Percent)	Project (Percent)
No overnight detention	44.5	86.1
1 night	20.7	9.9
2−4 nights	19.2	3.0
5−39 nights	14.4	0.7
40−100 nights	1.1	0.3
Over 100 nights	0.0	0.0

Source: Roger Baron and Floyd Feeney, *Juvenile Diversion Through Family Counseling* (Washington, D.C.: U.S. Department of Justice, 1976), p. 9.

As can be seen, not all of the control group was put into detention and not all of the project group escaped detention. However, a significant difference between the two groups did exist in avoiding detention altogether— 44.5 percent for the control group and 86.1 percent for the project group. Thus, while there is not perfect control, or even the fine measure of control we expect in an experiment, there is a clear difference between the control and project group. Ideally, *none* of the project group should have been placed in overnight detention and *all* of the control group should have been. However, in evaluation research, as well as any other kind of research, the investigator would not want to do anything to the subjects that might harm them, and since the researchers clearly believed detention was harmful, if they had insisted on placing an additional 44.5 percent of the youths in the control group in overnight detention, they would have been doing them harm by their own definition.

Under these circumstances, it would seem to be a better idea simply to compare groups that either did or did not actually come under the project conditions or control condition. That is, youths who were not placed in overnight detention and were not petitioned to juvenile court would make up the project group while those who did spend overnight in detention and were petitioned to court could be the comparison group. The problem with such a comparison is that the project was to evaluate whether the *current procedures* in the juvenile justice system were inferior to the diversion and counseling program. Since under the old juvenile justice program there was a sizable proportion of youths who did not spend overnight in detention, as well as not being petitioned to juvenile court, it was necessary to maintain the *general* pattern of the procedures currently being employed in the juvenile justice system. Another problem in evaluating how the project worked, based simply on those who did and did not have overnight detention or court petitions, was that under the old system it was usually the *more serious offenders* who had to spend overnight in detention or received court petitions. So if a comparison was made with only the group that did or did not have the more severe dispositions, the evaluation would have been based on the characteristics of the *offenders* and *not the programs.*

The design and execution of evaluation of pilot projects will depend on the nature of the new program being evaluated and the old program. If many of the features of the old program are similar to those of the new, it is more difficult to have as precise an evaluation. However, in situations where there is no old program or a significantly different one, a pilot project can be almost the same as a true experimental design. The closer a pilot project is to an experimental or quasiexperimental design, not only is it possible to better evaluate the effects of the program but of the underlying theory as well.

Measuring Goals

In virtually all evaluation research the "bottom line" is whether or not the program has achieved its goals. Since goals tend to be more general statements, it is necessary to establish criteria that can be somehow measured to reflect goal accomplishment. That is, criteria must be *operationally defined* in the same way that pure research operationally defines concepts.[9] In our example of the juvenile diversion program, the goal of *reducing delinquency* was operationally defined in terms of *reducing recidivism.* That is, delinquency was operationally defined as being apprehended for delinquency. Now, it may be argued that being arrested for delinquency and committing delinquency are two different things, and so the criterion for reducing delinquency was a false one in terms of the goals; however, it is certainly the case that being arrested for delinquency is *one* measure of delinquency, and since delinquency is a socially defined category, it is clear that arrests are a measure of social definitions. Whatever the case, though, the criterion for measuring the goal must be some reflection of the goal itself.

In her discussion of evaluation research, Moursund has provided an excellent model of the relationship between goal measurement and criteria. First, the goals are clearly stated, and then criteria for measuring the goals are listed.[10] For example, in evaluating an elementary school reading program, the following goals were stated:

1. To develop enough reading ability to be able to move into intermediate school programs.
2. To begin to be able to enjoy some activities in and out of school that involve reading skills.[11]

Accompanying these goals was a set of desired **outcomes** that could be observed, the accomplishment of which would serve as the criteria for meeting the goals. The following outcomes were considered appropriate for measuring goal accomplishment:

1. To be able to recognize a basic 600-word vocabulary.
2. To be able to sound out new words according to the rules of phonics.

3. To be able to read and understand material at the third-grade level of difficulty.
4. To give evidence of enjoying the activity of reading.
5. To show eagerness to improve reading skills.[12]

In order to have good criteria, they must do two things: (1) relate logically to the goal and (2) be clear enough to easily tell whether they have been satisfied.[13] If we look at the first goal and the first outcome to be used as a criterion, we can see the connection between the two. Assuming that a 600-word vocabulary is required to move into intermediate school programs, it is clear that if a child masters such a vocabulary, he or she will have the necessary reading ability for the higher school level, thereby meeting the goal. Likewise, the criterion is clearly measurable in that a child either will or will not have the ability to recognize a basic 600-word vocabulary.

One of the dangers in evaluation research is the tendency of the measuring devices to determine the goals. What happens is that in their eagerness to be successful, programmers will set up goals in terms of what can be easily measured and accomplished. Thus, instead of establishing a meaningful goal, the goal will simply be something that can be measured by known research methods. For instance, suppose a social goal is to improve health services to the elderly. A program is established to provide transportation between a retirement community and a hospital in the form of a shuttle-bus service, the goal of the program being "to improve transportation for the elderly between their homes and medical facilities." The criterion for the program goal is stated as, "to have a shuttle bus running every hour from 9 A.M. to 4 P.M. from the retirement community to the hospital." Such a criterion is linked to the **program goal** and it is easily measured—either the buses run according to the schedule or they do not. However, the *social goal of improved health services* may not have even been addressed. The real issue with the health services may have been the high costs, lack of sufficient medical personnel, or any number of other far more difficult problems, and so even if the transportation was improved, there would be no real changes in the quality of the health services. Thus, in addition to evaluating the program goals, it is important to determine whether they are linked to a real problem or merely a problem that could be easily evaluated.

Choosing an Evaluation Method

An all-too-common problem in pure research also crops up in evaluation research. Rather than selecting the most appropriate method or methods for the research, the researcher chooses his or her favorite one. Instead of asking, "What research tools could be best used to evaluate this program?" the programmer asks, "How can I evaluate this program using a survey?" or some other method he or she loves best. It makes about as much sense as asking how one can build a brick house using a saw, but it is a persistent bad habit among researchers.

The ideal situation in evaluation research is when the programmer and researcher work together to set up the program so that it can be fully evaluated without interfering with program procedures or goals. Pilot projects using a control group make for an excellent evaluation research program in the form of a field experiment, and even though a researcher may prefer some other methodology, some form of project experiment provides the best knowledge as to what effect a program has on a pattern of social behavior.

Usually a good evaluation requires more than a single methodology, certain techniques working best with one aspect of the project, and other techniques working best with other aspects. For example, if the evaluation involves a large number of people, a pretest and posttest may both involve surveys to measure changes and goal accomplishment. However, in the very same project, participant observation might be the best way to determine whether or not the procedures have actually been implemented in the way intended. Thus, by combining experimental design, survey methods, and participant observation, the evaluation has covered all of the major parts of the program, using the most appropriate technique for each aspect.

The choice of method always depends on what the researcher needs to find out. **Program implementation** usually requires some kind of direct observational technique, and goal measurement is best determined by a testing device, whether it is a questionnaire, intensive interview schedule, or a sociometric test of some kind. Also, where more than a single method can be used to measure the same thing, it is often wise to use multiple measures, for as we have seen throughout this book, some methods can "see" certain aspects of social behavior while other methods "see" others, and by backing up evaluation research by multiple methods, we can be better assured of an accurate assessment of a program.

Summary of Procedures

Having seen the various features of evaluation research, we will now retrace our steps and summarize the procedures of the method. Obviously, there will be variations depending on the nature of the evaluation and where the researcher enters the picture in terms of the program's development.

Step 1   Determine the underlying theory directing the program and how the theory is operationalized in program procedures.

Step 2   Determine the goals of the program and the criteria for accomplishing the goals.

Step 3   Determine the procedures the program intends to employ to meet the goals.

Step 4   Establish a control group to compare with the program group.

Step 5 Choose a method or methods to measure program implementation and goal accomplishment.

Step 6 Determine whether the program has been implemented in the intended manner.

Step 7 Determine whether stated goals have been accomplished, and compare project group with the control group.

This summary provides a checklist for evaluation research, and different parts might have to be omitted. As we pointed out elsewhere in this chapter, programs are not always grounded in theory, and so Step 1 may be nothing more than determining that a program has no theory. With highly complex programs, additional procedures for evaluation may have to be incorporated.

The Politics of Evaluation Research

In pure research if a favored theory proves to be invalid, losses are measured in hurt feelings and damaged egos. However, if evaluation research shows that a program cannot accomplish its intended goals or at least not as well as other programs, losses are measured in terms of lost revenues and jobs. As a result of the possible losses incurred when a program is determined to have failed, there is a greater tendency for all involved in the endeavor to make sure any evaluation is positive. To this end, criteria for success are established at easily achieved levels, information is doctored, and anything that at first appears to be a failure is rationalized away as a result of factors having nothing to do with the program.

It is not the case that evil people are involved in programs, but rather the funding structure of most programs is such that there is a great deal of pressure to always be successful—or at least partially so. Since most funding comes from government agencies, the money for programs is monitored by Congress—elected officials who want to make sure that their constituencies are satisfied with the way their tax dollars are spent. If a million dollars is spent on a program that is a monumental flop, elected officials can be blamed for wasting tax dollars by groups who make it their business to serve as "watch dogs" for public monies. That is at the top of the funding structure.

At the other end of the structure is the program administrator whose proposal for making the world a better place has been funded by the government, and at the very bottom is the person who has been hired to work on the program. If the program is successful, it will be funded again, with everybody involved in the project benefiting.

In the middle of the structure is the government agency funding the program. Since its budget is dependent on Congress, it is cautious not to fund anything that might blow up in its face. And if it happens to back a losing project, it would be as quick to find redeeming values in the program as would the programmers. Additionally, the government funding agency has to keep track of every penny it spends and therefore has a great number of forms to be filled out, thereby adding to the workload of the programmers. One meddling agency became so involved in a project that it effectively destroyed its operation. In order to keep track of the money spent in a program with juvenile gangs (as well as justifying how funds were being spent), the agency required the programmers to have the people working on the project complete "gang member contact" forms. The more gang members contacted by the project staff the better. Unfortunately, the entire program was geared to working with the gang leadership, and by sending staff all over to have their "contact forms" filled out, they were unable to carry out the program procedures.

Into this maze of interests, careers, and politics steps the evaluation researcher. Ideally, the researcher is only supposed to say whether the program met its goals or not. If the program has met its goals, then everyone throughout the entire structure is happy. On the other hand, if the program is an unqualified failure, the *ideal* would be that the programmers try something else. The money had been well-spent since we now know what does *not* work, and we can keep on searching. However, a failed program does not receive such a gracious and practical understanding. Instead, there is consternation over spending money on something that did not work. Programmers are not funded again for future projects, agency bureaucrats are accused of unwisely spending money, and eventually politicians are pointed out for betraying the public trust. Therefore, it becomes clear why there is pressure on evaluation researchers to "find" only success—if not total, at least partial. Moreover, if the researcher "fudges" a little in his or her findings, no one is going to be overly eager to expose it.

The next logical step is the cooperation of the evaluation researcher in the interest structure. In one program observed by the authors, the evaluation portion of a project was funded so that the money supporting the evaluation research team, a private organization, would depend on the success of the project. The three-year project was to be evaluated for renewal of funding at the end of each year. As long as there was evidence as compiled by the evaluation research team that the program was working, the project would be funded again, along with funds for the researchers. If the researchers reported at the end of the first year that the program was a failure, they would cut off their own funds. Not surprisingly, the evaluations at the end of the first and second years "found" that the program was working quite well. They may have been accurate evaluations, but since the very survival of the research team depended on the program's success, any evaluation it made would have to be highly suspect if it "found" the program to be achieving its goals.

The real danger in the structure of interests in programs and their evaluation is that it becomes increasingly difficult to tell which programs are effective and which are not. Since there is pressure to find success in all programs, we can presume that a number of mediocre programs have been deemed successful. At the same time, there probably have been a number of effective programs evaluated as equally successful, but we have no clear idea of which programs do in fact work because the evaluations look very much the same. Thus, the very structure that claims to spend its money in the wisest manner actually generates a set of conditions that does the opposite.

Perhaps the best way out of this dilemma is to understand how wasteful and unproductive it actually is. By rewarding programmers who have found clear evidence that a program does not work in the same way that they are rewarded for "successes," there would be less pressure to produce a triumph where there has been defeat. Billions have been spent on cancer research, and while there have been some partial successes, most research has found what does not work. We certainly do not consider it a failure in cancer research to seal off one more dead end in searching for a cancer cure or prevention method. If social science programs that were unqualified failures were treated as scientific successes in the sense that they told us what does not work, there would be less waste of money and far more social progress.

Summary

Evaluation research is really nothing more than social science research methods applied to social programs. At the very base of such programs is some kind of theory that provides the conceptual framework for the project. In one sense, program procedures are operationalized concepts, and so applied research can be almost identical to pure in such circumstances. However, too often programs are only vaguely linked to theory, and so the researcher is left measuring narrow program objectives instead of general principles.

Since the primary purpose of evaluation research is to determine the effectiveness and efficiency of a program, the focus is on whether or not the procedures have been implemented and, if put to work, can achieve a set of goals stated by the program. The more specific and clear the goals, the easier it is to determine whether or not they have been met. The evaluation researcher examines a set of criteria established to determine goal-achievement, and if the criteria have been met, then the program's objectives are considered to have been accomplished. Alternatively, if the criteria are not met, the program is determined to be a failure.

Unfortunately, the simplicity of evaluation research is not quite what it seems to be. The structure of funding for programs stresses success, even in cases where there is clear evidence that failure is the predominate feature of a program's operation. As a result, there is a great deal of pressure on evaluation researchers to "find" at least some success in the most dismal of programs. Criteria are changed so that initially evaluated failures are transformed into partial or whole triumphs. This kind of unfortunate influence leads to poor information, financial waste, and a generally unethical atmosphere for evaluation research. By understanding the value of documenting bona fide failures and the cumulative knowledge to be gained by *both* successful and unsuccessful programs, not to mention the financial savings, researchers can eventually convince those in policymaking positions that the best research is the most honest. Thus, what in one context is an ethical decision, in another context becomes a very practical one.

Glossary

effectiveness The extent to which a program can accomplish its stated goals.

efficiency The extent to which a program is "cost effective" or can accomplish its goals at a given level of quality while minimizing costs.

evaluation Determining the extent to which a program has been implemented and has effectively and efficiently accomplished its goals.

outcomes Measurable indicators of program goals used in determining the worth of a program.

pilot program A small-scale program used to test the effectiveness and efficiency of an idea before launching large-scale programs.

program goals The overall objectives of a program in terms of services or changes caused by the program.

program implementation In evaluation research, it refers to the extent to which the various parts of a program were put into action.

project group Similar to "experimental group" in experimental designs and used for the same purpose in evaluation research. It is the group that is subjected to the conditions of a program, and compared with a "control group" not subjected to the program.

Notes

1. Janet P. Moursund, *Evaluation: An Introduction to Research Design* (Monterey, Ca.: Brooks/Cole, 1973), pp. 8−9.
2. Peter M. Blau and W. Richard Scott, *Formal Organizations* (San Francisco: Chandler, 1962), pp. 33−34.
3. Moursund, op. cit., p. 8.
4. Roger Baron and Floyd Feeney, *Juvenile Diversion Through Family Counseling* (Washington, D.C.: U.S. Department of Justice, 1976).
5. Edwin Lemert, *Human Deviance, Social Problems, and Social Control* (Englewood Cliffs, N.J.: Prentice-Hall, 1967).
6. Edwin Sutherland and Donald R. Cressey, *Criminology*, 10th ed. (New York: Lippincott, 1978).
7. Donald R. Cressey and Robert A. McDermott, *Diversion from the Juvenile Justice System*, Project Report for National Assessment of Juvenile Corrections (Ann Arbor: University of Michigan, June, 1973).
8. Baron and Feeney, op. cit., p. 8.
9. Moursund, op. cit., p. 18−19.
10. Ibid., p. 18.
11. Ibid.

12. Ibid.
13. Ibid., p. 19.
14. Malcolm Klein, *Street Gangs and Street Workers* (Englewood Cliffs, N.J.: Prentice-Hall, 1971).

19

Ethics in
Social Research

In Chapter 18, we saw the pressures on evaluation researchers to "find" success in social intervention programs whether such programs were effective or not. On an intuitive level we recognize any tampering with research findings as clearly being *unethical*. To a large extent, social research ethics involve honesty in research findings, but it is insufficient to say that all there is to ethics in research is honesty.

When conducting research in which humans are the subjects of the inquiry, we must be quite careful not to create harmful conditions in the research process. At one extreme we can clearly understand that a social science researcher would not set a plague on a town to study community reaction to disaster, for even though it may be argued that such an experiment would tell us a good deal about reactions to catastrophe, our ethical standards clearly forbid such an experiment. More realistically, there is a question of ethics in experiments in which the subjects are temporarily misled in order to minimize researcher effect. Is it ethical to lie to subjects about the nature of a research project even though they will not be harmed?

Another problem in ethics that social science researchers must wrestle with involves political and quasipolitical features of research. Research sponsored by government agencies has been designed to gather information to be used to control populations. If such information was seen to be clearly for the good of the people, such as how to reduce the infant mortality rate by taking sanitary measures and following a proper diet, there would probably be little in the way of ethical doubts. However, in other facets of ethics where there are conflicting and opposite beliefs and values,—for example, the issues of birth-control and abortion—how then do researchers deal with the ethical issues involved? What if a demographer could clearly show that with the birth rate at current levels, a given population would suffer starvation in five years, resulting in the death of millions, and that a birth-control program would not only improve the lives of the people, but would also prevent the starvation disaster? Should social science researchers involve themselves in controversial issues or not? Or even more ethically problematical, what if the information gathered by a social science researcher were to be used by a dictatorship to keep the people docile? Should the researcher stop his or her research, even though the same findings could also be used for a beneficial purpose?

Weighing the greater good is often an issue with researchers. One researcher, in a study of drug offenders in a rehabilitation program, was given a stash of heroin to hide. Should he have turned over the heroin to the authorities and thereby terminated the research or should he have refused to hide the drug and destroyed his rapport with the drug offenders? If he had turned the heroin in, the men who gave it to him would have been sent to prison; his refusal to hide it would have broken the rapport with the drug offenders and not have solved the problem of the heroin; and if he cooperated in hiding the heroin, he would have involved himself in a felony crime. No matter what the researcher did, he was caught in a dilemma. Or take another example. A researcher was involved in examining a minority-group program on campus when he found that some of the leaders of the program were misappropriating funds for their own use; they were stealing money from the program. If the researcher had been reported this information in his research, it was highly probable that the program would have been shut down. On the other hand, by not saying anything, he was hurting the minority students who severely needed the money to continue their education. No matter what he did, someone would be hurt.

Another kind of ethical issue has to do with the value of a certain ethic in general, so that specific cases maintaining the ethic is questionable. For example, before a subject is involved in a research project, it is a general ethic that the person be informed of the nature of the research. However, what if a researcher is studying political corruption and the only way he or she can gather data about misdeeds is secretly? Is the general ethic maintained or is the greater good seen to be in ignoring the ethic and gathering material on corruption? Is it the case, as some argue, that if the organization and people being studied are moral that the research should be moral as well, but if the subjects are immoral then there are no holds barred in the research? If so, then by what measuring stick do we judge the morality of those we study? Obviously, the answers to this and other ethical problems are not simple, and they certainly are not final. The discussions in this chapter are meant to sensitize the student researcher to ethical problems, but as anyone who does research will understand, there is no way to fully deal with all of the solutions to ethical problems encountered in actual research.

Honesty: The First Ethic

Of all the various ethical concepts we could examine, simple honesty is the most important. This is true not only from a moral point of view but also from a practical one as well. It is not the honesty of a Goody Two-Shoes who tattles on self as well as others; rather, it is the honesty of the dedicated researcher who wants to uncover the most valid information he or she can. Similarly, it is an honesty with oneself and others about the nature of the research and what part all parties will play. Finally, it is an honesty of reporting what actually happened in the research, even if it did not follow all of the stipulated procedures, ethical and otherwise.

Truth in Findings

One of the most insidious of all lies in social research is doctoring one's findings to "prove" a theory. Such dishonesty not only misleads other researchers who will build on these findings but also it casts a pall of doubt over all other of the researcher's findings. One of the most notorious examples of such dishonesty involved a researcher who claimed to have researched separated pairs of identical twins, in an attempt to "discover" whether hereditary or environmental factors were more important in human development. By using identical twins, genetically the same, who grew up in different environments because they were separated at birth, it would be possible for him to test them as adults to find out whether their heredity or environment was the stronger determining factor in the development of their personalities. After examining several sets of separated identical twins, he concluded that even though the twins grew up in different environments, they tested out to be very similar. Thus, he concluded, heredity was more important than environment. Later on, another research report by different researchers was published with similar findings. After investigations, it was learned that not only was the original research false but also that the subsequent research by the "other researchers" was published by the first researcher using false names.[1] In other words, the so-called research on the separated identical twins was totally dishonest from beginning to end.

On the one hand, the research misled other researchers to citing and following up on what appeared to be very strong evidence for hereditary patterns of human behavior. This led to a great deal of wasted time and effort, not to mention the consternation created because the follow-up research did not find the kind of relationships reported in the phony study. Perhaps the cruelest blow was to the advocates of genetic transmission of personality characteristics—those researchers who agreed with the phony findings. This is because one discredited study cast doubt on all of their findings, no matter how honestly their own studies were carried out. In fact, if someone really did conduct a study using separated identical twins and found the genetic factors to be more important than social ones, nobody would believe it! And so instead of providing support for his position, the dishonest researcher probably did more than anyone else to discredit it.

It is fairly easy to speculate on motives for publishing dishonest findings, but it is important to single out at least some and examine them. In the last chapter, we saw the financial pressures on evaluation researchers to "find" successful results of a program; in theoretical research dependent on fundings, there are equal pressures to be "right." Such motivations stem from the structure of funding that correlates "being good" with "being right." However, in the long run, as we saw in Chapter 18, the only good research is that which tells us what is true and what is false. Good money is thrown after bad in situations where researchers are pressured to always find the predicted correlation. Since a great deal of excellent research has been published that indicates findings other than what was predicted, there certainly is evidence that no one's reputation is going to be damaged by publishing honest findings. In fact, such findings are the real breakthroughs in social science since they tell us to start looking in new directions and develop new theories.

Watch Dogs

At this point we might want to demand some kind of "watch dog" to monitor research findings, but such a move could be easily defeated by dishonest researchers. If someone wanted to, it would be a simple matter to make up data, especially in cases where there is a large sample of quantitative data. By tossing enough false numbers, a researcher would be able to alter the level of significance in one test or another to have the numbers come out pretty much the way he or she wanted. Unless the watch dog was as knowledgeable about the method as the researcher, there would be little chance that the watch dog could do much about the cheating. Furthermore, when we talk about such banal measures as watch dogs, all we really do is to pass the responsibility for ethical behavior onto the watchers, and we can only ask "Who's going to watch the watchers?" As we saw in our discussion of evaluation research, the interest structure is such that everyone from top to bottom is rooting for a successful program, and there are really no rewards for exposing dishonest research.

Professional Ethics

So what do we mean by **professional ethics?** Most professional organizations, such as the American Sociological Association, have codes of ethics that state that they will tell the truth and not intentionally hurt anyone. Likewise, as we will later discuss in detail, there is an elaborate set of rules for protecting human subjects that is supposed to guarantee that the conduct of the research will meet certain ethical standards, such as informing subjects as to the nature of the research. However, a written code or a legalistic set of research conditions has little to do with professional ethics. On the one hand, an organization's code is something like the Boy Scout's Code, a ritualistic litany of norms that may be voiced but are not understood to be binding in terms of actually living in the real world. The legalistic set of rules one acknowledges by filling out forms and providing written evidence of compilance is even more ritualistic than an organization's code in that it is seen as troublesome paperwork rather than a legitimate effort to maintain ethics. Besides, if one has a legalistic bent, there are enough "loopholes" in such documents for one to run amok over all kinds of important ethical standards.

By "professional ethics" we mean a deep commitment to telling the truth for the sake of knowledge and an equal commitment to humanity that results in taking the necessary steps to guarantee that one's research will not harm others. This is not a naive proclamation of idealistic ardor, but rather a realization that all means of maintaining any kind of ethics ultimately depend on the ethical understanding of the researcher. All the watch dogs, codes, and forms cannot serve as a substitute, nor can they even be effective, without a researcher's goal of valid knowledge gathered with respect shown to humanity.

Truth to Subjects

During the reign of the Nazis in Europe, millions of Jews, Slavs, Gypsies, and other were murdered in the death camps. One of the more common methods of mass murder was to tell the people they were going to take a shower and clean up before being assigned to their quarters. When the victims were in the "shower room," the Nazis turned on a lethal gas through the shower heads, killing the men, women, and children inside. In the same camps, Nazi "scientists" conducted experiments on human subjects to determine how much pain a person could take before he or she died, the effects of high altitude on unpressurized airplane cabins, and similar horrendous experiments. When the American, French, Russian, and British soldiers liberated the concentration camps, they were shocked, and even the German civilians who vaguely suspected what was happening in the camps were incredulous when they were taken to see the handiwork of the "master race."

So terrible were the savage and inhumane practices of the Nazis, especially the "experiments" conducted under the name of science, that they have served as a vivid reminder of the lengths people can go when there is a disregard for the value of human life. To prevent a recurrence of such outrages in the name of science, there has developed a mounting sensitivity to the effects of research on humans. Since even the most well-meaning research might have a negative effect on subjects, the decision to participate in research has been turned over to the subjects.

Originally, the focus on the protection of human subjects was in the area of experimentation, especially where drugs might be used or in which the emotional effect could have be lasting and negative. The most famous example of emotionally disturbing experiments were those conducted by psychologist Stanley Milgram. Ironically, Milgram set out to test the effects of authority in order to better understand why the German people followed the Nazi regime to the extremes they did. In order to test the effects of authority, he set up an experiment in which the experimenter represented the "authority figure." The experimental situation was devised so that the subjects thought they were administering electric shocks to a fellow subject who had a weak heart. The "fellow subject" was a person in league with the experimenter, who pretended to be receiving electric shocks whenever the real subject pressed a button. If the subject refused to administer the shocks after a certain level, the experimenter "ordered" him to do so "in the name of science," and to an unexpected degree, the experimental subjects followed orders. After the experiment was concluded, Milgram explained that no actual shocks had been given and that the other "subject" was just acting.

The issue the Milgram experiments raised was that of misleading subjects and putting them in a situation in which they would do something that was emotionally upsetting. Moreover, it showed the degree to which subjects trusted experimenters and would do what they asked, even if those requests were against their own ethical and moral beliefs.

Informed Consent

In order to minimize the possibility of harm to research subjects, elaborate precautions have been devised to ensure that research subjects *clearly* understand what they are getting themselves into. The *protocols* for the protection of human subjects are elaborate and detailed, and if they are followed in letter and spirit, there is little doubt that the people who are subjects in the research will not know what they are doing.

In order to see what is meant by **informed consent,** the following sample **consent form** is provided.

Sample Consent Form

You are invited to participate in a study of (state what is being studied). We hope to learn (state what the study is designed to discover or establish). You were selected as a possible participant in this study because (state why the subject was selected).

If you decide to participate, we (or: Dr. _____ and his/her associates) will (describe the procedures to be followed, including their purposes, how long they will take, and their frequency). (Describe the discomforts and inconveniences reasonably to be expected. If benefits are mentioned, add:) We cannot and do not guarantee or promise that you will receive any benefits from this study.

(Describe appropriate alternative procedures that might be advantageous to the subject, if any. Any standard treatment that is being withheld must be disclosed.)

Any information that is obtained in connection with this study and that can be identified with you will remain confidential and will be disclosed only with your permission or as required by law. If you give us your permission by signing this document, we plan to disclose (state the persons or agencies to whom the information will be furnished, the nature of the information to be furnished, and the purpose of the disclosure).

(If the subject will receive compensation, describe the amount or nature.) (If there is a possibility of additional costs to the subject because of participation, describe it.)

Your decisions whether or not to participate will not prejudice your future relations with the (institution) (and the named cooperating institution, if any). If you decide to participate, you are free to withdraw your consent and to discontinue participation at any time without prejudice.

If you have any questions, we expect you to ask us. If you have any additional questions later, Dr. _____ (give phone number or address) will be happy to answer them.

You will be given a copy of this form to keep. (Optional)

YOU ARE MAKING A DECISION WHETHER OR NOT TO PARTICIPATE. YOUR
SIGNATURE INDICATES THAT YOU HAVE DECIDED TO PARTICIPATE HAVING
READ THE INFORMATION PROVIDED.

_____   _____
Date   Signature

                                 _____
                                 Relationship to subject

                                 (This line should not appear on forms that
                                 will be given to subjects consenting for
                                 themselves.)

_____   _____
Signature of Witness   Signature of Investigator
(If any)

Source: Policy & Procedures for the Protection of Human Subjects, SDSU Committee on Protection
of Human Subjects, May 1978, San Diego State University.

Given the detail in the document, it would appear that the protection
issue has gone a bit far, but every item in the form has a specific purpose
relating to informed consent. The more obvious features require the researcher
to write out exactly what the research will involve and what he or she is going
to do to the subject. Some of the more subtle issues involved are letting
subjects know that they can quit whenever they want and that their refusal to
participate will not affect their relations with the researcher. On the first point,
some subjects believe that once they are involved in a research project, they
have to stay with it—after all, they signed an agreement to do so. Consent
forms make it clear that this is not the case. It may also seem strange to include
a statement saying that future relations with the researcher will not be
prejudiced by refusal to participate. Again, the consent form is addressing a
very important issue, since many research subjects are students. In fact, one of
the most researched groups in existence is college students. Since a student's
professor may ask him or her to participate in a research project as a subject,
students feel they have to or jepordize their grade. Thus, in order not to
intimidate students into experiments, surveys or other research they may feel
is not in their interest, the researcher uses the consent form to let people know
that there is no deception or coercion involved.

Before going on with some of the other aspects of the human subject
protection form, it should be pointed out that most of the research conducted
by social scientists is in no way harmful to the subjects nor are researchers
intimidating characters who flog students into being research subjects. Most

students enjoy participating in research, especially social science students who can learn a good deal about techniques of research from the subject's point of view. Questionnaires provide students with an opportunity to express their views and experiences, and most experiments are very interesting situations. The concern for protecting human subjects is simply to give the subjects a clear choice to participate or not from a position of full knowledge.

CONFIDENTIALITY   A very difficult issue in social science ethics is **confidentiality.** The fourth paragraph of the sample form reveals the unfortunate position of most researchers in relation to this matter. For many types of research, confidentiality is not that much of a problem. However, when illegal acts are involved, confidentiality cannot always be maintained. Where there is a marked legal interest in research findings, especially that involving the study of deviance, the researcher is in the strange position of attempting to learn about illegal behavior while saying that confidentiality can be maintained as long as there is no legal inquiry into the matter. For example, if a researcher were studying illegal drug use among hospital personnel—how much they use, how they get it, and so forth—it would seem to be almost impossible to get any subjects to cooperate, especially if they had to sign their names to a document that states that the researcher may have to reveal the information if a court asks him or her to do so.

The unfortunate aspect of the confidentiality matter is not with the researcher tattling on someone because the researcher's interest is in general patterns, and he or she could care less if a particular subject admitted to deviance or criminality. Rather, the problem is that, unlike attorneys and psychiatrists who are legally protected from divulging confidential information, most social science researchers are legally vulnerable. In fact, they are in a very similar legal situation to journalists. Even if researchers have no intention of revealing confidential sources, they have no legal protection against being forced to do so. Perhaps in the future social scientists will have the same legal protection as attorneys and psychiatrists do now, but until that time, social science researchers will often be at risk to keep confidentiality.

Another side to confidentiality is a very practical one. If a subject is not given some assurances of confidentiality, he or she is unlikely to agree to participate in a research project, especially one involving information that the person believes to be of a personal nature. In one study of the effects of confidentiality guarantees, it was found that statements of absolute confidentiality had a positive effect on people's willingness to answer questions. Compared to subjects under research conditions in which either no mention of confidentiality was made or only conditional confidentiality was given, those research subjects who were given promises of absolute confidentiality were more willing to answer sensitive questions.[2]

Ironically, the legal situation that does not guarantee information received by social scientists can be kept confidential may have led to tighter confidentiality among the social scientists themselves. In studies dealing with sensitive information, especially in large surveys, questionnaires and interviews are kept anonymous. It is often literally impossible to know who filled out what. With thousands of interviews or completed questionnaires on hand, none of which has any identifying characteristic that might reveal the subject, there is virtually absolute confidentiality. Moreover, since most questionnaire data is coded and put onto computer cards, tapes, or discs, there is no need to keep all of the bulky questionnaires around once they have been coded and stored for computer processing. Thus, even if a social scientist wanted to, he or she could not identify any particular individual's response.

Keeping anonymity, and therefore confidentiality, in field studies is a bit more difficult. One argument is that social scientists are not obliged to withhold information about someone who breaks the law. It is a naturally occurring phenomenon, and the fact that the researcher happened to be on hand during the commission of the crime does not exclude him or her from being a witness in court and reporting what was seen. A first response may be that such a condition is unfair, citing the situation of the psychiatrist and attorney. Moreover, how can a researcher really understand crime and deviance without firsthand study? When the researcher loses access to information because of the inability to guarantee complete confidentiality, the long-range result will be a lack of study, analysis, and understanding of certain parts of social life. There is merit to such an argument, especially since it is the chosen *method* that puts the researcher in a position where he or she can identify a particular person, for a survey researcher who found the same thing can still maintain anonymity by sheer numbers. That is, if a participant observer researcher saw a person commit a robbery, for example, he or she could identify the robber, but if a survey researcher found the same information on a questionnaire, the robber could not be identified since the questionnaire is part of a large sample, all anonymous. The survey researcher can maintain confidentiality simply by having no idea of who responded affirmatively to having committed a robbery while the participant observer, who somehow gained access to a gang of robbers, cannot. It would be inconsistent to demand that the participant observer give up confidentiality while the survey researcher need not do the same. However, that is the current situation in social science research, assuming a court demanded a researcher to testify against a robbery defendant.*

A related issue in confidentiality and criminal or deviant behavior has to do with the differing ethical standards for different types of crimes. Social scientists may individually and collectively balk at having to break confidentiality if their studies involve victimless crimes such as drug use, gambling, or

---

*There are special circumstances where researchers under federal sponsorship may be granted immunity against breaking confidentiality, but this is not the general state of affairs for social science researchers.

prostitution, but may not feel the same about breaking confidentiality in other criminal areas. For example, suppose a researcher were studying the Ku Klux Klan in a particular area, and learned that they were going to lynch a black man because he was dating a white woman. Ethical standards of confidentiality would probably not be the same in that kind of situation as in a study of marijuana users, for example, even though both situations involve law violations. No matter what method was employed, if the act is considered to be clearly harmful and/or evil, most social scientists would interfere. The dilemma arises when we attempt to develop a consistent set of guidelines that are applicable to all research situations under all circumstances. No matter what the result, whether we give social scientists full legal confidentiality guarantees or the limited ones we now have, there will be situations where either individual or collective ethics will take exception to some facet of social behavior.

Taking Risks

In the world of action and adventure, people risk their fortunes, lives, limbs, and social status.[3] When people knowingly take risks, they expect to get something in return, whether it be a fortune at the gambling table or the thrill of a free fall in skydiving. Social risk is involved in virtually every other kind of risk, for when we chance anything involving our selves, whether it is our body, money, or claims of ability, we also stand to lose our social standing in the eyes of others. Of course, as in other risk-taking situations, we can stand to gain in social esteem by risking the loss of it.

When people knowingly take risks, then, there appear to be at least two distinct features: (1) they expect to get something in return, and (2) they are aware of what might be lost. Given these two features of risk-taking, social science research presents an unusual type of situation where risk might be involved. First of all, there is little chance that a research subject will get anything in return, except perhaps an interesting experience. In research where subjects are paid to participate in projects, there is a monetary reward, but unlike the kinds of risk-taking situations that people willingly enter for excitement, fame, or gain, there are seldom any intrinsic rewards for research subjects. Second, when people agree to be research subjects, they are wholly dependent on the researcher to advise them of either known or potential risks. Rarely do researchers knowingly conduct research in which they believe there is a high probability that the subjects will suffer any lasting harm. At worst, researchers may know there will be some stress or embarassment, but these are considered minor and short-lived, the entire problem to be resolved by the end of the research. However, in order to assure that research risks are fully known to the subjects, researchers carefully examine their procedures to determine possible risks and explain them to the subjects, thus providing the subjects with the opportunity to evaluate the risks involved and to decide on their own whether or not they wish to take the chances described.

In order to see more clearly how risks are defined in research, we will use an excerpt from a protocol for the protection of human subjects. In addition to the risks we have already discussed, there is also psychological risk, explained in the listing of what is to be considered in assessing risks.

DEFINITIONS OF RISKS

Psychological Risk
Research that interrupts the normal activity of human subjects resulting in immediate and/or long-term stress that would not otherwise be experienced by the individual.

1. Stress involves any situation that poses a threat to desired goals or homeostatic organismic conditions and thus places strong adaptive demands on the individual.
2. Stress can be experienced during the actual experimental situation (immediate) and/or as a result of participation in the experiment (long-term).

Some examples of situations that may result in stress are:

a. Threat to self-esteem
b. Exposure to noxious events
c. Request or demand for behaviors that are discrepant with individual's values, morals, and/or ethics
d. The requirement of excess physical effort

Social Risk to Individuals
Social risk to individuals is the extent to which an individual subject is exposed to deprivation with respect to desired relationships with and within both formal and informal social groups, or normal opportunities for such relationships. Such depriviations include (but are not limited to) derogatory labeling, overt hostile reactions by others, diminished access to otherwise available roles, negative effects on social standing or mobility, reduced opportunity to communication, lost or endangered membership in such groups.

Social Risk to Groups
Social risk to groups to the extent to which a subject formal or informal group, as a collective, is exposed to loss with respect to factors affecting the viability and vitality of the group. Such loss includes (but is not limited to) derogatory labeling, overt hostile reactions from the social environment, reduced access to resources, diminished ability to recruit and retain members, negative effects on morale and other aspects of internal cohesion and organization, violation of legally required procedures or risk of damage claims through civil action where there is corporate liability, reduced opportunities for communication, distortion of group activities relative to established group purposes and functions.[4]

As we review these definitions of risk, it may seem that social science research is something akin to the Four Horsemen of the Apocalypse. However, these definitions of risk are complete so that researchers will *consider the possible* ways in which their research will affect individuals or groups. The question should be seen as one of research effect, and in the context of reasonable expectation. For example, if a man were being interviewed at his front door and a loose brick fell and hit him on the head, one could argue that the research was responsible since were it not for the interview being conducted, the person would not have been hurt. Other "what if" scenarios are endless, and no research would be possible if every conceivable contingency were examined. That is not the purpose of the **guidelines for protecting human subjects,** and it would be absurd to treat them as such. Their purpose is to draw attention to and urge precaution about research-generated risks, nothing more.

A more difficult problem concerning risks in social science research has to do with actions a group takes of its own accord, which would harm it if exposed by research. For instance, in researching a well-known national evangelist's organization, two researchers discovered that the organization was cheating in its procedures for documenting the number of conversions it was making. Since the evangelical organization's pitch to local churches was its ability to bring them new members through converting those who attended its rallies, "counting souls"—documenting the number of new converts— became an important part of the revival meetings. Thus, those who "took the walk" and claimed their conversion to Christianity had to be carefully counted and documented. Only new converts counted, and there had to be substantial evidence of the sincerity of their conversion. However, the researchers found that not only were a number of "converts" people who had "taken the walk" in previous meetings, but if a person "took the walk" and claimed to be interested but not wholly converted, he or she too was counted. As a result, a number of "conversions" claimed by the evangelist's organization were phony.[5] *By making this information available*, the researchers did something to create (1) derogatory labeling, and (2) diminished the organization's ability to recruit and retain members, by exposing fraud.

In one context, we could consider such research to have created risk because were it not for the research, the negative results would not have occurred. However, there was *no* distortion of the group's activities, and even though we can certainly see that the group distorted their own purposes and functions, the researchers did not. They simply reported what they found. Thus, while the research findings may have had an adverse effect on the group under study, the research did not create the behaviors that led to the findings, and so it was not a breach of ethics.

Spying and Researcher Effect

In our example of the researchers who found the evangelist organization to be cheating in their salvation records, there was no informed consent or knowledge by the group being studied. The findings were based on researchers who posed as "converts" during one of the revival meetings.[6] The researchers believed the only way they could test their hypothesis that the organization was not accurately reflecting its ability to make conversions was to send in someone pretending to be a convert and see what happened. By doing so, the researchers had found what they suspected, but they did it without the knowledge of the subject organization. It was argued, and probably accurately, that had they openly told the organization what they were doing, they would have been denied access and never learned about the deceptive recordkeeping practices. Therefore, in order to do the research effectively, they had to "spy" on the organization.

There are two interrelated issues here. First is the issue of research without consent, and second is that of the effect of informed consent. When research is conducted on a group or organization without its knowing about it, it can be seen as a form of "spying," and even though it might be argued that the research has no risk-producing effects (other than revelations it may bring) and so there is nothing to inform the subject group about, it is still a form of espionage. Moreover, if the group were informed, there would be an effect on the very behavior of interest. Research on informed consent has shown that even in interviews dealing with sensitive subjects, a standard consent form signed before the interview affected the subjects' responses.[7] Thus, if a group engaged in deviant behavior, such as the evangelical organization, any informed consent would result in changing the behavior to be observed.

Normal Roles

Another understanding of the same research technique is that even though the researchers did not announce their intentions, they entered the organization in a "consumer role" and did nothing by way of behavior that was different from a normal consumer. True, in the case of the revival study, the "converts" did not have the same mental and emotional commitment as did the bulk of genuine converts, but their behavior was essentially the same. Likewise, in other studies where the researcher happens to be in a normal role, whether entered for the purpose of research or, as in the case of many student researchers, in the role already and deciding to study it, there will be research without informed consent.

How far researchers can take the "normal role" argument depends on what is considered a normal role and whether or not doing research in such a role reconstitutes that role to the extent that it is no longer "normal." One of the more interesting research projects in which the researcher entered a "normal role" involved sociologist Laud Humphreys. Humphreys' study of male homosexual behavior was conducted in public restrooms where he researched impersonal sex between men. The observations occurred in the unusual role Humphreys assumed of the "watch queen," a voyeur role that was normal in the context of the setting and situation.[8] Apparently, the men who were having sexual relations with one another in the bathroom stalls were used to the presence of a watch queen, and so Humphreys' being there did not concern them. And since the watch queen doubled as a lookout, they were glad to have him. More than likely, had they known that the watch queen was really a researcher, they may not have wanted him to be there.

Another aspect of Humphreys' research, one that was generally condemned as unethical, involved his follow-up research after his observations were made. By noting the license plates on the cars near the public restroom in which the men had had sex, Humphreys was able to find the names and addresses of the men he had observed. He believed that by surveying the men involved, he would be able to learn something about their background, socioeconomic status, and attitudes that would be useful to his study.[9] Having their names and addresses simply made it possible, and by using their license plates to identify them, he was able to maintain his anonymity as a researcher.

The fact that Humphreys openly explained his research techniques is strong evidence that he believed he had done nothing unethical, and his findings certainly shed a great deal of light on an area no one knew much about. However, by arguing that the findings justified the methods, we open the door to virtually any kind of research techniques or experimental conditions. Those involved in the Watergate scandal used very much the same logic—namely, that what they were doing was justified by the ends they were pursuing. By their own logic, even the so-called scientists in the Nazi concentration camps who tortured human subjects believed that the ends justified the means. This is not to compare Humphreys' research with Watergate or the Nazis, for no one was harmed nor were the identities of any of the research subjects ever made known in Humphreys' study. However, to the extent that social scientists argue that they know best what is and is not in the interests the subjects of their study and point to the results of their study to justify the techniques employed, we risk trampling on human rights.

The Bureaucratization of Ethics

Perhaps the most crucial issue in the discussion of ethics in social research is the bureaucratic guidelines that are supposed to "guarantee" that all reviewed research procedures meet certain requirements. There is little or no essential disagreement that human subjects should be protected—all agree they should. However, the blanket policies that are in human-subject protocols sometimes fail to recognize the differences in research methods and what constitutes protecting people in one situation or another.

In arguing that the protection of human subjects is misapplied in participant observation research, one study pointed out that certain kinds of important findings are made next to impossible.[10] Citing an example of a study by the Department of Housing and Urban Development (HUD) in which black and white researchers posed as "renters" and found that realtors discriminated against blacks,[11] it was shown that such research would have been impossible were the researchers bounded by the guidelines set down by the Department of Health, Education and Welfare (HEW)* that regulate most social science research. Had the researchers been forced to provide informed consent to the realtors they were investigating, they would have had to say something to the effect of, "Hello, we're testing the hypothesis that you realtors discriminate against black renters, and we'd like to know if you'd mind if we watched you to see if we're correct. By the way, this research is being conducted under the auspices of the Department of Housing and Urban Development." Obviously, the realtors would not have been discriminatory had they been aware of the research.

When the guidelines for protecting human subjects were being drawn up, it is doubtful that the protection of human subjects was meant to conceal illegal activities such as those found in the HUD study, but a literal reading of the guidelines, which state, "Any social, psychological, or financial harm which might result from research is considered to be a risk," suggests that, given the hypothesis and findings of the HUD study on discrimination, there clearly was risk to the subjects (the realtors who were violating the law). In a reply to that criticism of the human-subject protection guidelines, it was argued that the section dealing with risk points out that only research "that increases the ordinary risks of daily life" is subject to the informed consent procedures.[12] However, since, as in the case of the discriminatory realtors, the findings of the research increased the risks to the realtors if they continued discrimination and the research was not a part of daily life, the research could be said to have increased the ordinary risks of the realtors' daily life.[13] That being the case, the HUD study could be interpreted to be in violation of the informed consent procedures where risk was decided to be involved.

The spirit of the ethic protecting human subjects can be lost in bureaucratic nitpicking, and so instead of seeing how to best protect human subjects, researchers become plagued with how to satisfy committees who make judgment as to meeting guidelines. The next logical step is the ritualization of complying with the procedures while losing the substance of the ethic behind the protocols. Thus, what began as an honest attempt to make sure that research did not put people in risky situations without their knowledge has come to be seen as a system to be beaten. At the same time, rather than asking fundamental theoretical questions and devising research to answer such questions, the researcher becomes obsessed with procedures that will meet the formal requirements of the guidelines for protecting human subjects—guidelines that in many cases are only vaguely protective, since what is to be examined is a normal part of a group's activities. Changes in the guidelines have improved the situation some, but there are still a number of problems.

There is no simple way out of the dilemma. On the one hand, it is

*Now two separate departments: Health and Human Services and Education.

imperative to have clear guidelines for ethics in research; on the other hand, the literal reading of virtually any guidelines will lead to problems and exceptions. However, it would be a substantial improvement to have better legal guarantees for confidentiality so that researchers could honestly say that under no circumstances would the identity of any person, group, or organization be made known. Likewise, it is important to recognize that guidelines that were originally established for experimental research, especially in psychology and medicine, are not applicable in the same way to all social science research, most notably participant observation research. Just those two changes would solve many of the problems in the area of human rights.

Summary

This chapter has focused on validity, risk, and informed consent. While scientific knowledge seeks valid and truthful information, it is recognized that the pursuit of such knowledge must be tempered with respect for human feelings. We are not studying bugs or rocks, and we cannot treat human beings as though they were animals or objects. Whenever there is risk involved in research, as long as that risk is due to the research procedures, and not just the research findings, those who are subject to the risk should be well informed. Among social scientists there is little disagreement over that matter.

However, it is in the implementation of ethics, especially the format provided by the Department of Health, Education and Welfare, that social scientists disagree. On the one hand, there are those who believe that ethical research can only be guaranteed if the guidelines are followed to the letter; on the other hand, there are those who see the guidelines as doing little to protect human subjects and much to thwart necessary research. Hampered by the inability to guarantee confidentiality, researchers are in the position of either ignoring the risk of breaking the law by refusing court-ordered exposure of confidential information or simply avoiding research where that would be a problem. Likewise, where suspected deviance or illegality can only be uncovered by covert research, researchers face the dilemma of following the procedures for protecting human subjects and the certainty of not gathering valid information or simply ignoring protection of subjects in order to learn the truth. Until these and similar problems are resolved, the issue of ethics will continue to plague research.

Glossary

anonymity Keeping the identity of the research subjects anonymous by not recording names. (See also *confidentiality*)

confidentiality Overall concept of not revealing the identity of persons or places; this protects subjects and organizations from embarassment and/or legal harassment.

consent form A form prepared by the researcher to give to the research subject informing him or her of the research procedures, risks, and other salient aspects of the research so that the subject will be fully aware of what he or she is getting into.

deception A researcher's knowingly misinforming the research subject either by omission of information or misrepresentation of information. In research in certain areas (such as political corruption, consumer fraud), deception is not considered unethical.

informed consent The concept in research ethics that stresses that the research subject be fully knowledgeable about the research procedures before giving consent. Avoids consent through misinformation (*deception*) or coercion.

professional ethics A code or set of rules for conducting research along moral guidelines.

protection of human-subject guidelines A standardized set of research requirements for informing and protecting research subjects. (Also called *protocols.*)

risks Any potential harm or losses that may be suffered due to participation in research. Included in such risks are social, psychological, legal, financial, and physical harm.

Notes

1. Sir Cyril Burt's identical-twin study was found to be a complete fraud, and it was Burt who, under a pseudonym, published "confirming evidence" of his original study. See, for example, L.S. Hearnshaw, *Cyril Burt, Psychologist* (Ithica, N.Y.: Cornell University Press, 1979), and D.D. Dorfman, "The Cyril Burt Question: New Findings," *Science* 201 (1978): 1177–1186.
2. Eleanor Singer, "Informed Consent: Consequences for Response Rate and Response Quality in Social Surveys," *American Sociological Review* 43 (April 1978): 144–162.
3. Stanford M. Lyman and Marvin B. Scott, *A Sociology of the Absurd* (New York: Appleton-Ceentury-Crofts, 1970), pp. 145–157.
4. San Diego State University Committee on Protection of Human Subjects, "Policy and Procedures for the Protection of Human Subjects," Appendix A (May, 1978, San Diego State University). For a more general statement of guidelines for the protection of human subjects, see *Code of Federal Regulations*, "Protection of Human Subjects," *Federal Register* 44 (1979): 47692–47698.
5. David L. Altheide and John Johnson, "Counting Souls: A Study of Counseling at Evangelical Crusades," *Pacific Sociological Review* (July 1977): 328–348.
6. Ibid., p. 334.
7. Singer, op. cit., p. 154.
8. Laud Humphreys, *Tearoom Trade* (Chicago: Aldine, 1970).
9. Ibid.
10. Troy Duster, David Matza, and David Wellman, "Field Work and the Protection of Human Subjects," *The American Sociologist* 14 (August 1979): 136–142.
11. Reported in the *Washington Post*, September 21, 1978.
12. Theodore N. Greenstein, "A Comment on Duster, Matza, and Wellman: Protection of Human Subjects in Field Research," *American Sociologist* 15 (May 1980): 113–114.
13. Troy Duster, David Matza, and David Wellman, "Interpretations, Regulations, and Facts" (Rejoinder to Greenstein), *American Sociologist* 15 (May 1980): 114.

20

The Student Research Paper

$\mathbf{A}$t the end of the term, many students will be required to turn in a paper based on their research. Usually instructors want the papers done in a certain style, using a particular format for references and many other things that students may consider to be unnecessarily fussy. After all, what does it matter how a paper is presented as long as it is clear? Well, the format that professors use is devised to clarify the research, and once we understand how a style and format work, we think it will be clear that such formal arrangement of findings actually makes it much easier because a format provides an order that the student can easily follow. Just imagine how much more difficult it would be if a professor simply said, "Write a research paper," and provided no information about how to organize it. Where would you begin or end? Without some guide, how would you know where to put everything or in what order? Thus, rather than looking at format as some kind of straightjacket, it should be seen as a road map, a guide to tell you where to start and end and the route to follow along the way.

Another issue that has dismayed both students and instructors is simple neatness. A smudged paper with narrow margins held together with a safety pin looks bad. But even if the proper format is followed, a sloppy presentation takes something away from even the best paper. To help you do a neat job, we will provide some hints on how to enhance a paper's appearance.

Organizing the Research

At the very beginning of our consideration of research, we discussed how to organize in order to execute the necessary procedures. Likewise, at the completion of research, everything has to be organized to communicate the findings of others. For novices, it is important to get started on the right foot, and there are books available on the details of how to prepare and present a paper. *The Student Sociologist's Handbook*[1] and *Encounter with Sociology: The Term Paper*[2] are two excellent works highly recommended for social science students.

Assuming that at the end of the research project the student has a mass of data, all sorts of completed analyses, and a clear knowledge of what the research all means, the problem remaining is one of organization and communication. To put all of the pieces together, consider the following steps:

1. State the problem and relevant literature.
2. Describe the methodology.
3. Show what was found.
4. Discuss the implications.

Looking at these four steps, we see pretty much the same steps we followed in research.

Stating the Problem and Reviewing the Literature

The very first thing in a research project is to construct a theoretical problem. Similarly, in preparing a paper, we explain why we chose a particular problem and why it is important in extending our knowledge in social science. This sets the stage for what will follow in the paper and tells the reader something interesting. For example, the following sentence started off an article on women and employment:

> The belief that discrimination against women results from structural factors is a central tenet of many recent labor market studies, particularly those in the tradition of institutional economics.[3]

Right off the bat, the author tells the reader why the research he is doing is important. He is going to examine the relationship between discrimination against women and the social structure. Later in the introduction, the same author said:

> In this paper, I evaluate one of the central tenets of segmented labor market theory—that women are overrepresented in marginal industries—by assessing several explicit hypotheses with detailed census data.[4]

So after reading a few lines, we know the general problem and the specific manner in which the researcher will examine it. We now have a context for understanding the significance of the research.

Having stated the problem we are going to discuss, now is the time to review the literature that has examined the same or similar phenomena as our study. Usually, the researcher reviews the literature before the research has begun so as to get an idea of where to proceed and to see if there are any pitfalls to watch out for. However, researchers will often go back over the literature after the research is completed to see if they can account for some unexpected findings. Whatever the case, though, it is important to describe other research in the area and to tell where our research fits. Not only does this heighten the relevance of our own work in a scholastic community, it may also show how our research blazes a new path that no one else has thought of.

As a practical question, students wonder exactly how much literature review should be put in a paper. To some extent this will depend on the topic and the way it is being examined. Some areas have an immense amount of research while others have hardly any. For instance, in an article about Soviet criminality and geography, the author pointed out a twenty-five years hiatus of criminological scholarship during the Stalinist era.[5] As a result, there was very little criminological literature on the Soviet Union available to review. On the other hand, if a student chooses to study social class and values (that is, attitudes), there is an immense amount of literature and hundreds of studies. It would take far too long to review every book and article on social class and beliefs systems, and so the literature review would narrow its focus to those items that are most similar to the research being presented. At the same time, it is possible to summarize several studies that found the same thing or that used the same theoretical and methodological approach. What is important in reviewing the literature is to provide an overall picture of what has been done and how our own work adds to knowledge in that area.

To get started on a literature review, the best place to begin is with one of several indexes available. Do not attempt to randomly select journals or books without some kind of index, for to do so wastes a lot of time and effort. For journal and magazine articles, the *Social Sciences and Humanities Index* available in most college libraries is a good place to look, and if you cannot find what you are looking for there, ask your librarian for help. The librarian can tell you what other indexes and bibliographies for periodicals are available in the library. Also, the two books mentioned earlier in this chapter, *The Student Sociologist's Handbook* and *Encounter with Sociology*, provide a listing of several places to conduct a literature search. For books dealing with your area of research, the card catalogue under the Subject Index (*not* Title/Author) provides a good overview. Once a book is identified as being relevant to your research and when you go to find the book in the stacks, take a look at other books in the same area to see if any of them are related to your research as well.

When you have found an item relevant to your research, the very first thing to do is to write down all of the pertinent information. This is extremely important and easy to overlook. Be sure to include the following:

a. Title of article/book
b. Name of author(s)
c. Title of journal or book publisher's name and place of publication
d. Volume and number of journal
e. Date of publication
f. Page numbers of relevant materials

Once this information is down, you can always go back and find the resource again, and you have everything you need when writing your references. If you forget, it will simply mean more work.

With an article, the first thing to examine is the abstract that precedes the body of the article itself to see whether or not the research in it is pertinent to your's. If it is, jot down the findings in general terms, usually provided in the abstract, and check to see what kind of methodology was employed. In cases where the research appears to be especially relevant, you will probably want to read the entire article to get all of the necessary details, but for the most part, the abstract should tell you what you want to know. If you are not sure, take a careful look at the study's findings and discussion. Again, it is important to write down everything you will want to remember, and by doing so immediately, you will save time later on.

A useful shortcut through a lot of the literature review is to look at the review of an article that is similar to your own. By following up the footnotes, you can branch off into the most relevant areas and at the same time see how the professionals review the literature. The only problem with sticking with someone else's review is that any published article or book is going to have somewhat dated citations. Thus, while following up another's literature review is useful for understanding and learning, only by doing it yourself is it possible to make sure that you have the very latest findings.

Describing the Methodology

Having stated the problem and described what other research has found, now is the time to explain the research methods employed. First, state exactly why you chose a certain method. Then, explain how you used the method in your study, giving the details in summary fashion. Be sure to include the unit of analysis, sample, setting, time-frame, and all other major features. Some methods will require more emphasis on certain elements than others. For example, in ethnographic studies, the time-frame is wholly different from that in survey research. If an ethnographic study is using participant observation as the primary source of data gathering, the researcher is going to want to be in the field as long as possible to observe patterns and change; but the survey researcher will want to be in and out of the field as quickly as possible so that his or her findings will not be affected by any changes. Therefore, in a paper describing an ethnographic study, the researcher will want to go into detail about the length of time spent in the field and why, whereas the survey researcher will probably spend a good deal of time discussing how a sample was taken, but only briefly deal with the time element.

While describing the research methods, it is important to explain what may have gone wrong as well as what went right. This tells the reader what to look out for if he or she wants to conduct research in the same area. For example, the wording of a question in an interview schedule may have been found to be confusing to the research subjects, and by explaining the nature of the problem, you can prevent other researchers from making the same mistake.

Also in describing the methodology, it is important to explain the analytic device. Sometimes this will be a simple chi-square that needs little elaboration, but in other cases where an elaborate path or multiple regression model is employed, it is necessary to outline the model and any formulas used. In certain cases, especially those where other research has used different analytic tests, it is important to explain why one test was used instead of another.

Presenting Findings

The presentation of findings is the heart of any research paper. It is important to present only the relevant findings and stick with the research problem. Participant observation research usually accumulates far more data than is directly relevant to the research problem, and it is easy for the researcher to get carried away in his or her presentation of findings, including just about everything that was observed, whether it is directly pertinent or not. Likewise, in surveys, the researcher may have far more cross-tabulations of data than is called for by the initial research problem. Once the data is on computer cards, discs, or tapes, it is a simple matter to generate all kinds of tables and tests, many of which are only tangentially related to the research problem. The temptation is to include all of these superfluous tables in one's findings, but all they do is clutter the paper and confuse the problem.

Probably the best way to summarize findings is through the use of tables and charts. Sometimes more dramatic graphics can be used to present findings, such as having figures of people represent so many thousands in a population or bar graphs with different textures illustrating different features of a community's services. The main purpose of any figure in findings is to clearly show, in summary form, exactly what the research has found. Keep in mind that the simpler the illustration, the easier it is for the reader to understand the significance of the findings.

In studies using qualitative data where tables and graphs usually are not employed, the researcher has to summarize findings by written description. Usually it helps to provide examples from the data that typify a certain observed pattern. In this way, the reader can better see what the pattern looks like. At the same time, the qualitative researcher should provide any negative cases found, also using examples, to show how strong or weak a pattern really is. If there are a number of exceptions to a given pattern, there is probably a competing pattern or pluralistic groupings in the research field, and so while presenting findings, the researcher will want to clearly show the different patterns, using examples for illustrations.

One way qualitative data can be graphically illustrated is to make an outline chart depicting different types and subtypes of patterns. In an ethnographic study of nude beaches, Douglas, Rasmussen, and Flanagan found several types of voyeurism and voyeurs.[6] The following is a list showing the different types and subtypes:

Voyeurs and Voyeurism
Cliff-dweller voyeurs
Airplane voyeurs
Camera voyeurs
    plain-bathing-suit cop
    crotch-watchers
    nude camera-voyeur
    straight camera-voyeurs
    TV-news voyeurism
Hobnail boot voyeurs
Shirt-and-tie voyeurs
Swimsuit voyeurs

Such tables summarize several types of forms found in the research, and even though there are no numbers accompanying the patterns, it is still clear that several different types and subtypes of behaviors can be distinguished.

Discussing Findings

It is rare when one's findings follow a perfectly predictable line. Instead, some hypotheses are supported, others are rejected, and still others are somewhere in between. In other words there are qualifications, reexaminations, of assumptions and suggestions for further research. Researchers use the discussion portion of their papers to pull together and summarize what was found. For example, the following is an excerpt from the discussion section of a study of "tracking" in schools:

> It is clear, however, that achievement-related criteria are not the sole, or even major, bases of curriculum assignment. Students of similar potential often are placed, for as yet undetermined reasons, in different tracks. In such cases, curriculum assignment expands opportunities for one group and constricts them for the other. At the same time, *direct* socioeconomic ascription in track placement is almost negligible. Thus, to a considerable degree the benefits associated with enrollment in a college program are available *entirely independent* of status origins *and* academic achievement. This suggests that neither functional nor conflict theories adequately characterize the role of curriculum differentiation in educational and social stratification.[7]

As can be seen in the above excerpt, the authors pull together general findings and point out the inadequacy of different theories to explain their findings.

An important point to remember in writing a discussion is that it is a summary, and as such it should not be a rambling monologue about the research. Sometimes researchers ramble on and on in their discussions, losing not only the focus of the paper but also the interest of the reader. Thus, before beginning the discussion, jot down an outline of the key points you want to make and stick with the outline. In this way, your discussion will be a crisp summary focusing on the crucial points.

References and Footnotes

Many students consider footnotes and references to be the bane of their existence. They usually see no reason to put in a lot of extraneous, awkward inserts into a paper that is difficult enough to write as it is. However, in any research paper, references are extremely important, for they provide a scholarly context for the work and tell the reader exactly the path taken by the researcher in developing and executing his or her study. Besides, once you learn the correct forms, references and footnotes are quite simple and are well worth the little time they take.

References

References simply denote the source of a statement in a paper. In citing another study or a theory, the writer inserts a parenthetical notation telling the reader where the finding or idea came from. By using a standard format for references, it is clear to the reader exactly what a given notation means.

The format used in the social sciences can be found on the inside cover of any recent issue of the *American Sociological Review*. The following is a portion of that format:

REFERENCE FORMAT

A. *In the text:* All source references are to be identified at the appropriate point in the text by the last name of the author, year of publication, and pagination where needed. Identify subsequent citations of the same source in the same way as the first, not using "ibid.," "op. cit.," or "loc. cit." Examples follow:

  1. If author's name is in the text, follow it with year in parentheses. (". . . Duncan (1959). . . .")

  2. If author's name is not in the text, insert, in parentheses, the last name and year, separated by a comma. (". . . (Goffman, 1979) . . .") or (". . . (cf. Gouldner, 1963) . . .")

  3. Pagination (without "p." or "pp.") follows year of publication after a colon. (". . . Kuhn (1970:71) . . .") or (". . . (Garfinkel, 1967:243) . . .")

  4. Give both last names for dual authors; for more than two use "et al." in the text. When two authors have the same last name, use identifying initial in the text. For institutional authorship, supply minimum identification from the beginning of the complete citation. (". . . (U.S. Bureau of the Census, 1963:117) . . .")

  5. Separate a series of references with semicolons and enclose them within a single pair of parentheses. (". . . (Burgess, 1968; Marwell et al., 1971; Cohen, 1962) . . .")

B. *In the appendix:* List all source citations by author, and within author by year of publication, in an appendix titled "References." The reference appendix must be complete and include all references in the text. The use of "et al." is not acceptable in the appendix; list the names of all authors. (See A.4. for text format.) If there is more than one reference to the same author and year, distinguish them by the letters, a, b, etc., added to the year. (". . . Levy (1965a:331) . . .") Give the publisher's name in as brief a form as is fully intelligible. For example, John A. Wiley and Sons should be "Wiley." If the cited material is unpublished, use "forthcoming" with name of journal or publisher; otherwise use "unpublished."

Use no underlining, italics, or abbreviations. Examples follow:

1. Books: Jud, Gerald J., Edgar Mills, Jr. and Genevieve Walters Burch

                    1970   Ex-Pastors, Philadelphia: Pilgrim Press.

             U.S. Bureau of the Census

                    1960   Characteristics of Population. Volume 1. Washington, D.C.: U.S. Government Printing Office.

             Bernard, Claude

                  (1865)

                    1957   An Introduction to the Study of Experimental Medicine. Tr. Henry Copley Green, New York: Dover.

2. Periodicals: Conger, Rand

             Forthcoming   "The effects of positive feedback on direction and amount of verbalization in a social setting." Pacific Sociological Review.

             Merton, Robert K.

                  1963a   "The ambivalence of scientists." Bulletin of the Johns Hopkins Hospital 112:77−97.

                  1963b   "Resistance to the systematic study of multiple discoveries in science." European Journal Journal of Sociology 4:237−82.

3. Collections: Davie, M.

                  1938   "The pattern of urban growth." Pp. 113−61 in G. Murdock (ed.), Studies of Society. New Haven: Yale University Press. Revised 1980 ASR[8]

    At first, all of this may appear to be very complicated and overly technical, but this format is much simpler than trying to put all the references at the bottom of the page along with footnotes. The following excerpt shows what a text using this format looks like:

The societal view of rape has been significantly altered by the feminist movement (Geis, 1977:4—18). A focal point of feminist theory is the reconceptualization of rape from a "sex" crime to a "violent" crime (Millet, 1971). The emphasis on violence is in the context of a humanistic, feminist view, a critique applicable to men who see violence as a proper means to an end. Rape is seeen as epiphenomenal to violence. Griffin (1971) and Greer (1973) took a more specific look at rape and violence, seeing them as one part of the subjugation of women by men. However, it was Susan Brownmiller's (1975) work, *Against Our Will: Men, Women and Rape*, which had the most impact on attitudes toward rape.[9]

As can be seen, there is really very little in the text that has to be done in order to cite a source of information. In the "References" appendix, it is a simple matter to look up the complete source since they are listed in alphabetical order.

Footnotes

When references are put in the format just discussed, there are relatively few notes at the bottom of the page—or footnotes. Exactly what is a footnote, then, if not a reference? It can be a lot of things, but for the most part a footnote is some kind of tangential point elaboration, or illustration that would break up the flow of the paper were it inserted in the text rather than at the bottom of the page.

The mechanics of footnote placement is awkward since the writer must estimate a certain amount of space at the bottom of the page, hoping it will be sufficient to contain the entire note without leaving too little or too much space. One way to solve this problem is to put all footnotes in a separate appendix under "Notes" in addition to having a "References" appendix. However, since for student papers footnotes are minimal, putting them at the bottom of the page may not be too difficult. To do so, simply put a number in the text corresponding to the note's number in sequence (for example, the fifth footnote is denoted with a "5") to the right and above the end of the sentence where it is to be inserted. The following examples show different kinds of footnotes:

A. footnote showing a relationship possibility that might exist but did not

(Text) Thus, our contemporary middle-class women show similarities to the middle-class men in the 1940s in their acceptance of a larger range of sexual experiences.[15]

_____

(Footnote)[15] We thought that this might be related to the later age at which they begin their sexual activity. Controlling for initial age, however, did not affect the relationship.
(Source: Martin S. Weinberg and Colin J. Williams, "Sexual Embourgeoisment? Social Class and Sexual Activity: 1938—1970," *American Sociological Review* 45 (February, 1980): 44.)

B. footnote using illustration of variation in point

(Text) When an American movie involves persons who are foreign, it is rare that they are restricted to the language they would likely speak. Instead, English is used but often with a corresponding "accent." The accent stands for the foreignness.[47]

(Footnote)[47] Also there are class arrangements. In American films, a "good" New York or New England accent can readily be used as evidence of British nationality. In English productions of Greek plays, Cockney comes to be used for working-class Greeks, "received pronunciation" for the better classes. (Source: Erving Goffman, *Frame Analysis*, New York: Harper and Row, 1974. p. 240.)

C. footnote as clarification and elaboration

(Text) His discussion dealt with a variety of forms of deviance and was not restricted to criminality.[28]

(Footnote)[28] In centering attention both upon deviant behavior and social attributions of deviance status, Spitzer steered clear of vulgar labeling theory, which implies that deviant labels are applied to persons quite apart from whether they engage in non-conforming acts. (Source: Don C. Gibbons, *The Criminological Enterprise*, Englewood Cliffs, N.J.: Prentice-Hall, 1979. p. 175.)

As can be seen from the above examples, there is a wide variety of uses for footnotes, but for the most part, in student papers they should only be employed where absolutely necessary.

Putting It All Together

Having spent a good deal of time on the research for a paper, students sometimes ruin the effect of their work by turning in sloppy papers. Words are misspelled, the pages are smudged, and the whole things is a mess. It's like showing up at a formal dinner in a T-shirt.

Students may argue that the real substance in any paper is in the ideas and data, and that is certainly true. However, the purpose is to communicate the findings, and anything that distracts from communication reduces the chances of being understood. Besides, instructors, like everyone else, tend to take a paper more seriously if it is presented in a clear and neat fashion. Sloppy work, looking like the best effort of a seven-year-old, simply is not taken as seriously as a presentation that shows care in its language, organization, and all other aspects that make up its total appearance.

Perhaps the greatest irony in a poor presentation is that a really first-class-looking paper is not that much more difficult to do. A first draft can be as sloppy as you like—just get everything down and in some order. Once the first draft is completed, go over it to check spelling and grammar. Use a thesaurus or a combination dictionary/thesaurus to make sure words are correctly spelled and to vary word usage—repetitive language makes for dull reading. Once that is done, and figures and tables are checked so that everything adds up, you can begin typing your final draft.

The following are a few hints that take little effort (and in some cases less effort than a sloppy paper) but result in a much better-looking final draft:

1. Clean the type on your typewriter—there are many different products available to do this with, and it only takes a few minutes.
2. Use a good bond paper, but not the erasable kind—it smudges easily.
3. To make corrections, use a correction tape or liquid correction fluid instead of making erasures—it is easier and looks much better.
4. To make tables and diagrams, get a template and some triangles for squaring off corners and making parallel lines.
5. Rather than buying folders for your paper, simply staple the pages together in the upper lefthand corner. They look more professional and are a lot easier for your instructor to read.

Summary

The goal of all social science research is to develop and communicate knowledge. In this final chapter, we have simply reviewed standardized ways to enhance communication between the researcher and his or her audience, whether it is simply his or her instructor or the more general community of social scientists. Not only do the standard formats help the readers understand what the researcher has to say; they are extremely helpful for the researcher in organizing his or her ideas as well. Thus, rather than viewing them as hinderances to creativity and originality, which they certainly are not, the formats should be seen as practical devices for helping the researcher put everything together.

As a final note, it is important that anyone who puts a serious effort into research should be taken seriously. Most students do not treat themselves seriously in that even though they may conduct excellent research, they really do not believe it is significant. However, if a student has followed the procedures of proper research, there is no reason that a his or her research could not be as significant as even the most experienced social scientists. Furthermore, students often have a special creativity and perspective that we sometimes lose as we become comfortable in certain static ideas about the world. Having this more open approach can lead to areas and views that have been overlooked, and so in some ways students are in a position to make important contributions to knowledge. That being the case, students should want their research papers to appear to be serious efforts, and not simply something that was hurried through to satisfy a course requirement. By taking some minimal efforts and precautions in preparing their work, students can produce papers that communicate the care they took in the research as well. A well-prepared paper is a statement of the research's importance.

By this point, a student should not only be able to carry out his or her own research, but also to understand that of others. All of the research papers, articles, books, and reports are the result of using some form of the methodologies we have discussed in this book. As you study research methods—from the simple but elegant to the complex and elaborate—though, it is good to remember that at one time, all researchers took an introductory course such as this one and examined some aspect of social life to better understand it.

Notes

1. Pauline Bart and Linda Frankel, *The Student Sociologist's Handbook* (Morristown, N.J.: General Learning Press, 1976).
2. Leonard Becker, Jr., and Clair Gustafson, *Encounter with Sociology: The Term Paper*, (San Francisco, Ca.: Boyd and Fraser, 1976).
3. William P. Bridges, "Industry Marginality and Female Employment: A New Appraisal," *American Sociological Review* 45 (February 1980): 58.
4. Ibid.
5. Louise Shelly, "The Geography of Soviet Criminality," *American Sociological Review* 45 (February 1980): 111−122.
6. Jack D. Douglas and Paul K. Rasmussen with Carol Ann Flanagan, *The Nude Beach* (Beverly Hills, Ca.: Sage, 1977) pp. 114−126.
7. Karl L. Alexander, Martha Cook, and Edward L. McDill, "Curriculum Tracking and Educational Stratification," *American Sociological Review* 43 (February 1978): 65.
8. The format is from the inside cover of the *American Sociological Review* 45 (February, 1980).
9. William B. Sanders, *Rape and Woman's Identity* (Beverly Hills, Ca.: Sage, 1980), p. 22.

Appendix A: Table of Random Numbers

45534 87140 24552 61060 48580 32859 85255 75210 88020 72481 45463 24538 30048 97997 40874 59446 66607 91201 94655 89288 76895

68510 36473 30558 24833 92992 41236 89256 58122 55356 73315 69100 15825 47455 58610 27923 34947 81793 46978 41528 27169 65084

76861 72002 79889 92849 92732 59411 99892 50028 86863 73615 11109 28557 23851 13257 48534 17170 53511 29687 37208 38166 87642

99557 25963 98145 54650 64112 22823 73238 33498 44311 22126 80797 28304 52822 75977 34411 50589 72743 27679 98710 31613 62194

55655 21394 98094 94456 95398 28096 44420 54312 82383 68489 16913 57139 67636 73127 79904 21422 34502 85612 22293 44391 65208

39220 14135 19917 81413 83037 39265 34939 57161 66496 98466 71399 15682 43672 66388 24484 33020 94695 72520 57990 41498 27520

83414 70782 75509 53857 27832 31174 25405 46174 83358 97696 19566 28075 79518 97320 86488 97959 76784 58666 71752 28540 46459

79856 82716 26780 70771 68470 67380 70811 50530 18122 21249 90652 44657 33164 73228 63179 70174 45862 46588 96445 91337 70533

40901 91126 76242 24781 63156 84361 72382 30940 95834 92467 15083 62786 69774 51662 85661 56358 14186 29581 77255 39859 38868

48012 25024 89237 94046 71669 56431 44759 43855 51168 47461 63307 15043 97712 52781 97794 70026 47613 60787 97803 47547 45850

80946 42472 90616 14163 54057 44132 27732 71515 67044 93773 32805 96820 64711 74825 93216 81629 46862 74567 69205 57380 17347

52952 12880 75895 65316 43670 94656 70930 13895 85172 74371 89770 86220 77456 23204 16503 33722 88091 49093 65227 43934 35583

37892 93895 49297 47547 23584 20703 38325 82293 60223 87639 77680 99535 71318 33311 87988 18943 78611 51366 95398 46455 21647

83188 37028 71579 54199 50582 83350 43784 72552 74028 57886 87445 92777 33662 55106 46008 29998 45512 50781 31679 89335 78100

```
51785  28804  30411  99416  35628  52409  72256  46482  59617  49271  49072  26525  58331  41590  40148  76387  93150  67520  29603  61189  83206

74541  22312  81554  35871  47674  55014  69315  79411  37869  86051  75774  35685  49754  70850  46261  40903  21988  44310  60620  18269  43542

56194  88173  81574  70260  33484  87330  91914  73285  12192  47579  58005  27456  36474  80950  99897  16047  90120  13627  89695  70152  79437

62497  50615  28710  48504  63047  14676  92119  79289  15908  16289  91494  18300  15114  66870  82198  61327  23568  89695  70152  13627  63017

97836  74183  93934  89168  65872  43285  99580  27932  28331  43134  16944  90126  55612  75631  94959  67238  97953  32249  29621  80382  75275

43409  94287  71059  67893  75054  85956  92113  54286  70236  76809  71965  43534  63605  75230  56003  97669  79703  15811  82925  80201  18507

89528  80971  59677  13418  33044  67028  28125  62082  92605  51509  75288  65419  23112  26399  29850  45484  23396  59626  43815  44470  71180

77744  52314  41663  91098  35989  67372  56737  20193  79068  56377  51713  55265  50140  76865  77863  23883  82098  35475  29926  96480  44096

79244  33064  24117  17136  99807  93327  72333  71920  79831  23714  42556  79407  10913  44244  62657  58263  30166  10829  39863  49420  75456

10850  30041  80788  64235  54248  12761  36353  77653  36625  54992  73189  20964  18753  74464  63664  35861  90864  31254  91683  14918  55210

99280  57798  15835  56500  30794  95812  60810  81430  75627  26206  89849  98385  30992  40905  32147  62535  44027  28365  88153  93278  35970

41173  47371  77631  69422  25265  87965  68926  17142  75229  32955  76153  85563  67590  79703  17411  31834  34306  10839  41640  80453  37435

39733  87518  27595  84018  52460  77807  70327  10141  10573  55990  80054  94184  93643  62790  59920  84624  28606  45866  57141  40296  26206

18622  65636  62872  43333  24954  63482  70759  82525  54137  48421  68181  55149  91089  78170  26178  12493  89914  44134  37892  59520  72962
```

54787 47309 25874 70550 56757 67095 98923 11451 59790 54985 60289 59207 74472 29685 91108 27793 14265 71043 63194 16446 30706

72908 81703 30898 80868 65464 48957 33784 16391 79570 40326 74966 21050 24855 65711 18838 78357 60951 35582 70506 67035 36729

10217 67134 13822 15410 84559 67425 85328 73309 87846 23547 83489 83726 23347 86067 23833 37033 64164 94772 72184 51502 77623

37775 53886 98968 63826 40388 87665 25354 55797 94642 75607 75411 94412 37944 17898 88975 84876 39395 47196 62150 65748 51312

15155 66047 68923 81981 40422 20526 34699 83044 27161 90990 22631 82849 17257 17915 11289 65515 59967 45513 93360 88713 76878

89982 98870 45398 81479 98186 78117 25625 71016 29972 27078 90756 69731 26094 98907 25502 16762 24638 73298 40181 92450 85383

92098 80447 29619 42874 22826 55667 94068 60748 11419 89297 60494 20044 63448 94539 39207 93023 67430 73616 65016 49495 68920

62385 91081 44961 82031 44424 51192 29527 96131 48928 54445 22025 15117 45789 94923 91041 36339 23727 34781 43823 90767 48786

45261 60618 85844 88128 25292 26949 40391 26731 95634 14200 43723 41607 70467 79118 65396 49642 71473 33811 43031 24220 59223

32306 95018 28218 55312 80675 56733 21749 54960 86426 83071 12066 42177 93714 72216 14415 96503 97628 28894 21681 87579

52637 38215 21306 48236 30809 91559 59753 15088 77656 71783 74265 68743 11413 55670 74931 33525 38705 89968 94947 75433 95990

95312 19441 67955 59516 37799 31264 73315 94881 62496 97097 55861 34577 73325 43326 25418 52462 90701 66567 35203 54784 12738

32707 59044 91038 80868 75620 35966 45856 37986 57310 88191 51508 42475 87886 28636 83899 23860 90627 75889 40063 12986 61455

21014 28613 95494 84414 81256 78238 92898 37263 27771 41547 29150 27483 86827 69292 13982 73299 89792 31157 52701 23039 26973

```
89679 13890 27904 90360 30388 80991 41332 10096 55627 15495 85289 43203 10011 97725 37556 33654 71100 28860 57522 34584 54595

68722 80324 71470 85238 61527 46897 36336 35051 19588 53090 17078 97134 32450 60268 52537 47838 83371 18408 77528 14271 33354

41735 61838 95775 22894 56641 80602 44573 56090 66542 91325 36540 13465 47759 98884 95799 99473 46606 30846 88928 79374 16750

17538 18489 28148 28553 33606 71356 49353 97236 73928 84769 81507 36229 80212 27108 48670 52518 75154 11418 45540 60585 88142

58505 96914 16279 36356 46408 85252 34974 38120 28594 88410 62210 72474 57176 70814 21099 23821 85047 94595 71668 46840 56176

14710 39190 23859 66405 26071 78920 94553 84919 57395 37530 89086 22845 84237 21755 18650 87980 82709 49971 50312 38827 46392

16480 19916 47424 44895 90921 48754 70606 41005 31116 86568 58172 60115 39819 39594 56071 33656 57045 68675 23036 29307 27929

38871 96064 71145 60532 32208 42004 73217 94812 41743 53646 88862 23468 57875 97975 61952 82656 74542 80247 73617 54861

19098 68155 14487 29329 41345 17536 57538 46718 68113 47059 46331 69127 36958 35932 41510 71668 45668 50319 53291 16875 58874

52907 98130 22218 45741 26886 57011 67347 78577 16230 29047 31489 38405 64935 45083 51344 84040 86550 34153 18606 23013 81977

79139 37677 59997 94341 47269 32565 46923 60591 37760 21833 39893 27197 68047 74491 14854 54068 32428 24660 47189 94952 55905

40889 52436 53945 70535 51842 12870 70171 93513 59184 18580 49890 68080 62427 18094 87578 45996 60841 99441 55959 55418 40590

69201 51515 87015 97160 18797 61051 81380 94712 52219 37623 31795 18179 59693 89223 85051 14520 84203 63138 56368 60295 42418

65930 92585 81964 44364 11224 94290 23356 29434 44304 87350 39976 82496 30364 14126 94081 13492 39708 96858 33036 33802

89880 44550 88481 24370 34649 89153 29143 61838 23901 39546 97409 74442 15601 81344 26347 54703 55593 28729 51291 79667 16957
```

Appendix B: The Chi-Square Distribution

Values of χ^2 for Various Values of P and Degrees of Freedom n

Degrees of Freedom n	P			
	0.10	0.05	0.02	0.01
1	2.706	3.841	5.412	6.635
2	4.605	5.991	7.824	9.210
3	6.251	7.815	9.837	11.341
4	7.779	9.488	11.668	13.277
5	9.236	11.070	13.388	15.086
6	10.645	12.592	15.033	16.812
7	12.017	14.067	16.622	18.475
8	13.362	15.507	18.168	20.090
9	14.684	16.919	19.679	21.666
10	15.987	18.307	21.161	23.209
11	17.275	19.675	22.618	24.725
12	18.549	21.026	24.054	26.217
13	19.812	22.362	25.472	27.688
14	21.064	23.685	26.873	29.141
15	22.307	24.996	28.259	30.578
16	23.542	26.296	29.633	32.000
17	24.769	27.587	30.995	33.409
18	25.989	28.869	32.346	34.805
19	27.204	30.144	33.687	36.191
20	28.412	31.410	35.020	37.566
21	29.615	32.671	36.343	38.932
22	30.813	33.924	37.659	40.289
23	32.007	35.172	38.968	41.638
24	33.196	36.415	40.270	42.980
25	34.382	37.652	41.566	44.314
26	35.563	36.885	42.856	45.642
27	36.741	40.113	44.140	46.693
28	37.916	41.337	45.419	48.278
29	39.087	42.557	46.693	49.588
30	40.256	43.773	47.962	50.892

Abridged from R. A. Fisher and F. Yates, *Statistical Tables for Biological, Agricultural and Medical Research*, 6th edition, London: Longman Group Ltd., 1974, Table IV, p. 47. (Previously published by Oliver & Boyd, Edinburgh.)

Index

Page numbers in boldface type indicate the page on which a term appears in an end-of-the-chapter Glossary.

episodes, qualitative, assembling into disciplined abstractions, 205–206, 209–210

episodic record, 233–234

epistemic relationship, 66–67, 68, **73**

epsilon, 277, **278**

equipment, in situation, 207

erosion measures, 232, **240**

ethics, 391–407
  bureaucratization of, 404–406
  and misdirected experiment, 180
  and natural experiment, 177
  professional, 394, 407

evaluation, 375, **388**

evaluation research, 47, 177–179, 375–387
  politics of, 385–387

evaluative assertion analysis, 195–197, **201–202**

evasions, 225–226, 230, **240**

exhaustive categories, 68–69, 70, 82, 83

expected frequencies, 322–323, **328–329**

experimental condition, 164, 166
  see also experimental treatment

experimental design, 164–168
  in evaluation research, 384

experimental group, 164–166, **182**

experimental notations, 172–173

experimental treatment, 164, **182**
  see also experimental condition

experimental variable, 164, **182**
  see also independent variable

experiments, 48–49, 162–182
  for explanatory study, 48
  and human subjects, 162, 177, 180
  logic of, 162–164, 175, 179
  problems with, 168–171
  questionnaires in, 76
  in studying social change, 49

expertise, 6

explanation, as goal, 18, 38, 48

explanatory study, 38–39, 48, **53**

exploration, as goal, 37, 48

exploratory study, 37, 46, **53**
  and generating hypotheses, 37
  vs. pilot study, 39–40

external validity, 169, 174, **182**
  problems that affect, 169–171

F

face-to-face interview, 48, 153–156, 157*t*

face validity, 88, **91**, 284

Feeney, Floyd, 381

field methods, 204–221
  see also specific method

field notes, and tape recorder, 332
  see also note taking; notes

field research, anonymity in, 399
  described in student paper, 412
  questionnaires in, 76

file, 254, **257**

filmed documents, content analysis of, 187

final sampling units, 98, **123**

fixed-choice question (see open-ended question)

Flanagan, Carol Ann, 413

follow-up mailings, 151–152, **158**

follow-up survey, 48

footnotes, in student paper, 414–415, 417–418

formal organization, 18
  as unit of analysis, 44, 46, 97

formula, 303

fourfold table (see two-by-two table)

Freeman, Linton C., 308, 309

frequency distribution, 261–263, **278**

friendship, in researcher-subject relationship, 227–228, 230

fronts, 226–227, 230, **240**

funded research, 47, 48
  and ethics, 393
  evaluation, and politics, 385–386

funnel technique, 144, **158**

G

gamma, 309–315, 320, **329**

Garfinkel, Harold, 179–180

generalizability, in experiments, 168–169
  see also external variable

generalizations, survey for, 127

generic forms, 210, **221**

Goffman, Erving, 204, 224, 240, 365

Goodman, Leo A., 309

investigative social research *(cont.)*
  strategies and tactics in, 227−228
involvement shield, 210
Irwin, John, 363
item, 76−77, **91**
  brevity of, 85
  positive nature of, 85
  relevancy of, for respondents, 84−85
  in scale or index, 284
  See also questions

J

jargon, 219
Job Control Language (JCL), 336−338, 352, **353**

K

key linkage, 365, **372**
keypunch machine, 244−246, **257**
Kitano, Harry, 26, 27
knowledge, social science, 2, 3−4
  sources of, 5−9
known researcher, 211, 212, 214
Kruskal, William H., 309

L

labeling theory, 378, 379
laboratory experiment, 169, **182**
lambda, 305−309, 320, 324, **329**
language, and learning social meaning, 219
leading question, 84, **91**
legal issues, and confidentiality, 398
Lenski, Gerhard, 64, 65
letters, cover, 149
  lost, technique of, 175−177
lies, 226, 230
Likert, Rensis, 287
Likert scale, 282, 287−288, **298**
linkages, 363−365, **372**
literature review, 410−412
Loether, Herman J., 271, 272, 273
Lofland, John, 205, 209, 210, 356
logic, of experiments, 162−164, 175, 179

logic *(cont.)*
  model of, in social science theory, 29−31
longitudinal study, 41−42, 46, 48, **54**
loopholing, 226
lost letters technique, 175−177
Lowe, George D., 42, 293, 295

M

McGaw, Dickinson, 276
macro (analysis), 46, **54,** 67
McTavish, Donald G., 271, 272, 273
mail survey, 45, 129, 146, 147−153, **158**
  advantages and disadvantages of, 147, 148*t*
  and response rate, 147−150
Malec, Michael A., 262, 308
marginals, 271, 273, 323, **329**
Marx, Karl, 19, 24
matching, 165, **182**
  with random assignment, 166
matrix question, 133−134, 141, **158**
maturation problem, 41, 46, 54, 171, **182**
mean, 106, 267, 268, **278,** 302
meanings, social, 370−371
measurement, 78, **91**
measurement, levels of, 68−72, 78−80
  see also specific level
measurement terminology, 76−78
measures of central tendency, 265−269
  comparison of, 267−269
  see also mean; median; ;mode
median, 265−267, 268, **278−279**
member role, 213
memory, questions relying on, 84
metaanalysis, 198
methodological notes, 359, **372**
methodology, 12, **14**
  importance of accurately describing, 201
  and theory, 29
micro (analysis), 45, **54,** 67
Milgram, Stanley, 169, 395
Miller, Delbert C., 288
misdirected experiment, 179−180, **182**
misinformation, 225, **240**

situation (cont.)
  size of, 207
  and space, 207
  and time, 207−208
skip interval, 116, **124**
slang, informant's, 219
  in questions, 145
snowball sample, 120−121, **124**
social action, 11−12, **14**
  patterns of, 4−5
social change, 2, 13, 19
  experiment for, 49
  longitudinal study for, 48
  panel study for, 48
social class, as concept, 24
social data, and physical data, 11−12
social desirability, 142, **159**
social integration, 59−60, 61, 63
social meanings, 219, **221**
social problems, 3, **14**
  and social science problems, 3−5
social processes, 368−370
social risk, 401
social science, 2, 4, **14**
social science knowledge, 2, 3−4
social science problems, 3, **14**
  and social problems, 3−5
Social Sciences and Humanities Index, 411
social types, 207
socioeconomic status, 64−66
Solomon Four-Group Design, 171−173,
  182
space, and situation, 207
special classes, 362−363, **372**
specification field, 337, **353**
spiritual authority, as source of
  knowledge, 7
sponsors, survey, and response rate, 148
SPSS (*see* Statistical Package for the Social
  Sciences)
spying, 402−403
square root calculation, 334
standard deviation, 106−110, 111, **124,**
  325−328, **329**
  characteristics of, 107−110
standard error, 103, 109−112, **124,**
  327−328, **329**
standardized questionnaires, 127, **159**

standing pattern of behavior, 216, 217, **221**
statistic, 99, 112, **124**
Statistical Abstract of the United States,
  201
statistical independence, 276−**279**
statistical methods, development of new,
  198
  see also specific method
Statistical Package for the Social Sciences
  (SPSS), 243, 332, 335−352
  and labeling, 340−342
  and secondary analysis, 185
  and setting up job, 336−340
  and table building, 343−352
statistics, 302−329
  descriptive, 303−304, 328
  inferential, 303, 321−325, 329
  as language, 302−303
  simple, with SPSS, 341
  symbols in, 302−303
status concept, 215
Stevens, S. S., 78
strategies, 205, 208−209, **221**
stratified sample, 97, 116−118, 120*t*, **124**
stub (in table), 270, **279**
student research paper, 409−420
  description of methodology in, 412
  discussing findings in, 414
  footnotes in, 414−415, 417−418
  neatness of, 409, 418−419
  presenting findings in, 412−414
  references in, 414−417
  review of literature in, 410−412
  statement of problem in, 410
Student Sociologist Handbook, The (Bart
  and Frankel), 409, 411
subjects, and experiments, 162, 177, 180
  truth to, 395−396
suicide, 58−60, 62, 63, 68, 198
summated ratings scale, 282, 283,
  286−287, 292, 293, **299**
survey, 35, 38, 48, **54,** 127−**159**
  and anonymity, 399
  for attitudes, 38, 48
  for evaluation research, 384
  follow-up, 48
  mail, 45, 129, 146, 147−153, 158
  as observation, 67